Seventh Edition

S0-BIQ-855

Shared Meaning

An Introduction to Speech Communication

Margot Olson, Ph.D.

Appalachian State University

Mary Forrest, Ed.D.

Eastfield College
Dallas County Community College District

KENDALL/HUNT PUBLISHING COMPANY
4050 Westmark Drive   Dubuque, Iowa 52002

Chapter opener photos © 2006 JupiterImages Corporation, unless otherwise noted

Cover photo courtesy of Stefan Olson

Copyright © 1986 by Mary Forrest and Margot Olson

Copyright © 1991, 1994, 1996, 1999, 2002, 2006 by Kendall/Hunt Publishing Company

ISBN 0-7575-2628-4

All rights reserved. No part of this publication may be reproduced,
stored in a retrieval system, or transmitted, in any form or by any
means, electronic, mechanical, photocopying, recording, or otherwise,
without the prior written permission of the copyright owner.

Printed in the United States of America
10   9   8   7   6   5   4   3   2   1

OVERVIEW

CONTENTS

PREFACE

Speech communication—talking with one other person, in small groups, and before an audience—is an area of study appropriate for every individual. One cannot exist as a normally functioning individual without engaging in the processes of verbal and nonverbal communication. With our global economy, with the technology of computers and satellites to carry messages instantly around the globe, with the ease of international travel provided by modern transportation, and with the changing demographics of our society which bring together people with greater differences in background and experience, knowledge of and experience with speech communication is not an option for a literate person. Becoming more competent as a communicator provides confidence in experiencing new situations and encountering people with diverse cultural backgrounds. Basic speech communication skills are essential in the multi-cultural settings of the 21st century which include international, national, regional, ethnic, economic, religious, age, gender, sexual orientation, and other factors related to competent intercultural communication.

Skill in speech communication is often taken for granted. College curriculums sometimes ignore the very important area of speech communication or require only a single "speech" course as a graduation requirement. When a single speech course is recommended to students, the selection of content becomes extremely important. Should the more informal speaking situations of day-to-day living be emphasized, should the more formal speaker-audience situation be emphasized, or should a combination of both be presented? This book provides a means of integrating interpersonal and small group communication with speaker-audience communication while allowing the instructor to provide emphasis in areas most relevant to specific student populations by selecting appropriate activities and chapters for reading.

It is our philosophy that all individuals require interpersonal communication skills, including small group communication, to function in today's world. Emphasis on using the basic speech communication skills in a variety of settings, especially cross-cultural situations, is a necessity. We have observed that many individuals fear the experience of presenting a message to an audience. To provide exposure to skills helpful in day-to-day living and to provide experiences in speaking before an audience, activities in speaker-audience communication have been integrated with activities in the interpersonal and multi-cultural communication areas. This integration allows the student to gradually move from making a somewhat informal statement before an audience to eventually providing the audience with a formal message, all the while participating in intrapersonal, interpersonal, small group speaking, and critical listening experiences.

To provide the necessary guidance for making a public speech, the last unit of this book has been designed to provide the traditional coverage of speaker-audience communication. The integrated approach avoids the often frightening impact of the assignment to make an informative or persuasive speech to a formal audience and allows formal presentation skills to evolve gradually. This text can be effectively used for interpersonal communication courses, for the integrated speech communication approach, or for a two-semester or two-quarter course of interpersonal communication followed by speaker-audience communication. It can also be used in public speaking courses where exposure to more general communication skills is desirable. By selecting relevant activities and readings from the introductory, listening and nonverbal, interpersonal, small group, and speaker-audience units, a course can be designed to meet the speech communication needs of most student populations.

Special thanks are due to Eastfield College students who contributed ideas for speeches as examples and who contributed photographs to illustrate the book. Further thanks are due to

Ric Masten who willingly allowed us to use his poetry to further illustrate the material in the book. We know our readers will enjoy the special meaning that Ric has conveyed through his unique way of seeing and then describing in verse the world around him. Finally, we wish to dedicate this book to our children, Laci Forrest Secor, Jason Forrest, Tonia Olson, and Stefan Olson.

Mary Forrest
Margot Olson

COMMUNICATION DEFINED

Overview

Communication is a term to which most readers of this book will have attached some meaning. In fact, even at this point in the study of communication, most readers could produce an adequate and informed definition of the term. Communication—talking, writing, gesturing—is a part of every college student's life. Communication, not necessarily good communication, is as natural as sleeping and eating and is taken for granted by most. Communication is an area of study where students can gain considerable insight and growth as they experience and learn new skills. With the spread of technology making the world a global village, communication becomes even more critical in relating to people who represent cultural differences. Sharing meaning is generally more complex as the parties to the exchange have less in common.

Consider the reflections of the poet, Ric Masten, in his poem "Conversation." Through the sensitivities of a poet, we can recognize a communication situation which we have all experienced. Communication is much more than talking and listening: it involves relationships with others and reactions to ordinary day-to-day situations as well as to complex business and social situations. The speaker has a responsibility to facilitate listening. Was the speaker delivering a message that was boring or too complex to hold the attention of the receiver? The listener also shares responsibility

Conversation

i have just wandered back
into our conversation
and find that you are still rattling on
about something or other
i think i must have been gone at least
twenty minutes
and you never missed me
now this might say something
about my acting ability
or it might say something about
your sensitivity
one thing troubles me though
when it is my turn to rattle on for twenty
minutes which i have been known to do
have you been missing too?

—Ric Masten
Speaking Poems published by Sunflower Ink,
Carmel, CA

for the communication exchange. Was the listener responding appropriately by sending nonverbal and verbal messages that indicated lack of interest or understanding? As we interact more and more with people representing differences in our society, sensitivity to the sending and receiving of messages becomes more critical in order to have shared meaning.

The following three chapters are included to provide a foundation for the study of communication by providing a definition of the term communication. The chapters deal with the meaning of the term, the physical and intellectual processes which provide the human organism the ability to communicate, and the effect on the communication process of the individual's image of self. The chapters are based on the research and thinking of many communicators who have shared careful reflections with others. The purpose of the chapters is to provide a foundation needed not only to acquire knowledge about the communication process, but more importantly, to put into practice techniques and skills that will improve one's ability to communicate within our complex, multi-cultural modern society. Each person, regardless of goals in life, must achieve a minimum level of competence in communication in order to survive. Communication is so vital to every aspect of a full and rewarding life that it is important to achieve more than a minimum effectiveness. Communication can be improved by studying basic concepts of communicating with an audience, in small groups, and on a one-to-one basis. Even study of the listening process, both as the sender and receiver of the message, can facilitate communication.

Literacy is usually defined as the ability to read, write, and speak and to compute or solve mathematical problems at a level which enables the individual to function in work and in society. According to the National Adult Literary Survey (National Institute for Literacy, n.d.) more than 44 million American adults are functionally illiterate and face much higher rates of unemployment, poverty, welfare, and crime. On the other hand, research has shown that education is highly correlated with income. According to USA Today (Reilly & Ahrens, 2005), paychecks increase with education—those without a high school diploma earn an average of $18,734 annually, those with a high school diploma earn an average of $27, 915 annually, and those with a four-year college degree earn an average of $51, 206. Standards, which have been compiled by the National Institute for Literacy (n.d.), include such speech communication skills as speaking so others can understand, listen actively, observe critically, plan, cooperate with others, advocate and influence, and resolve conflict. Speech communication is definitely an area of study where lifelong learning is essential in order to reap the maximum benefits from social, cultural, and economic opportunities.

Ability to communicate effectively provides an advantage in reaching personal goals, achieving occupational success, and participating in the rich cultural life of our multi-faceted society. Often money is seen as the great divider between the "haves" and "have nots" in regard to leading a rich and interesting life. More likely, the divider is education since those who are educated can live proactively and use critical thinking skills in making decisions. Perhaps, you have chosen to enter a profession such as law, medicine, or teaching, or to become a skilled tradesperson or public service worker. And perhaps you plan to be a parent and an active community member. In several of your many roles, you may be called upon to give a speech, to participate in a planning activity involving a small group, or even to introduce someone. In all your roles, you will need to participate on a one-to-one basis and you will need to listen. Communication involves demanding, complex behaviors that study, practice, and concentration can improve. A study of communication will provide a basis for better understanding oneself and for more rewarding interaction with others. Communication is an area of study that cannot be removed from processes of daily living; the study of communication is relevant for anyone seeking to expand opportunities and to maximize competence in all areas of living.

A good speaker is not born a good speaker, just as a good athlete is not born a good athlete. Both are born with potential that must be developed. If a magic formula exists for becoming an effective communicator, it includes practice, awareness, interest, and enthusiasm. Our society is becoming more complex as time moves forward; speech communication is an essential skill for maximizing the potential you have and becoming a self-actualized person. Our society is rich with opportunities to expand horizons and to explore the exciting differences that abound as our globe shrinks and we all enjoy broader horizons.

CHAPTER 1

THE MEANING OF COMMUNICATION

Communication is the sharing of meaning. When one person is able to transmit a thought to another person who attaches some meaning to the thought, communication has occurred. The sharing of meaning between two individuals is not always accurate. Each thought transmitted has the potential to take on one or more meanings. An effective communicator takes great care in choosing the symbols, that is, the words and gestures, that enable the listener to attach the expected meaning to the thought.

GOAL
Define communication.

Some insight into the question of whether meaning has been shared may be gained by considering the following question: Does a falling tree create sound in an isolated forest? Some would argue that a tree that falls in a forest devoid of listeners creates no sound, and there are others who would argue that sound is created independently of the presence of listeners. There can be no resolution of the controversy until the two debaters recognize that they have attached differing meanings to the word "sound." One of them believes that sound must stimulate the eardrum and be transmitted to the brain of some organism; the other believes that sound results from the movement of air waves. Were the two debaters communicating? It seems safe to assume that they were communicating to some extent, but more effective communication would have resulted from clarification of the seemingly simple term "sound."

To provide an adequate basis for study, the definition of communication must be expanded by illustrating a model for a simple communication exchange, by discussing common delivery systems and types of communication domains and by presenting the functions of communication in today's world. Within these contexts, the concept of communication will take on an expanded, more complete meaning that will form the foundation required to bring about more fulfilling communication domains.

The Communication Model

A communication exchange is the sending of a message from one person to another. When the message is a part of a conversation, many exchanges will often follow rapidly one after another. The communication exchange between two individuals can be illustrated in a simple form by developing a visual model of the process. To provide a concrete basis for the example, consider the following "conversation."

Person 1: "I'm tired."
Person 2: "You look dead."

Sending the Message

The communication exchange begins when one person has a thought, a feeling, or perhaps a description of an object or event that needs to be transmitted to another person. The originator, that is, the sender in the communication

exchange, is the first element of the model (Figure 1.1).

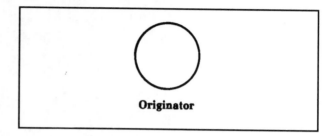

Figure 1.1

The originator must translate the thought, idea, or description into symbols, that will convey the intended meaning. Finding the right symbols, usually words, is called encoding (Figure 1.2).

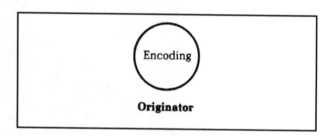

Figure 1.2

Once the encoding process is completed the message has been prepared. At this point in the process, message refers to the symbols that the originator will use to send the thought, idea, or description to another person. In the exchange given above, the originator has encoded certain physiological feelings and has used the verbal symbols, "I'm tired," to send the message (Figure 1.3).

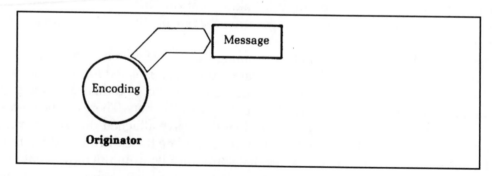

Figure 1.3

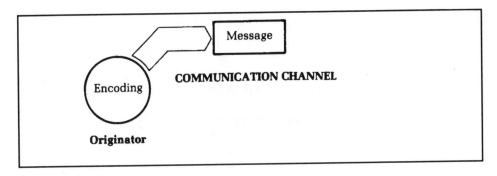

Figure 1.4

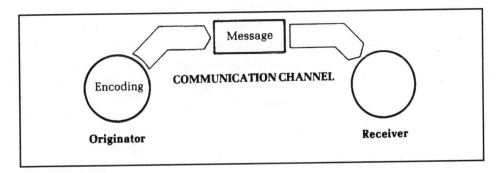

Figure 1.5

The message is sent by the originator via a communication channel. There are a number of ways to send messages. Speaking, writing, and gesturing are the most common (Figure 1.4).

RECEIVING THE MESSAGE

For communication to take place, there must be a receiver of the message (Figure 1.5).

The receiver must interpret the symbols used by the originator to transmit the idea, thought, or description. The process of giving meaning to the symbols representing the message is called decoding. It is in one sense the opposite process of encoding; it enables the originator and receiver to share meaning and thus to communicate (Figure 1.6).

RESPONDING TO THE MESSAGE

An acknowledgment that the message was received and decoded is called feedback. The feedback may be a frown or a nod, or it may take the form of a question or statement (Figure 1.7).

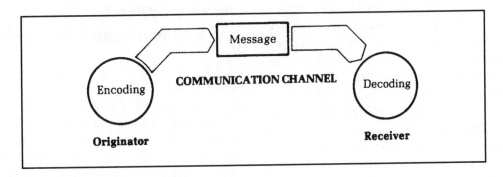

Figure 1.6

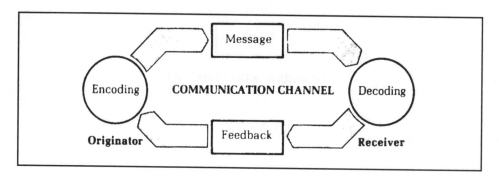

Figure 1.7

In the exchange given at the beginning of this section the receiver decoded the message and to show agreement transmitted feedback in the form of a statement, "You look dead." If the feedback results in another message from the originator, a continuing exchange of messages and feedback will occur. Both parties involved in the transaction will be originators and receivers and will contribute messages and feedback.

DISTORTIONS OF THE MESSAGE

The communication exchange can be upset by interfering stimuli occurring when the message or feedback is sent. Such interfering stimuli act as a "roadblock" which defeats the encoding and decoding processes. The distortion is often called "noise," and in the communication model illustrates a potential cause of misunderstanding. Noise affecting communication exchanges can be either physical or psychological.

Physical noise can be caused by distractions in the surrounding environment or by damage to the sensory receptors. Interference from an environmental factor would include noises from loud machinery, or a television blaring its message through a conversation. Damage to sensory receptors is manifested by impairment of hearing or poor vision. Such physical interference can result in partial reception of a message and can lead to misunderstanding.

Psychological noise is caused by mental characteristics of the individual that make it difficult to encode and decode messages properly.

GOAL
Identify elements (communication model) involved in any communication process.

For instance, the originator may have experienced anxiety over expressing a thought and, therefore, selected the wrong words in the encoding process, or social rules may inhibit the originator's ability to express an opinion accurately. Feelings of hostility, conflict, or prejudice will often result in distortion as the receiver gives a different meaning to the message than that intended by the originator. Generally, there is less psychological noise, or barriers to communication, and more effective communication among persons with similar backgrounds, values, language, attitudes, and experiences.

The communication model is a very simple way to demonstrate a very complex process. Its purpose is not to simplify the process. Its value lies primarily in the introduction and illustration of some terms—originator, encoding, message, communication channel, receiver, decoding, feedback and noise—that will be used as the meaning of communication is further expanded.

Delivery Systems and Communication Domains

Communication is a constantly occurring series of events. As students read this text, for example, concepts of communication are being transmitted. Reflective students, who stop reading to ponder an idea, are actually communicating within themselves. This example illustrates two ways that a single communication event can be analyzed: according to the type of delivery system used, and according to the type of domain. The delivery system is the means by which a message can be encoded. There are basically three types of delivery systems: written, verbal, and nonverbal. The delivery systems are used to transmit messages from original sources, such as statements made in conversations between two persons, or from secondary sources such as television or newspaper reports. A communication domain is characterized by the receiver or receivers of the message. Communication domains are generally classified in four ways: intrapersonal, interpersonal, small group, and speaker-audience. Both the mode of delivery and the type of domain are important considerations in developing effective communication skills.

DELIVERY SYSTEMS

The three delivery systems—written, verbal, and nonverbal—are alike in that they rely on symbols to transmit a message. To be effective, the symbols used in written, verbal, and nonverbal communication must be common to both the originator and the receiver of a message. Written and verbal communication both rely on words for the expression of meaning. In nonverbal communication meaning is shared through gestures, facial expressions, listening behaviors, and such artifacts as clothing, hairstyles, and possessions.

The term speech communication generally refers to verbal and nonverbal messages. In speech communication, however, writing ability is needed for note-taking, which is an important listening skill, and for the preparation of public speeches. To be an effective communicator it is necessary to acquire special skills in all three of the delivery systems, and to be aware of the power of the media as secondary delivery systems. A brief look at each of the three primary delivery systems and the media as means of transmitting messages will expand the meaning of communication.

Written Communication

In general, written communication requires greater facility with words and language than does verbal communication. The reason for this

GOAL
Recognize how written and spoken communication styles differ.

is the absence of immediate feedback from the receiver to the originator. Often a message is expressed in writing because a spoken message is impossible. To avoid misunderstanding, the originator of the written message must anticipate the decoding process by asking, "What will these words mean to the receiver of the message?" The originator of written communication often has the opportunity to use dictionaries and other writing aids, to ask others to review a message, and to rewrite before sending the message to the ultimate receiver. Interestingly, speech communication skills can sometimes be useful in developing written as well as spoken messages.

Verbal Communication

Just as the study of English composition emphasizes written composition, speech communication generally emphasizes the verbal aspects of transmitting messages. Verbal communication is taken for granted by most people because they acquire the ability to use a spoken language naturally and at a very young age. They fail to realize, however, that many of their day-to-day problems could be lessened by paying greater attention to verbal communication skills. This is not to imply that a speech communication course will solve all life's problems. Even the experts in the field of speech communication suffer the problems of communicating poorly.

Nonverbal Communication

Nonverbal communication occurs simultaneously with verbal communication in face-to-face situations. Even a totally paralyzed person would be communicating nonverbally that a physical disability exists. Many nonverbal reactions occur spontaneously. Most people in conversation naturally smile, nod, or point without asking themselves each time if the response is appropriate or inappropriate. An understanding of the role that nonverbal messages play in the total communication exchange is useful not only in encoding messages but also in decoding the messages sent by others.

The Media

"The media" are mechanical means of transmitting messages such as television, radio, films, newspapers, magazines, and books. Computer networks offer another avenue to access information. Media are considered secondary delivery systems because the receiver of the message does not receive it from the originator in a face-to-face encounter. For most people contact with the media will be primarily as passive receivers of messages. In our roles as passive receivers, the media, especially television, have influenced what we know, what we buy, what we eat, how we live, when we leave home, and even when we go to the bathroom. The media have powerful influences too on personal courses of action and decision making of major consequence in the lives of nearly everyone. Images of professions, fashions, and lifestyles are presented and often form the basis for, or at least contribute to, the goals and aspirations of receivers.

The impact of both print and nonprint media on communication is enormous. Many homes in the United States contain more televisions than occupants; publishers are reporting higher and higher circulation and advertising revenues. More and more households and educational institutions are acquiring computers. Mass media do much to provide a common bond among and within nations. The receiver, however, must realize first that all messages may not be accurate and unbiased, and then must develop evaluative skills to use in screening messages. The underlying purpose of much of the popular media is sales. Often the sales motivation leads to an overemphasis on subjects that draw attention and to neglect of issues of more importance.

The competition to break news to the public is so fierce that the lives of noteworthy people are perhaps misrepresented or endangered and their right to privacy is possibly violated. The years 1997–98 provide two examples of media frenzy that some people found repulsive, annoying, and distasteful. The death of Diana, Princess of Wales, and the Clinton sex scandals occupied the media, engrossed the public, and will provide good fodder for lively debates. Some said that the relentless badgering of the press caused the reckless behavior which

resulted in Diana's death. Some said that Bill Clinton should be judged for his political activities and that his sexual behavior was a private matter between him and his wife. Some said that the media goes too far in disclosing personal business of celebrities and manipulating public interest. Whatever position you might have taken in judging the media, let us hope that the skills presented in this text will provide some basis for deciding when and when not to give credibility to the media.

Much that the listener learns in a speech communication course directed toward participation in firsthand sending and receiving of messages can be applied to messages received via some form of media. Listening skills are especially relevant to evaluating any message; a knowledge of purposes of messages and how

---

Hands

i think of my poems and songs
as hands
and if I don't hold them out to you
i find i won't be touched

If i keep them
in my pocket i would never get to see you
seeing me
seeing you

and though i know from experience
many of you
for a myriad of reasons
will laugh
and spit
and walk away unmoved
still
to meet those of you
who do reach out
is well worth the risk and pain

so
here are my hands
do what you will

—Ric Masten
The Voice of the Hive published by Sunflower Ink,
Carmel, CA

to construct them helps in understanding and retaining information, and background in interpersonal and small group communication aids in the interpretation of the subtle messages underlying some television entertainment and reading material. The media have an impact on the quality of life that most people never consider. Do not be surprised when a child spells relief as R-O-L-A-I-D-S, tells you to buy Downy to soften clothes, or thinks the name of a popular sportscar is Zoom-Zoom.

COMMUNICATION DOMAINS

Speech communication is often studied within areas representing four domains—intrapersonal, interpersonal, small groups, and speaker-audience. The division into four domains may be viewed as a progression from communicating with oneself, with one other person, with several people, and with large groups of listeners. It should be obvious that the communication situation changes drastically through the progression from sending messages to oneself to the delivery of a formal message to an audience. Communication apprehension is often a stumbling block to becoming an effective communicator in each of the four domains.

Intrapersonal Communication

Intrapersonal communication, that is, communication that occurs within each individual, is going on continuously. It might be considered the most basic of the four communication domains because it forms the basis of messages to be shared with other individuals. The message must first be established within the individual before it can be transmitted to a receiver. Thoughts, or messages within the individual, need not be shared with others, however. Much time spent in thought has the purpose of developing insights into personal problems, establishing attitudes about issues, or contemplating knowledge that has been gained from personal experiences and the media.

Intrapersonal communication can occur in isolation or in the midst of other people. The

---

GOAL
Differentiate areas of communication: intrapersonal, interpersonal, small group and public speaking.

---

distinguishing characteristic of intrapersonal communication is that it is maintained within the individual and is not shared with others. In the study of speech communication, intrapersonal communication is often studied along with the other three types of encounters. In interpersonal communication, for example, much emphasis is placed upon individual reflection of attitudes, values, and behaviors. In small group communication, private thought is often given to ways of expressing viewpoints and influencing other members. The planning of the formal message for delivery to an audience is done through careful and reflective study of the material to be presented. Although the study of intrapersonal communication is not always pointed out, it cannot be ignored as an essential element of study in all aspects of speech communication.

Interpersonal Communication

Interpersonal communication occurs when two people recognize the presence of the other and share their thoughts. Interpersonal communication is usually informal and unplanned. The messages are often personal, as when one friend reveals thoughts and feelings to another friend. The messages take the form too of requests for services or information, or of answering the requests of others. Many interpersonal communication techniques have the potential to improve the communication process that people depend on in fulfilling their day-to-day physical and psychological needs. The many newspaper reports of interpersonal conflicts that eventually result in violence are ample evidence that skill in interpersonal communication is often lacking in American society.

Small Group Communication

Small group communication occurs when several people get together for a purpose. The purpose can be social, but often involves discussion of a particular topic or an attempt to solve problems. A small group generally forms when meaningful interaction among members occurs because they have something in common. Meaningful interaction in small groups will generally include face-to-face contact, purposeful discussion, a common goal, and an established way of interacting.

Examples of small groups include families, committees in social and work organizations, clubs, and work teams. To be successful, small groups must include people who maintain their individuality while working cooperatively toward achieving group goals. A study of small group communication will reveal information about leadership styles, ways to involve all members of the group, techniques for sharing responsibility, and methods that are useful in reaching conclusions.

Speaker-Audience Communication

The presentation of a message to an audience (i.e., public speaking) is a more formal situation than interpersonal and small group communication. It generally involves advance preparation and there is little or no verbal interaction between the speaker and audience. The message generally involves a body of material that will be appropriate for a large group of people. The language used to relay the message is more general than it is specific because it must be decoded by a group rather than an individual. It is one speaking situation that permits formulation of thoughts in time to revise and work toward maximizing the effectiveness of the message. There are many specific guidelines available to help the speaker prepare a message for a large audience. Careful preparation in speaker-audience communication increases the chances that the message will be successfully delivered to the listeners.

Communication Apprehension

Communication apprehension refers to a state where a speaker feels extreme anxiety about a communication encounter. Shyness, nervousness, or stage fright might be used to describe communication apprehension in different settings. Although intrapersonal communication anxiety may seem impossible, apprehension can occur in all four of the previously described domains. Apprehension leads to fear which can result in embarrassing physi-

ological reactions such as irregular breathing, perspiration, increased heart rate, stomach spasms, twitching muscles, and squeaky voice. Consider some of the following suggestions for overcoming communication apprehension.

In *intrapersonal communication*, thinking and feeling are the key components. When anxiety results, generally thoughts and feelings relate to the need to face difficult situations. Often the communicator finds reasons, that is, excuses, to avoid making a decision or facing up to an unpleasant situation. To avoid apprehension, the intrapersonal communicator must face situations head on—no Scarlett O'Hara reaction that problems can wait. Occasionally, problems or difficult situations will solve themselves but such procrastination is a bad habit to adopt. Being proactive—controlling events—is generally better than being reactive—letting events control you.

In *interpersonal communication*, anxiety often results from shyness or nervousness about conversation skills. Some people seem to have a natural talent for conversation; others feel at a loss about what to say in some situations. With guidance, motivation, and effort, a person can make significant improvement in conversational interactions. Techniques will be presented in part 3 of this text which will contribute to improving confidence in interpersonal encounters. Knowledge and practice will help eliminate feelings of shyness in meeting new people and carrying on conversations with people from all backgrounds and interests. Employment interviews are a particularly threatening interpersonal encounter since the stakes can be quite high. You can prepare by thinking of answers to probable questions and by thinking, in advance, of appropriate questions to ask. You might even role-play to improve your confidence in an interview format.

In *small group communication*, some individuals will fade into the background. They listen and send nonverbal messages, such as a nod or a smile, but they fail to speak and participate in the group encounter. More outgoing people have an obligation to include everyone. Often the apprehensive group member can be brought into a conversation by the more gregarious members. Once the ice is broken, shyness will be overcome. All members of a group must be made to feel that they have something to contribute. As presented in part 4 of this text, groups gain strength by discovering and building on the unique characteristics of everyone present. Reticent members of groups need to feel comfortable that a place for them exists in the tasks that lead to reaching group goals.

In *speaker-audience communication*, performance anxiety, or stage fright, affects nearly all speakers. Stage fright in delivering a message to an audience is similar to apprehension which is felt by athletes, musicians, or even test-takers. Numerous surveys have shown public speaking to be such a highly feared event that most people avoid it. Part 5 of this text will provide numerous strategies to use in preparing to make a public speech. Typically, preparation and rehearsal will lead to confidence which overcomes the debilitating effects of stage fright and turns stage fright into a motivational tool.

The communication model can be adapted to fit the four domains. All involve the components illustrated by the model, the major variation being the number of receivers and extent of feedback. The study of the four domains brings to attention the context variations in speech communication and suggests ways to maximize effectiveness in a variety of situations and ways to reduce communication apprehension.

Functions of Communication

The use of speech to communicate evolved first as a survival technique among very early populations of human beings. Today many people take for granted the fulfillment of their most basic needs. According to Abraham Maslow (1954), humans are motivated by the desire to fulfill five levels of basic needs.

1. **Physiological**—the need for air, water, food, rest, and reproduction of the species
2. **Safety**—the need for shelter, clothing, and protection from threats of life
3. **Social**—the need to belong and to be accepted, appreciated, and loved by others
4. **Self-Esteem**—the need to respect oneself and be respected by others
5. **Self-Actualization**—the need to fulfill one's potential and achieve all that is possible

The more basic needs in Maslow's list must be met before fulfillment of the higher needs can be attempted. Individuals who are concerned with studying about improving speech communication skills have probably achieved adequate physiological and safety needs to survive. They are interested in fulfilling social, self-esteem, or self-actualization needs. Communication will be particularly necessary to gain and give needed information, to persuade or influence others, to consider alternative solutions to problems and make decisions, and for social and entertainment purposes.

INFORMATION

To understand and function in the world, human beings must acquire a great store of information. Consider location of places and things, procedures for accomplishing specific tasks, and characteristics of cherished objects and pastimes. Much knowledge is acquired through discovery. Touching a hot flame is one way of acquiring the information that fire burns human skin. Because of the vast quantities of information to be acquired today, however, it is generally more efficient to gain and share information through written or spoken word—by using the ability to communicate—than by personal experience. Re-inventing the wheel takes too much time.

PERSUASION

Another aspect of contemporary living relates to the influence each person attempts to exert on others. It is important to be able to justify positions and opinions. This does not imply the ability to influence others for personal gain, but rather the ability to supply descriptions of the logic that forms the basis of one's behavior. There are times, too, when personal beliefs lead one to attempt to change the attitudes and values of others. The ability to influence and to judge the influence others exert is an important communication skill. In one word, this important function of communication might be summarized by the term "opinion." If I believe strongly in an issue, say physical fitness, then I will likely try to influence others to exercise more and improve their diets. I will use statistics, examples, case studies, and personal experience to influence them.

DECISION MAKING

Decisions are based on knowledge and opinions. The knowledge and opinions that one gathers are often the basis for discussion of alternatives in the decision-making process. An individual's choice of a solution, therefore, depends to a great extent on skill in gathering appropriate information, in evaluating opinions, and in discussing effects of potential solutions. Considering the many decisions facing the individual in contemporary society, communication skill has a tremendous influence on life outcomes. How does one make the decision to rent or own a home? The individual will talk to friends and family, will ask experts, will read books or articles, and will do a financial and goals analysis as part of the process of deciding to own or rent.

Communication

communication is my thing
and i'll gladly show you
how my knuckles bleed
as i go from door to door—knocking
and it pleases me to tell you
how i've wept into an open phone

is anybody home?
is anybody home?
communication is my thing

but once
while running my prepared speech
i paused for effect and heard breathing
you were there
i mean really there
and i became afraid

so hanging up
i went outside and looked around
until i found three deadly stones
and then i set off with my trusty sling
communication—that's my thing

—Ric Masten
Even As We Speak published by Sunflower Ink,
Carmel, CA

ENTERTAINMENT

Last, communication has a social or entertainment function in achieving the fulfillment of human needs. Perhaps skill in this area is not crucial since entertainment is available from the professionals who produce theater, movies, television, and books. However, greater pleasure is generally gained from such performances when the receiver's ability to decode the message is adequately developed. And nearly everyone interacts at a social level with friends and acquaintances. So again communication skill is an important ingredient in maximizing the benefits of social functions in daily life.

Summary

Communication is the sharing of meaning. To improve one's ability to verbally share meaning with and among others is the goal underlying the study of speech communication. The learning task can be simplified by more fully developing the meaning of the term communication and by considering and understanding the speech communication model, the systems for delivering messages, the types of communication domains, and the functions of communication in everyday living. Good communicators recognize that many barriers exist which impede the satisfactory sharing of meaning. Study of communication helps to eliminate barriers and increase effectiveness in a variety of communication situations.

The speech communication model includes the very important concepts of originator, receiver, encoding, decoding, message, feedback, channel, and noise. The three major delivery systems are written, verbal, and nonverbal messages. The media, including newspapers, books, and television, are powerful secondary means for message delivery. The types of communication domains are intrapersonal, interpersonal, small group, and speaker-audience. Communication serves the functions in everyday living of presenting information, revealing opinions, providing input and discussion for decision making, and creating entertainment.

CHAPTER 2

LANGUAGE IN COMMUNICATION

Nearly everyone has developed some capacity to communicate verbally with others. Being able to share meaning with others through talking is more or less taken for granted until thought is given to the underlying processes. Just what is it that enables human beings to symbolize meaning and transmit messages and be understood by others? A brief look at an area of study called language will reveal some of the bases for communication and some of the reasons that barriers, that is, communication breakdowns, occur.

Language, in very general terms, refers to words and the rules of grammar that determine their usage. A study of language as it relates to speech communication is enhanced by first investigating an area called sensation, then by looking at the relationship of sensation and perception, and finally by noting how language or symbolization depends upon processes of sensation and perception.

Sensation

Sensation refers to messages sent to the brain via body receptors associated with sight, hearing, touch, smell, and taste. The sensory receptors—the eyes, ears, skin and muscles, nose, and tongue—are the link between the human brain and surrounding environment. The meaning of the messages sent to the brain via the sensory receptors must be learned. One is not born, for example, knowing that the taste of lemon is sour or that the touch of fur is soft.

All the senses contribute to some extent to the speech communication process. Sight transmits nonverbal messages to the brain for interpretation. Since the brain receives approximately two-thirds of its messages from visual stimuli, sight is probably the most important of the five senses. Hearing, of course, transmits verbal messages to the brain for interpretation. Unlike visual messages, where the eye must be directed toward the object, sounds are received from all directions. Smell, touch, and taste sometimes play an important role in the communication process, also. Consider, for example, possible messages implied by a strong perfume, a firm handshake, or the taste of salt air at the seashore.

What happens when people find themselves in an environment characterized by a particularly noxious smell (e.g., a chemistry lab after an exercise with sulfur)? At first they are repulsed by the odor, but gradually they become accustomed to the smell and it no longer bothers them.

An Exercise in Perception: The Parable of the Six Blind Men of Indostan

It was six men of Indostan
    To learning much inclined
Who went to see the Elephant
    (Though all of them were blind),
That each by observation
    Might satisfy his mind.

The First approached the Elephant,
    And happening to fall
Against his broad and sturdy side,
    At once began to bawl:
"God bless me! but the Elephant
    Is very like a wall."

The Second, feeling of the tusk
    Cried, "Ho! what have we here
So very round and smooth and sharp?
    To me 'tis very clear
This wonder of an Elephant
    Is very like a spear."

The Third approached the animal
    And, happening to take
The squirming trunk within his hands
    Thus boldly up he spake:
"I see," quoth he, "the Elephant
    Is very like a snake!"

The Fourth reached out an eager hand,
    and felt about the knee:
"What most this wondrous beast is like
    Is very plain," quoth he;
"'Tis clear enough the Elephant
    Is very like a tree!"

The Fifth, who chanced to touch the ear,
    Said, "E'en the blindest man
Can tell what this resembles most;
    Deny the fact who can
This marvel of an Elephant
    Is very like a fan!"

The Sixth no sooner had begun
    About the beast to grope
Then seizing on the swinging tail
    That fell within his scope:
"I see," quoth he, "the Elephant
    Is very like a rope!'

And so these men of Indostan
    Disputed loud and long,
Each in his own opinion
    Exceeding stiff and strong.
Though each was partly in the right,
    They all were in the wrong!

Source: John Godfrey Saxe. Poems, Boston. 1852.

When a newcomer walks into the area, a typical comment might be, "How can you stand this place?" They are able to stand it because of the body's ability to adapt to a constant stimulus. As a stimulus remains the same, fewer and fewer nerve impulses are sent to the brain. The senses of smell and touch more readily adapt to constant stimulation than the other senses. Because the eye is constantly moving, sensory adaptation of vision is unlikely.

At any point in time, the body's receptors for sight, sound, touch, smell, and taste are receiving stimulation from many sources. Concentrate, for a moment, on each of your senses—what do you see around you, what are the sounds you can hear, how does your skin feel against your clothes and surrounding objects, are there any distinguishable odors around you, what tastes are you experiencing?

There was probably so much going on around you that you were unaware of most of it. Hopefully you were concentrating on your reading and experienced very little awareness of other stimuli. Focusing on specific aspects of the environment to the exclusion of other aspects is the process of selective attention. Fortunately, at least for most people, the neglect of unimportant sensations allows the human mind to focus on and process what is interpreted as the most relevant of the multitude of potential stimuli.

Perception

Sensation and the processes of sensory adaptation and selective attention bring the relevant stimuli from the environment to the

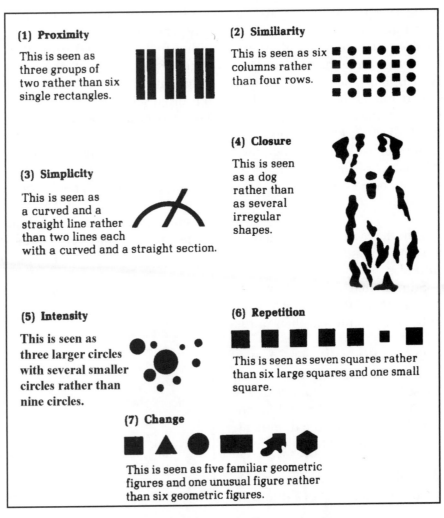

Figure 2.1. Environmental *Effects* on Perception

brain. What is done with the stimuli and the meanings attached to them is the process of perception. The meanings attached to the stimuli are based on the individual's knowledge, background, and experiences. Thus behavior and the individual's focus on the world are a combination of what occurs in the environment and what has previously occurred within the individual. Further understanding of the perceptual process may be gained by considering some aspects of environment and characteristics of the perceiver that affect perception.

PERCEPTION AND ENVIRONMENT

To be given meaning, stimuli must be selected, organized, interpreted, and judged. It may be that the chance a given stimulus has to gain meaning is similar in probability to the chance a given fish egg has to hatch. Both are dependent on what goes on in the surrounding environment. A dripping faucet, for example, will seldom be heard among the activities of the day. During the quiet of the night it takes on the impact of a steadily beating hammer on a tin roof. Figure 2.1 and the list below include factors that affect the chance of a given stimulus to reach the point of being interpreted and judged.

1. **Proximity**—Stimuli placed closely together are likely to stand out against a less dominant background.
2. **Similarity**—Stimuli that can be grouped according to some related characteristic will tend to be more dominant than unrelated stimuli.
3. **Simplicity**—Stimuli that have fewer distinguishing features will tend to be more dominant than those that are quite complex.
4. **Closure**—Stimuli with gaps that fit into an established pattern will be more dominant than other partial stimuli with no obvious pattern.
5. **Intensity**—Stimuli that exceed what might be considered the normal range of a stimulus

---

GOAL
Describe how perception affects communication.

---

will be more dominant than those within the normal range.
6. **Repetition**—Stimuli that occur again and again are more likely to become dominant than a single occurrence of a similar stimulus.
7. **Change**—Stimuli that are new in a somewhat familiar surrounding are more likely to become dominant than whatever preceded them.

The impact of a selected stimulus in the perceptual process also depends on its interaction with other stimuli. Seldom does an individual focus attention on a single aspect of a given stimulus. All the senses together react and form a total perceptual experience.

PERCEPTION AND THE INDIVIDUAL

The characteristics of the stimuli themselves affect what is perceived. In addition, the individual's past and present experiences and state of mind affect the interpretation and judgment of stimuli in the perceptual process. It is often said that we see what we want to see. This may be a simplification, but much research has demonstrated that individual perceptions are most certainly related to individual characteristics. Everyone has read about or witnessed different people giving a description of the "same" event. The result is generally as many versions as there are individuals. Perhaps our suspicions should be aroused when two

---

On This Bus

my god
it just occurred to me
underneath
our clothes
everyone on this bus
is stark naked

–Ric Masten
Stark Naked published by Sunflower Ink,
Carmel, CA

individuals reveal identical accounts of an event! The factors listed below have been shown by researchers to influence an individual's perception of events.

- **Expectancy**—Because of prior experience with sets of circumstances that are similar to a set of current circumstances, individuals anticipate what will probably occur and may react according to what is anticipated rather than what is reality. For example, an adult son might return home after a long absence, go to his old bedroom, and be surprised that it is now a computer room.
- **Habit**—Because of routine ways of reacting to a given stimulus, individuals often fail to perceive subtle differences in a similar stimulus and react in the way they are accustomed to reacting. For example, even a good student proofing a paper often overlooks misspelled words because of their similarity to the correct spelling.
- **Motive**—The dominance of a particular motive will often cause individuals to perceive stimuli associated with fulfilling immediate needs. For example, individuals who become hungry on a motor trip will begin taking notice of signs and other indicators of restaurants and food that would otherwise have been overlooked.
- **Constancy**—The world is composed of many features that are uniform. Because of this, individuals automatically adjust a distorted shape to see it as it generally exists. For example, a plate seen from across a table has the shape of an ellipse but would readily be called a circle by most observers.
- **Relativity**—Individuals will often categorize stimuli in relation to surrounding stimuli. For example, a basketball player will seem like a giant among average people but will appear normal among teammates.
- **Familiarity**—From a group of competing stimuli, individuals are likely to perceive more readily those that they routinely encounter and, therefore, relate to. For example, individuals will readily perceive their own names from among the chatter of a large group of people.

What the individual recognizes from the environment and then interprets is affected by many internal and external factors. The important point to remember, at least in regard to communication, is that people send and react to

---

Real Life Situation
You are exposed to constantly changing people, places, and events in your surroundings.

Your Perceptions
Past Experiences—You have certain expectations of how individuals and groups should behave and how things ought to be in specific situations.
Self-Concept—You have an idea of who you are and what you are and of the kind of person you would like to be.
Objectives—You have present goals that you are trying to achieve in specific situations.
Obligations—You have obligations and know what others expect of you in a given situation.
Sentiments—You have prejudices, likes, dislikes, and loyalties for specific individuals and groups.

Your Interpretation of the Situation
You need to be aware of and to recognize your own involvement in a situation and then interpret the situation objectively.

messages according to their own perspectives, and that many barriers emerge or communication breakdowns occur when others make the wrong assumption that everyone sees the world in the same way that they see it.

To show the impact of perception in communication, consider the following statement by African-American psychometrician, Lloyd Bond (1995), in reference to scoring paradigms for high-stakes performance tests of candidates for the prestigious National Board for Professional Teaching Standards: "...it would take an extraordinary effort on my part to give the same evaluation to two individuals who are identical in every way, except that one has a high British accent and the other a deep southern drawl" (p. 23). Can it be that Bond is saying that judgments about images projected in communication encounters are difficult to erase even by persons highly trained in objectivity and elimination of bias?

EXTRASENSORY PERCEPTION

Another area of perception that many people find interesting is extrasensory perception, ESP. ESP is the ability to gain information through means that fall outside the realm of scientific law. It includes clairvoyance, knowledge of things that are out of sight; precognition, prediction of future events; and telepathy, the reading of someone else's mind. Most scientists are quite skeptical about extrasensory perception and feel that events attributed to ESP are explainable through coincidence and chance occurrence. Some communicators who are extremely sensitive to their surroundings seem to possess the skills of extrasensory perception. It is likely, however, that such people merely attend to stimuli and perceive their environment with much deeper concentration than the majority of the population.

Language

Language is the use of symbols to convey meaning. Through use of language, humans have been able to make the intellectual, cultural, and technological achievements that set them apart from other animal species. Language provides, as well, the basis for establishing social and emotional ties that are essential for a truly healthy psychological being. Good communicators understand sensation, perception, and language to such an extent that barriers to understanding and sharing are often minimized, reduced, or even eliminated.

Sensations, primarily sight and sound, allow humans to receive verbal and nonverbal messages from others. Those messages that are perceived are given meaning by the receiver. Verbal messages use language to convey the sender's meaning. Confusion, breakdowns, and barriers to sharing meaning often result from cultural experiences and diverse backgrounds where people learn different symbols, verbal and nonverbal, to express themselves. To understand language better and to improve speech communication skills, it is useful to consider words, their meanings, the circumstances that influence the ways different people use language, and the acceptable usage of language as a basis for sharing meaning. Finally, several recommendations to facilitate using language to convey thoughts will be presented.

WHAT ARE WORDS?

Words are the symbols for objects, events, and feelings; they are not the objects, events, and feelings themselves. A problem that occurs in using language is the substitution in an individual's mind of the word for the object, event, or feeling itself. For example, the actual presence of a snake is, perhaps, reason to experience fear. Hearing the word "snake" in the absence of the creature should not cause fear; but often does.

Words enable humans to translate thoughts and experiences into a form that can be shared with other individuals. What is communicated is based on the combination of words and gestures used to transmit the messages. The words and gestures represent the thought or experience; they are not the thought or experience itself.

GOAL
Illustrate how the use of language affects communication.

Words do create visual images in the minds of both the originator and receiver. The visual image may account for the fear that some people feel when they hear the word snake. For some the visual image is, in effect, the same experience as seeing the object or event itself. Creating strong visual images through verbal communication can be extremely successful as a way of increasing the ability of the receiver to share meaning with the originator of a message. The visual potential of words can create more interesting and successful communication domains.

Think for a moment of the benefits provided the human race by this amazing ability to use words to represent objects, events, and feelings. Without the symbolic code provided by words, conversation would not exist. There would be no way to describe past events or discuss future expectations. Storing memories and experiences would be difficult if not impossible, and transmission of knowledge from generation to generation would probably not exist. Words and their associated visual images, then, enable the human race to describe and represent past, present, and future experiences, thoughts, and expectations.

WHAT IS MEANING?

Words themselves do not possess meaning. The meanings attached to words exist within the person who is perceiving the words. Many words, in fact, are associated with several meanings, and the same object, event, or feeling may be described in a variety of ways. Words have no meaning until the individuals who use them attach some meaning to them. Each person, through past experiences with a word or combination of words, attaches a unique and personal meaning to every message.

The fact that words do not possess exact meanings common to all communicators is an underlying cause of communication breakdowns. As messages are sent, communicators fail to consider the origin of meaning of the words they select. They fail to consider that the meaning of each word originates in their own experiences with the word in the past. It is unlikely that the receivers of their messages have experienced the same sets of prior experiences with the word. In formulating and interpreting verbal messages, it is important to remember that the same word may represent more than one thing, that meanings exist within individuals, and that two individuals will often assign different interpretations to the same set of words.

Context, or the interaction of words with one another, is an extremely important way of determining meaning. Context is essential to interpreting words with several meanings, and it is a way to check the meaning that seems to be intended by a message. Many communication breakdowns occur when words or groups of words are removed from their contexts. This can occur when messages are repeated from person to person, or when the receiver hears a part of the message and then suddenly stops listening.

Another factor to consider in looking at the meanings associated with words is whether the thing represented exists in the real world as well as the mind, or exists only in the mind. For example, the object referred to by the word "table" exists in reality as well as psychologically. It is possible to point at and touch a table. On the other hand, feelings do not exist as actual objects. They exist only within the individual. One cannot locate and see actual objects referred to by words like love, fear, or spirit. Communication breakdown or confusion is more likely to result from words whose meanings exist only internally. Whenever possible, use words that represent concrete objects to add clarity to the communication process.

HOW BARRIERS RESULT FROM LANGUAGE USAGE

Language development in the human begins in early infancy. Although cooing and gurgling sounds are emitted earlier, the first words are usually spoken between twelve and eighteen months of age. Young children acquire the language patterns of those with whom they interact. Therefore, they acquire the particulars of their native tongue as well as the characteristics of the region in which they grow up. They acquire certain peculiarities of language that associate them with a particular geographic region. The New England accent of Senator

Speaker		Listener
I live in a new house.		*What type of architecture?*
It's a colonial style.		*Is it one-story or two-story?*
It's one-story.		*Does it have shutters?*
It has shutters.		*Is it painted a dark or light color?*
It's white with dark shutters.		*Why didn't you just tell me you had a new, one-story, white colonial house with dark shutters?*
Oh, why doesn't anyone ever understand me?		

Figure 2.2. What Is Meaning?

Edward Kennedy and the southern drawl of former President Jimmy Carter are very obvious examples of regional variations. More subtle influences are recognized by experts who notice that one individual "sits in the first row" and another "sits on the first row," or that some people use bags for groceries and others use sacks.

A second influence on language usage is socioeconomic position. In fact, many initial impressions of background and education are made on the basis of language, particularly the way the individual uses sounds to form words and chooses words to form thoughts. Eliza Doolittle's change from pauper to aristocrat in *My Fair Lady* could not have occurred without the extensive language training provided by Professor Higgins.

In addition to regional and socioeconomic influences on language, group associations often result in specialized vocabularies and speaking habits. Some occupations, for example, require development of new language skills to understand and be understood. Computers are a part of everyone's lives whether or not they directly use computers.

Spiders

when i was a little kid
another little kid told me
that if i poured water down a tarantula hole
i could get him to come out
so i did
> *and he did*
and bit me

since then spiders
have not been among my favorite things

last year i had occasion
to spend some time with an entomologist
that's a bug freak
and this nut was really into spiders
> *beautiful creatures*
that walk smoothly
four feet on the floor
not jerky like people
this dude didn't live in a house
he lived in a big jar full of 'em

and i got to thinking
that if someone ran up to us in the street
yelling
> *spiders!*
we'd 'a' both known

what he was hollering about
but we would 'a' knocked each other down
running in different directions

> *when it comes to words*
> *it's a miracle we communicate at all*

—Ric Masten
Even As We Speak published by Sunflower Ink,
Carmel, CA

How frustrating it is to hear that "the computer is down." We all know that phrase will lead to some degree of inconvenience. Computers involve a specialized language thatc the general public is more and more able to decipher. The computer experts, however, can choose to help the uninitiated to understand or cause them to be totally confused.

A fourth influence on language usage is the particular circumstances of each communication encounter. The age, sex, or cultural background of the listener will affect the way the speaker expresses thoughts and feelings. For example, young people often show their respect for an older person by reacting more formally than they would in a similar situation with a peer, and it seems inappropriate to most people to tell dirty jokes to the clergy. There are many conventions accepted within subgroups of society concerning what is proper and what is not proper in given situations. As individuals interact interpersonally, in small groups, or with an audience of listeners, their choice of words and use of language are constantly being adapted to provide the most appropriate presentation of the intended message within a particular cultural setting.

A fifth circumstance affecting language usage may be the limitations of the language itself. The Sapir-Whorf hypothesis (Whorf, 1956) was formulated to reflect the notion that our use of concepts to express ourselves is limited to those concepts for which we have words. There are numerous concepts for which words exist in other languages but do not exist in English. For example, one group of people in the Philippine Islands uses a different name to identify each of ninety-two varieties of rice. To English-speaking people, rice in its raw form is distinguishable in only a few categories by the use of adjectives. Because of its lesser importance to Americans, rice is more or less rice. In contrast, however, consider our vocabulary for describing motor vehicles: coupe, convertible, fastback, pickup, and so on.

Language is a complex system for communicating ideas, thoughts, and feelings to others. Words, with their associated meanings, are the foundation of language, but the ways in which the words are selected and used communicate also. Native region, background and education, occupation or group membership, unwritten rules concerning appropriate ways of speaking in given situations, and possibly limitations of the language itself affect what one individual says and another comprehends.

Ignoring the variances in communication background that we encounter in our multicultural society and global economy creates barriers to effective communication. A natural tendency is to reject or ignore those situations we encounter where differences dominate. The path of least resistance, the expenditure of the least effort, occurs when we choose paths that are comfortable yet not challenging. Consider a traveler, outside a zone of familiarity, who wishes to have a meal. If this traveler were you and you had a choice of three nationally franchised restaurants or a local name that you had never heard of, all things like appearance and cost being equal, which would you choose? Choosing the local name involves risk, open-mindedness, and the excitement of change. The national franchises provide consistency, stability, and absolutely nothing to broaden your experience. Most people stick with the familiar; their comfort level creates a barrier. By improving your communication skills, your self-esteem will soar and you will want to encounter different experiences and people with different backgrounds than your own.

Acceptable Usage of Language

People are judged by the way they talk. Many inferences, right and wrong, about people are made from their choice and way of saying words. Sophistication of vocabulary, fluency, and the way that words are said can make a powerful impression on the listener. The impression might be one of intelligence, "putting on airs," formality, conscientious preparation, snobbishness, scholarship, and others.

Language is sometimes classified as formal, standard, and slang. Formal language is primarily written or used in professional presentations. It can be found in technical journals, at professional meetings, and in legal reports. Formal language is well organized, follows precisely defined guidelines for preparation, and relies on vocabulary often understood only by members of specific groups. Standard language is the use of language according to generally accepted rules of grammar and pronunciation. It is understood by society as a whole and does nothing to draw particular attention to the speaker. General American speech is the term often used to describe the standards of speaking adopted by radio and television announcers, actors, and others with a national image.

Slang is primarily language spoken only among persons sharing close personal relationships or common backgrounds. Its use by and clarity for members of specialized groups makes it similar in one way to formal language. Slang is characterized by careless use of language, shortening of words and phrases for ease of speech, and the assignment of new meanings to words considered standard. Consider the examples of words sharing similar meanings but representing different usage, shown in the box following.

The different ways of speaking American English within the United States are referred to as dialects. Dialects differ from rules of general American speech in the use of vocabulary, the ways sounds are made and fit together to form words, and the way words fit together to form sentences. There are many dialects in use in the United States. In fact, it might be said that everyone speaks a particular dialect. Examples of obvious dialects include the Southern drawl, Brooklynese, urban Black, and Hispanic influence of Mexican, Puerto Rican, and Cuban cultures. When used in situations where meaning is shared adequately between originator and receivers, dialects cannot be judged as inferior modes of speaking. The difficulty with dialects is that they impair communication when spoken among persons unfamiliar with their use. Not only is meaning lost, but inappropriate impressions of intelligence and individual worth are often made. A speaker's dialect often leads to stereotyping by the receiver.

Whether to learn and use the rules of general American speech is an individual decision. Individuals must evaluate goals and determine the audiences with whom they plan to interact. If it appears that messages will be directed toward a broad cross section of American society, then mastery of general American speech will be important. General American speech, as defined by dictionaries and handbooks of grammar, is probably the most common basis for communication in the mobile society of today and will be understood more readily by a cross section of society.

Whereas some communicators have to overcome background and experience to use correct grammar and to reduce regional dialects and expressions, we all have the choice of whether

Comparison of Words and Meaning		
Formal	**Standard**	**Slang**
seminar	meeting	get-together
gain composure	relax	chill
intoxicants	liquor	booze
error	mistake	goof
theater	movie	show
exhausted	tired	wiped-out

or not to use profanity and other, less potentially offensive fillers in our speech. Profanity refers to meaningless words with associations which are intended to add emphasis to a communication exchange at the expense of group associations, religious beliefs, or other putdowns. Profanity may be acceptable in interpersonal communication with intimate acquaintances who are accustomed to a particular person's communication patterns, but profanity has no place in communication outside the intimate level or in the workplace. Often use of profanity is interpreted as an indication of poor education and lack of knowledge of appropriate behavior. Fillers, on the other hand, are sounds or words like "uhm," "ah," "you know," or "bottom line." Since fillers are not intended to offend, they are, perhaps, more acceptable. Profanity and fillers add nothing and are best omitted. Whatever the situation, to maximally share meaning, it is important to realize that individual cultural, social, and economic differences can cause mistaken meaning, or even no meaning, to be attached to a given message by a specific receiver.

Use of Language to Remove Barriers

In considering individual differences in sensation, perception, and language, it almost seems as if communication among individuals could not exist. Somehow it does and considering everything, it works quite well. There are barriers in communication, however, that can often be overcome by careful choice of words to represent a message. Eight guidelines for the use of language to convey meaning, often in settings of varied cultures, are given below.

GOAL

Identify ways to eliminate barriers to communication.

1. Use feedback to check the accuracy of interpretation. This is important to sender and receiver. As sender, pay attention to the feedback the receiver provides. As receiver, provide feedback that will give the sender an indication of your understanding.

2. Do not react reflexively to what you hear. Remember that words are not the actual objects, events, or feelings, and that meanings given to words are unique within each individual.

3. Remember that you do not know everything there is to know. The message you are receiving may not relate to your prior experience and knowledge. You may need to request additional information to attach personal significance to the message.

4. Keep in mind that situations change. As you send and receive messages, be aware that the prior experiences on which you are basing your descriptions and interpretations might have become invalid.

5. Use context to substantiate the intended message. Many words in the English

language have several meanings and many words sound very much like others. As speaker, do not assume the listener is aware of the context: provide the context. As listener, pay attention to context as a means of checking your interpretation of the message.

6. Avoid extreme reactions to messages. Often it is easier to interpret a given message and react as if it were a "yes-no" situation. A less extreme reaction will often more accurately reflect your true perception as well as avoid communication breakdown.

7. Remember that communication is more accurate between two persons sharing common experiences. Therefore, communication is clearer when words are selected that will make sense to the listener. Communication breakdown will be less likely to occur when messages are clear and relevant to the receiver.

8. Avoid intentional distortion of messages. Some communicators are creative enough to manipulate words meaning one thing into thoughts meaning something else. Such use of language is dishonest and really cannot be called communication.

9. Stay focused on your message. Avoid such communication pitfalls as indecision, vacillation, rambling, and introduction of inappropriate topics. Devious communicators use such tactics to get the focus off the real message. Sincere communicators avoid such ploys by keeping focused on the message.

Language is essential to the way our world operates. Misunderstandings are often humorous but can be disastrous. When accurate communication is the goal, it is necessary to consider how the listener will react to the symbols used to transmit the message. It is unwise to assume that symbols will be understood as intended.

Summary

The meaning given to the words used to communicate a thought or feeling is based on the entire set of reactions that occur in the receiver's mind. The meaning is based on the sensations of sight, sound, touch, taste, and smell that reach the receiver's brain. It is based on how the selected sensations are perceived, that is, how the receiver uses experience and knowledge to organize, interpret, and judge the sensations. The basis for understanding is language, or the use of symbols, both verbal and nonverbal, that represent specific objects, events, or feelings.

Communication barriers or confusion often occur when the receiver's interpretation of words used to convey a message is different from the originator's intention. To communicate effectively, both originators and receivers must realize that no two people, no matter how similar their backgrounds, will assign exactly the same meaning to a given set of symbols. To communicate effectively, keep in mind individual differences in reception of stimuli, in perception of the interacting stimuli that reach the brain, and in unique interpretations given to the words of the common language.

Looking for Patterns

I collect small
typewritten words
and fly them
        looking for patterns

sometimes they rise from me
in clouds
like birds off a field
to circle and then wheel away
for no apparent reason
        and i
lie empty as a pasture
left behind
defined only by these dark fences
of mine
        western civilization
        waiting for the punch line
missing the point

—Ric Masten
Speaking Poems published by Sunflower Ink,
Carmel, CA

CHAPTER 3

Photograph by Venisa Jones

INTRAPERSONAL COMMUNICATION

The communication process is based on the perceptions of the originators and receivers of messages. These perceptions include stimulation of the sensory receptors for hearing, seeing, tasting, smelling, and touching, as well as the background, experiences, and knowledge composing the communicator's perception of self. Perception of self includes the feelings people have about themselves and the feelings they think others have about them. After the basic sensory processes, perception of self may be the most important aspect of the communication process. When two persons are communicating, there may be as many as six perceptions of self interacting. Consider for a moment the various perceptions of self listed below (Barnlund, 1962).

1. YOUR image of the other person
2. YOUR image of yourself
3. YOUR impression of the other person's image of you
4. OTHER person's image of you
5. OTHER person's image of self
6. OTHER person's impression of your image of him or her

Perception of self forms the foundation of intrapersonal communication.

The communication process, as complicated as it may seem, is facilitated when the communicators have accurate impressions of themselves. When a clear impression of self exists it is easier to concentrate on the messages being sent and received. Speculation about others' impressions diminishes considerably, and feelings of greater confidence generally exist. Persons who have accurate and clear perceptions of self will be able to do the best they can with the abilities and characteristics they possess. Number "2" from the previous list is probably the most important of the six perceptions.

It can be a difficult task to analyze one's own image. It is probably worthwhile, however, as part of the process of working toward the improvement of communication skill. To assist the process of personal image clarification, it is useful to examine more fully perception of self, to contrast self-confidence as a communicator with defensiveness, to review the effect of credibility as it affects the sharing of meaning, and to explore the relationship of intrapersonal communication and perception of self.

GOAL
Explain how self-concept, self-esteem, and self-image affect communication.

Perception of Self

Perception of self is your idea of who you are and what you are. It is much more than name, age, occupation, marital status, eye color, height, and so forth. It is a combination of physical features, intellectual abilities, values, style of establishing and maintaining relationships, way of expressing thoughts and opinions, selections of clothing and other personal property, and everything else that makes one person unique and distinguishable from every other. Perception of self is referred to as self-concept, self-image, and self-esteem—terms which are frequently used interchangeably. In this book, we have chosen to use self-esteem since it implies a positive connotation in contrast to the neutral implications of self-concept and self-image.

Self-esteem begins developing as the infant becomes aware of the world and begins interacting with significant others in the surrounding environment. It is formulated primarily by successes and failures in different types of experiences, by the types of feedback received from others, and by perception of various roles and behaviors that are expected. The determination of feelings and worth begins early in life, but can be modified and even changed radically throughout life.

Figure 3.1. Perceptions of Self

Self-esteem is sometimes measured along a line that is called negative at one end and positive at the other. In theory at least, the many factors contributing to self-esteem can be analyzed and, in a sense, weighed to determine where on the line from negative to positive an individual's self-esteem falls. This is a useful measure. An important point to consider, however, is that nearly everyone possesses some negative and some positive feelings about specific aspects of self-esteem. Even the most confident persons harbor some self-doubt; even the most downtrodden individuals should be able to identify something positive about themselves. Before taking a serious look at your own self-esteem, a review of information about public versus private self, the self-fulfilling prophecy, and the effect of self-esteem on communication might prove helpful.

PUBLIC VERSUS PRIVATE SELF

Each individual has a self that is presented to others and a self that remains hidden from others: the public versus private selves. Differing public and private selves may be exemplified by the attitudes toward housecleaning and guests many families seem to hold. Many individuals present a public image of pride in a neat and orderly home; yet their private image allows for some clutter and disorderliness. The public image is often a combination of the private image and the role the individual is playing in a given situation.

In addition to the public and private selves, there are parts of the self that are known and other parts that are unknown. For example, an individual might be quite aware of a dialect representing a specific regional upbringing, but be totally unaware of habitually coughing before saying something. It is hard to admit or even realize that there are some aspects of self that are unknown to the individual, but it is probably true.

By combining the public and private selves with the known and unknown selves, a model for analyzing self-esteem can be developed. The model, called the Johari Window (Luft, 1969), is shown in the following diagram. The name of the model, Johari Window, comes from the names of the two men who developed the concept, Joseph Luft and Harry Ingham. The four parts of the Johari Window are more fully described below.

1. The open section refers to the image that is revealed to others and known by self. Examples of the open section include pride in housekeeping, leisure activities that are selected, profession entered, topics chosen for conversation, and dress selected for special occasions.
2. The hidden section refers to those things known to self but not revealed to others. Allowing some disorderliness when no guests are expected is an example of the hidden section. Other examples include writing letters instead of taking notes during a lecture, being friendly to someone you dislike, and accepting committee assignments with a false display of enthusiasm.
3. The blind section refers to those aspects of self that are revealed to others but remain unknown to self. Some examples include always coughing before speaking, having a

	Known to Self	Not Known to Self
Known to Others	Open	Blind
Not Known to Others	Hidden	Unknown

Figure 3.2. Johari Window

rip in the back of your pants, and feeling confident in a situation where others find you inadequate.

4. The unknown section refers to those aspects of self that are unknown to both self and others. Reactions to events never occurring in prior experience would comprise the majority of examples. In many cases, giving your first public speech, confronting a dishonest friend, or reacting to a dangerous fire are examples of the unknown self.

By analyzing what is known and by trying to learn some things that are currently unknown, self-esteem can be studied. Ideally, the open section of the model will grow as one learns more about self and is able to share this knowledge with others. The open section will become more honest, as well, as the individual accepts those facts that were once hidden. More honestly revealed and clearly conceived self-esteem is described by the following diagram.

With different individuals and in different situations, the division of area in the various sections may change. Certainly differences would occur in the size of the open section in conversation with a lifelong friend as compared to conversation with a total stranger. This is to be expected. Generally speaking, however, communication is more successful when both individuals have large "open" areas in their Johari Windows and are able to reveal honest information and avoid role-playing behaviors. One possible contribution to noise in the communication channel (i.e., the hidden self) is thus significantly reduced.

SELF-FULFILLING PROPHECY

Often individuals will think ahead to possible outcomes of future events. The expectation may be positive—doing well on a test, having fun at a party, or creating interest among the audience for a public speech. Or the expectation may be negative—blowing an important job interview, having a miserable evening with family members, or disliking the food and service at a new restaurant. The expectation often results in behavior that makes the outcomes more likely to occur. Confidence in knowledge learned for a test may reduce test anxiety significantly and, therefore, make that high grade more probable. Nervousness about an important interview may mask true potential and make an otherwise promising candidate appear incompetent. The expectation and the resulting increased likelihood of its occurrence is known as the self-fulfilling prophecy.

The self-fulfilling prophecy works in two ways. First, perception of self may result in behavior on the part of the individual that influences outcomes. The preceding examples typify this effect. The self-fulfilling prophecy may occur also when others' perceptions of individuals influence outcomes. This commonly occurs when labels are attached to individuals by significant others. For example, average children may progress slowly in school because they have been told they are slow learners; or a beautiful young woman, having been teased and taunted for years because of braces on her teeth, may perceive herself as ugly. Outcomes, then, may be significantly influenced by the individual's perception of self as well as others' implied perceptions of the individual.

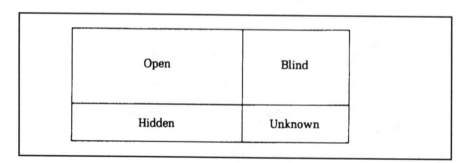

Figure 3.3. Johari Window

The self-fulfilling prophecy is helpful when it works in positive ways. Consideration of potential negative outcomes can be an important means of changing the direction of events that depend heavily on the expectations and attitudes of those involved. The effect of self-fulfilling prophecy on communication is significant. Preconceived ideas that an interpersonal relationship, a small group activity, or a public speech would go well or poorly will often contribute to the outcome.

EFFECTS OF SELF-ESTEEM ON COMMUNICATION

Two effects of self-esteem on communication have just been discussed: the importance of openness in facilitating the communication process, and the role of expectations in affecting outcomes in communication domains. In addition, there are some general characteristics that seem to be associated with communication experiences of individuals possessing healthy positive self-esteem.

Positive self-esteem or lack of it has a direct effect on both verbal and nonverbal communication. Fear can cause the vocal pitch to rise, the body to shake, the hands to get clammy, the knees to knock, and the stomach to churn. Fearful individuals are hesitant to speak out before an audience or in a group, and often stammer or speak incessantly in conversation.

Persons with positive self-esteem act differently. Although sometimes hesitant in new situations, they gradually begin to feel relaxed, to find ways to participate, and to enjoy themselves. Self-accepting persons participate in life. They are objective, spontaneous, and emotionally and intellectually honest. They do not brood about lost opportunities, lost causes, errors, and failures. They profit from mistakes and try to do things differently in the future.

Persons with positive self-esteem have their own values and principles, which they are willing to defend even in the face of strong opposition, but they are secure enough to modify their ideas if new evidence suggests a better way. They are capable of acting on their own judgment even when others disapprove. Persons with strong self-esteem see themselves as equals, not as inferior or superior persons. They realize

I, the Caterpillar

i the caterpillar
did see saint butterfly
i was working at my weaving
and i saw her flutter by
and i wondered that a thing
could be so fragile and so frail
dancing on the lilacs
all the way to jail

and i hung her
in a pale white cage
up in a broken tree
and i longed to climb inside her eyes
and listen to the sea
and i would give my body to be lifted
by her wings
but i the caterpillar
am tangled in my strings

for who
would have the grocer
check the items from the list
and when my loves are sleeping
there are eyelids to be kissed
and the yellow bus keeps coming
at four o'clock each day
and i the caterpillar
cannot get away
and if i had a pair of wings
and knew i wouldn't fall
then the simple act of flying
doesn't mean much at all
and if i jumped without them
well i wonder what we'd find
in all the empty rooms
i would go and leave behind

so i the caterpillar
will keep working at my trade
and i won't know what i'm weaving
until i get it made
if i don't believe in butterflies
i can tell you this
we all will do what we must do
simply to exist
i, the caterpillar
and saint butterfly

—Ric Masten

Notice Me! published by Sunflower Ink, Carmel, CA

that they are of value to other people. To be an effective communicator in speaker-audience, small group, interpersonal, and probably even intrapersonal situations, it is important to feel good about oneself.

Self-Confidence versus Defensiveness

Perception of self influences behavior in nearly every situation. From perception of self comes an individual's feelings about what can and cannot be accomplished. Feelings about potential for success versus failure in a situation is called self-confidence. Whether an individual will take a flying leap off a diving tower at the campus pool is dependent to a large extent on confidence in survival. Applying for jobs, meeting new people, or volunteering for a special task are all based on self-confidence or perception of ability to meet the challenge. Because nearly every aspect of living involves some form of communication, self-confidence plays an important role. To assess importance of self-confidence, a look at defensive behaviors, stress management, and ways of improving self-esteem is useful.

DEFENSIVENESS

Defensive behavior, a way of covering up inadequacies, often arises when self-confidence is low. Just as the word implies, it is a way of defending or protecting oneself when seemingly under attack. It is a means of justifying behavior perceived to be inadequate in a given situation and, therefore, eliminating any threat to self-esteem. Defensive behaviors, then, result from the degree of confidence perceived appropriate by the individual for a given situation. They are a way to distort reality so that it appears to be congruent with the perceived self-image the individual holds in that situation.

The problem with defensive behaviors is their detrimental effect on the communication process. They add noise to the communication process and make sending and receiving messages either difficult or impossible. Defensive behaviors involve either avoidance or attack. In avoidance the individual "flees the enemy" by withdrawing from or ignoring the situation. In attacking, the individual finds a way to threaten the other individual's self-esteem. Some common defensive behaviors follow.

- **Fantasy**—To avoid a threatening situation, we dream of an unreal, yet pleasing world. When a parent reprimands a child, the child might dream of running away.
- **Repression**—Instead of accepting a threatening situation, we ignore it. Instead of paying all the bills this month, we ignore some and face them later.
- **Apathy**—Rather than face a threatening situation, we pretend that it does not matter. If a student fails an exam, the student might decide that course does not really matter.
- **Helplessness**—Rather than admit that a task or situation may be difficult, we avoid it. Instead of trying to get a real estate license, an energetic sales assistant might never attempt to move ahead.
- **Compensation**—We may perform some action in an attempt to make up for a shortcoming, or to draw attention away from it. A teenager, not successful academically, might work harder to be a good athlete.
- **Rationalization**—To avoid accepting the truth about an inadequacy, we create an explanation that makes it appear acceptable. A woman might withhold affection from her lover and decide that she was justified because of his insensitivity.
- **Verbal Aggression**—To avoid a threatening situation, we sometimes draw attention from ourselves by verbalizing another's apparent or contrived shortcomings. An employee who is being reprimanded might tell the boss a thing or two.
- **Displacement**—Rather than face the individual who threatens our self-esteem, we turn hostility toward another individual or object that will be less harmful. A frustrated motorist might kick the family dog.

Defensive behaviors are sometimes healthy. There are times when the self-esteem must be protected in one of the above ways. Almost always, however, attempting to reduce such behaviors will be more productive.

STRESS MANAGEMENT

Stress is a state of imbalance between external demands and our internal capabilities. Stress refers to *strain*, *pressure*, **and** *tension*, both psychological and physical, which weaken the body's ability to cope. Stress is often caused by deadlines, procrastination, job or school, finances, and home and social life. One major cause of stress is change resulting not only from negative outcomes but also from positive outcomes. For example, stress is bound to be associated with the loss of a job but it is also evident to varying degrees when a promotion occurs. Stress results from the unknowns that accompany both situations. Other general causes of stress include lack of time—too much to do and not enough hours to do it; lack of direction—no purpose to life or no goals to guide decision making; frustration—needing and wanting things that you cannot have; monotony—asking the question, "is this all there is?"; and lack of control—feeling that you cannot make your own decisions. Stress is a state of imbalance between demands from outside sources and capability to meet those demands.

The body reacts to stress, both mentally and physically, resulting in nonverbal and verbal signs that are often clearly evident in communication domains. Mental and emotional reactions include guilt, anxiety, and worry. Stress can physically tear down the body's defenses causing deterioration and greater susceptibility to disease. Behaviorally, we can observe such signs of stress as twitching, sweaty palms, hesitation in speaking, and upset stomach. Each individual must learn to deal with stress so that the negative side effects are minimized. Everyone must learn to relax yet realize that some stress is positive and that it provides motivation to achieve. Some mornings, for example, it is the stress of getting to school or work on time that gets us out of bed.

There are several common signs of stress. Have you experienced any of the following?

1. Headaches
2. Feeling rushed, trapped, nervous, or bored
3. Nausea or stomach pains
4. Grinding teeth, clenched jaw
5. Appetite change
6. Weight gain or loss
7. Fatigue
8. Muscle tension, sitting stiffly
9. Gripping the steering wheel
10. Use of drugs or alcohol
11. Sleeplessness
12. Irritability and edginess

GOAL
Recognize the debilitating effects of stress in communication.

If so, it may be that you would benefit by consciously attempting to gain control of those aspects of your life that are causing stress.

Consider the following negative ways that people deal with stress.

1. Alcohol/drugs—change perception of reality.
2. Food—over-eating can be consoling.
3. Cigarettes—relieve tension.
4. Caffeine—stimulant.
5. Withdrawing—avoid problems entirely.
6. Procrastination—other activities take valuable time.
7. Indulgence—more satisfying activities.
8. Worry—fret and imagine the worst.
9. Projection—transfer frustration to others.

Some practical tips to consider as you combat stress are listed as follows:

1. Get a complete physical.
2. Work off your tensions.
3. Slow down and get as much rest as you can.
4. Eat correctly.
5. Modify your routine.
6. Take mental breaks during the day.
7. Talk about stress or problems with others.
8. Accentuate the positive.

Everyone experiences stress. How you handle stress makes the difference. All of the above suggestions take conscious effort, however, and require commitment and follow through. Eating one nutritious meal, for example, and then reverting to a routine of fast foods is not the objective. A routine of nutritious meals served and eaten in a relaxing setting might have a stress-reducing effect.

In *The Seven Habits of Highly Effective People,* Covey (1989) ends with a habit he calls "Sharpen the Saw." He suggests that a saw is very ineffective in cutting wood if it is not maintained well—sharpened regularly. He suggests that people are the same. If we do not take care of our physical, mental, social/emotional, or spiritual sides, then we will not be able to realize our potential or do our best. In our busy world, it is hard to take time to preserve ourselves. Many of us let families, work, and social responsibilities take all of our time and energy. The more we neglect the four aspects of self, the less we can achieve in the other areas. All of the practical tips for combating stress which were listed previously in this section could easily be placed in one or more of the four aspects of self which Covey emphasizes for us. Sharpen the saw underlies the essence of burnout and renewal.

GOAL
Describe ways to improve self-esteem.

Other approaches to controlling stress relate to relaxation techniques rather than changes in life style. Several of these include meditation, concentrated breathing, guided imagery, relaxation tapes, biofeedback machines, and stress cards. These techniques require training for their effective use. Many courses and books on these topics are available, and many people have found them to be effective in alleviating the physical and psychological ravages of stress.

Several of the concepts associated with time management have application in controlling stress. You might begin with taking charge of your life and having a plan. Write down your plan in specific terms so that progress is observable. Make certain that the plan is realistic and set a deadline. This strategy puts you in control and relieves the stress of ambiguity. Once goals are established, begin using your time effectively. Handle paper only once. Wear a watch and use it. Delegate as much as you can. Shorten non-productive time. Avoid procrastination. Do not be overwhelmed by attempting all your goals at once or by the difficulty of the task. Divide tasks into small manageable steps, use your high energy time to work on the goal, and reward yourself when closure is achieved.

Stress can be positive in that it is motivating; but it can change us negatively by affecting self-image, the ways we interact with people, and even our health—coronary disease often linked to stress has increased dramatically in America. It takes conscious effort to balance the demands of living, to bounce back when things go wrong, to work with others harmoniously, and to maintain confidence in ourselves.

IMPROVING SELF-ESTEEM

One way to reduce the avoidance and attacking behaviors associated with defensiveness and to manage stress more effectively is to develop and maintain strong self-esteem. When improvement in self-esteem is desirable, there must be a certain amount of analysis and knowledge to determine realistic personal goals. In addition, the will to work toward the desired objective must exist. It may not be an easy task to replace long-established negative images with more positive images. In evaluating progress, it may be more rewarding to judge gains made toward a goal rather than to make success or failure dependent on achieving the goal itself.

A certain amount of self analysis is required to determine areas of self-esteem that are inaccurately perceived. It is important for individuals to have realistic expectations of what they are able to do. Negative aspects of self-esteem are often the result of setting expectations too high. It is important, too, to have accurate perceptions of self. Many competent individuals have negative self-images, not from inadequacies, but because of inability to make clear and accurate judgments of their own worth. A boost in self-esteem might result from a more realistic judgment of self.

Feedback is a good way to determine the reliability of self-perception. Feedback from others that is always more positive than personal perceptions is a good indicator that personal perceptions have been unrealistically low. To develop positive self-esteem it is important to interact as often as possible with others. Through interaction with others feedback about behavior is readily acquired. Most people are striving for praise and recognition. Those with positive self-esteem realize that they may not always receive praise in situations involving communication. They are not destroyed by this realization and often try repeatedly to achieve important personal goals. Self-esteem can be realistically built by attending to the comments of actions, ideas, beliefs, and mannerisms received from others.

Consider the following suggestions for improving your own self-esteem.

1. **Be your own best friend.** Self-esteem will be high if you learn to appreciate your own special talents and those qualities you bring to relationships.
2. **Leave old baggage behind.** Everyone suffers from past experiences that may not have been as positive as hoped for. Old baggage is good to remember so that the same mistake is not repeated but old baggage should stay in the past.
3. **Create a personal mission.** Set goals for yourself so that you have something to work towards. Break long-term goals down into short-term goals. Achieving small steps towards goals definitely helps self-esteem.
4. **Visualize success.** Athletes are trained to visualize the perfect performance. You can, in your own mind, savor feelings of success. Self-fulfilling prophecy does have power in building self-esteem.
5. **Build a network of friends.** Having a few really close friends gives you a support group to help you through tough situations. Confiding problems and doubts to others relieves stress and often their humor can lighten your load.
6. **Take care of your body.** Proper eating and exercise can stimulate the brain's production of serotonin which improves moods, can help the immune system so that you stay healthier, and give you added energy to take care of life's problems.

Numerous lists can be compiled with dozens of suggestions for achieving higher self-esteem. Simply put, you can build self-esteem by acting happy and by taking time to nurture yourself. Often a little extra time on yourself is such a boost that it compensates for time taken away from work, family, and responsibilities.

The Counselor

i was talking to myself again
in front of the mirror
but the glass man only
moved his lips with mine
and said nothing that would help

so i came to you to hear
what it was i had to tell myself
i chose you above everyone else
because i knew
that you would say

    one can
    only
    help oneself

and that is exactly
the kind of smart-ass remark
i will not take off a mirror

—Ric Masten
Speaking Poems published by Sunflower Ink,
Carmel, CA

SELF-CONFIDENCE

No matter where on the continuum of ability an individual falls in regard to a specific task or situation, realistic yet positive self-esteem will result in self-confidence. Self-confidence is knowing what can be done and then giving it a good try. Negative self-esteem distorts reality and can result in inaccurate decisions. Failures can result because no attempt was made, or because there was little chance of accomplishing a given task.

Just as no one has totally positive and perfect self-esteem, no one is totally self-confident in every situation. There will be times when individuals with generally positive self-esteem feel a lack of confidence in a given situation. Yet a person who is self-accepting will experience a minimum of such situations, and approach even difficult situations with as much confidence as possible. Self confidence in communication domains can be improved by experience. Often it takes only one successful experience to alleviate the self-doubt that produced anxiety and possibly even avoidance in the past.

Credibility and the Roles We Play

CREDIBILITY

In all communication it is extremely important that listeners perceive the speaker as believable. If for some reason the speaker is perceived as untrustworthy, the intended message will be distorted as it is decoded by the listener. A speaker's goal is to transmit a specific message to another person. A listener is not likely to place much value in messages from speakers who are disliked, distrusted, or disbelieved.

The confidence of the listener in what a speaker has to say is termed credibility. It is the believability of a message in a given situation. The speaker must have an accurate perception of self and listener characteristics if credibility is to be maximized. An analysis of listener qualities and expectations allows the speaker to present a message in a way that will seem credible. Credibility is important in both informative and persuasive communication situations. Listeners find it hard to accept information from speakers who do not seem knowledgeable about what they are saying. Likewise, it is difficult to convince others of an opinion if they lack trust in the speaker. If you want to describe the benefits of contact lenses over glasses, you might tell the listener that you wear contact lenses, that you live with someone that wears them, or that you work in the eyecare field. Telling us that you read about contacts on the Internet will not seem credible.

Credibility can be maximized by considering the perception by the listener of the speaker's character, competence, and composure. Character refers to the personal characteristics a speaker represents. Sincerity, honesty, and reliability are especially important for establishing credibility. Competence refers to the authority, wisdom, and knowledge demonstrated when a speaker communicates. To establish credibility, it is important to be accurate, to document information with other sources, and to quote trustworthy sources. Composure refers to the speaker's ability to appear confident. Speakers will be more readily accepted by listeners if they are able to project an image of enthusiasm and poise in speaking style. Ability to be credible is tied very closely to both self-esteem and self-confidence. To be sincere, accurate, and enthusiastic in presenting a message to one other, a small group, or a large audience, it is important for speakers to perceive themselves as projecting a credible image. Many times, credibility will not be obvious. The speaker must take responsibility for insuring that the listener is aware of the speaker's background and experience with a topic.

ROLES WE PLAY

Roles, referring to the fulfillment of a proper activity or expected function, affect our credibility in different situations. We act differently when we represent only ourselves as opposed to representing our school, family, or place of work. Research (Brown and Walberg, 1993) has shown, for example, that young children will try harder on standardized tests when asked to work hard for their schools and their families instead of just for themselves. The major types of roles played include, of course, being yourself as well as personal roles, professional roles, and community roles. Think of the various relationships you might have: son, father, brother, employee, supervisor, volunteer, coach, and teacher to name a few. In each of these roles you perceive yourself to have specific responsibilities and others perceive you to have specific responsibilities. Communication is important to resolve discrepancies that might exist between your perceived responsibilities in a role and the expectations of others. Young children usually expect parents to care for them; young adults often resent involvement of parents in their life decisions; and older adults often find themselves needing the support of their children.

GOAL
Recognize the effect on credibility of the different roles that each of us plays.

Clarity of roles is sometimes difficult to establish especially in periods of transition. To establish credibility, you often have to assert yourself and establish your qualifications for that particular role.

Within the major roles we play, we often reflect certain attitudes (Adler and Towne, 1978) which affect credibility. Do you ever find yourself or others demonstrating the following behaviors in conflict situations?

1. **Avoiders**—finding other activities.
2. **Pseudo-Accommodators**—pretending that there is no conflict.
3. **Guilt Makers**—making others feel responsible.
4. **Subject Changers**—shifting focus away from conflict.
5. **Distractors**—using unrelated topics.
6. **Mind Readers**—analyzing others' feelings.
7. **Trappers**—arranging circumstances and then attacking reaction.
8. **Crisis Ticklers**—hinting at the problem.
9. **Gunnysackers**—storing up resentment and releasing it all at once.
10. **Trivial Tyrannizers**—doing many insignificant things to irritate.
11. **Jokers**—"kidding around."
12. **Beltliners**—focusing on other subjects that are sensitive.
13. **Blamers**—finding fault.
14. **Contract Tyrannizers**—failing to adjust relationships.
15. **Kitchen Sink Fighters**—avoiding real issue.
16. **Withholders**—avoiding honestly.
17. **Benedict Arnolds**—degrading others behind their backs.

These "roles" are usually negative, detract from communication, and cause conflict. To be perceived as credible, avoid such behaviors.

Intrapersonal Communication and Self-Esteem

Intrapersonal communication refers to the conversations speakers have with themselves. In developing communication skills, the self-analysis that is required involves intrapersonal communication. Positive change in communication takes, rather it requires, application of content and skills to personal habits and characteristics. Knowing what self-fulfilling prophecy means is not the same as realizing how self-fulfilling prophecy affects behavior. Your attempt to understand how you react to situations where preconceived outcomes may affect behavior requires intrapersonal communication.

As you consider your self-esteem through the process of intrapersonal communication, try to look at yourself as if you were outside your body. You may discover habits and speech patterns that are comfortable but not necessarily effective. Change, if you realize its necessity, is never easy because it involves the risks of disappointment and failure. Becoming an effective communicator is likely to require determination, perseverance, discipline, and effort—intrapersonally. It depends on the person and how important the desire to improve communication skills becomes. It requires conversations within the individual and the setting of unique personal goals.

Intrapersonal communication might be more realistically called self-talk. Self-talk can be both positive and negative. If you believe what you say to yourself, then negative self-talk will be self-defeating and positive self-talk will be enabling. Which of the following examples of self-talk seem more comfortable to you?

I can't do this.	I can do anything.
I'm so stupid.	I can handle this.
I feel tired.	I feel energized.

Hopefully, you picked the second column which represents POSITIVE self-talk. If not, now is the time to begin to use positive self-talk. You must begin to think in the PRESENT tense, to make your thoughts POSITIVE, and to make your thoughts PERSONAL.

Say: I exercise now.	Don't say: I will exercise tomorrow.
Say: I finish things on time.	Don't say: I won't procrastinate.
Say: I'm a worthy person.	Don't say: They don't appreciate me.

Further suggestions for positive self-talk are the following:

To Build Motivation:	I can do this.
To Build Teamwork:	I fix the process, not the person.
To Build Relationships:	I forgive and I feel free.
To Build Success:	I am a winner.
To Build Self-Esteem:	I feel good about myself.
To Build Well-Being:	I easily let go of my tensions.

One way to encourage yourself is to look at the philosophies of famous people. Zelinski (1997) recognized the following inspirational quotations from three famous people as particularly motivating. Television celebrity Jack Parr was quoted as saying, "my life is filled with many obstacles. The greatest obstacle is me" (p. 107). Poet Ralph Waldo Emerson said, "we are always getting ready to live, but not really living" (p. 47). Psychologist Abraham Maslow, whose hierarchy of needs was cited in chapter 1, suggested that "our ability to satisfy our needs is dependent on first knowing what it is that we need; we should know our needs well. . . . In the average person they are more often unconscious than conscious . . . although they may, with suitable techniques, and with sophisticated people, become conscious" (pp. 107–108).

Zelinski (1997) furthered mentioned that "the way to higher self-esteem is to change your attitude about the way things are and the way you are. If you can start achieving something in your life, your esteem is bound to go up. . . . With higher self-esteem, you will be more motivated to go out and get what you want in life" (p. 110). It is easy to be negative. It takes initiative and self-control to be positive. Negativity sucks away energy that is lost and never recovered. There is generally a solution to every problem. It just takes creativity and positive self-talk to find the solution. Try it and try to get those around you to improve in this area of intrapersonal communication.

Increasing your self-awareness or developing positive self-esteem is the most vital result of intrapersonal communication. To become an effective communicator, you must do more than learn what it takes to organize a speech, improve your listening skills, work in small groups, and react effectively in interpersonal situations—you must improve yourself in the process. It means taking a close look at the way you see yourself. It means many intrapersonal communication encounters. Happiness is a goal most of us strive to achieve. Happiness is not dependent on wealth, beauty, or intellect. Significant events like a wedding or graduation often bring momentary happiness. Sustained happiness, however, is based on high self-esteem, a positive outlook on life, meeting challenges, and a belief that you are worthy of happiness.

Summary

The communication situation is affected by the perceptions and expectations of all concerned. Participants bring their own values and attitudes to the situation. Further, the physical states of participants affect their role in the communication situation. And self-esteem, the way individuals feel about themselves, is a critical factor in the communication experience.

Self-esteem is determined by the value individuals place on their own worth. Almost everyone has value that can be perceived by others. This value affects what is said and how things are said in one-to-one situations, small group discussions, and even speaker-audience situations. A clear perception of self often leads to greater openness and self-confidence in communication situations. There is less distortion from defensive behaviors, and speaker credibility can be established more easily and effectively. Success as a communicator depends to a very great extent on intrapersonal communication—the application of the knowledge and skills to the behavioral patterns of the individual.

Activity 1

Information about Communication

Preparation: Read part 1: Communication Defined. Prepare yourself for a test by answering the practice items given below.

Practice Items

PART 1: OVERVIEW

1. Why is it important to study communication?

2. If a magic formula existed for becoming a good communicator, what might the formula be?

CHAPTER 1

1. When does a communication exchange begin?

2. What is meant by the term "noise" in the communication process?

3. What causes noise to occur in the communication process?

4. What are the three types of delivery systems in communication?

5. How do written and spoken communication differ?

6. What is the influence of media on everyday life?

7. Why is intrapersonal communication considered to be the most basic of the four communication domains?

8. What is the definition of interpersonal communication?

9. How do Abraham Maslow's five levels of basic needs relate to the communication process?

CHAPTER 2

1. What is the relationship of perception with the communication process?

2. What is meant by the phrase, "We see what we want to see"?

3. What is a definition of language?

4. Why do people scream when they hear the word "snake"?

5. Why do barriers occur in the communication process?

6. How does study of communication reduce barriers to communication?

7. What are five important influences on language usage?

8. In what ways are people judged by their use of language?

9. What are eight ways that language can be improved to convey meaning?

CHAPTER 3

1. What are the six perceptions of self that occur during a communication encounter?

2. To what does the term self-esteem refer?

3. What is the Johari Window as it relates to communication?

4. How can the hidden self cause noise in the communication process?

5. What effect does self-fulfilling prophecy have on the communication process

6. Why is it important to the communication process to have positive self-esteem?

7. What are some common defensive behaviors in communication experiences?

8. What are the six major causes of stress?

9. What are eight ways that the body reacts physically to stress?

10. What is an example of how stress can negatively affect the way we interact with people?

11. What is an example of how stress can be a positive factor in our lives?

12. Why is credibility so important in communication?

13. List the major categories for roles you play in relationships (e.g., father).

14. How can credibility be achieved in communication?

15. How do roles we play affect self-esteem?

16. How is intrapersonal communication affected by a communicator's self-esteem?

17. Why does positive self-talk improve confidence and self-esteem?

18. What factors related to self-esteem result in personal happiness?

Group Activity: Follow course instructions to complete the test for part 1.

Individual Activity: Make arrangements with your instructor to complete the test for part 1.

Activity 2

Speech Communication Goals

Preparation: As you begin your study of speech communication, you have a set of feelings about your present skill in various speaking situations. It is interesting to record these initial feelings and to compare them to your feelings about your speech communication skills at the end of the course.

For each statement below, rate yourself as you feel at this moment. Indicate your feelings by circling the appropriate number to the left of the statement. Think carefully and be honest with yourself. These results are for you alone.

5=Strongly Disagree   4=Disagree   3=Don't Know   2=Agree   1=Strongly Agree

1.	1 2 3 4 5	I am able to define communication.
2.	1 2 3 4 5	I am able to identify elements (communication model) involved in any communication process.
3.	1 2 3 4 5	I am able to recognize how written and spoken communication styles differ.
4.	1 2 3 4 5	I am able to differentiate areas of communication: intrapersonal, interpersonal, small group, and public speaking.
5.	1 2 3 4 5	I am able to describe how perception affects communication.
6.	1 2 3 4 5	I am able to illustrate how the use of language affects communication.
7.	1 2 3 4 5	I am able to identify ways to eliminate barriers to communication.
8.	1 2 3 4 5	I am able to explain how self-concept, self-esteem, and self-image affect communication.
9.	1 2 3 4 5	*I am able to recognize the debilitating effects of stress in communication.*
10.	1 2 3 4 5	I am able to describe ways to improve self-esteem.
11.	1 2 3 4 5	*I am able to recognize the effect on credibility of the different roles that each of us plays.*
12.	1 2 3 4 5	I am able to define and distinguish between hearing and listening.
13.	1 2 3 4 5	I am able to demonstrate and employ appropriate listening skills (passive, active, social, critical, discriminative, empathic) in the family, community, workplace.
14.	1 2 3 4 5	I am able to apply principles associated with various types of nonverbal communication.
15.	1 2 3 4 5	I am able to develop effective nonverbal skills for various speaking situations.
16.	1 2 3 4 5	*I am able to illustrate effective ways to handle time management.*
17.	1 2 3 4 5	I am able to demonstrate ability in the use of appropriate feedback (body motion, vocal expression) to help the listener.
18.	1 2 3 4 5	I am able to recognize the importance of vocal quality when talking on the telephone.
19.	1 2 3 4 5	I am able to develop strategies for improving interpersonal relationships.
20.	1 2 3 4 5	I am able to distinguish between feeling and thinking.
21.	1 2 3 4 5	I am able to explain how self-disclosure enhances relationships.
22.	1 2 3 4 5	*I am able to differentiate among passive, aggressive, and assertive communication strategies.*
23.	1 2 3 4 5	I am able to demonstrate effective interviewing skills.
24.	1 2 3 4 5	*I am able to recognize the impact of values on communication.*
25.	1 2 3 4 5	*I am able to explain the importance of ethics (honesty) on communication exchanges.*

26.	1 2 3 4 5	I am able to describe how interpersonal relationships develop and disintegrate.
27.	1 2 3 4 5	I am able to distinguish between empathy and sympathy.
28.	1 2 3 4 5	I am able to demonstrate styles of conflict management.
29.	1 2 3 4 5	*I am able to describe the benefits of embracing a diverse culture.*
30.	1 2 3 4 5	I am able to discuss how cultural differences affect the way we communicate.
31.	1 2 3 4 5	I am able to employ strategies for overcoming cultural barriers to communication.
32.	1 2 3 4 5	I am able to discuss the impact of gender differences on communication between males and females.
33.	1 2 3 4 5	I am able to summarize characteristics of a small group.
34.	1 2 3 4 5	I am able to describe situations in which a group decision is superior to individual decision making.
35.	1 2 3 4 5	I am able to participate effectively in groups through effective listening and by using critical and reflective thinking.
36.	1 2 3 4 5	*I am able to distinguish between productive and non-productive behaviors in a small group.*
37.	1 2 3 4 5	*I am able to identify consequences of roles, skills, and attitudes on group participation.*
38.	1 2 3 4 5	I am able to identify application of leadership styles to real-world situations.
39.	1 2 3 4 5	*I am able to demonstrate use of brainstorming to generate possible solutions to problems.*
40.	1 2 3 4 5	*I am able to conduct an effective meeting through the use of organized planning skills.*
41.	1 2 3 4 5	I am able to adapt to the purpose, occasion, and audience of a public speaking situation.
42.	1 2 3 4 5	I am able to demonstrate ability to use research and data bases to gather support material for speeches.
43.	1 2 3 4 5	I am able to draft, organize, revise, edit, and present formal public speeches.
44.	1 2 3 4 5	I am able to demonstrate effective delivery techniques for public speaking.
45.	1 2 3 4 5	I am able to use various types of visual aids in the delivery of public speeches.
46.	1 2 3 4 5	I am able to develop strategies for building speech confidence.
47.	1 2 3 4 5	I am able to deliver an effective informative speech.
48.	1 2 3 4 5	I am able to deliver an effective persuasive speech.
49.	1 2 3 4 5	*I am able to define the concept of dissonance as it is used in persuasive speaking.*
50.	1 2 3 4 5	*I am able to differentiate fact and opinion.*

Note: Statements in regular type are adapted from Dallas County Community College District core curriculum; statements in italics have been added by the authors.

Group and Individual Activities: The statements above can be viewed in one sense as general goals for speech communication improvement. As you attempt to improve your communication skills, keep in mind those areas in which you feel weaker than others.

Another copy of Speech Communication Goals will be included as a final course activity. Make it a priority to gain confidence as you study speech communication.

Activity 3

Getting to Know Your Listeners

Preparation: Prepare yourself to make a number of new acquaintances. Getting acquainted with each of your classmates often makes the task of practicing new communication skills easier and more enjoyable.

Group Activity: Option 1—Introducing Yourself

Form a large circle including everyone in the class. You will introduce yourself four times. During the first time around the circle, state your name and your present or planned occupation. The next time around the circle, give your name and your favorite leisure activity. Next, give your name and the reason you enrolled in the speech communication course. Next, give your name preceded by an adjective beginning with the same letter as your first name. Finally, give the adjective and first name of each classmate in the circle.

Example: Nancy Falk, insurance adjuster
Nancy Falk, tennis
Nancy Falk, requirement for graduation
"Noble" Nancy

Group Activity: Option 2—Introducing a Classmate

Form groups of two by pairing with people you have not met previously. Include the instructor. During the next twenty minutes take turns interviewing each other. As interviewer, ask questions to get to know your partner. Try to learn at least three unique things about the interviewee. The following ideas could be used.

1. What is something in which you take pride (e.g., making the debate team)?

2. Who are the three most important people in your life?

3. What two activities do you like to do best when money is no object?

4. What are two things you would like people to remember about you?

5. What would you do if given a gift of $100,000?

Prepare to introduce your partner to the group by giving your partner's name and several of the unique characteristics you discovered. After completing the interviews, form a large circle including everyone in the class. When it is your turn, introduce your partner to the group.

Group Activity: Option 3—Discovering Interests

Prior to this activity, all participants must turn in a card which contains a phrase or sentence which describes some special interest or characteristic of themselves. For example, you might write, "I love Cavalier King Charles Spaniels" or "I raise tarantulas as a hobby" or "My right leg is a prosthesis." The example you share should be something that will set you apart from the others. For example, "I just graduated from high school" is not distinctive enough to set you apart in a college class. Someone must be responsible for taking the cards and making a sheet where each person's entry is preceded by a blank. Enough copies must be made so that each participant has one.

When you come together for the second time, each of you will be challenged to meet the others and find the name which goes with each interest or characteristic. IT IS NOT FAIR TO COPY THE ANSWERS FROM THE OTHERS. The first person who finishes should read the completed list to the group. Hopefully, along the way many new friendships will be started.

Individual Activity: Before, during, or after class, introduce yourself to your classmates. As your classmates introduce themselves to you, write down their names and answers to the questions from *option* 1. Learn all their names so you will begin to become well acquainted with your classmates.

Activity 4

Perception of Self—Your Life Line

Preparation: You have a choice as to how you will spend your future years. Hopefully you will make the most of them. The intent of long life should be positive. How you live your life is vital.

Take a piece of paper and draw a line down the page. The top of the line represents your birth; write the date next to it. The bottom of the line signifies the date of your death. Next to it, write the number of years you hope to live. Next to your age, write the estimated year of your death. Let us hope you want a long life and a useful one. Place "present" at the point where you are now on the line between your birth and death. Then write today's date at that point. This line is your life line.

Right of today's date, above the line, record ten significant accomplishments or events from your life up to the present. To the left of today's date, below the line, indicate some events you would like to experience or goals you would like to accomplish before your death. Examine your life line. Study and think about it. How much are you willing to invest for a life of meaning?

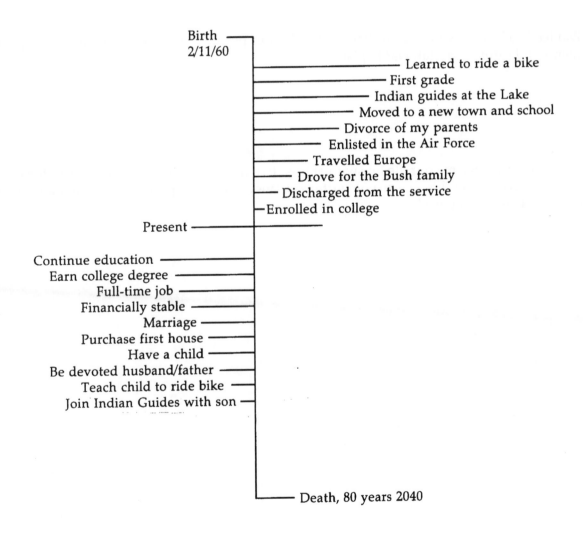

Group Activity: During class share life lines with each of your classmates. To keep track of those you have seen, place your initials on the bottom of each life line. Use the experience of viewing others' life lines as you more fully consider your own perception of past accomplishments and future expectations. Then discuss the following questions with the entire class and revise your life line if you wish.

1. Have others indicated accomplishments and expectations which you considered too trivial to list? What are they?

2. Were you honest in listing your accomplishments and expectations? Which would you change? Are there additions and deletions you would make? If so, what are they?

3. Did feedback about your life line help to clarify your perception of your own past accomplishments and future expectations? Explain.

Individual Activity: Share your life line with at least five friends or family members. Use the experience of discussing your life line as you write your answers to the questions included above and revise your life line if you wish.

Activity 5

Setting Personal Goals

Preparation: Perhaps you have heard stories of people who have been classified as "overnight successes." When you hear this term, of whom do you think? What qualities do these people possess that make them successful? Emmett Smith, a football player and a business executive, was asked by a news reporter to name a characteristic he knew he had that continued to make him successful. He said he was determined. To achieve all that he has, Emmett said that he had to keep his mind focused on a plan or goal and persistently work toward it. Success like that of Emmett Smith does NOT happen overnight. Without determination, it will not happen at all.

1. Using the outline below, list three people you perceive as highly successful. List at least one famous person and at least one example that you know on a more personal level (e.g., family member, community leader).

2. Then list the qualities or characteristics which enabled them to achieve their goals.

Person	Qualities
1.	A.
	B.
	C.
2.	A.
	B.
	C.
3.	A.
	B.
	C.

3. Look at your life line that you completed for activity 4. Focus on the present and look toward your future. Imagine that there are no limits to what you can achieve. Now describe your future DREAM.

4. Now, list the three to five steps you would have to take to make this DREAM become a reality. If you have listed a material possession, how would you acquire this property?

   A.

   B.

C.

D.

E.

5. Look at your life line again and focus on the word "present." Your future life will be the result of the completion of smaller goals. Take the GOAL closest to the word present and write it below.

6. Now list three to five steps to make this GOAL become a reality.
   A.

   B.

   C.

   D.

   E.

Group Activity: During class form groups of three to discuss success.

1. Tell a success story to your group and describe the characteristics this person has.
2. Next, describe your lifelong dream and how you plan to achieve this dream. Do members of the small group agree with what you believe you would have to do to get what you want? Are you being realistic? If not, why not? Should you revise your dream or the steps it will take to achieve it?
3. Finally, discuss the present goal that you took from your life line. Reveal the three to five steps that it will take to achieve that goal. Ask your listeners for input. Are you being realistic? If not, why not? You may want to alter your plan after listening to the suggestions.

Individual Activity: Find two other people who will listen to you describe your dream and your goal and the steps it will take to achieve them. Write a summary of their reactions to each of the parts listed under Group Activity. Also, write a summary of the revisions you would make based on the discussion you had.

Activity 6

Positive Self-Talk

Preparation: Some psychologists believe that as we grow up in families, study in school with teachers and peers, and later work with co-workers in careers, we hear more negative than positive sentences over and over again. In his book, *What to Say When You Talk to Yourself,* Helmstelter (1986) labeled such sentences as "seed" sentences.

Some examples of positive sentences follow:

> You are so pretty.
> That shirt looks great on you.
> Your family is so close.
> You are so smart.

Some examples of negative sentences follow:

> You need to lose a few pounds.
> Your clothes look like you slept in them.
> Your family is just a bunch of losers.
> You are really dumb.

Some sentences grow into patterns and beliefs that we carry with us throughout our lives. Some of these are positive and some are negative. An example follows of how purposeful self-talk can work.

Joanne used a word picture to image herself at her ideal weight. She imagined herself in her Size 10 red-sequined evening dress. In her mind's eye, she could see every detail that she wanted to attain. She even put a picture of an attractive woman who was wearing a red-sequined gown on her refrigerator. During the second stage of reaching her goal. Joanne used positive self-talk by telling herself "When I feel like snacking, I will eat fruit." The combination of describing and seeing her goal and focusing on repetitive steps caused her to become a Size 10. The positive self-talk created energy which created productive behavior.

Planting productive ideas in your mind over and over again becomes habit and the habit causes you to automatically say the right thing to yourself at the right time. Ideally, you will then do the right behavior for yourself. You feel empowered to accomplish your priorities and reach your goals. Think back over your life and you can no doubt recall many powerful words and phrases that have already caused you to make changes. Write out several, both positive and negative, that have influenced who you are.

1.
2.
3.
4.
5.

Now that you are aware of some "seed" sentences from your life, you can begin to feed yourself your own positive "seed" sentences. Once you recognize the negative messages, you can begin to use positive and purposeful self-talk to supply yourself with motivation. Motivation is a driving force which enables us to achieve our goals. Purposeful and positive self-talk is a way to overcome some stresses and stay motivated. No doubt you have had success with one of your goals because you talked to yourself in a positive way. Write the details of this process.

1. What was the experience?

2. Describe your feelings.

3. What choice did you decide to make?

4. What did you say to yourself that helped you take the right action or make the right choice?

5. What repetitive steps were used to achieve your goal?

A list of priorities is provided below that you may have dealt with or be dealing with right now in your personal or professional life. Check the issues you have faced and are currently facing and are motivated to improve. You may also add your own priorities to your list.

_____ Keeping an energetic attitude.	_____ Getting organized.
_____ Reducing conflict at home.	_____ Finding personal time.
_____ Handling negative people.	_____ Improving physical times.
_____ Stopping procrastination.	_____ Reducing stress.
_____ Dealing with rejection.	_____
_____ Losing weight.	_____
_____ Building positive self-esteem.	_____

Now select one that you want to work on immediately and write at least three sentences that reflect positive self-talk. Selected priority: _____

1.

2.

3.

Group Activity: Join a group of three others to make a group of four. Share your success story. Describe the type of self-talk which helped you succeed. Choose one of the stories, which reveals the power of positive self-talk, and share it with the larger group. To conclude, form a generalization about the power of self-talk as an intrapersonal communication tool.

Individual Activity: Share your success story with a friend or family member. Describe your goal, also. Write a response to the issue of self-talk as an intrapersonal tool.

Activity 7

How to Manage Stress

The purpose of this activity is to examine stress and the positive and negative ways that people deal with stress. Review the Chapter 3 section on stress.

Group Activity: In small groups, discuss ways people deal with stress that are healthy and unhealthy.

Ways that People Deal with Stress

NEGATIVE	POSITIVE
1.	1.
2.	2.
3.	3.
4.	4.
5.	5.
6.	6.

Next select a scenario (e.g., an argument that a member of your group has had or a task that seemed insurmountable) that you can use to role-play the negative way that one might handle a problem and then the positive way that the stress might have been handled. Let members of your group take on the roles and develop a dialog to demonstrate the two approaches. Using the following suggestions, brainstorm and list specific ways to handle the problem in a positive way.

1. How can you alter the source of stress in the scene? You would need to remove the source of stress by changing something. Examples include problem solving, planning and time management, or direct communication with those involved.

2. How could you avoid the stressful situation or not even be there? Could you walk away, let it go, assert yourself and say "no" to someone?

3. How could you prepare yourself to accept this stress physically and mentally? Consider each of the following:

   A. Physical Preparation

      a. Proper diet

      b. Regular exercise

      c. Relaxation techniques

    B. Mental Resistance

      a. Positive affirmations

      b. Taking time for mental health

    C. Social Experiences

    D. Spiritual Resistance

4. How can you change the way you perceive the situation or yourself? Should you change unrealistic expectations? Can you build a more positive self-esteem? Can you change the way you look at a situation by bringing humor into the scene instead of looking at it with an "ain't it awful" attitude? Can you remember that in time most situations will improve or do not seem as bad as they first appeared?

Return to the entire group. Select a group member to introduce the scenario. Play out the scenario revealing the negative stress that occurred. Share any additional negative strategies that apply to the situation. Then play out the scenario revealing the positive strategies that your group felt best fit the problem. Share any additional positive strategies that apply to the situation.

Individual Activity: Select an intrapersonal, interpersonal, or small group situation which has caused you major stress. Follow the group instructions to find a alternative way of the handling the stress which might have been more positive. In writing, describe the original situation. Then write out four possible ways that you might have handled the situation with less stress.

Activity 8

Speaking Activity—
Making an Introduction

Preparation: There may be occasions when you will have to introduce another person to a group. You may introduce a speaker or you may bring a new member into an established group. A formal introduction of another person should be made with confidence and without hesitation. This implies preparation and rehearsal. It is hard to make a speaker or guest comfortable if you forget relevant information and the person being introduced has to fill in parts you have forgotten. An introduction of another person should include the information shown below.

I.   **Attention device**—Capture the attention of the listeners by mentioning something about the individual that is especially catching. It need not be humorous. Include also a statement of purpose for your introduction.

II.   **Factual details**—This section of the introduction will depend on the specific occasion. It is the place to list accomplishments and specific information about the person's life.

III.   **Summary**—Briefly review the most relevant of the factual details and let your listeners know that the introduction of the person is complete.

To create an even flow of information, parts of the introduction should be designed to complement the personality of the person being introduced and to have relevance to the listeners. It is generally inappropriate to merely read an individual's resume as an introduction. It is important to summarize across categories rather than listing accomplishment after accomplishment. For example, rather than saying the names of numerous memberships held by the speaker, you might say, "... belongs to numerous non-profit organizations such as X and Y."

Choose a person in the class that you would like to get to know. During class or by arranging a specific time outside of class, interview the person. During the interview find out as much as possible about the person. Or look at yourself in an objective manner and determine your own characteristics, experiences, or background that would interest an audience. In preparing, you may want to use a single outstanding accomplishment or some of the characteristics below.

1.	Age	11.	Ambition (e.g., architect)
2.	Marital status	12.	Political (e.g., Republican)
3.	Children	13.	Clubs (e.g., P.T.A.)
4.	Occupation	14.	Sports (e.g., tennis)
5.	Religion	15.	Friends (e.g., card players)
6.	Geographic roots	16.	Hobbies (e.g., reading)
7.	Hometown (e.g., Dallas)	17.	Interests (e.g., family)
8.	Dwelling (e.g., apartment)	18.	Talents (e.g., writing)
9.	Major (e.g., music)	19.	Admire (e.g., educated people)
10.	Class (e.g., freshman)	20.	Dislikes (e.g., communists)

When you have your material, prepare an outline like the following example with attention device, factual details, and summary. Limit material to what can be presented in two to three minutes. Practice in front of an imaginary audience until you are comfortable with the presentation.

An Introduction of Myself

Topic Outline	Script
I. Introduction—attention device	
A. Gain attention of audience	My name is Rita. I have also been known by those on my volleyball team as "Too-Tall" Rita.
B. Statement of main purpose	I would like to tell you a little about myself so that we will communicate better during our semester together.
II. Body—factual details	
A. First main idea—early life	I was born in Burlington, NC, on October 2, 1959. My family moved to Pensacola, Florida, when I was eight years old. I was raised there and graduated from high school in 1977.
B. Second main idea—recent events	For three years I dated a wonderful guy named Jeff and we married in 1978. I attended Pensacola Junior College while my husband worked for his family business. Jeff decided he would like to pursue a bachelor's degree; therefore, I quit school to work and help him attain his goal. He graduated in 1982 which is the same year that our first child, Philip, was born. Two years later our daughter, Chrissie, was born. Jeff and I both worked for the family business, thinking this was the future we wanted. After several years, however, we decided to "take the plunge" and truly assert our independence! Jeff was offered a job in Dallas and we moved in June, 1989. For financial security, I began to work for this college where, through a special friendship, I was ENCOURAGED to pursue my dream of becoming an elementary school teacher. I quit work and returned fulltime to college.
C. Third main idea—future plans	I see my future as teaching; launching my children to be happy, self-confident, independent people; travelling abroad; and continuing to live happily with my husband, Jeff. I would also like to see world peace and a protected environment.
III. Conclusion—summary	
A. Summary of main ideas	With a positive outlook on life, Jeff, Philip, Chrissie and I can be happy while living and growing together.
B. Closing remarks	That my mother began college during middle adulthood is an inspiration to me. She came to America at age 16 and earned her bachelor's degree at age 40.

Group Activity: During class, make your two-to-three minute introduction of a classmate or yourself. You may use note cards and visual aids if you wish.

Individual Activity: Make an appointment with your instructor to plan a specific time to present a two-to-three minute speech to introduce yourself. You may use note cards and visual aids.

NOTE: Evaluation criteria for this Speaking Activity are located in the Appendix.

LISTENING AND NONVERBAL MESSAGES

Overview

The human race communicates with verbal and nonverbal symbols simultaneously. Verbal symbols are the sounds and combinations of sounds that form the words that comprise spoken messages. Nonverbal symbols are all communication techniques other than the actual words used by a speaker. These include facial expressions, vocal qualities, and all forms of body movement.

Jonathan Swift was a master at describing nonverbal messages. Although Swift is better known for his satire of eighteenth century political customs, in *Gulliver's Travels* he skillfully described the adventures of a man lost first among tiny human creatures, then giants, and later other variations of the human race. Gulliver was able to communicate effectively enough in these foreign lands to save his life and fulfill his basic needs.

> I answered in a few words but to no Purpose, and made a Sign with my Hand that was loose, putting it to the other, and then to my own Head and Body, to signify that I desired my Liberty. It appeared that he understood me well enough; for he shook his Head by way of Disapprobation, and held his Hand in a Posture to show that I must be carried as Prisoner. . . . I gave Tokens to let them know that they might do with me what they pleased.

Imagine yourself in a foreign land, among strange creatures, and with no knowledge of the language. Your only option, save fainting, would be to call on your ability to send accurate nonverbal messages.

Jonathan Swift was a keen observer of another aspect of communication: listening, or the processing of verbal messages. He recognized the poor listening skills that some of his countrymen seemed to demonstrate. He created a country of people of the same body proportions as Gulliver but who had great difficulty communicating.

> I observed here and there many in the Habit of Servants, with a blown Bladder fastened like a Flail to the End of a short Stick, which they carried in their Hands. In each Bladder was a small Quantity of dried Pease, or little Pebbles (as I was afterwards informed). With these Bladders they now and then flapped the Mouths and Ears of those who stood near them, of which Practice I could not then conceive the Meaning. It seems, the Minds of these People are so taken up with intense Speculations, that they neither can speak, or attend to the Discourses of others, without being

rouzed by some external Taction upon the Organs of Speech and Hearing; for which Reason, those Persons who are able to afford it, always keep a Flapper in their Family.

How many of us need a "Flapper" to keep our minds off "intense speculations" when supposedly listening to some form of verbal communication? The study of communication often excludes many aspects of nonverbal communication and emphasizes only speaking and other verbal skills. This does not seem rational when such nonverbal messages as postures, facial expressions, and gestures form a second language that everyone uses; and when even the best message given through the eloquent lips of the practiced speaker is lost when listeners are without their Flappers.

In the opening years of the 21st Century, profiling has become a very intense topic which has its basis in nonverbal communication and even listening to some extent. Profiling refers to the observation of nonverbal characteristics, a synthesis of the data gathered, and a conclusion about the background or probable intentions of the person. It is very similar to stereotyping, although much more scientific in its underlying predictive research. While profiling may seem harmless in the business sector—does it really matter if an individual fits the profile of someone who is a good prospect for selling a specific brand of product? Are you a Lexus sedan type, a bright red convertible type, or just the basic pick-up truck type? Where profiling and the Constitutional rights guaranteed to citizens of the United States become controversial is in the identification of persons suspected to be criminals or terrorists on the basis of nonverbal characteristics. As you study nonverbal communication, consider the strength of the messages sent and the implications, both correct and incorrect, that arise from them.

Cultural differences are also evident in the listening process and the observation of nonverbal characteristics. We use an area called vocalics to identity accents and regional variations in language. Colorful forms of dress which deviate from general attire create interest and add to the richness of our culture. One excellent way to learn more about people whose backgrounds differ from yours is to participate in the festivals that groups of people have to celebrate their traditions. Listen to the stories and music, talk to the sponsors of the events, and observe the festivities. Enjoy unusual foods and beverages and play games that are different. Most cultures celebrate similar events, just in different ways. Nonverbal communication then, is defined here as those aspects of communication that require skills other than those involved in the formation and sending of verbal messages. These two basic areas of communication, listening and nonverbal messages, are critical to the development of adequate skill in sending verbal messages in interpersonal, small group, and speaker-audience communication situations.

LISTENING BEHAVIOR

If oral communication is to exist, an internal process called listening must occur. Most communicators take listening for granted. Originators of messages assume that their receivers are paying attention; receivers of messages assume that their attending skills are adequate. But listening is much more than the sensory process of hearing. It means processing what is heard so that meaning can be determined and a reaction can be made.

Communicators often hear but do not listen. For example, listeners will routinely say, "I don't care" to a question about dinner or a television program, and later react with surprise because their opinions were not considered in the choices made. Or the receiver of a message will appear to be giving full attention to what is being said, only to inquire about a specific point just made by the speaker. The receivers of the messages clearly heard but failed to give the attention required at the perceptual level to change hearing to listening. Listening is a skill that can be studied, practiced, and improved. Through effective listening, it is possible to learn more, be more appreciative of pleasant sounds in the environment and be more sensitive to messages received.

The Listening Process

To appreciate the significance of listening in the communication process, it is useful to make clear distinctions between the concepts of hearing and listening and between the concepts of not hearing and not listening. Basically, the two pairs of concepts are distinguishable as sensory versus perceptual processes. Hearing and not hearing are sensory processes; listening and not listening, perceptual processes. For listening to occur, then, a message must not only be transmitted to the brain via sensory processes but also be attended to and interpreted. The listening process in action is influenced by the type of situation and by the characteristics and habits of the listener.

Some Definitions

- **Listening.** Listening depends on the ability of the potential receiver of a message to hear what is said and then to perceive the message as relevant enough to decode. Listening can be defined concisely as the attachment of meaning to spoken words. In greater detail, listening is defined as the selective process of giving attention to the spoken words, attaching meaning, and responding with understanding. Listening is the prerequisite to the decoding process referred to in the communication model.

- **Not listening.** Not listening does not imply failure to hear but failure to attend to stimuli and to attach meaning to spoken words and, therefore, failure to respond with understanding. Think for a moment about the concepts of listening, not listening, hearing, and not hearing. Communicators will sometimes claim that they failed to hear when, in fact, they failed to listen. In general usage, the two concepts, not hearing and not listening, are often inappropriately

> **GOAL**
> *Define and distinguish between hearing and listening.*

used to mean the same thing: failure to attend to and attach meaning to relevant stimuli.

Types of Listening

Assuming that listening takes place at all, it occurs with different intensities within the receiver of the message. The intensity will depend on the importance of a particular message as it competes for the listener's attention. A major distinction in listening intensity can be made between passive and active listening.

- **Passive Listening.** Passive listening refers to those forms of listening in which many people engage simply because they happen to be present. This can occur, for example, when someone is talking or when music is playing. The potential receiver of the message is minimally, if at all, concerned about the listening process. This type of listening is barely more than hearing.

- **Active Listening.** Active listening involves listening with a purpose, such as understanding, evaluation, enjoyment, or giving feedback. It can occur while listening to a lecture, judging a television commercial, watching a movie, or helping a friend with a problem. The main goal of active listening is to understand the meaning intended by the speaker. There must be a willingness to listen and a desire to try to understand the message as it is intended. Active listening is dependent to a great extent on acquiring desirable listening skills. Active listening can occur in either a social or a serious setting.

> **GOAL**
> Demonstrate and employ appropriate listening skills (passive, active, social, critical, discriminative, empathic) in the family, community, workplace.

Social listening refers to situations where enjoyment or appreciation of what is to be heard is the primary objective. Social listening, for example, takes place during casual conversations or while attending to messages meant to entertain. Social listening enables individuals to enlarge experiences, expand interests, develop an awareness of cultural and ethnic influences, and mature socially. Being an effective listener in social situations can improve the image others hold of a person as well as result in increased self-confidence. A good listener is always in demand in social situations.

Serious listening is appropriate for situations where it is important to expand knowledge or gather information for decision making. Serious listening, for example, occurs when a friend gives a detailed set of instructions or a boss tells an employee how to complete a task. The goal of serious listening is usually to attend to as many details and receive as much information as possible. Language facility and vocabulary can be improved by close attention to the ways that other people report information and analyze situations. Serious listening can be critical, discriminative, or empathic.

Critical listening occurs when the receiver of a message attempts to analyze evidence presented by the speaker and make critical judgments about the accuracy and quality of the material. Critical listening involves the abilities to distinguish between fact and opinion, to distinguish between emotional and logical arguments, to detect bias and prejudice, to evaluate a speaker's arguments, to recognize propaganda, to draw inferences, to make judgments, and to evaluate sales "gimmicks." Critical listening is extremely important in gathering information needed to make decisions. Messages must be heard, listened to, and then screened for appropriateness to the decision at hand.

The purpose of discriminative listening is comprehension—understanding and remembering. In discriminative listening, such skills as understanding meanings of words from context, understanding the relationship of details to main points, following steps when given directions, following the sequence of the message, listening for details, listening to a question with an intent to answer, recognizing repetition of the same idea in different words, repeating what has been heard, taking notes, and outlining are emphasized. Discriminative listening is particularly important for students who find themselves in learning situations where the bulk of course content is given in lectures.

Empathic listening requires an attitude of care and concern as well as time and attention to the personal messages of friends or family members. When supporting your relationships with others is your listening goal, you are likely to be using empathic listening skills. Empathic listening shows that you are feeling some of the same emotions as the speaker. If a friend has just been jilted in a relationship, an empathic listener would not say, "not to worry, there are many more fish in the sea!" "Ending a relationship is always a difficult time and I am here for you when you need some support" is an empathic response. More on the topic of empathy and empathic listening is included in chapter 8.

The types of listening situations reveal a wide range of attending behaviors—from barely more than hearing through general conversation to understanding and evaluation of sometimes complex messages. The listener must exert various degrees of energy in the various situations. It is not appropriate to use passive listening skills when taking notes in an important meeting or class.

LISTENING CHARACTERISTICS AND HABITS

There are many different ways to listen. Ability to listen effectively in the different serious listening situations is acquired in part by practice. In addition to skill developed through practice, listening effectiveness is determined to some extent by physical characteristics, cultural variables, and by experiences of the listener. Habits, that is, responses that are automatic for an individual, also affect listening skill. Many listening habits result in effective attending behaviors, but many others result in ineffective attention to the message being received. Several poor listening habits may even be practiced simultaneously.

Characteristics Affecting Listening

If a person has normal hearing, there is little relationship between age and ability to listen. However, there are some age-related variables, the primary one being attention span. Young children have considerably shorter attention spans than young adults. Also, when a person reaches old age, listening ability may be negatively

Silence

it began with idle conversation
the exchanging of different points of view
two chinese brain-washers
using chop sticks
deftly
speaking loudly softly

and then the wind died
and we hung like tattered flags
full of word holes
resting now
in the beauty which was the silence
smiling into space

listening to the thunder which was the silence
wondering
who would speak first

listening to the screaming which was the
silence
listening to the laughter
of this brutal thing

listening to eternity

trapped
gathering dust
wrinkling
we
will
sit here
forever

—Ric Masten
Stark Naked published by Sunflower Ink,
Carmel, CA

affected by reduced reception within some ranges of sounds.

Personality characteristics of the listener can affect listening effectiveness. Understanding of verbal messages can be reduced by defensive behaviors, whereas objectivity tends to increase understanding. Listeners who have personal worries, feelings of insecurity, or a sense of failure tend to be poorer listeners than those who are optimistic and free from momentary worries.

Interests and attitudes toward the material affect listening effectiveness too, since people are more likely to attend to material they perceive as interesting or important.

Fatigue is another characteristic that often affects listening ability. When a listener is mentally or physically tired, reduced attention span proportionately decreases ability to listen. Fatigue can cause a temporary loss of desire to attend to and understand the message sent by the speaker. It is wise to be rested when important messages require attention.

Listening Habits

Daydreaming is probably the most troublesome listening fault. A speaker will mention a person or thing that will trigger an association in the listener's mind. The association will divert attention from the speaker and cause some of the message to be lost. When the listener returns attention to the speaker, what is heard no longer seems to relate to the original message. Consider your own behavior as you attempt to listen to a group discussion. You may hear the word "travel" as it applies to payment for local expenses and begin dreaming about your summer vacation. By the time you return, the group may be discussing a menu for a party. Off you go again, thinking about what you plan to eat for your evening meal.

Closed-mindedness is another serious listening problem. Close-mindedness operates when positions listeners hold dear are threatened. Close-minded people refuse to listen to ideas, viewpoints, and values that are different from their own. If one has a strong belief that credit spending leads to financial doom, then it is difficult to listen to a message arguing that borrowing money can be a useful practice. There is a tendency to think, "I know all I want to know on this subject," and then to think about something else. Important facts are shut out whether they are right or wrong. Generally a speaker is not seeking agreement on the issue, but is seeking close attention and fair appraisal on the part of the listener. If listeners are aware of their biases and convictions, they can attempt to have open minds when such topics are discussed.

Faking attention is a protective device that listeners use from time to time. They pretend to listen by showing an alert facial expression, maintaining eye contact, and occasionally nodding the head. Actually their minds are somewhere else. Listeners who find themselves having difficulty remembering what has been said should check themselves to determine if they have been faking attention. How many times have you asked a question only to realize that you missed the answer by faking attention and failing to listen?

Failure to attend to an uninteresting or difficult message is a common listening problem. Listeners who find themselves in such communication situations should try to make the best use of their time by actively listening, discussing material where appropriate, and asking questions if possible. Something might be learned and prove useful in the future. Certainly there is no potential for gain if listeners fail to attend to the message. This problem will occur when messages have been designed with a different audience in mind and are thus "over the head" of the listener.

Distractions often affect listening effectiveness. A poor listener habitually fails to attend to messages when distractions occur. Untrained listeners will be disturbed by poor speaker delivery, traffic noise, noise in adjoining rooms, or even visual stimuli like glaring lights. When distractions occur, the effective listener will modify internal behavior in an attempt to attend fully to the message sent by the speaker. Rather than dwell on that interesting conversation across the room, for example, it is wise to concentrate on the message of immediate concern.

Some people listen only for facts and avoid evaluation of the message. If facts are important, the listener should attend to them. If it is more important to analyze the message, evaluation should occur as the message is processed. A similar problem occurs when the listener attempts to outline or take note of everything said by a speaker. It is often more effective to listen for several minutes and then make note of key ideas and concepts rather than attempt to outline the message point by point. Such emphasis on specific facts often results in retention of insignificant details rather than knowledge of an entire process.

Developing Listening Skills

Now that the distinction has been made between the processes of hearing and listening, the various types of listening situations have been introduced, and characteristics and habits that affect listening have been discussed, it is relevant to discuss ways to improve listening skills, and some ways that the listening process leads to distortion of messages.

LISTENING IMPROVEMENT

Because so much time is spent in listening, it seems reasonable to attempt to improve listening behavior. Through effective listening, it is possible to learn more, to become better informed, and to gain in sophistication. In direct communication with others, an improvement in listening will likely lead to a widening circle of friends. In attending to speaker-audience and small group messages, an improvement in listening can lead to increased knowledge and ability to make decisions. Good listening habits result in greater dependability and fewer embarrassments since fewer errors are made, directions are more clearly followed, and more informed messages can be made.

Social Listening

There are ways to improve the listening that occurs in interpersonal relationships at the social level. The following list includes some hints that can be used to improve ability to listen in a more informal setting. Many of the recommendations make sense in both serious and social listening situations. The important point is to practice them where appropriate.

1. Do not make it appear that you have all the answers. Some listeners always appear to want to win an argument rather than to solve a problem or receive information.
2. Avoid the attitude that you are superior to the speaker in power, position, wealth, or intellect. Try to make others realize that you respect their opinions.
3. Try not to appear uninterested or show lack of concern. Do not pass judgment on others

for their ideas. Avoid blaming or praising based upon your own values.

4. Be willing to reconsider your own abilities, ideas, and values based upon the rationales you have been given.
5. Be spontaneous, straightforward, and honest with other communicators. Do not base your reactions on hidden motives.
6. Avoid nonverbal behaviors that create a negative climate. Try not to avoid eye contact, turn the body away, shake the head, wring hands, or engage in other nonverbal movements with negative meanings.

Serious Listening

The following list includes a number of hints that can be practiced to improve serious listening behaviors. These can be practiced until they no longer require direct thought but occur almost automatically.

1. Be physically prepared to listen. Evaluative listening especially takes energy and it is important to be rested for the experience.
2. Set listening goals. A message will make more sense if there is an understanding of how the input can be useful.
3. Recognize any prejudices you might have and determine how the message relates to your values. Keeping an open mind is essential to the listening process. Listening to a message does not mean acceptance—it represents maturity, self-confidence, and open-mindedness.
4. Try to understand the meaning of the message even if it is unclear. When the message is difficult to understand, it is useful to write down questions to be asked.
5. Be a responsive listener. Nonverbal expressions such as nods, smiles, or puzzled expressions can reveal understanding or lack of understanding.
6. Always shut out distractions. Noises, other people, or daydreaming often take the listener's attention away from the message.
7. Be alert to the nonverbal language of the speaker. Movements, posture, and facial expressions contribute to the message.

Critical Listening

Critical listening is especially important since it permits the assessment of evidence or ideas that are essential in making valid decisions. It is more than just receiving and understanding a verbal message. It is an attempt to analyze verbal messages received. All suggestions and instructions from others are based upon their values, knowledge, and experiences. Listeners cannot accept uncritically what they hear. They must take responsibility for evaluating the information they receive.

Different people have different values. When listening critically, it is essential to be aware of the speaker's values and to be ready to reconsider one's own values. If the speaker's values reflect a specific position on an issue, then it may be that the message reflects the same position. Values are seldom verbalized but are definitely implied. It is sometimes useful to point out differences in values and to discuss them openly.

It is useful too in developing critical listening skill to learn to recognize differences in statements of facts and statements of opinions. Communicators rarely specify whether their messages are facts or opinions and some develop great skill in making opinions sound like facts. A factual statement must be backed by evidence. This evidence can be directly observable, or can be found in written reports, books, or documents.

Some questions you might try to answer as you critically listen, analyze, and evaluate are given below.

1. Is the speaker's opinion backed by evidence (e.g., quotations, examples, statistics, facts that support the main ideas)?
2. Are conclusions based on relevant facts?
3. What will the speaker gain from acceptance of the conclusion (e.g., a salesman)?
4. Is the speaker qualified to draw the conclusion?
5. Can the evidence presented be countered by opposing evidence?
6. Does the speaker use correct reasoning (e.g., moving from specifics to more general statements, emphasizing similarities and differences, or showing that one event was the cause of another)?

7. Is propaganda used to gain acceptance?
8. Is the message of value to you personally?

Attention to these questions might prove helpful in situations requiring critical listening. Critical listening is a part of the critical thinking process. Critical listening is the evaluation of verbal messages; critical thinking, the evaluation of all types of input relating to a particular issue. Critical listening is essential in judging worth of verbal input used to make decisions.

Discriminative Listening

In discriminative listening, a major goal is to understand and remember. Note taking is an extremely useful tool in discriminative listening. Without a photographic memory it is often difficult to remember the key ideas of a message, not to mention less important details or supporting evidence. Notes can provide an adequate stimulus for recall of important details of lectures and speakers. When a complete record seems important and the speaker does not object, however, it may be appropriate to record the message on audio tape.

Since note taking is the more usual course of action, an awareness of some note-taking techniques that facilitate discriminative listening can be useful. First, be brief. Second, be clear and well-organized. Soon after the listening experience, review and fill in from memory important, missing information. In taking notes from lectures in a formal classroom setting the steps listed below are suggested.

1. Be prepared by completing reading assignments and reviewing previous notes.
2. Immediately before the lecture, write down the date, the topic heading, and any other information you have.
3. Use the same format each time; listen for words like first, next, important, and significant to indicate main ideas; jot down important details and examples; leave space between main ideas so that other notes can be added; and be sure to make notes of the conclusion or summary.
4. Review lecture notes and include omissions, spell out unusual abbreviations, and coordinate them with notes from the text.

The Enlightened

when I was younger
I would shoot the rapids
on any subject
showboating in the shallows
and later on
enjoyed being in over my head
discussing the depth
of wider deeper places

however
having spent half my life
working both sides of this river
i feel i know the pools and eddies
fairly well
and when the conversation flows these days
i find it impossible
to wade right in

but don't misunderstand
this silence
for i do enjoy being here with you
listening
to the things you have to say

and in some small way
comprehending perhaps
why the so-called enlightened
simply stand
by the water
smiling
    vacantly

—Ric Masten
The Voice Of The Hive published by
Sunflower Ink, Carmel, CA

Even in situations where someone gives you a brief set of instructions, careful note taking will improve your chances of retaining and understanding important information.

DISTORTED MESSAGES

Internal or external interference with the communication process is often called "noise." The interference can be caused by environmental distractions, physiological impairment, semantic problems, psychological and social problems, and chains of communication. When noise interferes with the communication process, it becomes more and more difficult to send and receive accurate messages. Therefore, listening is improved by eliminating factors that cause noise and distort messages.

Environmental Distractions

Environmental distractions are the result of outside interference that makes it difficult for the listener to receive the message. Have you ever tried to listen to a news broadcast while someone was vacuuming the rug? If so, you have experienced noise in the communication channels. Such physical noise may not be so important in listening to a television broadcast. It is probably much more important when listening to an instructor describe the questions for an upcoming test. When environmental distractions affect reception of a message it is essential to attempt to eliminate the interference. This might be done by moving closer to the message source, by increasing the volume of the message, or by removing the distraction from the immediate surroundings. Speakers can help listeners by taking responsibility for elimination of environmental distractions.

Physiological Impairment and Semantic Problems

Deaf people cannot receive messages in the way that a person with normal hearing can. People with speech impediments may be difficult to understand. These are examples of physiological impairments that make the listening process more difficult. Semantic problems, on the other hand, occur because of word choice. It is often difficult to find just the right words to express a thought. Differences in language use, culture, experience, and education affect meanings that communicator and receiver assign to different words. The listener who has difficulty interpreting the words used in a message may ask for clarification. With tact, such requests can be made without causing embarrassment to other participants in the communication encounter. Speakers can help listeners by paying attention to impairments and semantics represented in the group receiving the message.

Psychological and Social Problems

Sometimes people have difficulty communicating because of their prior experiences or backgrounds. For example, people often become nervous in unfamiliar situations and both their listening and speaking skills are likely to suffer. Low self-esteem may affect speaking and listening skills as well. These are examples of psychological problems that make it difficult for the listener to receive a clear message. Social problems in listening result from preconceived and unchangeable ideas about individuals or groups of people. Thoughts like "nice girls don't do things like that," or "all women belong at home," can get in the way of open and honest communication. We tend to "not listen" if the ideas expressed are those to which we are violently opposed. The conscientious listener must learn to keep an open mind as a message is listened to and to remain nonjudgmental until the message has been totally delivered. Listening to and understanding a message does NOT mean that the message is accepted or will be acted upon. Speakers can help listeners by being inclusive and understanding cultural variables that exist in their audiences.

Communication Chains

Within organizations and among members of groups, information is constantly being transmitted from person to person. At work the most remote person in the company eventually hears about the boss's interpretation of the new telephone policy. At home the teenage children often spread news of the new telephone policy among themselves. Chains of communication are the ways that messages can be transmitted from individual to individual. The three most common ways of spreading information are the single-strand chain, gossip chain, and branching chain.

A single-strand chain is the process where person "A" tells person "B," person "B" tells person "C," person "C" tells person "D," and so on. A single-strand chain can be pictured as a single line of people, each hearing the message from only one person and telling it only to one other person. A great deal of distortion will result in the original message if the single-strand chain is very long.

The gossip chain occurs when person "A" tells person "B," person "A" tells person "C," person "A" tells person "D," and so on. The gossip chain can be pictured as a circle of listeners with gossiper in the middle. The person who transmits the message will often distort the message as it is told over and over to many different individuals.

The branching chain is a combination of the single-strand and gossip chains. In the branching chain, person "A" tells persons "B" and "C," person "B" tells person "D," person "C" tells persons "E" and "F," and so on. The originator of the message can be pictured in the center of a number of ropes leading outward. Some of the ropes are short, some long, and some indicate further branching as they radiate outward.

Designated chains of communication often exist in organizations. Bosses, for example, are expected to provide their employees with certain information. In contrast to the more formal chain of communication, informal chains exist where individuals somewhat randomly pass messages on to others. The number of times the message is repeated, whether by the same person as in the gossip chain, or by different people as in the single-strand chain, increases the amount of distortion that occurs as details are changed, omitted, or added.

In looking at distortion that occurs along the different types of communication chains, it is important to note that the message exists as the speaker thinks of it, as the speaker says it, as the listener perceives it, and as the listener remembers it. To increase the accuracy of a message as it is transmitted, keep the following in mind.

1. Take notes to help recall specific details.
2. Make the message as simple as possible.
3. Arrange details in a logical order.
4. Emphasize the important details.
5. Repeat the major details in a review process after the message has been relayed.

Gossip is transmitted from person to person along communication chains. Gossip refers to idle, usually senseless, and groundless talk about others. Schools, work settings, and family gatherings are places that provide opportunities for spread of gossip. Often the purpose of gossip is to be hurtful. Gossip might be classified as a form of workplace violence which results in pain and confusion. The problem with gossip, in addition to its potential harm, is that it reduces productivity and it undermines values. Before believing gossip, it is ESSENTIAL that you affirm what you have heard by checking with the subject of the gossip. Let us assume that you have just heard that your manager at work is disagreeing with a change in policies, touted to increase the profits of your division, because she is afraid she will lose her job. Before judging her for her failure to see the big picture or before spreading the gossip further, you must verify the truth or falseness of this claim. Go to the subject and find out if a potentially harmful event is in fact true. Do NOT make decisions based on unverified information.

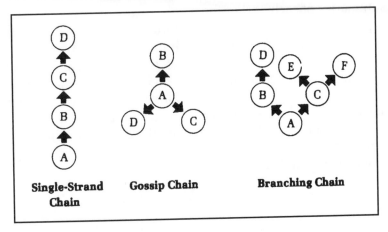

Figure 4.1. Communication Chains

Noise in the communication process, whether physical, social, psychological, or caused by repetition of a message, interferes with the listener's ability to comprehend and understand with accuracy. The listener must make a conscious effort to compensate for distortion by moving away from physical noise, by asking questions to clarify what is not understood, and by remaining open-minded when the message does not match values.

AVOIDING DISTRACTIONS

Listening is hard work. It takes concentrated effort to eliminate distractions and to keep the mind from wandering away from the message. It is an easy way out to place the blame for poor listening on the speaker's "worthless message." The listener must take responsibility for attending to the message.

One problem that occurs when concentrating on a spoken message is that the mind of the receiver is working faster than the speaker is able to talk. People are able to think about four times faster than they are able to speak. Speakers comfortably talk at about 125 words a minute; thinkers can easily process about 500 words a minute. The mind that is merely receiving a message is underutilized and often directs unused potential toward other interests, then returns to the message, strays again, and so forth.

Some suggestions for keeping the mind actively involved in a message are listed below.

1. Evaluate the support and rationale underlying the speaker's message.
2. Make mental summaries of each part of the message as it is presented.
3. Relate each part of the message to parts that preceded it.
4. Relate the message to your personal experiences.
5. Determine what parts of the message are more important than others.
6. Remind yourself to be open-minded and pay attention even when you disagree.

7. Reflect on vocabulary and sentence structure as they supply the context for validating your impressions.

In one sentence, the idea is to develop techniques you can use to stay tuned to the speaker's message and avoid the cycle of straying off, coming back, straying off, and so forth. Effective listening requires an actively involved mind, not just a passively receptive mind.

Summary

Listening and hearing are different processes in the individual. Hearing goes little beyond awareness of sound. There is practically no personal involvement in the hearing process. It is through listening that verbal messages are perceived, processed, and reacted to. If one gets tired of listening to a classroom lecture, for example, the instructor can be "tuned out" and participation can be reduced to hearing. Input that arrives via the process of hearing only has minimal imprint on one's memory. Very little conscious decoding occurs.

The different types of listening require different degrees of concentration, are appropriate for specific types of situations, and are affected to some extent by interest, fatigue, cultural variables, and personality traits.

Listening skills can be developed and improved at both the social and serious levels. To make effective use of time spent in serious listening situations, it is particularly important to develop good critical and discriminative listening skills. To be a good listener it is useful to be aware of ways that messages can be distorted by environmental factors; physiological impairment; and semantic, psychological, and social problems, as well as the ways that repetition of the same message changes its meaning. Finally, one means of improving listening may be as simple as keeping your mind actively involved in the message.

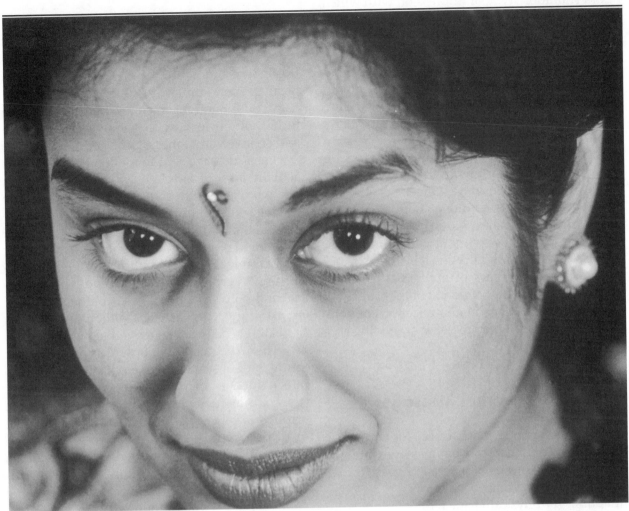

CHAPTER 5

Photograph by Beau Twilighten

NONVERBAL MESSAGES

There is much more to the communication process than speaking. In addition to speaking, communicators are involved in listening to others and in sending and interpreting nonverbal messages. To receive meaning from a spoken message it is necessary to listen, of course, and to read movement, facial expressions, gestures, and other nonverbal signs that add meaning to the spoken message. Listeners are senders of nonverbal messages also. Without uttering a sound receivers of messages can respond, thereby giving feedback to the speaker.

Think of your own experiences as a speaker. You may have been in the middle of a conversation that you had planned to go one way and, because of a movement, a look, or a gesture on the part of the receiver, changed what you intended to say. As a receiver of a message you have, no doubt, frowned or looked confused and caused the speaker to clarify what was said. Nonverbal messages are sent continually by all persons involved in the communication process. Even the seeming lack of a nonverbal message can communicate the "cold shoulder" type of impression with which all communicators are familiar.

For most speakers verbal messages are essential for communicating information about concrete objects and relationships. Nonverbal messages are generally more appropriate in enhancing or reinforcing expressions of feeling and emotions. Think about the difficulty many communicators have in verbally expressing emotional reactions. Such expression is made more easily and clearly with the aid of nonverbal expression. Consider someone saying "I love you" without the aid of nonverbal messages, and someone explaining a complex formula in mathematics without verbal messages. In the study of communication it is useful to recognize the many types of nonverbal behavior that contribute to the formation of the total message and to consider some implications of nonverbal messages in the processes of sending and receiving messages.

Types of Nonverbal Messages

Included among those aspects of nonverbal communication that convey messages are (a) body motion (kinesics), (b) personal space (proxemics), (c) touching behavior (haptics), (e) physical characteristics, (f) artifacts, and (g) environment (Knapp, 1978). Also, taste and smell (olfactory) send nonverbal messages. Further, perception of time (chronemics) is another area included in some discussions of nonverbal communication (Burgoon, Butler, and Woodall, 1989). Many important messages are transmitted through nonverbal language. Although people differ to some extent in meanings associated with specific types of nonverbal language, researchers have concluded that common meanings are associated with many expressions and movements. In spite of the fact that nonverbal messages are easily misunderstood and must be interpreted within the context in which they occur, they play an essential part in communication. One can usually decide not to send verbal messages but cannot choose to cease sending nonverbal messages. Even silence says something.

GOAL

Apply principles associated with various types of nonverbal communication.

KINESICS

Body motion (kinesics) includes facial expressions and eye contact, whole head movements, gestures, trunk movements, and posture (Eisenberg and Smith, 1971). Although communicators spend much less time speaking than in using body motions to communicate, they give little thought to how they move as they send and receive verbal messages.

Each message sent to a potential receiver is actually a set of messages. A sender may say a few words, point to something, and frown. The receiver must interpret the words as well as the pointing and frowning behaviors. The same words and pointing movement accompanied by a smile might have an entirely different meaning and interpretation. As the sender of the verbal and nonverbal messages is in the process of transmitting, the listener, although silent, is revealing reactions via nonverbal messages.

There is no firm consensus on whether body motions and their associated meanings are natural human characteristics or whether they are learned responses unique to specific groups of people. Much evidence points to the conclusion that body motions are learned behaviors. This is supported by observations that people of different backgrounds assign different meanings to the same body motions. For example, one individual might attract the attention of a waiter in a restaurant with a nod and a direct look in the eye, whereas another might slightly raise an arm and point at the waiter.

Most communicators have a good intuitive knowledge of those behaviors that are common within their specific cultures. According to some researchers, for example, crossed arms generally suggest defensiveness and indicate negative communication. Anxiety and lack of confidence are indicated by cuticle picking, nail biting, pencil chewing, and fidgeting with jewelry or hair. Rapid movements often express fear. Aggressiveness or dominance is suggested by a pointing finger. Boredom and impatience are indicated by tapping of fingers or clicking of a ballpoint pen. A flirtation might be enhanced by arranging the hair or smoothing a dress. Confidence is displayed by an erect posture with shoulders held back.

Certain physical behaviors are sometimes associated with occupations. Professional people like lawyers or professors often seem to be evaluating or thinking. They might lean forward, sit on the edge of a chair, or support the head with a hand on the cheek. Athletes often seem to display their strength. They might stand with legs apart, feet solidly on the ground, and muscles flexed. Some body motions are subtle and some are quite obvious. Whatever, they merit conscious attention by the communicator who strives to be perceptive and to clarify the meaning of the total message.

PROXEMICS

It has been said that each person has a personal space (proxemics) that can be conceptualized as an invisible bubble (Sommer, 1969). The invisible bubble defines the territory that individuals claim as their own. Others should not enter the invisible bubble without an invitation. Consider the somewhat common situation where two people in a casual conversation tend to move very slowly across the room. In such cases the individual who is backing away is experiencing an invasion of personal space and is attempting to restore the boundaries of the bubble.

Edward Hall (1959, 1966) has concluded that comfortable distances between persons in communication situations are related to the nature of the message. In the American population he has identified four interpersonal distances, each with a close and far phase, that correspond to certain types of messages.

1. Intimate, close (3 to 6 inches)—soft whisper, secretive, intimate
   Intimate, far (6 to 18 inches)—audible whisper, very confidential

2. Personal, close (18 to 30 inches)—soft voice, confidential
   Personal, far (30 to 48 inches)—soft voice, personal information

3. Social, close (4 to 7 feet)—full voice, impersonal
   Social, far (7 to 12 feet)—full voice, formal

4. Public, close (12 to 25 feet)—pronounced volume needed
   Public, far (25 feet and beyond)—amplification usually needed

These classifications may be reduced by calling 1 and 2 the intimate zone; 3 and 4 the personal zone; 5 and 6 the social zone; and 7 and 8 the public zone.

Communication occurs most effectively when the personal space of the individuals involved is not invaded. In general, the intimate zone should not be violated by those who are not intimate. Persons in a crowded bus are probably having their intimate zone violated and find the closeness uncomfortable. By avoiding eye contact in such close situations, crowded individuals are sometimes attempting to maintain a sense of control over personal space. The personal zone is acceptable for party conversation, for talk among classmates, and for discussion among close friends. It generally

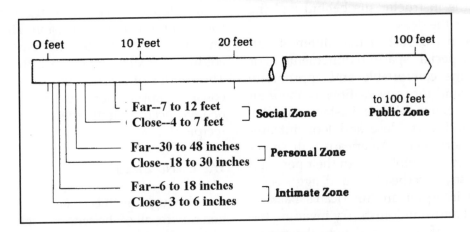

Figure 5.1. Zones of Distance

Space Bubble

Figure 5.2. Invisible Bubble Defining Personal Space

connotes a close and trusting relationship. More general conversation and business transactions will occur at the social distance. The public distance is established between the public speaker or actor and the audience.

Personal space has much to do with the ways that furniture is arranged and buildings are designed. Territoriality is a term that is often used to denote perception of ownership of space or objects. It affects the choice of seating within groups and the comfort that individuals feel in certain situations. Members of a family will often display ownership of territory within their homes by claiming a specific chair or room. Consider the behaviors of people in public places. In a nearly vacant library, for example, few people would select a chair immediately next to one of the other patrons. Most individuals would select a seat that allowed them to maximize their personal bubbles. Or consider a student who visits an instructor's office for a conference. Many students are more comfortable when both the instructor and student sit on easy chairs rather than when the instructor sits behind and the student across the desk.

It has been established that different cultures have special space requirements. For Americans, the comfortable and appropriate distance to stand for conversations is about an arm's length. Some Middle Eastern cultures, however, stand very close and look intently into each other's eyes. Americans will sometimes interpret such violations of their personal space as pushy, overbearing, and aggressive. Others may interpret an American's backing away as cold and standoffish. Try invading the personal space of others and note the verbal and nonverbal communication that results.

HAPTICS

Communication by touch (haptics) has always had a special significance to human beings. The handshake is one of the most common forms of touch we experience. Think of handshakes you have experienced—limp, firm, bone-crushing, sweaty, long, short, fingers only—and how you interpret the differences. In teaching job-search skills, instructors often include how to shake hands. Touch is certainly the earliest form of communication available to the human infant. Orphaned babies placed in institutions have died for lack of cuddling and holding. Through the experience of touching, a child is reassured, comforted, accepted, and made to feel loved.

Early touching experiences of the infant and child may be directly related to the effectiveness of adult interpersonal communication. Early experiences establish the first patterns of interpersonal relationships. They often determine individuals' confidence in themselves and amount of trust in others. For adults, touching is one of the most valuable forms of nonverbal expression. Through touch, one can communicate such emotions as fear, coldness, anxiety, love, warmth, and security. The sender of a touch message, must always consider appropriateness of the gesture and behave according to the expectations of the recipient.

TASTE AND SMELL

Although touch is a very strong communication device, all of the senses—sight, sound, taste, and smell (olfactory)—contribute information to a communication encounter. Sight and sound are obvious since we give meaning to what we see around us and what we hear in our environment.

What of the other two senses, taste and smell? Taste communicates through the pleasure of food and through the air. Can you taste the salt air as you approach the beach? Do certain food tastes bring memories to your mind? Likewise, we smell the salt air and we smell the aromas of cooking. Some real estate agents use taste and smell effectively in selling residential property. Imagine walking into a house and smelling coffee or freshly baked muffins and then discovering a note that you should help yourself to a snack as you evaluate the house. Wouldn't you want to live in such a pleasing home? Body odors also contribute to communication. The scents of some soaps and deodorants are pleasing; that locker room odor, on the other hand, is a turn-off.

PARALANGUAGE

Paralanguage refers to qualities or tones of the voice and speaking styles not directly related to the specific words that are said. It includes the sounds associated with laughing and crying. The loudness, pitch, rate, and rhythm of the voice are the vocal qualities most obvious to the average communicator. The concept of speaking styles refers to pauses, fillers like "ah," "uh," "and a," and drawling or clipping words.

Nasality is a vocal quality that falls under the nonverbal category of paralanguage. We often think that a person whose voice has nasal qualities is suffering from congested sinuses. One very famous person whose voice seems "nasal" to many of us is Willie Nelson. Willie himself, in his autobiography (Nelson, 1988), made the following comments:

A lot of people think I sing nasal. It's not true. It may sound nasal to some ears, but actually it's the sound that comes from deep down in the diaphragm. That's where you get the most strength. It's the result of controlling your breathing, which is the secret to many things, including peace of mind. (p. 22)

Later in his life story Willie, in describing a bitter argument with one of his wives, made another observation about paralanguage.

The Beautiful

wherever she went
in that crowded
    chattering room
the conversation dimmed
as if something were wrong
with the electricity

she was that beautiful
the men running their eyes over her
like hands
the women bunching up
    into small clenched fists
    shouting at each other
    about babies
    and pregnancy

the poet in me must have been showing
because she came over
    and she leaned close
    with an unlit cigarette
and as i fumbled for a light
she said
quite confidently

    it's like i had a goiter

—Ric Masten
The Voice of the Hive published by Sunflower Ink,
Carmel, CA

If you hit somebody, or they hit you, it's over with. It's out of your system. But if you speak mean angry words, it goes to the bone and stays there. Just your tone of voice can do damage. Maybe you hardly notice how harsh you sound, but the other person never forgets it. They'll always hear your words and your tone and remember what you meant. (p. 152)

Paralanguage is a powerful part of nonverbal communication.

Specific reactions to messages often result more from the tone of voice of the sender than from the actual words said. Loudness or softness of voice conveys meaning by providing emphasis to certain verbal messages. Shouting is often associated with anger; quietness, with disappointment. Pitch describes the highness or lowness of the voice. A high-pitched voice is often associated with whining, fear, or anxiety. A low-pitched voice conveys relaxation and calmness. Pitch differs, too, at the end of statements and questions. Listen carefully at the end of a question—normally pitch will rise. Rate refers to the speed of what is said. Quick speech generally indicates urgency; slow speech, a hesitation. Rhythm refers to the way that loudness, pitch, and speed are varied. With little variety a monotone effect will result.

PHYSICAL CHARACTERISTICS

Physical characteristics are those qualities of an individual that generally stay the same. Physical characteristics are in part acquired through heredity. For example, individuals can do little to alter permanently height, bone structure, or eye color. Other physical characteristics are acquired as one passes through the developmental phases of life, or as one makes decisions about physical appearance. For example, length of hair, posture, and aspects of appearance related to grooming can be determined to a considerable extent by the individual.

Both types of physical characteristics—those over which an individual has control and those over which little control is possible—provide nonverbal messages in a communication situation. For example, the condition of a person's hands communicates something about the type of work in which the person is involved. The length, style, and condition of a person's hair reveal information about the person's lifestyle—casual versus structured, progressive versus conservative. Physical characteristics and their corresponding messages interact with what, in communication, are called artifacts.

ARTIFACTS

Artifacts are those objects which communicators display while sending and receiving messages. These include such items as clothing, jewelry, and makeup that directly interact with physical appearance. First impressions of individuals are often relayed via the nonverbal messages associated with an individual's overall appearance. Such judgments can relate to a person's socioeconomic status, values, and interests. First impressions made on the basis of physical characteristics and artifacts, however, are often proved to be accurate.

The topic of clothing as it relates to image and success continually receives attention in the popular press. John T. Molloy (1975, 1977) has been called "America's first wardrobe engineer" by Time magazine. He has conducted numerous investigations of reactions to specific ways of dressing that create desired images. He feels that most men and women who seek to advance in the corporate structure dress for failure. Molloy (1975, p. 15) made the following statement as he expressed the effect of dress on image.

I can help you look successful, fatherly, honest, sexy, or even use clothes to mask or overcome detrimental physical characteristics or quirks. I have successfully applied these techniques on behalf of national political figures of both parties, executives of many of America's leading corporations, diplomats of foreign governments stationed in the United States, foreign executives seeking to do business here, television personalities, salesmen, courtroom lawyers, defendants in major criminal trials, professional associations, and, of course, private individuals.

Molloy is convinced that people who look successful and educated receive better treatment in nearly all business and social situations. He bases his conclusions on studies where reactions to individuals wearing different types of clothing have been recorded. His message is quite persuasive and leaves the reader feeling that such artifacts as clothing can, in fact, make a strong statement to others. A study of the professional dress of women makes a statement about the status of women in the workplace. As more women entered the workforce in the 1960s, there was a trend to imitate the dress of men. Women wore dark business suits, starched cotton blouses, and silk bow ties. By the start of the new century, a new professional dress has emerged which is more colorful, more varied, and, many times, more feminine.

Figure 5.3. Messages about Values and Lifestyles

ENVIRONMENT

In addition to the objects that create the outward appearance of an individual, choices of other objects such as cars and furnishings, room arrangements, and preferences for specific places provide nonverbal messages. Communicators make inferences from the make and model of a car, the type of architecture of a home, and choice of a restaurant for an evening meal. For example, the message seems different when a couple selects a quiet, small, dimly lit restaurant for their date in contrast to a noisy, large, brightly lit restaurant. And does not the choice of a small economical car versus a mid-sized sportier model reveal something about the purchaser's values? The way we dress and things we own send messages to others about our values and life styles.

Color is a dimension of environment that is a very powerful communicator. Color preferences are very individualistic due to learned associations plus differences in the receptors in the eyes. "Color blindness" is a term often used to indicate differences in the level of color differentiation across people. Leading to many disputes about what matches or not, color blindness occurs in varying degrees and occurs more often in males. Like many design dimensions, sensitivity to color can be acquired with experience. Color associations vary across cultures. For example, white represents purity and is associated with weddings in the United States but is associated with death in Japan. Red is associated with death in Korea but represents danger in the United States. Teachers use red ink to mark mistakes on papers! Lighting interacts with the intensity of color. Dim lighting will reduce the intensity of vivid colors. When assessing the strength of color associations in the United States, think about the use of pale blue for baby boys and pale red (pink) for baby girls. Any parent who dressed a baby boy in pink would be considered weird, but baby girls can wear pale blue.

Numerous studies have been conducted over the years in an attempt to relate choices of environmental factors to other traits. The relationships, however, are so complex that it is difficult to make specific conclusions. Many factors, preferences, and constraints interact. Nevertheless such choices do provide information in a communication situation and, right or wrong, contribute to perceptions of what is going on.

CHRONEMICS

Perception of time (chronemics) in nonverbal communication seems to diverge along two different dimensions: cultural which refers to punctuality and scheduling and psychological which refers to orientation to past, present, and future. The messages one sends concerning

---

Time Warp

when i assured them all
i'd return next June

the children cried:
"gone so long?"

the elders sighed:
"back so soon?"

—Ric Masten
They Are All Gone Now published by Sunflower Ink, Carmel, CA

these dimensions communicate about personal characteristics, priorities, and values.

Punctuality and scheduling relate to the individual's management of time. Is one on time for appointments; does one over commit so that an appearance of constant rushing is obvious? Does one make time for helping friends and family or are others' needs always subordinate? Cultural differences in study of time relate to the importance of or value placed on punctuality and scheduling. In some cultures, trains arrive and leave the station almost to the second the schedule indicates; in other cultures, trains arrive and leave the station when they arrive and leave. International travellers must behave quite differently if travelling by train in Switzerland than if travelling by train in Mexico. Orientation to past, present, and future is related somewhat to age and also to cultural values. As Americans, in general, age, they seem to become less future oriented and more past oriented. In some cultures, where tradition is paramount, past orientations are more obvious. Across American culture, a future orientation is pervasive. There is emphasis on such factors as educational degrees, insurance policies, and upward mobility. Compare your own time orientation to cultural and psychological time. How do you manage time and how do you relate past, present, and future? Ghandi has suggested that people should live as if they were to die tomorrow and should learn as if they were to live forever.

Some Implications of Nonverbal Messages

The study of nonverbal messages has intrigued scholars for years. Nierenberg and Calero (1971) have a bibliography in their book, *How to Read a Person Like a Book*, with references dating as far back as 1822 (e.g., *Practical Illustration of Rhetorical Gestures*, by Henry Soddons). Other books contain extensive bibliographies and reviews of research and opinions concerning nonverbal messages. For purposes of this review, information about universality of nonverbal messages,

conflicting verbal and nonverbal messages, awareness of one's own nonverbal messages, body language, and time management will be covered.

Our multi-cultural society of the 21st century requires a sensitivity to communication styles of people from differing backgrounds. Noverbal communication is an area where differences might be crucial to sending and receiving nonverbal messages. The elder George Bush created a serious faux-pas while visiting Australia in 1992. Using the symbol common in the United States for victory, that is, holding up two fingers to form a "V," he made this gesture as he drove through the Australian capital. Unfortunately, in Australia, the "V" sign is used as the middle finger is used in the US. Of course, the Australians had differing reactions to that event and Bush later apologized. All of the areas of nonverbal communication have potential for difference meanings cross-culturally. Punctuality, eye contact, sounds of bodily functions, exposure of skin in dress, and much more differ within various cultures. A good communicator will factor this possibility into the communication exchange when the nonverbal message does not compute.

CONFLICTING MESSAGES

The major goal of communication is to send and receive messages that are clear and accurate. This requires speaking ability and listening ability as well as the ability to receive and interpret nonverbal messages. If you notice a gesture, an article of clothing, or a facial expression, it might be a planned action of the communicator meant to send a message, a subconscious movement of the communicator, or a random motion of no importance. One problem with nonverbal messages is that we are not sure if they are intended or not. Another problem in interpreting nonverbal messages is the possibility that verbal and nonverbal messages may conflict.

GOAL
Develop effective nonverbal skills for various speaking situations.

Consider the person who has just had a foot trampled while sitting on a bus. The trampler, with face set in a worried manner, might say, "I'm sorry." The person with the crushed foot is likely to be

Flags

she dresses in flags
and comes on
like a mack truck
she paints
her eyelids green
and her mouth
is a loudspeaker
rasping out profanity

at cocktail parties
she is everywhere
like a sheep dog
working a flock
barking
nipping at your sleeve
spilling your drink
bestowing
wet sloppy kisses

but i
       have received
       secret messages
       carefully written
       from the shy
       quiet woman
       who hides
       in this bizarre
       gaudy castle

—Ric Masten

Even As We Speak published by Sunflower Ink,
Carmel, CA

grinding teeth in pain while saying, "No problem. My foot is fine." The actual message of pain was communicated fairly clearly. Conflicts between verbal and nonverbal messages can go much deeper. There are situations where it is hard to determine which message, the verbal or nonverbal, is the more accurate.

Examples of verbal and nonverbal messages that are hard to interpret often occur during heated discussions, arguments, or what might be called personality clashes in situations where appearances of friendship must be upheld. For example, a mother and daughter in the company of friends might have a discussion over a matter on which they disagree. The ver-

bal messages might mask the true extent of the problem while the nonverbal messages may be subtly revealing that a conflict situation exists. Unfortunately for the sender who tries to mask the conflict, not only the intended receiver but everyone observing the transaction can give meaning to such sometimes not so subtle nonverbal messages.

In situations where verbal and nonverbal messages seem to conflict, it is generally the nonverbal message that is the more truthful (Nierenberg and Calero, 1971). To clarify situations where conflicting messages occur, it is useful to try two things. First, interpret the total nonverbal message or the cluster of individual signs that follow one another. Often more accurate meanings can be gathered from nonverbal messages that seem to go together. Isolated movements and gestures that result from an individual's habits do not necessarily carry the meaning normally assigned to them (e.g., blinking eyes may be due to a physical impairment). Second, initiate a verbal response by asking a question aimed at clearing up the confusion. Such questions as, "are you certain about that," "let me see if I understand what you've said," or "could you expand on that," are useful to clarify a message that includes conflicting verbal and nonverbal components. Understanding nonverbal messages is a difficult task. Each can be contradicted, made clearer, or confused by the verbal and other nonverbal messages it accompanies.

AWARENESS OF ONE'S OWN NONVERBAL MESSAGES

Have you ever thought about the nonverbal messages that you send and the meanings others might attach to them? If communicators become aware of the nonverbal messages they are sending, they become more aware of their own reactions to situations and are able to communicate better. Very often nonverbal messages cause receivers of messages to react in specific yet unanticipated ways.

Each movement or motion is, in a sense, a word in a nonverbal language. It is a language that is hard to speak fluently. It contains a great deal of "noise" that distorts messages. Although it is hard to see oneself speak in nonverbal ways, like other languages, practice makes it easier to understand. Try looking at yourself as you speak to other people, in small groups, and to large audiences. What do you see? Do you have habits that might interfere with the nonverbal messages you send? What type of messages do you send? What does your clothing say? What messages do you send through the qualities of your voice? How close do you get to people in different kinds of situations? Do you ever communicate through touch?

People who become aware of their own nonverbal messages can sometimes improve the clarity of the messages they convey. Consider an individual who sits somewhat rigidly with arms folded in conference with another individual. Realizing this and the message of resistance that it probably conveys, the first individual might change posture to indicate an attitude of openness toward the topic of discussion. It seems only logical that the communication process will be more effective if both parties feel that each is receptive and open to discussion.

Like learning a foreign language, the process of self-observation and conscious knowledge of nonverbal messages will take time. It seems a hard task to concentrate on both the content of a message and how to express it both verbally and nonverbally. It might be easier to begin noticing your own nonverbal behaviors as you listen in situations that do not require total concentration. For example, take a look at yourself as you chat with a close friend and as you chat with an authority figure. Are your nonverbal behaviors different? If so, should they be different?

BODY LANGUAGE

Body language has been a prevalent topic in the popular press for several years. Books like *Body Language* (Fast, 1970) have been best sellers and popular periodicals have included many articles on body language or, as it was called earlier in this chapter, body motions or movements. The scientific community has done much work in this area of communication too. Psychologists, sociologists, anthropologists and communication theorists have studied the meanings attached to gestures, facial expressions, posture, eye movement, and other non-verbal expressions. Of the areas differentiated in the earlier section on nonverbal messages the area of body language (i.e., body motion) has probably received more attention and created wider interest than any of the others.

Communication scholars often break Body Language into five different types:

- *Emblems* represent actual words. An arm outstretched with the palm of the hand in vertical position facing the viewer means "STOP!"
- *Regulators* represent movements that affect the continuity of a communication exchange. Shaking the head sideways sends the message of "No," and tells the speaker to reconsider the message.
- *Illustrators* represent movements, usually with the hands, that add clarity to the verbal message. Giving emphasis to the concept of "hugeness" might be done by stretching the arms far apart.
- *Affect Displays* represent movements, usually of the face, that illustrate emotion. A smile is a universal symbol of a positive emotion.
- *Adaptors* represent other nonverbal signals that do not enhance the message but happen during a communication exchange. Blinking eyes might indicate dirty contact lenses, scratching relieves itching, or squirming is a reaction to uncomfortable furnishings.

Because of the popularity of the study of body language by both scholars and the general public, perhaps it deserves further discussion here. It is impossible in this limited space to cover the entire domain of body language. Therefore, a few of the more common and possibly the more interesting generalizations about body language will be presented. Nierenberg and Calero (1971), in *How to Read a Person Like a Book*, discuss a number of different behavioral states and the body language associated with them. Among these behavioral states are openness, cooperation, frustration, confidence, nervousness, and courtship.

Openness

The human behaviors associated with openness are similar to those behaviors of animals that communicate submissiveness by lying on their backs and exposing their stomachs and necks. Open arms with palms exposed are a particularly common and easily observable indication of openness. It is, in fact, a posture that is commonly displayed in religious statues. An unbuttoned coat is another symbol of openness. A general demeanor of being relaxed often expresses openness. In group situations openness may be shown by members drawing closer together.

Cooperation

The state of being cooperative is similar to that of being open. It seems that true cooperation requires an openness to exploring the situation. A cooperative attitude is demonstrated by a posture that can be described as a "sprinter's position." It is a nonverbal indicator of being ready for action by leaning forward with feet on tiptoes. The cooperative gesture is further demonstrated by such behaviors as sitting and tilting the head in an attentive position. It can be especially useful to recognize behaviors that indicate a change from a cooperative attitude to a noncooperative attitude so that the situation can be restructured before it results in irreparable changes in attitude.

Frustration

Frustration is a behavior communicated nonverbally by most people at one time or another. It is communicated by a wide range of behaviors like short breaths, hands tightly clenched, wringing of hands, fistlike gestures, pointing index finger, palm to the back of the neck, and kicking the ground or an imaginary object. Frustration seems to be a mental state that is openly communicated both to oneself, even when alone, and to others. Frustrated people are generally seeking solutions. When reacting to others' frustrations, it is often helpful to send nonverbal messages that communicate reassurance and confidence.

Confidence

Confidence is demonstrated by a proud, erect stance that can be achieved by squaring the shoulders and straightening the back. A confident person also seems to have longer, more frequent eye contact and to blink less.

Steepling (joining of the fingertips and wrists); hands joined together behind the back with chin thrust upward; claiming territory by placing feet on a desk or one leg over the arm of a chair, or by placing personal articles in desired space; elevating oneself to a higher plane than another; and leaning back with hands supporting the head are other behaviors that communicate confidence. Many of these characteristics can be associated with authority figures who must display confidence as part of their roles.

Nervousness

Nervousness is the opposite of confidence. We have all noticed what might be called "uptight" messages from those around us. This is an instance where the verbal messages usually contradict the nonverbal messages. Most people resist admitting anxiety and often take offense when asked a direct question about how they seem to be feeling. Several indicators of nervousness are the following: clearing of the throat, the "whew" sound, extinguishing or leaving a cigarette burning, fidgeting in a chair, hands covering the mouth while speaking, tugging at clothing while seated, jingling money in pockets, and ear-tugging. When such behaviors are observed, it is sometimes useful to pause briefly and analyze the situation that is causing nervousness. Sometimes an objective look at a situation can greatly reduce anxiety.

Courtship

Persons engaged in courtship behaviors can be identified by a state of firm muscle tone, attempts at improving appearance, and a feeling of being at ease with each other. The posture of a couple in love seems to be less slumped than usual. The skin seems to take on a firmer look. There is an attempt to smooth the hair, straighten the clothing, and check reflections in mirrors or windows. Some gestures like direct eye contact are used to express an interest in involvement. Normally men and women who are romantically interested in each other have little difficulty expressing this emotion via nonverbal messages.

Jo-Ellen Dimitries (Dimitries and Mazarella, 1998) who has consulted in over 600 jury trials including Rodney King, John DuPont, McMartin

Preschool, and O. J. Simpson, has concluded the following concerning body language:

> Body language provides more basic information. Few people are aware of all their physical reactions to the world around them, and fewer still can always control those actions even if they want to. Manners and poise may be consciously learned, but facial expressions, eye blinking, leg crossing, and nervous tapping are difficult to consistently repress. I've seen enough people on the witness stand to know that it's nearly impossible to control body language, even if one's fate depends on it.
>
> Body language, then, tends to reveal inner character and emotions—fear, honesty, nervousness, joy, indecisiveness, frustration, and much more—that aren't obvious from grooming or attire. Although appearance and body language usually provide different types of information, the knowledge that can be obtained from each of them is equally important. Sometimes appearance and body language point in the same direction, sometimes in opposite directions. The important thing is to keep your eyes and your mind open. (pp. 43–44)

Body language, along with all the other nonverbal ways of communicating, provides a silent language that transmits meaning right along with verbal messages.

PERSUASIVE EDGE

In addition, consider the following nonverbal characteristics (Murphy, 2001) that might help you make your point in interpersonal, small group, or speaker audience situations.

1. Making the most of your physical characteristics might give you an edge.
2. Being older than your listener might help get your desired outcome.
3. Exuding tenacity and willpower might contribute to your goals.
4. Having confidence might put you a step ahead of the competition.
5. Being well dressed and well groomed might tip the scales in your favor.
6. Giving something for something in return might put you out in front.
7. Having some knowledge—doing your research—might help you negotiate.
8. Having good timing and lots of luck might be the answer.
9. Avoiding mean, aggressive, or rude behaviors might make a difference.
10. Sending positive nonverbal messages as you explain your reasons, offer your services, and give compliments might tilt the table in your favor.

TIME MANAGEMENT

GOAL
Illustrate effective ways to handle time management.

When management of time is mentioned, Alan Lakein's (1973) time management system described in *How to Get Control of Your Time and Your Life* immediately comes to mind. Lakein bases the development of his system for time management on simple premises:

- Time is life. To waste your time is to waste your life.
- There is no such thing as lack of time.

Everyone has the same amount of time each day. The variance among the accomplishments of different people is related directly to how they use their time.

Procrastination, or putting off to later what can easily be done now, is one of the primary causes of wasted time. For example, imagine that you have just finished the best term paper of your life but decide to print it later. With ample time right before class, you start to print and run out of paper. You have to turn the paper in late and lose points on your grade. Lakein lists seven reasons why people sometimes fail to begin or complete the really important goals they set.

1. Indulging yourself, doing something you really enjoy
2. Socializing, visiting with others

3. Reading, catching up on a backlog of unread materials
4. Doing it yourself, baking your own bread
5. Overdoing it, closely supervising others, allowing each visitor to take an extra 15 minutes of your time
6. Running away, paying your telephone bill in person, extending your lunch break, hand carrying a memo
7. Daydreaming, engaging in fantasies

Lakein goes on to mention that time is lost, also, through guilt, anger, and worry. The GREAT escape, however, is television. And another is the telephone.

Lakein suggests a straightforward method for using time to the best advantage.

1. Set aside a specific time each day for planning the use of your time.
2. Make a daily "TO DO" list.
3. Assign priority values to each item on your "TO DO" list, by labeling them A, B, or C. Ask, "is this necessary?" and "what would happen if I do not do it?"
   "A" items yield the most value.
   "B" items are of medium value.
   "C" items are of lowest value.
4. Start with the A's. Many of the B's can be delegated. Many of the C's can be ignored. Get a "C" drawer. Handle "C" items once a month or so, during a two or three hour block of time.

When using the time management system, it is essential that you get into the habit of planning your time every day. Some people find that an early hour in the morning is best; others plan later in the day for the following day. Habitually, using 10 minutes per day to schedule time helps to keep you working on "A" items rather than the sometimes simpler "C" items. Lakein suggests that you do leave some time unscheduled for interruptions.

To make maximum use of time, it is necessary to make conscious decisions about how your time will be spent. Control of time is the key but control requires planning. In all planning, you must make a list and set priorities. You must begin by looking at long-term goals and breaking them into more doable steps that will eventually lead to the goal. Be in control of

your destiny. Lakein points out five unsatisfactory approaches and one satisfactory approach to decision-making:

1. **Habit**—Being automatic and following routines
2. **Demands of others**—Letting others decide
3. **Escapism**—Daydreaming, blaming something or someone else
4. **Spur of the moment**—Deciding at the last minute
5. **Default**—Letting others make our choices
6. **Conscious decision**—Planning ahead and following through

Do not get caught in the traps, listed in items one through five above, but rather make well thought-out decisions, as suggested in item six above, that permit planning ahead and then follow-through. Lakein suggests that you take five minutes out of your day to begin tasks which are particularly distasteful or overwhelming. This gets you started and makes it easier to follow through the next day. Time control does not mean that you must be super-organized, super-busy, or preoccupied with every minute but rather that you are in control of how your time is spent.

Steven Covey (1989) in his popular book, *The Seven Habits of Highly Effective People*, has suggested that time management be taken even further than Lakein. Covey traces time management through an evolution from making lists to keeping calendars and prioritizing tasks. Covey then recommends that we go further and concentrate on enhancing relationships and accomplishing results. His time management matrix puts the things we do in perspective. Study the Time Management Quadrants shown above and decide which quadrant you emphasize in your planning.

Consider the following example: You have begun to hear the chirping sound that eventually emerges from the brakes of your car as they wear and need to be repaired. Are brakes important to the operation of your car? YES, they are important! Is the repair urgent? NO, the chirping begins as a warning so that you have time to take the proper steps. Therefore, at first, repairing the brakes goes in Quadrant II. That's great unless they stay there with no intervention on your part. The day that you miss school or work

Time Management Quadrants

I. Urgent, Important *Crises* *Deadlines* *Problems*	II. Not Urgent, Important *Prevention* *Relationships* *Planning*
III. Urgent, Not Important *Interruptions* *Some mail, meetings* *Pressing matters*	IV. Not Urgent, Not Important *Busywork* *Some mail, calls* *Time wasters*

or fail to pick up your children, they move to Quadrant I. Covey suggests that we concentrate on Quadrant II. Fixing the brakes in a Quadrant I situation is likely to take more time, cause more inconvenience, and be more expensive than making an appointment which will easily fit it into your schedule. Some health care issues are the same. Are you going to wait until a benign skin irritation turns into a melanoma or should you take preventative steps to avoid the cancer? Unfortunately, many of us cannot get out of Quadrant I. We should take steps to manage our time and relationships as Quadrant II activities.

The ways we manage time reflect habits which are hard to break. Time is a cultural factor, too, with differences related to such factors as family background, occupation, and age. For example, the older professional person may value punctuality and strict deadlines whereas some younger but equally successful professionals may have a more casual interpretation of time. It pays to consider how your boss is thinking before you take the casual approach. Technology has facilitated the concept of "multi-tasking," where somehow we mange to do several tasks at once. Although becoming illegal in many states and advised against by insurance companies, one common example of multi-tasking is driving and talking on cellphones. Also, we do a number of computer tasks simultaneously. As one function is running, we turn to another and then back and forth. Time management strategies can be evaluated on a conceptual basis and then adapted to fit into your own values toward time. The bottom line is that time is a finite variable and being in control of time is what matters. Recent

innovation for help in keeping control of time are the Palm Pilot and other handheld, minicomputers as well as scheduling systems to use on your personal computer. If the traditional paper and pencil systems fail to work for you, try one of the electronic systems. Whichever you use, all systems require constant updating and checking to keep on task.

Summary

Human beings rely heavily on verbal communication to transmit and receive messages. Nonverbal messages also play an essential role in the total communication process. Verbal communication is particularly appropriate for transmitting knowledge. Nonverbal messages are particularly appropriate for sharing emotions, feelings, and attitudes. Love, for example, can be communicated verbally but is more effectively communicated with the addition of nonverbal messages.

Nonverbal language is expressed through body motions, personal space, touching, taste and smell, paralanguage, physical characteristics, artifacts, environment, and time perception. Through nonverbal language, power, trustworthiness, status, love, affection, acceptance, hostility, and other emotions and attitudes can be communicated. Some individuals are more adept at both sending and receiving nonverbal messages than others. Hopefully, through an awareness that nonverbal messages are important aspects of communication, a greater sensitivity to one's own nonverbal messages and those of others can be developed.

CHAPTER 6

Goodshoot®

NONVERBAL TECHNIQUES TO HELP THE LISTENER

Listening is a complex process. To be an effective listener it is necessary to select and process those elements in the environment that provide the most important information. By studying and practicing good listening habits individuals can do much to improve their own skill as listeners. Speakers can do much also to help the listener attend to and retain the important aspects of a message. In fact, communication is enhanced when the speaker shares responsibility with the receiver for facilitating listening.

GOAL
Demonstrate ability in the use of appropriate feedback to help the listener.

Your total communication image is based on such factors as language, including grammar; enunciation, how you create the sounds which form words; vocal qualities such as volume and pitch; and your presentation style, including the confidence you portray. By considering the effects of nonverbal stimuli on the receiver of the message, the speaker can facilitate the listening process in interpersonal, small group, and speaker-audience situations. The goal of the speaker in facilitating listening is to eliminate factors that might be distracting and to present the message in a manner that maintains attention. The speaker's body motions, appearance, and vocal expressions are extremely important nonverbal factors in facilitating the listening process. The telephone call presents a particularly unique communication transaction where several aspects of nonverbal communication are emphasized and others are absent.

Body Motion

Body motions that contribute to the effectiveness of speakers as they send messages include posture, movements, gestures, eye contact, and facial expressions. Skill in facilitating the listening task of intended receivers can be developed by paying attention to the nonverbal messages sent with the verbal messages.

POSTURE

Posture can be described along dimensions from relaxed to rigid and erect to stooped. A relaxed posture indicates informality; a rigid posture, formality. An erect posture indicates pride and confidence; a stooped posture, timidness or lack of concern. In communication situations interest and confidence are two states that have direct effect on the attentiveness of the listener. Interest in the listener can be indicated by a somewhat rigid and erect posture. Lack of interest is indicated by a totally relaxed or stooped posture. An especially good example of posture as it relates to interest occurs as an instructor ends a somewhat dull lecture and says, "Now, let me tell you what to study for the test." The relaxed and possibly slouched postures of the students suddenly change to indicate attention.

In speaker-audience and small group situations, an erect but relaxed posture is probably the appropriate stance. The erect posture provides a mood of preparedness and confidence that helps to establish credibility. The somewhat relaxed posture removes the look of tenseness and nervousness that speakers often feel. Hands rattling change, kept in the pocket, or held behind the back tend to keep the speaker from being free and spontaneous. If standing, speakers should have weight distributed about equally on both feet. It is recommended that they not lean on a lectern or table. In fact, it is

often better not to use a lectern since it can create a barrier between the speaker and listeners.

In interpersonal situations, the appropriate posture can be quite varied. If passive listening is appropriate, a totally relaxed posture might be most effective. If a very serious dialogue is occurring, a rigid and upright posture might communicate the appropriate concern. In all speaking situations, a change in posture from somewhat passive to more alert is a good way to indicate readiness to speak or change roles. It should be noted that postures are acquired, in many cases, by copying the postures perceived to be used effectively by others in communication situations.

MOVEMENTS

A speaker's movements can enhance and hinder the communication process. Movements are probably most effectively used as a nonverbal emphasis of verbal statements—that is, telling the listener that a particular part of a message is especially important. By moving the body closer to the listener, for example, the speaker can send the nonverbal message that the upcoming verbal statements are particularly significant. By moving away from the listener, emphasis can be drawn to a message that indicates a cautionary or doubtful reaction. Constant movement, however, may be so distracting that it will weaken or "throw away" the entire message.

A public speaker's movements in most cases should be free and uninhibited. The speaker should feel free to move around in front of the audience. The speaker can emphasize points by moving toward the audience or by taking a step and pausing. The statement or word that comes immediately after the movement is the point that receives the emphasis. When a speaker's stand is used, the speaker should not hide behind it but should feel free to move around it to the side or even to the front. It is acceptable too to move away from the speaker's stand to refer to a chart or diagram on an easel or blackboard. In less formal small group and interpersonal communication situations, seemingly routine movements will not be as noticeable as they are in a speaker-audience situation. In all situations, a speaker's movement should be used to enhance and not to interfere with the message.

GESTURES

Gesturing is a type of nonverbal expression that most speakers use quite naturally. Gesturing that is spontaneous and unplanned is generally the best. Forced gestures alert the receiver of a message to the speaker's uneasiness. Gestures are particularly important in pointing out relevant visual elements of the surroundings, and as a way of reinforcing parts of the spoken message. The listener often relies on gestures to add specifically to somewhat vague verbal messages. For example, gardeners might reinforce messages concerning huge tomatoes by pointing out one of particularly large size, by making emphatic gestures as they say the word "huge," or by using their hands to show the approximate size.

Beginning public speakers often complain that they do not know how to use their hands effectively in making gestures. They prefer to put them in their pockets or hide them behind their backs. If hands are left by the side, there is often a natural, free, and uninhibited gesturing that comes as the result of involvement in what the speaker is saying. If gesturing is difficult, the public speaker may consciously want to plan a gesture at a certain place in the speech. This can seem awkward to the speaker in the beginning, but as experience increases the gestures will seem more natural. It is helpful to speak as often as possible before an audience so that gestures can be practiced. This will lead to a more relaxed feeling and eventually gesturing will become entirely spontaneous in speaker-audience situations. In small group and interpersonal communication situations gestures are generally second nature. The speaker can, however, develop skill in the use of gestures as a means of reinforcing or further defining important concepts.

EYE CONTACT

Even more important than gesturing in facilitating the listening task is eye contact. Some speakers tend to look at the ceiling, floor, or anyplace but the eyes of their listener or listeners. Avoidance of the listener's eyes sends a message of extreme discomfort or lack of interest that does nothing but hinder communication. Ignoring the listener by failing to establish eye contact reduces the speaker's credibility and the chance to convince or inform the listener of anything.

Public speakers should maintain good eye contact as much of the time as possible by looking directly into the eyes of various members of the audience and not over their heads or at their feet. Staring at one particular person in the audience or one area of the audience should be avoided also. Often your audience includes a dominant person—for example, the instructor during a class presentation or your boss during a sales meeting. Focusing totally on this dominant listener makes this person feel discomfort. Any part of the audience that is constantly ignored will feel less and less involved with the message and find it more and more difficult to listen effectively. In small group communication, eye contact can be established with every group member at various points in a discussion. This is effective in helping each group member feel that the message is intended personally.

Looking Out/Looking In

he stripped the dark circles of mystery off
revealed his eyes
and thus he waited
exposed
>
> *and i did sing the song around*
> *until i found the chorus*
> *that speaks of windows*
>
> *looking out*
> *means looking in my friend*
> *and i'm all right now*
> *i'm fine*
> *i have seen the beauty that is mine*

you can watch the sky for signals
but look to the eyes for signs

—Ric Masten
Stark Naked published by Sunflower Ink,
Carmel, CA

In communication with one other person, constant eye contact becomes a stare and causes the listener to feel discomfort. In interpersonal situations, it is best to lose and reestablish eye contact in a way that seems natural for the situation. To be authentic in communication, eye contact with your listeners is essential to show that you care about them.

FACIAL EXPRESSIONS

Another important aspect of nonverbal communication and a definite way to help the listener is through facial expression. Facial expression should be consistent with the speaker's message. Without appropriate facial expression, the listener will doubt the sincerity of the speaker. When this occurs the ability to listen either critically or discriminately can be affected. A good example of the importance of facial expressions to the message occurs in films where a second language has been dubbed over the native language. The facial movements often seem inappropriate for the verbal message. Nonverbal expressions like frowns, smiles, grimaces, and appearances of excitement, happiness, or concern help the listener feel that the speaker is sincere. The feeling of sincerity generated by the speaker helps create interest in the message.

Speakers who are new to public speaking are sometimes nervous at first and find it difficult to present an expressive face. As speakers gain experience and appear before more groups, they become more relaxed and more expressive. As the speaker reveals involvement with the subject by facial expression as well as other nonverbal movements, the audience often senses the interest and becomes equally involved. It is generally unwise, however to laugh or "break out of character" in a formal speaking situation. In general, public speakers should concentrate on the message so intently that they remain in control of the situation even when the audience laughs or smiles. Certainly it is acceptable to smile and look happy but it is better not to lose composure completely by laughing on the platform because of something in the message. In less formal communication situations, facial expressions, like gestures, occur more naturally. A face that expresses involvement in the message can be a useful

Figure 6.1. Eye Contact

tool for creating a similar involvement in the listener.

Appearance

Impression management is a term that refers to choosing artifacts and manipulating physical characteristics so as to imply specific characteristics. The choice of artifacts, the manipulation of environment, and even the choice of a gift for someone, send a message about the individual. We all use impression management to some extent. In fact, there are many occasions when we manage our appearance to be at its best, not at its typical state. For a job interview, for meeting new people, for inviting guests to our home or office, we may maximize appearances to make an impression beyond what is typical. Impression management might be interpreted as phoney in a negative context and as taking pride or having self-respect in a positive context. Has anyone ever told you that "you clean up really well?" Grooming and demeanor have a definite impact on the communication exchange. Consideration for dressing for an employment interview can be an invaluable aid for life success.

GROOMING

Appearance can and often does contribute to the effectiveness or ineffectiveness of a speaker. In general, appearance becomes more and more important as the communication encounter moves from the intimate relationships of family and friends to that of the casual acquaintance, or the complete stranger. Speakers present a better appearance if they are groomed and dressed in a manner suitable to their listeners. Appearance should in no way detract from the message. An extremely short dress, a low-necked blouse, a sweatshirt with comments printed across the front, a ball cap that hides the eyes, or dirty tennis shoes can distract listeners.

Some people react negatively to certain types of dress and grooming. Every minute that a listener spends dwelling on the speaker's appearance is valuable time taken away from concentration on the message. Although many listeners will be quite tolerant of dress and grooming, it is important to give thought to the effect that appearance will have on a communication situation. What would you wear to court even for pleading "not guilty" to a routine traffic offense? Business dress and attention to grooming send the message that you respect the court. If there is some question about what will be appropriate dress, it is probably safer to dress conservatively. In general, attention to grooming and dress is definitely more important in formal speaking situations than in casual interpersonal encounters.

DEMEANOR

Demeanor refers to the manner in which individuals present themselves. Like grooming, a speaker's demeanor can have a definite effect on the first impressions of the listener. For example, public speakers who hesitate and shuffle up to the platform, appear overly nervous, self-conscious, bored, or indifferent, or spend too much time getting organized, tend to make the audience feel ill at ease. Public speakers who wish to attract the interest of their audiences should be ready to get out of their seats as soon as they are introduced and walk to the front of the group without greeting friends or shaking hands. Public speakers should appear confident but not smug, go directly to the platform, adjust notes, survey the audience to see if they are ready to listen, take a deep breath, and begin. When speeches are complete, speakers should state their conclusions. Without saying thank you (the audience should thank the speaker), speakers should pause to allow the audience a moment to collect their thoughts and reflect, and then they should return to their seats. Demeanor will affect listeners in less formal situations too.

A Place for Conservatives

I must admit it bothers me more
than just a little bit
to see an airline pilot with dandruff
sitting around
slightly wrinkled
chewing gum
looking like any one of us
    i mean
when you see the crew
go passing through the gate
don't you want the captain
    to be a tight-lipped man
    with close cropped hair
    eyes like steel doors slammed shut
    crisp white shirt
    slacks creased so sharply
    if you weren't careful
    you could get a nasty cut there
why i'd turn in my boarding pass
just like that
if some freaky long-haired cat
came bopping by
with an earring on one side
saying
    hey baby
    i'm gonna take us for a ride
believe me i'm finally convinced
there really is a place for conservatives
or would you go to a neurosurgeon
    who bit his fingernails—
    seen knocking his drink over all the time
    i mean
would you really want to do business
with either one of these guys
the morning after
he fought all night with his wife
    not on your life
    not me at least
    if i'm getting on that plane
    going under that knife
what we need here
are hard minded
cold blooded
machine-like people
in a culture as techno-
logically advanced as ours has become
    we cannot all afford to be human
—Ric Masten

Speaking Poems published by Sunflower Ink, Carmel, CA

Small groups and individuals will react to the manner in which speakers present themselves and will listen more or less effectively because of it. For example, a parent or spouse must often adopt an authoritarian demeanor to get household members to attend to a "clean up the house" message.

In general then, the speaker's appearance should be such that it does not distract listeners as they attempt to attend to the message. The speaker's demeanor should be confident so that the listener is at ease with the speaker's presence. The entire speaking process will be more effective if it is designed to enhance the receiver's ability to listen.

EMPLOYMENT INTERVIEWING

Reread the poem on the previous page, "A Place for Conservatives," as you consider the image you want to portray in going to an employment interview. The amount of information available for preparing for job interviews is overwhelming with dressing for success playing a large factor. Some sources give you a very stereotypical "uniform" to wear whereas others suggest that you carefully analyze the "setting and the audience." Would you want your interior designer to look like an investment banker or an officer of the court? You expect a design professional to wear a splash of color or to show sophistication through an achromatic color scheme of sophisticated neutral tones. Impression management is important in choosing dress for an important interview. When in doubt, be more conservative and always make sure that you will be comfortable, both physically and psychologically, in what you wear. With an interview, you may not have a chance to change that first impression. Get to know people who work in the business or profession and at the site where you are applying. The following paragraphs are included to list the stereotypical "uniform" for an employment interview. Take these suggestions as a starting point and modify your clothing choices to fit the type of environment and the business or profession where you will be interviewing.

Both men and women should consider their physical characteristics as a starting point. Consider those factors which can be changed—haircut and hair color, facial and body hair, appearance of nails, piercings, tattoos, body odor and cologne. Even posture in how you sit and stand makes a statement. Adjust these factors to fit the occasion. Generally, older people in the work force will be more formal in work dress whereas younger people will be more accepting of casualness. For example, when interviewing with a young person, you do not want to look like a parent.

Along with physical characteristics, men must consider suits, shirts, shoes, socks, ties, and belts. Hats are inappropriate in interior environments.

- Most interviews will require a suit. The level of conservatism in choice depends on the occupation. A conservative, dark suit will likely be your choice especially if the interview will be held in an indoor, business environment. If the job is outdoor-related, say in construction, and the interview will be at a work site, then a khaki suit might be a better choice as it will not show dust and dirt.

- The white, long-sleeved shirt is a safe bet to go with that conservative suit. However, consider the setting before wearing cufflinks or button-down collars. If you find yourself wearing the khaki suit mentioned above, the shirt can be more casual too. A nicely styled knit shirt might work.

- Your shoes need to be well-maintained in all settings and should never be athletic-type shoes even if they are totally clean. Choose a neutral color or black. Make sure your shoes are scuff-free and have good heels and soles.

- Your socks should coordinate with your shoes and never be white.

- Ties can vary depending on the setting. When in doubt, go with the plain, neutral pattern. The knot should be tight; length needs to be adjusted so that the tie ends at the top of your belt, and the tie should be wrinkle-free.

- The belt should be unobtrusive and coordinate with the colors chosen for your suit and shoes. No large, cowboy buckles allowed here.

Along with physical characteristics, women must consider suits, shoes, accessories, and make-up. While men's fashion stays more stable, women's fashion is constantly changing. Women must consider the importance of looking current in fashion yet not wearing tight and revealing clothing.

- Women should wear a skirted suit in dark, neutral tones to be safe. A neutral blouse or sweater can be worn if the suit coat is to be open. Hemlines need to be conservative for interviews. Women have more acceptance for livening their outfits than do men so consider the work environment when choosing.
- The shoes should be enclosed with low to medium heels. Consider open heeled or toed shoes depending on the season and norms. Never wear flipflop- type shoes even if dressy. Be prepared to walk a mile—you never know what kind of tour the interview will include.
- Accessories should enhance your appearance without distracting the interviewer. Large jewelry and any jewelry that makes noise is out.
- Make-up needs to be applied to match the level of light in the interview environment. You are not dressing for a dark, nightclub setting.

VOCAL EXPRESSION

The ways that speakers use their voices make a difference in whether or not one listener or an entire audience pays attention to what a speaker has to say. A listener does not pay attention to ideas, supporting materials, or language as much as to the sounds that are heard. These sounds are uttered with a particular volume, pitch, rate, articulation, pronunciation, and vocal quality which affect the listener's reaction to the message. Inadequate volume, monotonous pitch, rate that is too rapid, sloppy articulation, mispronounced words, a voice quality that is heavily marred by regionalisms, and other facets can cause the listener's ear to turn away from the message. For this reason a person who is trying to communicate should pay close attention to the vocal aspects of speech.

VOLUME

Volume refers to the loudness and softness of the communicator's voice. It is determined by the amount of air supporting the sound production. When there is a considerable amount of air to support a sound, it will be loud. When there is little air, the sound will be faint. When communicators speak so softly that they cannot be heard, they waste their own time as well as that of their listeners.

Often speakers, especially public speakers, will barely speak above a whisper. This may be caused by a poor self-esteem resulting from a feeling that the message has little value. If the intended listener does not hear what is being said, then no communication can take place. A flexible variation in volume is also important to the listening process. Without variation in volume, the speaker places the same emphasis on everything. This makes the message appear dull. Emphasis and contrast may be achieved by speaking softly or by stating an idea with increasing volume. The pattern of beginning a sentence with adequate volume and then fading at the end should be avoided, however.

PITCH

Pitch variation is also important. Pitch refers to the highness and lowness of the voice. As air passes over tensed vocal folds, they vibrate and sound is formed. The amount of tension present as the vocal folds vibrate determines the pitch of the speaker's voice. When tension is great, pitch will be high. Less tension creates a lower pitch. Common errors for speakers, especially public speakers, are a sameness of pitch that produces a monotonous voice, or a pitch that seems to strain the voice. A strained voice in a speaker-audience situation often results from a beginning speaker's nervousness before an audience and passes as confidence is gained. Feelings of insecurity often lead to improper pitch usage.

A speaker's optimum pitch level refers to those tones best suited to the individual's voice. Nothing, however, is more boring than a speaker who remains at the same pitch throughout a message. To create variety, a speaker should deviate both four or five pitches

$$\text{Vocal Expression} = \left(\begin{array}{c} \text{Volume} + \text{Pitch} + \text{Rate} + \text{Articulation} \\ + \text{Pronounciation} + \text{Vocal Quality} \end{array} \right) - \left(\begin{array}{c} \text{"Er"} + \text{"Uh"} \\ + \text{"You } Know \text{"} \end{array} \right)$$

OR

$$\text{Speaking Clearly} = \text{Rate} + \text{Inflection} + \text{Pitch} + \text{Tone}$$
SCRIPT

Figure 6.2. Vocal Expression

above and below the optimum pitch level. Creating variety is easier if the speaker has chosen a topic in which both personal and audience interest can be developed. If a speaker is eager to discuss the subject with the listeners it is likely that an energetic and animated voice will result.

RATE

Rate refers to the speed at which a message is delivered. A desirable rate of speaking is one that permits the listener to grasp what the speaker says. If the rate of speech is too slow, the listener's interest will wander; if too fast, much of the message will be lost. Rate of speech, within understandable ranges, can be used to alert the listener to certain behavioral states of the speaker. Rapid rate of speech indicates excitement or urgency; slow rate of speech, boredom.

Because of insecurity before an audience, beginning public speakers often tend to present their messages too rapidly. This causes them to be less interesting because they lack variety in speaking rate. Speakers who are sure that they know what they are talking about are better able to vary rate. By recording a speech on tape before the delivery date, the speaker can practice varying rate. If the speaker will listen objectively to the recording, corrections and improvements can be made. If it seems too fast to the speaker, who knows the subject, then it is sure to be too fast for the average listener. A speaker who tends to get nervous and talk too fast should make a conscious effort to slow down. Remember too that every second does not have to be filled with sound. Speakers in all

situations can pause to get their breath or collect their thoughts.

ARTICULATION AND PRONUNCIATION

Articulation is the process of forming individual sounds and joining them together. Pronunciation is the way that a whole word should be said. Articulation is primarily a matter of habit. Many people say "jist" instead of "just," or "git" instead of "get" because they are in the habit of articulating these words incorrectly. When speakers say "Illinois" with an "s" sound at the end, however, it is probably because they do not know the correct pronunciation.

When sounds are articulated correctly they do not need to sound overly precise or affected. Each sound is uttered to be distinct and easily recognizable, without adding sounds that should not be there (e.g., "warsh" instead of wash), without omitting sounds (e.g., "swimmin" instead of swimming), without substituting incorrect sounds (e.g., "git" instead of get), and without reversing the order of sounds (e.g., "hunderd" instead of hundred). When people learn to form sounds incorrectly, articulation problems like omissions, distortions, and slurring result.

Because mistakes in pronunciation are the result of lack of knowledge, many errors can be eliminated once the speaker learns the correct way to say the words. It is important to learn which letters or letter combinations are spoken or silent, how a word is correctly pronounced, when a syllable is accented, and which regional variations are acceptable. If a speaker knows the correct way to say a word but continues to err, then the problem is one of articulation, not pronunciation. When speakers include words unfamiliar to them in their messages, they are wise to consult a dictionary, a book called *A Pronouncing Dictionary of American English* (Kenyon and Knott, 1953), one of the many Internet dictionary sites, or a person known to be an expert in pronunciation.

VOCAL QUALITY

Finally, a speaker's vocal quality is significant to the way that listeners receive the message. Vocal quality is that special characteristic in a speaker's voice that makes it unique. The vocal quality can be defined as the resonance, or vibration, of the sounds formed in the vocal folds. The sounds pass through the resonating cavities—the throat, mouth and nose—and are altered and modified before being emitted. Size, shape, and texture of the resonating cavities determine the sound the listener hears. A voice with good quality is free from nasality, harshness, huskiness, hoarseness, breathiness, and shrillness. It is in general a voice that is pleasant and easy to listen to.

To listen to your own vocal quality, record it on tape or call your own answering machine and leave yourself a message. Your voice will probably not sound the way you think it should, but it will be you exactly as others hear you. The difference is caused by hearing yourself through bone rather than air as others do. Most people are so accustomed to their voices that they fail to hear them as others do. It is useful as a speaker to develop an awareness of how you sound and to change your voice if it is unpleasant. If you need help in improving the quality of your voice, you may want to consult an expert in the field such as a speech therapist. As you listen to yourself, count the fillers or trash words that you use. Often fillers are merely a bad habit, but they often make you sound unsure, nervous, or waffling.

Telephone Skills

The telephone, at work and at home, has become an integral part of our lives. The telephone is a wonderful invention making communication near and far available instantaneously. The telephone saves time and provides convenience in sending and receiving information. Yet the telephone can be a nuisance. The caller, in a sense, takes the prerogative and assumes that the receiver will be available for a conversation. As callers, we have all hesitated to place calls for fear of choosing an inopportune time. As receivers, we have had our sleep and meals and many tasks and conversations interrupted by callers. The cellphone is now adding another dimension for intrusion into our lives. The telephone should work positively for both caller and receiver. Instead, we tend to empower the telephone and let it dominate our lives.

By giving your telephone behaviors some thought, you can enhance your ability to communicate with this miracle of modern technology. Consider how you wish to be treated during telephone conversations, create a mental image of your listener, and imagine that person sitting with you in conversation. This makes you more aware of the total dynamics of the communication situation; and it helps in the realization that you are, in fact, talking to another human being and not to a piece of machinery. Even tele-marketing callers have feelings. A useful habit to develop in initiating a telephone conversation is to ask, "Is this a convenient time for you to talk?" That question allows the receiver of the call the opportunity to request another time for the conversation. On the other hand, if you receive a call at an inconvenient time, be assertive and let the caller know that another time would be more suitable.

In communicating by telephone, it is important, also, to consider your vocal quality. The receiver has only your words and voice quality to give meaning to the message. Pitch of the voice can convey such emotions as anger, fright, impatience, and anxiety whereas a normal pitch conveys understanding,

---

GOAL
Recognize the importance of vocal quality when talking on the telephone.

interest, confidence, and pleasantness. Inflection of the voice adds meaning, emphasis, and enthusiasm to otherwise monotonous, mechanical messages. Rate of speech is important for understanding. Speaking too slowly causes disconnected thoughts and loss of meaning; rapid speech can cause misunderstanding and poor pronunciation. The telephone is designed for the speaker's lips to be about half an inch from the mouthpiece and for using normal conversational voices. Use appropriate voice qualities but be yourself. After all, you might someday meet the person who created a mental image of you via a telephone encounter.

Whether representing yourself or your family or representing your place of employment, there are many acts of courtesy that we might all be well-advised to use during telephone communication. All of the suggestions seem so obvious when pointed out but represent responses that many of us use without thinking. Many of the suggestions are appropriate for business but do have some application to private phones as well.

1. Answer promptly, on the first ring if possible, and identify yourself with a pleasant greeting. Allow the receiver's phone to ring 10 times when you are calling.

    SAY: Dallas Company, Pam Walker, may I help you?
    DON'T SAY: Yes or Hello (without a name).

2. Treat every call as important by being courteous and practicing good listening skills. Do not try to carry on more than one conversation at a time.

    SAY: What can I do to help you today?
    DON'T SAY: What do you need? Just a minute. Now what was it? Oh, wait I have to talk to a customer.

3. Use the caller's name to add a touch of personal interest.

    SAY: Thank you for calling, Ms. Ross.
    DON'T SAY: OK, is that it?

4. Let the caller hang up first. Use a good ending for the call.

    SAY: Is there any other way that I might help?
    DON'T SAY: Bye (followed by a click of the receiver).

5. Handle transfer calls very carefully to avoid disconnections. Explain what you are doing.

    SAY: Will you hold the line, please? I'll transfer you to the Accounting Office.
    DON'T SAY: Just a minute (followed by the transfer).

6. When placing callers on hold, ask if that is acceptable and if so, provide a status report every 30 seconds or so. Place the headset facedown gently or use a "hold" button to minimize picking up office noise. Finally, express your appreciation of the caller's patience.

    SAY: Will you wait? Or would you prefer that I call you back?
    DON'T SAY: This will take awhile, hold on.

7. Be tactful when answering calls for others. Identify yourself and be prepared to take a message.

    SAY: Mr. Jones' office, this is Ms. Allen. Mr. Jones will be out of the office for about 30 minutes. Is there someone else who might help you?
    DON'T SAY: Jones' desk. He's still on his coffee break. Call back in about 30 minutes. You'll have a chance of catching him before lunch.

8. Take accurate messages and request, rather than demand, information.

    SAY: May I have your name and phone number, please.
    DON'T SAY: What's your name? Repeat that number.

9. As caller, plan your calls before placing them. As a courtesy, identify yourself and be certain that you have reached the proper party. Using your full name and stating your association with the party you are calling helps the receiver identify you more quickly.

SAY: Hello, this is Sue Brown. I am calling to inquire about a recent order.
DON'T SAY: Hello, the red dress I ordered is too small.

10. Be courteous when wrong numbers are called. As caller, apologize for the inconvenience rather then hanging up without a word. As receiver, explain that you are not the proper party.

SAY: I was trying to reach the repair shop at Northwest Auto Sales. I am sorry that I have reached the wrong number.
DON'T SAY: Who is this? What's your phone number (followed by a click).

The telephone is a daily, ongoing, never-ending facet of our society. Even the Amish, a sub-group of our society that spurns modern technology, use telephones outside their homes. A drive through the rural highways of Amish country in Ohio reveals the somewhat unexpected placement of telephone booths at the intersections of country roads often with patrons in Amish garb using them.

Modern technology has given us two more oral communication devices with which to contend—the answering machine (including voice mail) and the cellular phone (including beepers)—along with additional considerations for thoughtful use. Consider the following suggestions for receiving and sending messages via an answering machine:

1. The outgoing message should be short. We are all familiar enough with the answering machine that we do not need to be told to leave a message at the sound of a beep. We know that people will return our calls only if they feel like it. It is nice if the answering machine contains a message identifying its owner but privacy may prohibit this. Consider saying, "You have reached the home of George and Margot Olson, please leave a message, good-bye." If you do not want to mention names, you could say your phone number instead. You are letting the caller know whose home was reached, you have invited a message, and you have signified closure.

2. The caller should be succinct, also. It is nice to have a long time interval in which to leave a message. However, abuse by wordy people might lead the recipient to provide only the shortest interval. Get to the point and leave your name, a number, and a time where you can be reached. Telling the purpose of the message is helpful, also. If privacy issues are a consideration, keep in mind that the message might fall on the ears of someone other than you intended.

3. If your call is not returned, lack of interest on the part of the receiver is not necessarily the reason. Consider other hypotheses such as forgetting to check the machine, faulty equipment, wrong numbers, accidental erasure, and irresponsible family members. Try calling again if you think the person has had time to receive the message but has not returned your call. Unless you have reason for concern or different information, leaving a second message is not necessary.

4. If you will be unable to check your messages for an extended period of time, you will need to consider disconnecting the answering machine or finding someone to check your messages. It often works to have business phone numbers transferred to another number or to indicate in your message who the caller should contact or when you will return to work.

The cellular phone is a fabulous invention for convenience and getting information shared immediately but has so much more potential for interrupting the receiver than does the stationary phone. It also has the capacity for annoying other people who must hear the ring or the background noise of the conversation. Now that smoking has been eliminated from many restaurants and we often avoid the question of smoking or non-smoking, when will we be asked if we wish to sit in the cellular or noncellular section? Will theaters have to be insulated in ways that sound waves from cellular frequencies do not penetrate? Will teachers have to include a section in their syllabuses that prohibits the ringing or use of cellular phones during class? The statistics already show that use of cellular phones while operating a vehicle increases the probability of automobile accidents. People who use cellular phones must consider the impact of their phone behaviors on the others around them. Turn off your cellular phone when the interruption of a call will be annoying to yourself or others; use a vibrator instead of a ringer if you must leave the device on in settings involving others; and leave meetings, dining rooms, theaters, classrooms, or other locations if you must answer where phone conversations do not have a place. Thoughtful use and consideration will provide the convenience while not creating a nuisance. Privacy issues are a further concern since sound frequencies used for the cellular phones can be intercepted.

Another type of message transmission that is taking the place of the usual phone interaction or message is electronic mail. Many people are finding e-mail more efficient than telephones for transmitting information that is factual and does not need clarification or discussion. A tradition, etiquette, and technical language are emerging to facilitate the use of e-mail. Once sent, e-mails do not disappear by striking the delete button so be aware of potential consequences of messages you decide to send. E-mails you send to one person can be easily forwarded to others without your consent. E-mail is best used to send factual, not emotional, information. The tone of written words can often be misleading when describing feelings. Use e-mail to say "the meeting is at 4:00" not to debate the value of the meeting. An obvious difference between e-mail and telephone is the lack of paralanguage as a part of the meaning of the e-mail message. E-mail is becoming an integral part of social and career lives which requires considerable maintenance so choices are often made about what to read and what to immediately delete. Be as brief and to the point as possible.

The telephone message is based upon voice quality and choice of words only; the setting and other important nonverbal clues are miss-ing. Therefore, the telephone must be used carefully in ways that communication exchanges are appropriate. Exchange of information is facilitated by phone conversations whereas emotionally sensitive conversations are better handled in direct interpersonal exchanges where visual access to nonverbal behaviors is available. Always smile when talking by phone, if your goal is to be perceived as pleasant, since the smiling face is reflected in your vocal quality.

Summary

The listening process is especially difficult in critical and discriminative listening situations when attention must be maintained and important points must be retained. The listener, of course, must take responsibility for attending to messages and can do much to improve attending and retention skills. In addition, the speaker who particularly wishes a message to have a significant effect can facilitate the listening process by paying particular attention to body motions, vocal expression, and appearance.

Such body motions as posture, movements, gestures, eye contact, and facial expressions can be used to draw emphasis to particular points of a message. The aspects of vocal expression that require special attention by the speaker are volume, pitch, rate, articulation, pronunciation, and vocal quality. Lack of vocal energy, lack of emphasis and variety, monotony in pitch, and a rate that drags can be dull and cause the listener's mind to wander. A speaker's appearance can be distracting to the listener if inappropriate for the situation. Aspects of vocal quality and energy affect the outcomes of telephone conversations.

When an attempt is made to emphasize a point, accomplished speakers will often change their volume; slow their rates of speaking; pause before and after a point; change body posture; step toward the audience; or maintain eye contact for a longer, steadier length of time. Combinations of several of these nonverbal aspects of communication can be used effectively to place emphasis on a special point. The listener who is aware of such techniques is then cued to pay attention to particularly important points.

Activity 1

Information about Listening and Nonverbal Messages

Preparation: Read Part 2: Listening and Nonverbal Messages. Prepare for a test by answering the practice items given below.

Practice Items

PART 2: OVERVIEW

1. Why has a focus on listening and nonverbal messages emerged during the last three decades?

CHAPTER 4

1. What is the difference between listening and not listening?
2. What is the difference between passive listening and not listening?
3. What are the definitions of five kinds of active listening: social, serious, critical, discriminative, and empathic?
4. What are two personal characteristics that affect listening?
5. What negative habits affect a person's ability to listen?
6. What are several ways to improve listening that occurs in interpersonal relationships at the social level?
7. What are several suggestions to follow in preparing for a serious listening experience?
8. What are questions to ask intrapersonally when listening critically or evaluating a message?
9. What are four suggestions for taking notes in discriminative listening experiences?
10. What is meant by "noise" as it relates to the following:
    a. environmental distractions,
    b. physiological impairments,
    c. semantic problems,
    d. psychological and social problems, and
    e. chains of command?
    f. gossip
11. What are specific ways a listener can avoid distractions?

CHAPTER 5

1. What are the general and technical labels (if known) for the eight areas of non-verbal communication?
2. How does body motion contribute to the communication process?
3. What are the eight distances described by Hall in regard to a communicator's personal space?
4. How do early touching experiences affect adult interpersonal communication situations?
5. What is paralanguage?
6. How do physical characteristics provide nonverbal messages in a communication situation?
7. What are examples of artifacts that send positive and negative messages during the communication process?

8. What environmental factors send nonverbal messages about a communicator?
9. In situations where verbal and nonverbal messages conflict, why is the nonverbal message generally more truthful?
10. How can you improve your own nonverbal messages?
11. What are some nonverbal indicators of the following reactions:
    a. openness,
    b. cooperation,
    c. frustration,
    d. confidence,
    e. nervousness, and
    f. courtship?
12. What seven time factors sometimes cause people to fail to begin or complete their really important goals?
13. What are the definitions of A, B, and C items as discussed in time management?
14. Why is Quadrant II the most important for time management?

CHAPTER 6

1. How do the following nonverbal characteristics contribute to the effectiveness of speakers as they send messages:
   a. posture,
   b. movement,
   c. gestures,
   d. eye contact, and
   e. facial expressions?
2. How do volume, pitch, rate, articulation, pronunciation, and vocal quality affect the listener's reaction to a message?
3. What is impression management?
4. How do the speaker's appearance and demeanor affect the listener's reaction to a message?
5. Which vocal qualities are appropriate for telephone conversations and what impression do these qualities make?
6. What are three suggestions for appropriate business telephoning with specific examples of what to say and not say?
7. How do cellular phones facilitate and hinder communication?

Group Activity: Follow course instructions to complete the test for part 2.

Individual Activity: Make arrangements with your instructor to complete the test for part 2.

Activity 2

Listening Myths

Preparation: Contrast the assumptions and facts given below.

The following are assumptions about the listening process.

1. You need to be intelligent to be an excellent listener.
2. You listen well automatically.
3. You will hear exactly what other people say to you.
4. Neither the personality of speaker nor listener affects the listening process.
5. You listen automatically so it is not necessary to study to acquire listening skills.
6. Only the words, not the vocal characteristics, matter in listening.

The facts below have been verified from research on listening.

1. A person of average intelligence can be a good listener.
2. Because they lack training, most people often listen poorly.
3. What is heard is affected by many variables including values, prejudices, and past experiences.
4. Listening is affected by the personalities of the communicators and ways they present themselves visually and orally.
5. Listening is a learned response that can be practiced until adequate skill is acquired.
6. Vocal characteristics of the speaker contribute to the meaning of the message.

Group Activity: The instructor will read an excerpt from literature to the group. Make a conscious effort to be a good listener. As you listen, record single words or phrases that have meaning to you. Become aware of how well you listen. At completion of the excerpt, answer the questions below. Then discuss your reaction to the assumptions and facts listed above.

1. What type of response does the excerpt from literature elicit from you?

2. Are some of the words or phrases related to something in your life?

3. Do you need to overcome certain habits that interfere with your ability to listen?

Individual Activity: Select an excerpt from literature and ask a friend to spend at least 10 minutes reading it to you. Follow the Group Activity instructions and write a one-page report of your reaction.

Activity 3

Listening Problems Checklist

Preparation: It is difficult to become a skilled active listener. Most people do not receive training in the art of listening. Thus, they spend a great deal of time experiencing listening difficulties but not realizing why. Attend a lecture, listen to a sermon, or listen to a news editorial lasting at least 10 minutes. Make a determined effort to be an active listener. Use the checklist below to identify factors which affected your listening behavior. For those problems you identity, make notes about ways that you might improve.

Listening Problems Checklist

_____ 1. Perceiving a topic as boring.

_____ 2. Criticizing a speaker's delivery instead of the message.

_____ 3. Becoming emotionally involved in the message.

_____ 4. Attending only to facts.

_____ 5. Attempting to answer questions before they are fully asked.

_____ 6. Trying to outline everything in the message.

_____ 7. Failing to adjust to distractions.

_____ 8. Faking attention.

_____ 9. Attending only to what is easy to understand.

_____ 10. Allowing emotionally laden words to distort the message.

_____ 11. Permitting personal prejudices to impair understanding.

_____ 12. Attending only to messages relating to personal interests.

_____ 13. Avoiding clarification by paraphrasing or questioning.

_____ 14. Sending nonverbal feedback that reveals lack of interest.

_____ 15. Interrupting whenever you think of a reaction.

Group Activity: Discuss with your classmates ways that you might improve your listening skill. Refer to specific problems in the checklist or to other problems you identify. Although you may not have the opportunity to repeat the same listening experience again, analysis of the past situation can be helpful for future situations.

Individual Activity: Write a one-page report summarizing the content of your listening experience and list ways that you might improve your listening skill. Refer to specific problems in the checklist or to other problems you identify. Although you may not have the opportunity to repeat the same listening experience again, analysis of the past situation can be helpful for future situations.

Activity 4

Communication Chains

Preparation: The following activity is often used to demonstrate the follies of gossip as well as the distortion of communication caused by different perceptions of verbal descriptions of an event. It is a useful demonstration of the listening process, also. As you participate or observe, remember that perceptions are based on the accumulation of background variables and experiences of the individuals involved. We attempt to make what we perceive fit into what we already know. Thus, each individual gives different emphasis to different stimuli.

Group Activity: Six volunteers are needed. The volunteers are asked to leave the room. They are permitted to determine the order in which they each enter the room as they are admitted one-by-one.

As each volunteer enters the room, the instructor will explain that each is to listen to a short summary of an event and then recount that summary to the next volunteer. When the first volunteer enters, the instructor will read the summary statement to the volunteer. The summary statement should contain about three sentences and total 60–70 words in length. It should be a statement that is full of factual information. The process is continued until all six volunteers have entered the room and the last volunteer has repeated the description. It is useful to have someone write down the last statement for reference. Students who are not volunteering should make notes of changes which occur as each volunteer repeats the message.

The following questions should be discussed (after the laughter dies away):

1. What is the effect of omitting information? What were some particularly glaring omissions?

2. What is the effect of adding information? What were some particularly noticeable additions?

3. What is the effect of distorting information? What were some of the most significant distortions which occurred?

4. Did language have an effect on the changes which occurred in the message? What regional accents, pronunciations, or lack thereof were evident?

5. When you hear something that appears to be gossip, how should you react? What can be done to maintain accuracy in messages like the one in this example?

6. Do members of the media add, delete, distort, or manipulate language to affect the listener's perception?

Individual Activity: Complete the instructions above for the group activity but use six of your friends, family members, or work associates. Write out the original message and the variations that occur from each participant. Write out your answers to the five questions listed above.

Activity 5

Violation of Expectations

Preparation: Nonverbal messages form a language of their own. We learn how to send and receive nonverbal messages. To show that nonverbal messages communicate, it is interesting to analyze a nonverbal behavior and change it in such a way that the receiver's expectations are violated.

Consider a scene in a quiet cafeteria at about 4:00 pm when very few people have arrived for dinner. You enter and obtain your food and sit side-by-side next to the only person dining in the room. The expectation is that you will create your own personal space and select a table quite distant from a sole occupant. The violation of expectations results when you invade the personal space of the only other occupant in the dining room. What type of reaction would you expect?

All of the areas of nonverbal communication can provide scenarios for violations of expectations. Think of a way that you can show how the powerful language of nonverbal signals communicates.

1. FIRST, think about the possible consequences of this activity. Do not create embarrassment or anger!
2. Review the areas of nonverbal communication: paralanguage, body movement, personal space, touching, artifacts, environment, physical characteristics, and time.
3. Plan a nonverbal behavior that will seem to one or more people to be unexpected. Again, do not create anger or embarrassment.
4. Write an approximately one-page, typed report which includes the following:
   A. Nonverbal Area with Definition
   B. Your Planned Behavior
   C. Expected Reaction of Others
   D. Actual Reaction of Others
   E. Relation of this Experience with Interpersonal Communication
5. Use what you have read and learned in class about nonverbal behavior. Remember that your professor is easily impressed by complete sentences and legible text. The way you present yourself, in writing as well as personally, communicates.

Group Activity: Bring your written report to class.

In small groups, or time permitting with the class as a whole, describe the behavior that you displayed and the expected and actual reactions of others. Consider these questions.

1. Which scenario reported by your classmates was extremely appropriate for demonstrating the expectations we have concerning nonverbal messages?
2. How powerful and how accurate is the language of nonverbal signals?
3. What are some common examples of discrepancy between related verbal and nonverbal messages?
4. How much attention do you pay to the nonverbal messages you send in intimate surroundings and in public surroundings?

Individual Activity: Along with your written report, write answers to questions #2, #3, and #4 above. Include, also, how you would revise your scenario to make it even better as a demonstration of nonverbal expectations.

Activity 6

Paralanguage

Preparation: A speaker's voice is basic to the art of public speaking and communication in general. Foremost, the speaker's voice should be audible and the listener should have no trouble hearing and understanding it. The voice should be flexible so that variation in pitch, inflection, and rate can be used to communicate a variety of ideas, meanings and emotions. Unless serious vocal problems exist, practice and experimentation with different ways of expressing thoughts will improve speaking ability.

To prepare for this activity, select a children's story, a personal adventure, or a folk tale passed down through your family that demonstrates one or more communication skills. Your selection should have an interesting beginning, a logical sequence of events, a spirited conflict, a definite climax, and a satisfying conclusion. The story should increase your listener's understanding of life, portray certain universal emotions or values, and show respect for character.

Practice telling the story by rehearsing your presentation. Keep the language simple. Make the story come alive. Try to keep your voice flexible as you express each character's thoughts. Vary the rate. Variety is essential if your goal is to communicate feeling and thought. As the action progresses, the tempo should increase and build toward an exciting climax. Use the pause to gain suspense or to allow a thought to sink in before continuing to the next event.

The listener's role is to create actively a vivid, multi-sensory image of characters and events based on your verbal and nonverbal performance. Since storytelling is a creative process shared by the sender and receiver, the audience will draw on their past experiences, beliefs, and understandings as the action of the story happens in their minds. The listener will respond to your voice, words, and actions. As the teller of the story, you must use the nonverbal feedback of the audience to spontaneously improvise the tones, wording, and pace of the story to meet the needs of the audience. The telling of a story is a live person-to-person oral and physical presentation of your material in such a way that the audience will give you attention and retain the essence of your message.

Overlearn your story. Think it through whenever you have a moment so that you will have no difficulty remembering the sequence of events when you stand before your audience. Bring a copy of your selection and your props to class.

Option 1—Retelling a Children's Story

Several classics appropriate for this activity are *The Ugly Duckling, The Little Engine that Could,* and *The Little Red Hen.* Also, given below are several currently popular selections that are particularly good for completing this activity.

Velveteen Rabbit	Margery Williams
The New Baby	Esther Wilkin
Pecos Bill	Stephen Kellogg
I Was So Mad	Mercer Mayer
Horton Hatches the Egg	Dr. Suess
Learn about Strangers	Jan and Stan Berenstain
What's Fair Is Fair	Jim Henson
The Giving Tree	Shel Silverstein
Susan in the Driver Seat	Kathy Giveault
The Foot Book	Dr. Suess

Go to the Doctor	Jan and Stan Berenstain
Half Child and Half Child	Lizi Boyd
The Secret Garden	F. H. Burnett

Read the story silently for enjoyment. Then reread the story slowly once or twice to visualize each scene. Try to visualize each event and character in the story until you feel you have lived the experience. Close the book and think silently through the story. Then read the story aloud using as much vocal variety and energy as possible.

Now prepare the story to be told or acted out, not read. Try to find props that will help an audience visualize the story. Use the outline below to help in preparation.

1. List the sequence of events.

2. Who are the characters?

3. What is the problem?

4. What is the complication?

5. What is the solution?

Option 2—Relating a Personal Adventure or a Family Folk Tale

We tell stories every day without even realizing it. Stories are a vehicle for interpreting experiences, events, and concepts as we live our daily lives. More than any other form of communication, the telling of our life stories is an integral and essential part of the human experience chronicling minor moments in our daily lives and including the grander nature of the human condition.

Dictionaries define a story as a narrative account of a real or imagined event or events. A story is generally agreed to be a specific structure of narrative with a style and set of characters. Through the sharing of our experiences, we use stories to pass on to one another wishes, beliefs, and values. Stories link us to our humanness and connect us to the past, present, and future.

As you think about a story that you would like to tell to your audience, consider the following ideas as a source of inspiration. Tell a story about one of the following:

1. Pet you once had which you do not have now

2. Getting into trouble for something you were told not to do

3. Trip that you would like to take again

4. Night your parents never found out about

5. Place where you go to take walks or have picnics

6. Oldest person you remember knowing as a child

7. Getting sick at a very inconvenient moment

8. Getting lied to or tricked by someone

9. Girlfriend or boyfriend you once thought about marrying

10. Forgetting about an important appointment or date

11. Teacher to whom you owe a lot

12. Your favorite year in school

13. A special family meal

14. A first impression that turned out to be totally wrong

15. Childhood hiding or special thinking space

16. Your choice

Or, you might recount a story that has been passed down through the generations of your family heritage.

Group Activity: When you get to class, form groups of four to six students. Choose one story from the individual selections to tell or act out as a group. Each member of the group should present a segment of the selected story, serving as narrator or taking a specific character, for a performance in front of the class.

At the end of the performance, ask the audience to guess the communication message. Have one member of the group elaborate on the communication skill or skills that were demonstrated. Be very specific as you describe examples; use dialogue from the story to make your point.

After all groups have completed their stories, the class members should discuss paralanguage used to enhance the telling and acting out of the stories.

1. Identify several effective variations in paralanguage that enhanced each performance.

2. What are the positive and negative effects of vocal variety and paralanguage when used in the story-telling experience?

3. Can you conclude that variety in pitch, rate, and rhythm in a voice makes the speaker more interesting to the listener?

4. Were fillers like "uh," and "stuff" distracting?

5. Give examples of famous storytellers who use effective paralanguage techniques.

Individual Activity: Listen to a tape of at least one famous storyteller and analyze effects of paralanguage techniques on holding your interest and creating images for you.

Locate a group to whom you can present the story that you have individually rehearsed. As you present the story, observe reactions of listeners and your own skill in making the presentation. Notice your vocal variety and paralanguage techniques. What are the positive effects of vocal variety such as pitch variation, rate, and rhythm in your voice? At the end of your performance, ask your audience to guess the communication skills used in your story. Then elaborate on the message as you perceive the author intended.

Prepare a one-page report describing your experience as a storyteller. Include the following points: the title of the story you listened to and the name of the famous storyteller, what you liked or disliked about the storyteller's voice, the title of the story you selected or prepared for presentation, your interpretation of the significance of the story for relating communication skills, the audience reaction, and your impression of the experience as a way to practice varying your voice and to demonstrate paralanguage techniques. Were you a good storyteller and how could you improve in the future? What improvements in your own paralanguage techniques would you like to make?

Activity 7

Artifacts and Environment

Preparation: Specific artifacts, objects worn by you and generally chosen by you, communicate a particular message. They represent who you are and send nonverbal messages to those around you. In a similar way, your environment says something very specific about who you are and what you value. The environments you choose generally represent your personality. As you actually choose your surroundings you communicate certain generalizations about your personality.

Following is a list of artifacts and specific environmental factors that may or may not be associated with your experiences. Comment on each of these and relate them to your lifestyle.

A. Artifacts

1. What kind of clothing do you prefer? Casual or formal? Describe.

2. Do you wear jewelry? Do you wear costume jewelry or real jewels?

3. Do you use artificial means to change your appearance (e.g., make-up, tans, dyes)?

4. What is your favorite kind of cologne or perfume? How expensive is it? What does this selection suggest?

5. If money were no object would you have your hair professionally styled or do it yourself?

B. Environmental Factors

1. What kind of car do you drive? Would this be your choice if you could have any car? If not, what would you buy?

2. Describe your house architecturally.

3. If you were designing your own house, what would it be like? What does this tell us about you?

4. What style furniture would you purchase for your house?

5. Would you prefer to buy paintings or cover the walls in paper?

6. If you purchased art, what would be your favorite kind?

7. Where do you travel when you have vacation time? If you could go any place, where would you go?

8. What kind of restaurants do you choose now? Would you go to a different kind of restaurant if you had more money? Name a few of your choices.

Group Activity: In groups of approximately five discuss your responses to artifacts and environmental factors. Discuss the nonverbal signals that you as a person send as a result of choices. Is this the message you wish to communicate to people you meet? If not, how would you like to change that message?

While still with your group, choose a spokesperson to present a short description of a selected group member's choices of artifacts and environment. Then meet with the entire class. Present the descriptions of the selected group member's choices of artifacts and environment. The class should try to guess the persons who were described.

Individual Activity: Find a friend or family member with whom to discuss your responses to the artifact and environmental factors. Discuss the nonverbal signals that you as a person send as a result of these choices. Write a one-page report describing your reaction to the messages you and your partner feel you communicate through your choices of artifacts and environment. Discuss your satisfaction with your image and any changes you might make.

Activity 8

Time Management

Preparation: View the film "How to Get Control of Your Time and Your Life." Integrate your knowledge of chronemics (see chapter 5) as you answer the following questions.

1. What is time?

2. Give examples of ways that we tell time.

3. How many hours do we have to live per week?

4. What is the first step in organizing your time?

5. Describe an A in your life at the time.

6. What is the second step for organizing your time?

7. Identify and describe a C in your life right now.

8. What is idea number five?

9. What is idea number six, a very crucial Laekin rule?

10. Describe the Swiss cheese technique.

11. Using Covey's four quadrants, list an example from your life that fits each quadrant.

12. List five examples from your life that should be moved from Covey's quadrant I to quadrant II.

13. How does psychological time (orientation to past, present, and future) affect your reaction to time?

14. How does cultural time (punctuality and scheduling) affect your reaction to time?

Group Activity: Discuss the film and your answers to the questions.

Individual Activity: Go to the Learning Resource Center and view the film "The Time of Your Life." Turn in your answers to the above questions and your notes on the film to your instructor.

Activity 9

Sending and
Interpreting Nonverbal Messages

Preparation: Write the name of a book, song, play, or movie on a 3 × 5 card. In selecting a title be sure that it contains no more than four words (e.g., "Little Brown Jug," *To Kill a Mockingbird, Death of a Salesman*).

Group Activity: The class will divide into two equal groups. Each group will choose a leader and give their titles to the leader. The leader will place these where players on the opposite team can draw one when it is their turn. The leader of Team A will draw the first card from those submitted by Team B and silently read it, keeping it a secret from team members but showing it to the opposing side so that they will know which of their titles is being enacted. The leader will pantomime in complete silence, using only bodily action to convey the title.

From the performance, the teammates will try to guess the title. They may ask questions but the contestant will reply only nonverbally by movement and gesture. The instructor will record the exact time in seconds that it takes for the team to guess the title. Three minutes is the maximum time allowed a single title. If the team doesn't guess in three minutes, they receive a score of 180 seconds and the opposing team gets a turn.

In this way, continue alternating teams until every member of each team has enacted a charade. At the end the instructor will tally the time sheet and announce the winning team.

Remember, as you play the game your purpose is to communicate the title to your team only through the use of nonverbal expression. Since you cannot use your voice, your actions must tell the whole story. Broad gestures and facial expression will help. Make all movements clear and definite.

Loosen up your body and become communicative. Relax, and put your whole self in the experience to have fun! As you play the game, consider the following questions.

1. Did you gain any insight into meanings associated with certain gestures and movements?

2. Did you have difficulty expressing a message nonverbally?

3. Did you want to send verbal messages as you enacted a title?

Individual Activity: Find at least three friends with whom to play the game of charades. Specify rules before playing, the only restriction being the necessity of the person enacting a title to be totally nonverbal. Play the game until each person has had at least two turns. Then write a one-page report describing your experience as sender and receiver of nonverbal messages. Include answers to the three questions included in the group activity.

Activity 10

Nonverbal Feedback

Preparation: Write brief answers to each of the following topics as you analyze your own nonverbal communication style.

1. Eye Contact:

2. Facial Expression:

3. Gestures:

4. Haptics (Touching):

5. Proxemics (Personal Space):

6. Chronemics (Time):

7. Appearance:

8. Individualism:

9. Authority:

10. Formality:

Next, give thought to how you would answer the items below which will form the basis for the following communication exchanges.

1. Hobbies you enjoy.

2. Foods and beverages you like.

3. Restaurants you like best.

4. Where you have traveled or would like to travel.

5. What you like or dislike about your daily routine.

6. How much education you want to complete.

7. Goals you have set for yourself for the next five years.

8. What you and your family take pride in.

9. Unfulfilled wishes and dreams that you have.

10. The aspect of your personality that most pleases you.

Be prepared to comment on these topics in activities where you can practice nonverbal communication skills in receiving both verbal and nonverbal messages.

Group Activity: The total group should divide into two subgroups of equal numbers. One subgroup should form an outer circle and the other, an inner circle. The members of the two subgroups should face each other. Using one of the topics given above, everyone in the outer circle will talk at the same time. The members of the inner circle will listen and respond nonverbally to what is said by the person opposite them in the outer circle. Members of the inner circle must establish eye contact with the person opposite them.

After a topic has been discussed for 1.5 minutes, the outer circle will rotate. The members of the outer circle will again speak for 1.5 minutes on another of the topics. The rotation should continue four or five times with the outer circle speaking and the inner circle listening and responding nonverbally. Then, the members of the inner circle should become the speakers and those in the outer circle, the listeners as the activity is repeated for another four or five rotations. Finally, the activity will be repeated again as the inner and outer circle pairs exchange views on a given topic.

After the three roles—speaker, listener, and speaker and listener—have been completed, the group will discuss each role.

1. Is it easier to listen or to talk?

2. Is it easier to participate in a communication exchange where you can both speak and listen?

3. Is the listener free of responsibility in the communication situation?

4. Was your role as listener similar to your usual role in everyday situations?

5. How did it feel to speak when you were receiving the full attention of the listener?

6. What nonverbal responses from the listener seemed best when you were the speaker?

7. Do most of your listeners in everyday situations give you similar attention?

8. What was the effect of interruptions in each of the three scenarios?

9. As speaker, how do you feel when you are interrupted?

10. As listener, how do you control your desire to interrupt?

11. Does the subject matter, especially the level of controversy, affect interruptions?

12. Can nonverbal messages "interrupt" a message?

13. How do cultural backgrounds affect the roles of listening and speaking?

Individual Activity: Locate at least four friends or family members who will cooperate with you in this activity. Meet with each of your partners individually. Allow them to select a topic of interest from those in the preparation section of this activity. Ask them to talk for several minutes on the topic as you attentively listen and respond nonverbally. Then switch roles as you speak on a selected topic and they follow your model as listener. Then engage in an exchange on a topic of mutual choice where you both interact as speakers and listeners. Finally, describe each of your twelve communication situations—speaker, listener, and speaker and listener with each of your partners—with a sentence or two. Then write a brief response (one paragraph) in answer to each of the 13 discussion questions that follow the group activity.

Activity 11

Speaking Activity— Demonstration Speech

Preparation: You will someday have the opportunity to demonstrate your special areas of expertise to others. In a demonstration bodily actions are used deliberately because the subject matter insists on it. It would be impossible to demonstrate karate without showing the different stances, hand and arm movements, and head positions. Much can be said but even more can be shown.

Since the purpose of presenting a demonstration is to use gesture and bodily motion to enhance communication, it is important to choose a subject about which you will feel confident talking and showing. Almost any topic will be suitable if you become skilled at explaining and demonstrating. For purposes of this activity you MUST select a topic that uses significant body movements or definite artifacts. Select a topic that you can SHOW as well as describe. Demonstrating psychological processes or non-manipulatable objects is NOT suitable. Some possibilities follow.

Topics for Demonstration Presentations

Archery	Feather flowers	Papier mache
Ballet	Fencing	Pool
Basketball	First aid	Polishing silver
Baton twirling	Fishing	Puppets
Book binding	Flower arranging	Scarf tying
Bottle art	Golf	Shaving
Bowling	Guitar playing	Shoe shining
Breathing exercises	Jogging	Scuba diving
Brushing teeth	Judo	Soap art
Changing a tire	Karate	Tennis
Chocolate cookies	Knitting	Tissue paper art
Christmas decorations	Magic	Tying a tie
Contact lenses	Modeling	Weaving
Cross stitch	Package wrapping	Wine tasting
Decoupage	Paper airplanes	Your choice

After you have chosen a topic it is best to stay with it even if you feel the subject is more difficult than you thought. We often think we know more about a subject than we really do. Often additional information on a topic is available at the library.

In preparing, first list the phases of the process in a step-by-step fashion that you can present in about four minutes. Remember that your audience may know little about the subject. Do not make assumptions about what you think they know. Explain and show every aspect of the process you are demonstrating. You may want to rehearse both the verbal and nonverbal messages in front of a mirror. Body actions should be spontaneous and never memorized. They should be motivated by a desire to help the listeners understand you. Practice the body actions until they become a natural part of your presentation. Be certain to introduce briefly the topic to be demonstrated and to summarize the process as you end your presentation. An example is given below.

Inexpensive Book Binding

Topic Outline	*Script*
I. Introduction	
A. Gain attention of audience	Look at these disorganized, ruined, torn documents. Some of this artwork is precious. Some of this writing is good. It should be preserved and kept.
B. Relate to audience	How many of you have ever wanted to have some of your creative writing or art professionally bound? There is a way you can bind your own books quickly and easily. Those of you who have young children at home or plan to teach in elementary school may decide to bind some of your children's works.
C. Statement of main purpose	The purpose of my speech is to teach you how to bind books inexpensively.
D. Preview first main idea	First, I will tell you what materials you will need.
E. Preview second main idea	Then I will demonstrate the steps to be followed in making a binding.
F. Preview third main idea	And finally, I will show you some examples of finished products.
II. Body	
A. First main idea	The materials required to make a book binding can be easily found around the house and are, therefore, inexpensive.
1. Support (visual aid)	I am certain that most of you will have masking tape, scissors. a ruler, and a stapler.
2. Support (visual aid)	In addition, you will need some type of heavy poster board or thin cardboard to use as a cover. The backs of writing tablets work very well.
3. Support (visual aid)	The only item you might have to purchase is some contact paper. There are many attractive colors and prints from which to choose.
4. Support (visual aid)	And, of course, you have to have the pages of the book you wish to bind.
B. Second main idea	Now I will demonstrate how to use these materials to bind a book.
1. Support (demonstrate)	First, take the pages of the book, place a blank sheet on the top and bottom and staple them together along the left side.

2. Support (demonstrate)   To construct the front and back cover, measure and cut out sections of poster board or cardboard so that they are about one-eighth inch larger than the pages of the book. Connect the two covers together with a strip of masking tape. Then cut out a piece of contact paper that is two-to-three inches longer and wider than the entire cover, both front and back. Peel the backing off the contact paper and place the entire cover in the center. Fold the edges and corners neatly over.

3. Support (demonstrate)   Now the covers are ready to be attached to the pages of the book. Tape the pages into place inside the covers. Then measure and cut a piece of contact paper to fit the inside of the front cover and extend over the blank cover sheet. Peel off the backing and attach the contact paper. Repeat this procedure with the back cover.

C. Third main idea   Now, I will show you some examples of the finished product.

   1. Support (visual aid)   This book is a story my son dictated to me about a birthday party he attended. He also did the illustrations.

   2. Support (visual aid)   This is an example of a predictable or patterned story I bound for a reading class where I was a teacher.

III. Conclusion

A. Summary of main ideas   I have listed the materials needed to bind books easily and inexpensively. I have shown you the steps involved in binding a book and I have provided several examples of finished products.

B. Closing remarks   In conclusion, I would like to stress how easy it is to bind a book. So go home, try it yourself, and create your own personal library.

Group Activity: After you have drawn for speaker places relax and enjoy the other presentations. When it is your time to speak approach the front of the room with confidence, and allow your gestures to occur naturally. Your objective in this presentation is to help your audience listen effectively.

As you present your ideas, try to make them clearer by showing the audience as well as telling them. If you use drawings, models, or objects, make certain that everyone can see them. For example, place drawings on the board as you speak, draw quickly and turn your body toward the audience as often as you can. Remember to stand to the side of the drawing and use the hand next to the poster to explain a point. Always erase your drawings or gather your other materials quickly after you complete the presentation.

Individual Activity: Make an appointment with your instructor to plan a specific time to make your presentation. Remember to do all that you can to make listening easy for your audience.

NOTE: Evaluation criteria for the speaking Activity are located in the Appendix.

INTERPERSONAL COMMUNICATION STRATEGIES_____

Overview

The emphasis in interpersonal communication is on the interaction of two individuals, that is, the face-to-face exchange between persons who are aware of each other's presence. Each person in the interpersonal communication situation becomes both a sender of messages and a receiver of messages (Patton and Giffin, 1974; p. 5). Interpersonal communication situations can exist when two people are alone, or in group situations where each person is paired with several others as the group as a whole interacts.

Interpersonal communication is generally more comfortable when one interacts with a person who shares similar interests and backgrounds—who shares commonalities. Starting a conversation with a stranger can be very stressful as one or both participants search for interesting points which will engage the other. Once a topic of common interest is uncovered, however, the conversation generally blooms. As differences between the two persons in the interpersonal exchange are greater, the likelihood of finding a point of common interest is smaller. People who send nonverbal signals that are stand-offish or cold-hearted or disinterested may actually be shy or feel intimidated by the situation. Generally speaking, people enjoy interaction. The hurdle to be jumped to initiate interaction is often very high and just needs to be knocked over and forgotten. Getting to know people takes effort and

---

Encounter

it was just that i was
very touchy that day
and really that's
all i can say
to explain why
while walking through
the sears and roebuck department store
i happened to get into
this fist fight with a mannequin

—Ric Masten
Speaking Poems published by Sunflower Ink,
Carmel, CA

---

developing interpersonal relationships that are lasting takes even more effort. Getting to know people who have different backgrounds and who have had different experiences expands your own interests and makes life richer.

Many variables, both verbal and nonverbal, affect the outcomes of interpersonal communication. Such things as appearance, movements, facial expressions, meanings of words, values, and tone of voice affect what is sent on the one hand and received on the other. Interpersonal communication is affected too by the current states of mind of the two individuals. Consider the poem, "Encounter," by Ric Masten, as he

On the Best-Seller List
and Only Three Pages Long

Chapter One.

On first meeting
reject them totally.

Chapter Two.

The next time around
be halfway civil.

Chapter Three.

Now let yourself
be completely captivated.

it's true
the world does not need
another How-to-Book
but if i were to write one
i would title it:

How to Make Friends
With Important People

and i would dedicate it
to you

—*Ric Masten*
They Are All Gone Now published by Sunflower
Ink, Carmel, CA

describes a state of mind that can destroy the potential of an interpersonal encounter. Problems in interpersonal communication often originate within individuals and are not caused by the "other" individuals or innocent mannequins who often receive the blame.

Many people feel uncomfortable in their interpersonal relationships. It may be that those individuals feel uncomfortable because they lack experience in skills needed for effective and rewarding interpersonal relationships. Imagine yourself as a person hired to operate a computer network. Would you not feel inept if you began your job with little or no training and tried to learn through trial and error? The situation in interpersonal communication for most of us is not as severe as that of an uninformed computer network analyst. Through the processes of maturing and modeling the behavior of others, people acquire some skill in developing and maintaining interpersonal communication skills. However, professionals in fields of contemporary psychology and communication have, in recent years, published many guides, manuals, texts, and other reading materials in areas related to

interpersonal communication. To discover these materials one need only visit the psychology and human development sections of any bookstore or open the covers of many popular periodicals.

To provide an introduction to several popular theories of psychology and communication related to interpersonal relationships, brief overviews of such areas as assertiveness training, stress management, values clarification, and related communication skills will be presented. If there is a common theme throughout these concepts in regard to interpersonal communication, it is the following: that all persons must identify their own position in every situation and take responsibility for that position. Stated somewhat differently, each person must assume responsibility for every action taken and in so doing, eliminate judgmental responses in dealing with the behavior of others. These thoughts will be clarified, expanded, and demonstrated on the pages that follow.

As you begin your study of interpersonal communication, reflect on the poem, "On the Best-Seller List…" and how your behavior with others might be similar to the description in the poem. Does it take three meetings to accept someone new into your life? Do you reject people on first meeting; then act somewhat more open on the second meeting; and, if they persist, you finally accept the person on the third meeting? Do they become "important people" once you let them into your life? If this scenario reflects your pattern, then think about all the people who never give you a second or third chance. Think of all the first meetings you have had and all of the relationships you have lost. Consider how often the second meeting never happens when people seem different and you perceive few commonalities with them.

The material is presented as a stimulus. It is presented to develop awareness in the reader of ideas espoused by scholars and practitioners in the fields of communication and human relations. However, inclusion of the material is not meant to imply that the suggestions and techniques are appropriate for everyone. The ideas have been helpful to some people but not to others. It is the responsibility of every reader to become aware of the materials and to evaluate the material in regard to personal needs. The reader is provided with information and experiences and must independently decide to discard the ideas or change behavior in interpersonal encounters.

CHAPTER 7

TAKING RESPONSIBILITY FOR ONESELF

I t is probably reasonable to assume that most communicators are striving to achieve rewarding interpersonal relationships with others. A common problem, however, is to determine responsibility for the causes of unsatisfactory encounters. Often individuals place the blame for unsatisfactory encounters on the other communicator, thus removing themselves from responsibility. It may well be that many "other" communicators do cause problems in interpersonal encounters. There are some techniques, however, that all

GOAL
Develop strategies for improving interpersonal relationships.

121

communicators can use in presenting themselves as they attempt to achieve successful interpersonal relationships in informal settings as well as such formal settings as the employment interview.

Some Interpersonal Skills

In taking responsibility for oneself, three interpersonal skills are particularly useful: owning feelings and thoughts, self-disclosure, and assertiveness. These skills enable communicators to place responsibility for effective communication in interpersonal situations on themselves and not on the "other" persons. They are skills that many individuals use quite naturally and effectively as they relate to others. As communication becomes more complex, for example in our fast-paced, multi-cultural society, taking responsibility for oneself facilitates shared meaning.

OWNING FEELINGS AND THOUGHTS

To take responsibility for their behavior communicators must be able to own their feelings and thoughts. Owning feelings and thoughts means accepting them rather than blaming others for them, or pretending they do not exist. When feelings and thoughts are owned, complete responsibility for them is accepted.

Feelings and thoughts are different. Feelings are the emotional factor that drives behavior. Thoughts, or thinking, are the logical factor that drives behavior. We are often asked if a decision was made by the heart or the mind. The emotional reaction will often lead to a different outcome than the logical reaction. Think about the possibility of a shopping spree—whether at a department store or a home improvement store. Your emotional side might justify a purchase— you've worked hard, you really need it, you deserve a special purchase. Your logical side might be saying that the credit card is nearly maxed out, there are bills to pay, and you promised a donation to a charity. How do we reconcile these two, often disparate, decision processes? Some researchers think, or do they feel, that people have a tendency to be domi-

nated by one or the other but are capable of both thinking and feeling. Knowing whether you are being driven by your heart or mind is useful in communication exchanges and in making decisions.

Owning feelings and thoughts shows a willingness to accept responsibility for self and a commitment to being nonjudgmental toward others. Therefore, it is the direct opposite of blaming others for the way one feels. Several examples of "owned" and "not owned" feelings and thoughts follow.

> **Owned:** I need to call my friends more.
> **Not-owned:** My friends don't pay enough attention to me.
> **Owned:** I am not being listened to by the people at this meeting.
> **Not-owned:** The people at this meeting are too irresponsible to listen.

When feelings and thoughts are owned, it becomes easier to identify and communicate attitudes and thoughts. When blame is placed on or projected to someone else, communicators are attempting to transfer responsibility for negative actions from themselves to others.

Denial of feelings and thoughts refers to a refusal to acknowledge the existence of personal thoughts or intents. Adding denial to the types of reactions from which communicators can select in a given situation results in the three possibilities illustrated below.

> **Owned:** I am upset.
> **Not-owned:** He upset me.
> **Denied:** I am not upset.

A goal for effective communicators then is to take responsibility, "to own up to" the messages they communicate verbally and nonverbally. Messages do not arise without purpose. Persons delivering messages have feelings and goals. In formulating messages in interpersonal relationships, it is useful to consider communication on three levels: the message, what was said or done to communicate; the feelings that accompanied the origination and delivery of the message; and the intent, what the sender intended to accomplish through delivery of

---

GOAL
Distinguish between feeling and thinking.

the message. As each component of the message is considered, the important choice of behavior is ownership, projection, or denial.

Taking responsibility for one's own behavior can be made easier by looking at events in literal terms, that is, by speaking operationally instead of abstractly (Narciso and Burkett, 1975). To make communication clearer, the actual circumstances associated with an event or happening can be described specifically, rather than expressed in abstract words like trust, love, tolerance, loyalty, or other constructs. Note the following examples.

> **Operational:** Since I haven't eaten for twenty-four hours, I would like to be served dinner.
> **Abstract:** Since I am hungry, let's eat right now.
> **Operational:** He arrives at work punctually at 8:00 A.M. or he has never stolen materials from the warehouse.
> **Abstract:** He's a loyal employee.

The operational description provides the factual information necessary for assuring clarity. Thus, it is important not only to own feelings and thoughts but to express feelings and thoughts in operational terms. Consider the example below in owning feelings and thoughts and translating them to operational terms.

> **Owned and Abstract:** I am an unhappy person. Because of my attitude toward work and family, I find it difficult to cope with the constant pressures of day-to-day living.
> **Owned and Operational:** I seldom smile or talk pleasantly to my family and coworkers. I dread getting up in the morning to face the chores ahead of me. I have nothing to look forward to but the same routine. I yell at my family and complain at every opportunity. I avoid speaking at work unless someone addresses me. I always point out the flaws in the behavior of my family and coworkers.

Compare these examples to the one below, which illustrates not-owned feelings expressed in abstract terms.

> **Not owned and abstract:** My children make too many demands of me and give nothing in return. Even though I work, my husband irritates me by expecting me to be solely responsible for maintaining our home and taking care of the children. The people I work with upset me by being totally inconsiderate.

In considering relationships with other people, the use of first person singular (i.e., I, me, my, etc.) is appropriate because it places responsibility clearly; and the use of operational terms is appropriate because they express the meaning intended by the speaker.

> **First person:** I am upset because my watch was broken.
> **Second person:** You upset me when you broke my watch.

It may be that maturity, true friendship, and emotional honesty cannot be attained until one realizes that judgment of others' actions is inappropriate. Most communicators, however, have learned to place emphasis on the other person in their relationships and strive to change the other person's behavior rather than their own. When feelings and thoughts are owned, individuals can more readily take responsibility for their own behavior. Effective interpersonal relationships often result when communicators are responsive to the feelings and thoughts of others, yet responsible for their own feelings and thoughts.

SELF-DISCLOSURE

GOAL
Explain how self-disclosure enhances relationships.

Once individuals have owned feelings and thoughts, thereby taking responsibility for their own behavior, to engage in interpersonal communication they must be able to reveal their feelings and thoughts, or to self-disclose. Self-disclosure can be defined as a willingness to make one's feelings known to others, or as the revelation of personal information by one person to another person. When communicators are able to self-disclose, that is, reveal personal information, they increase their awareness of their own personalities through feedback received from others. Self-disclosure requires courage, however, since feedback can be threatening as well as favorable.

From research on self-disclosure (Jourard, 1971), it has been concluded that persons with healthy personalities will have the ability to self-disclose to at least one other significant person. The fact that men have a shorter life expectancy than women may even be attributable in part to the interpersonal environments of men. The male role is often perceived as one of toughness, objectivity, ambition, unsentimentality, and lack of emotion. This male role prohibits the disclosure of inner experiences, thoughts, and feelings to others. Some men appear to hide their real selves both from themselves and others, and thus must bear the added stress and expend the energy required to keep their feelings hidden.

Self-disclosure can occur at several levels (Fensterheim and Baer, 1975; Lazarus, 1971; Powell, 1969). The levels of self-disclosure can be conceptualized as five concentric circles of increasing diameter with the smallest circle representing complete disclosure to one or a few significant others, and the largest circle representing disclosure at a superficial level to many people. Depending on ability to self-disclose, each person develops a configuration of circles for the various types of circumstances likely to be encountered. The five levels have been described in the following way (Powell, 1969).

1. Based on absolute openness and honesty between two intimate friends or marriage partners, self-disclosure is required for a close relationship.
2. Revelation of unique feelings that correspond with ideas, judgments, and convictions.
3. Communication of ideas and judgments but with caution of the recipient's reaction.
4. Reporting of facts with little or no revelation of personal feelings.
5. Conversation without communication, no sharing of anything of value.

When new acquaintances are met, communication generally begins at level five. As the relationship develops the two persons progress to a mutually satisfactory level of communication.

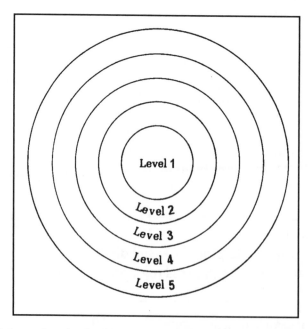

Figure 7.1. Each individual has a series of circles representing ability to self-disclose to others at various degrees of intimacy. Level 1 represents absolute openness; Level 5 represents random chatter of little value.

Communication problems sometimes arise, however, when an individual is unable to communicate at different levels when appropriate, or at the same level as the other person.

Self-disclosure of varying degrees can be useful at all five levels of communication. Even starting a conversation at the most superficial level involves self-disclosure. The sometimes difficult situation of beginning a conversation can be made easier by following the steps below, which are based on the concept of free information (Smith, 1975).

1. Ask a question about any topic that you feel may elicit an informative response from the other person. Three topics that often facilitate conversation are the situation, the other person, and yourself.
2. Follow up by expanding on any information that the other person has included in the answer. As a co-participant in the conversation, provide the other person with information to keep things going.
3. Continue the conversation based on information obtained from the responses of the other person and by providing information.
4. Sometimes interruptions are acceptable. Use interruptions wisely to clarify, agree, disagree, or to steer the topic away from something likely to be unacceptable.

For example, note the cues used by the conversants below.

Jake: Hello, have you had an exciting day?
Jane: Yes, I attended a really interesting speech class.
Jake: I didn't know you were taking speech. Have you made any speeches?
Jane: Yes, I've made two so far.
Jake: What topics did you research?

Compare this conversation with one where the other person fails to provide information.

Jake: Hello, have you had an exciting day?
Jane: No.
Jake: What class did you just attend?
Jane: Speech.
Jake: Have you made any speeches yet?
Jane: Yes.

Jake: How many speeches have you made?
Jane: Two.
Jake: What topics did you research?

Jake, on the other hand, might have facilitated the conversation by providing Jane with some information.

Jake: Hello, have you had an exciting day?
Jane: No.
Jake: Well, I have. I just came from speech class. One of the students gave a presentation on vitamin therapy.
Jane: That does sound interesting. I've read . . .

Self-disclosure requires a willingness to accept responsibility for thoughts and feelings as well as taking the risk of revealing such feelings and thoughts to others. Honest self-disclosure in interpersonal communication situations can eliminate possible noise from the communication channel and result in more fulfilling relationships. It requires an orientation where denial of feelings or placement of blame on others is unacceptable personal behavior. Appropriate levels of self-disclosure require an analysis of the level of intimacy of the relationship to

> *I do not speak like my poems. They are a bit affected like mother's telephone voice. I, too, prefer to meet the world as someone else. . . . nor do i behave in public as I do alone with a mirror, leaning over the sink, close to that other face, waiting for it to initiate a wink or give some small sign that didn't begin with me.*
>
> *The upstairs TV, the radio in the kitchen, might as well be off. No one is here.*
>
> *In the final year of his life, there was only one entry in my father's journal, dated July 24, 1940. "Tinker Bell is dead." . . . and to think the man drove me back and forth to school daily, and I never knew him. . . . nor do my children know me.*
>
> *But here now, if I get too personal, you would never recognize yourself.*
>
> —Ric Masten
> *Stark Naked* published by Sunflower Ink, Carmel, CA

determine appropriateness, level of trust, and willingness to risk.

ASSERTIVENESS

Because of preconceived notions about what others expect of an interpersonal communications encounter, many people have difficulty expressing their thoughts and feelings. The risk of a negative or adverse reaction on the part of the receiver of the message seems too threatening to allow honest self-disclosures. Such thoughts as, "he won't be interested in my opinion," "she looks like a tough person to convince," or "I'll look stupid if I say what I really think," interfere with an individual's ability to communicate. Several authors (Bloom, Coburn, and Pearlman, 1975; Fensterheim and Baer, 1975; Smith, 1975) have composed lists of assertiveness rights that they feel belong to everyone. Some common elements from the lists of assertiveness rights are the following:

- Saying no when you want to
- Making requests of others (who also have the right to say no)
- Discussing problems that arise
- Having your own opinion
- Expecting to receive respect from others
- Answering honestly about your feelings
- Changing your mind
- Admitting that you do not know or understand something

Since the purpose of assertive behavior is to facilitate honest and direct relationships with others, these rights form a basic framework for effective interpersonal communication.

Being assertive requires behavior much different than being passive or aggressive. A passive person is one who says nothing even in the face of put-downs by others. Passive behavior often results from lack of self-confidence and is manifested through intimidation by another or results from an attempt to "keep the peace" by saying nothing. An aggressive person, on the other hand, is pushy, demanding, controlling, argumentative, and even hostile toward others. An aggressive person has learned "get my own way" behaviors and is able to control others through such unpleasantness. Assertive behavior does not mean remaining silent, being pushy, being unruly, or exhibiting distasteful behavior. It is a quality related to belief in oneself and control over one's life. It means standing up for oneself. Four aspects of an assertive personality have been identified (Fensterheim and Baer, 1975, p. 20):

1. the freedom to let others know feelings, thoughts, and wants
2. the ability to talk openly and honestly with strangers, friends, and family
3. the capacity to make things happen rather than to wait for things to happen
4. acceptance of limitations while always striving to make a good effort.

Several books on assertiveness training (Anderson, 1998; Bloom, Coburn, and Pearlman, 1975; Bower and Bower, 1991; Covey, 1989; Fensterheim and Baer, 1975) offer many suggestions for developing or improving the skill of assertiveness. The techniques have been tried and proved successful in some situations. Communicators who feel uncomfortable with the list of assertive rights might consider investigating one or more of the sources described below.

In *The New Assertive Woman* (Bloom, Coburn, and Pearlman, 1975), the authors provide information about the meaning of assertiveness and include many specific examples of assertive responses that have been effective. They stress evaluating the current situation, making decisions about areas in which to become more assertive, and establishing goals to accomplish. Often the overall goal is preceded by a series of exercises or easier goals to lead to the overall goal. The authors make a contribution by building a case for developing assertive behavior and by providing a rationale for dismissing many of the games and excuses people use to avoid asserting themselves.

In the book *Don't Say YES When You Want to Say NO* (Fensterheim and Baer, 1975),

GOAL
Differentiate among passive, aggressive, and assertive communication strategies.

the authors review many aspects of everyday living—social relationships, close relationships, and work relationships—and describe positive approaches for changing ineffective behavior through assertiveness training. The book provides many case studies of situations where assertive behavior was effective and provides laboratory exercises for developing assertive behavior in those areas where difficulty is experienced.

In the book *When I say No, I Feel Guilty* (Smith, 1975), assertiveness training is approached by providing the reader with descriptions of skills that can be used to develop assertive behavior. The concepts of self-disclosure and free information, discussed earlier, are examples of assertive skills described in this book. Numerous dialogues are provided as examples of the verbal skills often used in many different everyday situations.

In Stephen Covey's (1989) book, *The Seven Habits of Highly Effective People*, two habits, relating to proactivity and setting goals, have relevance for establishing an assertive attitude. Being proactive means that you analyze situations and make things happen. This is in contrast to being reactive. A reactive person waits until events happen and then acts accordingly. Proactive people make choices; reactive people respond to circumstances. A proactive person is assertive and looks at alternatives. A reactive person just feels that nothing can be done. Another of the seven habits is "begin with the end in mind," a method of goal setting. Covey suggests that we think about what we would like to be said about us at our funeral. Covey provides a method of constructing a personal mission statement which reflects values and what type of person you want to be and what you want to accomplish. The personal mission statement provides a focus for proactive, assertive behavior.

Giving compliments and criticism takes skill on the part of an assertive communicator. In giving both compliments and criticism, it is important to be specific, be sincere, be personal, and be timely. Don't just say "good job" maybe weeks after the event, but say "I read your report today and, as one who reads these all the time, I can truly say that you did an exceptional job, especially in summarizing the statistics." In receiving a compliment, do not discount yourself or give all the credit to another. The box below provides examples of compliments and possible responses. In receiving criticism, avoid defensiveness or argument by saying, "you might be right about that" or "you have a right to that opinion" to give yourself time to evaluate the comments.

Walter Anderson (1998), who has been editor of *Parade*, suggested some assertive behaviors to use when you must give criticism.

- Can it be changed? If not, be silent.
- Choose a proper time and place where privacy exists and anger is absent.

Type of Compliment Categories and Compliment Responses

Compliment Categories		Compliment Responses	
Performance	"I loved your recital."	Ritual Acceptance	"Thank you."
Personality	"You are a brave person."	Pleased Acceptance	"I am glad you think so."
Appearance	"I love your new hairstyle."	Embarrassment	Blushing, Loss of Words
Possessions	"Your new car is awesome!"	Return Compliment	"I like your car too."
Attire	"That is a beautiful coat."	Magnified Acceptance	"Just wait to see my fur."
Service	"What a great contribution."	No Acknowledgment	Continues the Topic

- Reassure by beginning with praise.
- Be specific about the criticism.
- Express confidence and make change seem easy.
- Praise improvement. (p. 175)

Anderson further suggested four steps to follow when you are being criticized.

1. Focus on criticism only and not on critic.
2. Ask for details if you don't understand the specific criticism.
3. Evaluate—decide if this criticism is something you can or want to change.
4. Thank the critic for the advice and enlist help in improving. (p. 176)

Anderson feels that "a common fear regarding criticism is that it makes us a doormat—that accepting criticism, particularly harsh criticism, somehow demeans us. That's not necessarily true. If you exercise the steps outlined, you—not your critic—are in control" (p. 177).

Interruptions are another area where assertiveness can be beneficial. Consider the advice of Bower and Bower (1991) from their book, *Asserting Your-Self.*

1. Describe: "Did you know that you stopped me before I finished stating my point?"
2. Express: "When you do that, I feel foolish, as though my ideas are insignificant, and I feel like giving up."
3. Specify: "Let's try this: when one of us finishes speaking, the other will count silently one-two-three before jumping into the conversation. That way each of us can finish what he has to say without being interrupted. If either of us slips, we can remind each other—like I'm doing with you now. Okay?"
4. Consequences: Positive—"That way we'll both be able to have enjoyable conversations." Negative—"If this agreement doesn't work, I'll start interrupting you frequently just to get my point across." (pp. 114–115)

Bower and Bower (1991) recommend a look at the nonassertive messages that your body is sending. Observe yourself in a mirror to see if you are doing the following non-assertive mannerisms.

1. **Eye Contact**—blinking rapidly, staring fixedly, not looking, shifting head and eyes excessively, squinting your eyes.
2. **Facial Expression**—a pursed, tight-lipped mouth; tensing and wrinkling your forehead; swallowing repeatedly; clearing your throat excessively; wetting your lips.
3. **Gestures and Posture**—covering your mouth when speaking, scratching your head or rubbing your eye or the back of your neck, preening such as touching your hair or stroking your beard, tinkering with jewelry, adjusting clothing, shifting weight from one foot to another, wandering or pacing, freezing like a statue. (pp. 175–177)

Assertive behavior requires a look at oneself and the belief that individuals do have the right to change their own behavior and make decisions about positive changes that might be

---

Not Exactly a Command Performance

have you ever sat back
and looked at the life you were living
and saw that it was playing
like a really bad B movie?
appalled and taken back
by the inane lines you were saying
and the unrestrained way you were weeping
and waving your arms about
over acting

but what bothers you most
is the knowledge
that someone of your reputed good taste
would allow themselves to sit through such
    hogwash
unable to turn it off till they learn
how the damn thing comes out

—Ric Masten
Stark Naked published by Sunflower Ink,
Carmel, CA

made. They can take responsibility for present behavior. For example, persons who cannot hold jobs should not place the blame on others but should examine their own behavior to determine what they must do to keep their jobs. Individuals who are always angry with their families might analyze their own participation in the unpleasant situations rather than blaming other family members. Persons who are intimidated by salesclerks might try to determine the types of behavior they exhibit that allow them to be intimidated. An assertive person takes responsibility for behavior and therefore has the potential for revealing true feelings and thoughts, rather than masking them because of inhibitions and fears of repercussion. Remember, to be assertive, you must be specific and factual, you must take ownership by using "I" language, and you must offer a potential solution aimed at making both communicators happy. Assertive individuals are okay with changing their minds, not always having an answer, saying they do not understand, and answering "no."

The Interview

One very important and common situation in which interpersonal communication occurs is the interview. An interview is a communication encounter that has the general purpose of collecting information to be used either for reporting or decision-making purposes. The interview can be distinguished from general conversation by its more purposeful objective of collecting specific information and its generally predetermined format. All communicators will find themselves in interview situations at one time or another and many will fulfill the role of interviewer (i.e., the one who asks the questions) as well as interviewee (i.e., the one who answers the questions). It will be helpful to have some general knowledge of the various purposes of interviews and their structure as well as more detailed information about the employment interview. A few strategies to use in answering questions will be useful, also.

BASICS OF INTERVIEWING

Purpose

Within the context of gathering information for reporting and decision-making purposes, three distinct types of interviews can be distinguished: opinion, diagnosis, and employment.

Interviews that seek to establish the viewpoints of either individuals or groups have the specific purpose of collecting opinions. These interviews often sample the opinions of specific populations of individuals or focus on the views of one or a few experts in an area. Examples of interviews for collecting opinions would include questioning the parents of children in a particular school about their satisfaction with the reading curriculum, or recording the statements made by the principal in regard to reading achievement at the school.

The diagnostic interview has a somewhat different purpose. It is designed to collect information that permits some prescription to be made in regard to the needs of an individual or group. A very common example occurs between physician and patient as information is sought to determine an appropriate treatment. An example involving a group might include the gathering of information among individuals in a particular work unit with the objective of improving interpersonal relationships among peers.

The employment interview is used by those who hire to assess the potential of an applicant for a job, and by those seeking jobs to determine the desirability of the position. Although the common perception is that the applicant is being interviewed by the employer, often the applicant is interviewing the employer as well.

GOAL
Demonstrate effective interviewing skills.

Structure

In nearly all interview situations the interviewer has given some prior consideration to the type of information being sought and the use it will be given. Based on such considerations, a format for collecting the information is determined. In general, interviews may be classified as structured or unstructured. The highly structured interview is one where all questions have been predetermined and the interviewer's dialogue has been written out and rehearsed almost like a script. The unstructured interview allows the interviewer to say nearly anything that will elicit the type of information desired. And of course, there are many variations between the two extremes.

The structured interview is needed to provide consistency of information when there are several interviewers and many interviewees. When data from a number of individuals are to be combined, it is especially important that the responses be collected from all respondents under nearly identical conditions. This is the case in many scientific investigations that rely on interview data. The unstructured interview is probably most useful when there is only one interviewer and one interviewee and spontaneity is sought, as in a celebrity interview on television. Thus, the amount of structure given an interview is determined primarily by the use the information will have.

Within the general structure of an interview there is some variety in the way that questions are asked. The interviewer will usually ask a question, wait for a response, and make some written record of the response. In less structured interviews, the interviewer can interact with the respondent by restating questions for clarity and by restating some of the responses. Generally questions will be open or closed, neutral or leading, and general or specific. An open question has no predetermined alternative answers. The interviewee is free to formulate the answer. A closed question provides the respondent with specific choices from which to select the answer. Neutral questions are stated without biasing the respondent's answer in one way or another. Leading questions are stated in ways that suggest an answer to the respondent. General questions permit the interviewee to formulate answers from a broad domain. Specific questions direct the respondent to particular aspects of an issue. With the exception of the leading question, a well-constructed interview might include some of each type of question. To clarify the distinctions among question types, note the examples below.

Open: How would you describe the condition of the city's public parks?

Closed: Have you found the city's public parks to be poorly kept or well kept?

Neutral: Which should receive priority—city park maintenance or city park construction?

Leading: Is it wise to maintain existing city parks before building new city parks?

General: What can be done to improve the city's public parks?

Specific: What can be done to improve the playgrounds in the city's public parks?

Answering Questions

In studying interviewing as an information gathering technique, one often thinks only of the formulation of the questions. Strategies for answering the questions can prove useful, also. Consider the following suggestions for answering questions in an interview setting.

1. Listen for both content (what is asked) and intent (what is meant).
2. Acknowledge the question—that is, show that you understand or ask for clarification. Paraphrasing is one way to show understanding or reveal lack of understanding.
3. Answer the question directly, briefly, accurately, and completely.
4. Evaluate non-verbal behavior, especially facial expression, to verify that the interviewer is satisfied with the completeness of your answer.
5. Be prepared to offer proof, clarification, or support of your ideas. Your own experience is often a good way to do this.
6. Avoid verbal or non-verbal behaviors which indicate that you think a question is stupid or ill-conceived.
7. If you cannot answer a question, explain the reason simply and politely without being unresponsive, evasive, or flippant.
8. If you are responding to questions in writing, rather than orally, be sure to answer each question individually and clearly without padding answers or skipping around so much that you confuse the reader.

Listening skills and responsiveness to non-verbal behaviors are extremely important as you field the questions in an interview.

THE EMPLOYMENT INTERVIEW

A job applicant wishes to make the best possible impression on the potential employer. Four things are especially important in creating a positive image in the potential employer's eyes: the letter of application, the résumé, the interview, and the follow-up letter. It is important to tailor the application, résumé, interview behaviors, and follow-up letter to the specific situation. To be hired for a specific job, the applicant must often present the image that fits the job, and not expect the job to be adapted to fit the image.

Letter of Application

The letter of application is a written communication with the purpose of convincing the prospective employer that the applicant has potential for the job. The letter of application should be based on the following rules.

1. The letter should display such positive characteristics as confidence, dignity, and courtesy.
2. The letter and envelope should be addressed to a specific person and should include both name and title. Do not address letters to President, Personnel Manager, or To Whom It May Concern.
3. The letter is generally divided into three paragraphs: the reasons for wanting the particular position; personal qualities, education, and experience relevant for the position; and request for an interview and how to be reached.
4. The letter of application should be brief, specific, businesslike in tone, and clear.
5. The letter of application should be checked very carefully to ensure correct grammar, spelling, and punctuation; should be neatly typed; and should not include slang, jokes, or unusual stylistic practices. Be particularly careful to avoid slang since each generation has had its own slang and you might be writing to someone who will think your slang is just sloppiness.

The applicant might ask, as a final check, "What type of impression would this letter make on me if I were an employer?" See example of a Letter of Application on the following page.

Résumé

Again, in preparing the résumé, the applicant is attempting to catch the eye of the potential employer. With today's technology, the applicant can use word processing templates to format the résumé and can easily create a unique résumé to fit each job application. The résumé should include the following:

1. Personal—name and address.

   Enter your name as you would like to see it at the top of your résumé. Along with your complete mailing address (no abbreviations), include your e-mail address. The e-mail address is especially important if you are applying for a position in a computer-related industry. Include area codes for all phone numbers. Include phone numbers that will be answered by a person or by voice mail (answering machine). Include your work phone if you have privacy for a job-related conversation at your place of current employment.

2. Position Objective—brief phrase or sentence to describe the type of employment you are seeking.

   Change the position objective to merge your interests and skills with the characteristics of each particular employer. The position objective might be the first impression you make. Think of it as your main idea for a speech or your thesis statement for an essay. Create a vision in the mind of the reader. Some experts consider the resume objective optional.

3. Education—relevant high school, college, and special training.

   Include all applicable education, formal schooling, on-the-job training, continuing education, military, certifications, workshops, and seminars. Focus the reader on your academic credentials and your continued commitment to educational achievement. Begin with your highest level of education even if you did not complete the degree. If you have attended a college, generally high school graduation is omitted.

Dana Smith
6300 Fifth Street
Dallas, Texas 75214

Dr. A. J. Robins
Chief of Staff
City Hospital
114 Second Avenue
Dallas, Texas 75206

Dear Dr. Robins:

Your August 10 advertisement in the Dallas Morning News described your need for a laboratory technician. I am very much interested in this position since it would provide an excellent opportunity to begin my career in the medical field.

My recent training at Dallas University Medical School and internship at the Veteran's Administration Hospital as well as my strong desire to work in the field qualify me to perform successfully in such a position and contribute to your organization. My résumé is enclosed.

I would appreciate the opportunity to meet with you. My current address and telephone number are listed on my résumé.

Very truly yours,

Dana Smith

Letter of Application

List only the city and state of the college or school with the last attended institution listed first. List the title of your degree, diploma, or certificate exactly as it was awarded (see your transcript for exact wording). If the degree was not recent, you need not list the date you received it. You should list your grade-point average if it is "B" or higher. You can include such other educational activities as extracurricular involvement, internships, teaching or research grants or appointments, professional sororities or fraternities, and student government responsibilities.

4. Experience—chronological listing of previous jobs with dates and activities.

Include part-time as well as full-time employment and paid and unpaid positions of responsibility. Give the full name of the company including division or parent company if applicable. List only the city and the state for address purposes. Beginning with your most recent position list your title and describe your duties. Use job titles and descriptions which relate best to the job for which you are applying. List dates of employment with a starting date followed by an ending date or "present." Dates can include both months and years. However, if there are gaps in your work history, you may prefer to list years only. Begin sentences with action verbs, such as supervised, when describing duties and avoid the use of personal pronouns.

Résumé of John Jones
(—Address—)
(—Telephone—)

Position Objective:
Position leading to management and administrative responsibilities in sales division of a major industrial corporation.

Education:
Bachelor of Science Degree in Business Administration from Central Texas State University, June, 2000.

Associates of Arts and Science Degree in Mid-Management from City Community College, June, 1995.

Employment History:
1998 to Present: Sales manager for soft drink division of Lone Star Beverage Company, Plano, Texas. Responsible for personnel, distribution, and sales of over $500,000 in product.

References:
Mr. Jack Andrews   Dr. Ann Rogers
Vice President of Marketing   Professor of Business
Lone Star Beverage Company   Central Texas State University
(—Address—)   (—Address—)
(—Telephone—)   (—Telephone—)

Résumé

5. Optional Sections—relevant information that was not included in the education and experience sections. Do not include personal interests unless they contribute to the job. Loving travel, while interesting, might not seem appropriate for a medical job but might fit well with hotel management.

- Course Work—list titles of courses relevant to the position as well as computer classes taken. The computer listing is very important in contemporary employment opportunities.
- Abilities—include personal traits and proven professional skills such as communication skills or team-oriented.
- Memberships—involvement in organizations shows that you keep up-to-date

with current trends in your field or that you are willing to share your expertise with the community.

- Honors and Awards—include recognition you received for outstanding performance in an educational, professional, or volunteer setting. Making the dean's list, being top sales associate, being an officer in an organization, or receiving military honors shows your ability to achieve.
- Personal Interests—emphasizes relevant contributions outside the workplace: team sports, volunteering, service, community involvement. If you have stayed out of the workforce for caregiver responsibilities, entries in this section will show your continued growth.

6. References—permission should be obtained from those listed. A potential employer will generally request references if you are a serious candidate. Tell your references of your job interests and even share a copy of your résumé with them.

The résumé should be neatly typed with parallel construction of sentences and phrases and with parallel spacing of headings and margins. The résumé of persons entering a field or beginning a career is best presented as one page. The ten-page résumé is more appropriate for established professionals with many experiences and outstanding contributions. See example of a Résumé on the previous page.

Interview Behavior

The employment interview is an example of an interpersonal communication situation where owning feelings, self-disclosure, and assertiveness (not aggressiveness) are useful skills. It is important to begin with appropriate greetings (e.g., a firm handshake and "how do you do"). Although interviewers sometimes try to make applicants uncomfortable to note their reactions to stress, most will probably attempt to put the applicant at ease by offering a chair and making casual conversation. The interviewee should relax, maintain good posture, avoid chewing gum, and refrain from smoking. When preparing for the interview, the applicant should keep the following in mind:

1. Think very carefully about what to wear. How you look communicates. When in doubt, the more conservative route is usually recommended. Wear your clothes before the interview to discover defective zippers, pinching shoes, baggy socks that would be distracting.
2. Be sincere, natural, friendly, and relaxed.
3. Be specific and concrete in answering.
4. If unsure of a comment say, "I'm not sure I understand your question."
5. Articulate and pronounce words clearly and distinctly. Use correct grammar and avoid using slang or profanity. Speak conversationally. Be personable and energetic by varying vocal rate, pitch, and volume

meaningfully. Avoid "fillers" such as "like," "stuff," "ah" that detract.
6. Look the interviewer in the eyes and address by name occasionally.
7. Smile occasionally and show a pleasant personality. Be alert and spontaneous when the interviewer is speaking. React by using appropriate nonverbal expression.
8. Consider the questions to be asked by both interviewer and applicant. Examples of these are given in the Speaking Activity for Part Three.

Follow-Up Letter

If still interested in the position after the interview, consider writing a follow-up letter immediately. In the letter thank the interviewer and mention something positive about the company. Remark that you would like to be associated with such a company. Type the letter in business format and send it to the interviewer immediately.

Summary

An understanding of such communication skills as owning feelings, self-disclosure, and assertiveness are relevant for interpersonal encounters as informal as a conversation between two friends or as formal as an employment interview. Assertiveness training provides an experience in self-discovery that leads to a greater respect and appreciation for oneself. If individuals recognize and believe that they do have basic assertive rights, and that honesty with oneself and others is important, then the potential exists to develop effective relationships with others.

During and after discovery of oneself, interpersonal relationships are facilitated by speaking in the first person singular, by speaking in specific rather than abstract terms, and by self-disclosing personal information at a level appropriate for the situation. Since most individuals will participate in an employment interview at some time in their lives, an understanding of the purposes and structures of interviews is very important.

CHAPTER 8

RELATING TO OTHERS

Relating to others equals relationships. Although we often hear the term "relationship" in the context of a romantic relationship, the term is really broader and refers to interactions with others at various levels of intimacy. Friendship and intimacy are two concepts that define our close relationships. Friendship is very important for many reasons: fulfilling the need for security, combating loneliness, having a sense of belonging, feeling appreciated, finding a person to whom to self-disclose, and much more. Friendships are sometimes stronger than family ties. People often jokingly say we inherit our families but we choose our friends—even though family members will often be friends, there is a bit of truth in that. Intimacy refers to a state of frequent interaction, comfortable self-disclosure of more private details, high interdependence, and high emotional involvement. Friendships occur when we find others who seem caring, when others share viewpoints and interests with us, and when we sense that others seem to like us.

No matter how intimate the relationship becomes, the growth of the relationship can be defined by stages of development through initiation to possibly termination. A first stage of a relationship can be called the "entry stage" where two people meet and through some need such as avoiding loneliness, seeking friendship, or solving a

GOAL
Develop strategies for improving interpersonal relationships.

GOAL
Describe how interpersonal relationships develop and disintegrate.

Relating to Others Equals Relationships

Stages of Relationships

1. Entry Stage

2. Exploratory Stage

3. Bonding Stage

and sometimes

4. Termination Stage

---

mutual problem, a connection is made. Often convenience or physical proximity facilitate the entry stage. When moving to a new location, people often connect with coworkers and neighbors. Next is the "exploratory stage" where more information about the other person is sought. As you learn more about the other person, your interest either intensifies or diminishes. If the relationship is to continue, the two parties enter the "bonding stage" where trust, predictability, and mutual dependency develop. As bonding progresses, the relationship becomes more stable and permanent or enters the "termination stage." Until bonding occurs, the relationship might end but would hardly be missed. Terminating a relationship that has stabilized and achieved a sense of permanency is often painful. Signs are evident, however, when the two parties avoid each other, when predictions become inaccurate, or intimacy diminishes. When the relationship disintegrates yet remains important, renewal strategies, such as confronting problems, redefining roles, renegotiating rules, investigating change, and/or obtaining outside counseling, can reverse the termination and reestablish the bond. To endure, relationships take considerable work.

Communication skills such as assertiveness, self-disclosure, and owning feelings and thoughts facilitate the maintenance of relationships. Other communication skills that contribute to bonding between people are covered in this chapter. These include values clarification, ethics or honesty, behavioral flexibility, more on listening skills, empathy, and conflict management.

GOAL

Recognize the impact of values on communication.

Some Interpersonal Skills

All individuals possess sets of values that affect their abilities to share meaning with others in interpersonal relationships. To communicate effectively, speakers must consider not only their own values but also the values of those with whom they communicate. All too often people stop listening when persons with whom they are communicating display values contrary to their own. To share meaning with others, individuals must continue to listen even when messages seem contrary to their values. Effective communication requires a willingness to listen openly to what others are saying, especially in situations where hostility and conflict are apt to occur.

In addition to knowledge of one's own values and willingness to consider the values of others, additional skills useful for relating to others are ethics, behavioral flexibility, descriptive listening, and empathy. Ethics refer to the moral principles guiding communication—right versus wrong. Behavioral flexibility is the ability to select appropriate behaviors to fit given situations. It provides some latitude in communicating with persons whose values differ from one's own. Descriptive listening is a technique useful in helping others think through their problems and arrive at their own conclusions. It requires the listener to be nonjudgmental. Empathy is the ability to put oneself in the place of another. By empathizing one can, perhaps, better understand the values that motivate others.

VALUES CLARIFICATION

In today's diverse world and within the "melting pot" sense of inclusion embodied in the formation of the United States, having a sense of how values affect communication is essential. What exactly are values? Values are constructs and do not exist as concrete objects like books, cars, furniture, or food. They can be inferred by behavior and, perhaps, by self-disclosure of the individuals who hold them. When convenient they can be easily faked. Values affect self-esteem, and they contribute to the impressions held by others. Values are firmly held attitudes used in making choices among alternatives. They represent aspects of living that hold some worth and receive priority.

An example of a value is the importance many people place on pursuing higher education. People who value higher education give it priority in their lives. This importance of the value of education can be identified by observing the individual's contribution of time and resources to achieving the goal and asking the individual to describe feelings about education. The dedication can be faked, too, by displaying false behavioral clues and self-disclosing false evidence of the attitude.

People acquire values in several ways (Adell, 1976): experimentation, authority, rational thinking, personal decision, or intuition. Through experimentation, values are acquired by comparing the results of various ways of approaching similar situations. Behaviors associated with outcomes providing maximum benefits are likely to become a part of the value system. With the authoritarian approach to values, one accepts standards imposed by such important others as parents and leaders of society and religion. Values are acquired also through rational thought and selection on an intellectual level according to a set of moral standards. Or values can be acquired by thinking through what is important only to the individual and without regard to authority or a set of moral standards. Last, it is thought by some that values are acquired through intuition, or some insight, that leads people to select good rather than bad outcomes. Thus it seems that values can be acquired through comparison of results, authoritarian directives, rational thinking, personal decision, or perhaps intuition. It may well be that values are acquired from combinations of several of these general methods.

In considering the role of values in the communication process, the following points should be remembered.

1. Since they are internal states values cannot be seen. They do affect reactions to situations, events, and other people. For example, love of family cannot be seen but is an important value to many.
2. Behavior is influenced by an individual's set of values. A knowledge of values will contribute to an understanding and prediction of behavior. Knowing that one values fast cars may explain an individual's choice of a specific type of car.

Figure 8.1. These illustrations do not represent values; they reflect values. Values do not exist as concrete objects.

3. The intensity of values varies. Some values are very strongly held, whereas others are less important. Reactions to situations are affected by the value itself as well as the intensity of the value. For example, music perceived as too loud might be tolerated if liked and eliminated if disliked.
4. The specificity of values varies. Some values are quite specific and others are very general. One might value a more general area, like education, but see little value in taking specific groups of courses.
5. Behavior is often affected by the relative importance of the value. Some situations require choices among outcomes related to several important values. For example, one might feel that travel and education are extremely important. Given a limited amount of income, however, it might be necessary to choose between a trip or a semester in school.
6. The situation will affect the role of a specific value also. The chance to study with a famous professor might make choice between travel and education much easier.

Thus, values are internal states that affect observable behavior in various ways depending on the situation as well as the intensity, specificity, and relative importance of the value.

Values are an important aspect of interpersonal communication. A clearer picture of one's values can be a useful tool for achieving more fulfilling relationships with others. Values clarification (Howe and Howe, 1975; Simon, Howe, and Kirschenbaum, 1972) provides a process, comprised primarily of exercises that lead one to think through feelings, for discovering values. It does not tell a person what values should be held, but provides techniques for self-discovery. The process of values clarification leads to a better understanding of what is important and a better understanding of how to make choices. Do individuals value studying and striving for college degrees? Depending on the relative value of studying versus leisure, priorities can be assigned and choices can be made. Do they play golf or do an assignment? Can they do one or both? Given a limited amount of

money, do they pay golf club fees or college tuition?

Being aware of one's own set of values, decision-making processes, ways of setting priorities, and ways of reacting is important since values are directly related to self-esteem. One's image of self includes the things that are valued. A clarification of values helps one better perceive self, and therefore, enables self-disclosure. Better defined self-esteem has a direct relationship to communication abilities. Values determine topics for conversations, influence choices in work and leisure activities, and affect relationships with others.

Persons with whom one communicates are in the same position. Their skills in interpersonal communication are related to some extent to their perceptions of their own values. Their values will affect their own self-esteems, their behaviors, and their reactions to others' behavior. All messages and the resultant reactions are influenced by the values held by each participant in the communication situation.

In considering others' values communicators should try to recognize how closely they relate to their own. Perhaps a message from someone with different values should be given deeper consideration than a message from someone with the same values. An attempt to determine the values that motivate a message will provide added information for sharing the intended meaning of the message. Values are seldom verbally stated; they are implied. Recognition of the values motivating a message is an important interpersonal skill. Acquisition of this skill can begin through a better understanding of one's own values. When interacting with new people, across the cultures within our society, understand the values of those whose backgrounds and characteristics are different than yours. Remember that understanding does not require acceptance.

GOAL

Explain the importance of ethics (honesty) on communication exchanges.

ETHICS

Every society establishes standards of conduct that it expects of its citizens. When choices among alternatives are to be made by individuals, the standards of conduct of the society or the group to which the individual belongs will contribute to the decision. Many decisions, of course, are made among alternatives that are readily acceptable. Should I call my friend in another state or should I write a letter to offer my congratulations? Should I invite the new neighbors over for dessert and coffee or should I invite them to dinner? Other decisions require evaluation of choices according to standards of conduct expected of group membership. Should I admit my mistake or should I create a phony excuse to cover up? Should I get a job to support myself or should I steal my food and clothing?

Ethics is the term used to refer to the standards of conduct associated with various groups to which one might belong. Often reference is made to professional ethics. Physicians, for example, vow to follow a code of conduct developed centuries ago called the Hippocratic Oath. In this oath, physicians vow to ". . . follow the system of regimen which according to my ability and judgment, I consider for the benefit of my patients, and abstain from whatever is deleterious and mischievous." Attorneys are another group with whom a code of conduct, legal ethics, is associated. Colleges and universities will generally have a code of student conduct which expresses expectations of their students. Ethics require evaluation in making choices—what is right, what is wrong?

In speech communication, honesty is an appropriate synonym for ethics. Ethical communication provides the information others need to make choices. Omission of relevant information can be just as harmful to a relationship as lying. Honesty in interpersonal relationships forms the basis of trust. Dishonesty often occurs when individuals must relay a message which is likely to result in negative consequences. Dishonesty provides a method of avoidance but if and when discovered, the receiver of the message must add another criterion for interpreting the message—does it convey truth or falsehood? The introduction of dishonesty into a relationship adds strain and distorts communication. The sometimes senders of dishonest messages will often find themselves placed in the position of justifying their honest messages to others in order to prove their credibility.

The communication process can be facilitated by the listener who is accepting and open to messages which do have negative associations. If I as sender am confident that you as receiver will accept a negative message, I will be more likely to make a clear, concise statement. If I anticipate that you as receiver will react with anger, defensiveness, or any of the other protectionist responses, I possibly will be less clear and perhaps distort my message in order to avoid the negative reaction I perceive as probable.

Most people would rather receive a negative message than no message at all. In other words, if you are fearful of giving someone information that will be received as bad news, it is generally better in the long run to disclose the negative news immediately than to face perhaps worse consequences later. Consider a tenant who does not have the money to pay rent. Many tenants will just avoid the landlord and hope for the best. The landlord may be leaving messages which request some response. Being ignored just makes the landlord unhappier. Most people are willing to work out problems if they just have information and cooperation. Or, consider teenagers who find themselves in the dilemma of breaking parental curfews. Do they call home and perhaps have to listen to an upset parent or do they just come home late? Usually the parent is so stressed by the worry that the consequences will be worse by not calling.

Ethics in interpersonal communication requires honesty, the standard that our society and most subgroups within it anticipate. When a friend gives a compliment, a supervisor at work gives an evaluation, or a spouse expresses commitment, we expect that such messages will be true and honest. On the other hand, in our society we have grown to anticipate the possibility of dishonesty in some groups, salespersons, for example. When I hear from salespersons that their products are the best, that the "deal" I will receive is the best, that my car needs a major repair, or that the new jacket I am trying on is perfect for me, I know that there is a personal profit motive entering the communication process and that ethics are possibly being compromised. Not all of us can claim as did George Washington that we have never told a lie, but all of us can be aware of the importance of ethics in all communication and the relationship of honesty to credibility, clarity, trust, and openness.

BEHAVIORAL FLEXIBILITY

When people are behaviorally flexible they possess the ability to adapt readily to any situation. They are open-minded and able to keep channels of communication open. Behaviorally flexible persons are especially adept at successfully adjusting to new communication situations and at relating to people in new and different ways. They are able to behave in ways appropriate for the situation; they are not at a loss when past behavioral patterns are inappropriate. They adjust well to the diversity of a global economy.

When dealing with situations where different values are evident, behavioral flexibility encourages a continuance of dialogue rather than an embarrassed or flustered end to communication. Behavioral flexibility does not imply that communicators accept or appear to accept values or behavior of which they disapprove. It means only that they allow communication channels to remain open by displaying behavior that will maintain an exchange of both similar and different opinions. Consider the following example of a flexible and judgmental response to the same situation.

Speaker: People in this city are going to have to begin using their cars less. They need to plan fewer trips and carpool more. We need a law to limit driving.

Judgmental response: You are wrong. Freedom of choice is a right in our country. People have the right to drive cars when and where they want. A law to limit driving would be ridiculous and unconstitutional.

Flexible response: You expressed the need for people to change driving habits. That may be, but choice has always been a right of the individual. A law to limit driving would cause many hardships and limit the choices of those who wish to allocate resources to driving their own cars as they please.

To gain competence in behavioral flexibility it is useful to identify and focus on ways to behave differently in difficult or irritating situations. It is important also to recognize the behavioral choices available for a given set of circumstances. In many situations alternative reactions are possible. Behaviorally flexible individuals select the most appropriate behavior, not the habitual behavior. To provide experience in the area of behavioral flexibility, attempt to increase the number of times interaction is initiated and dialogue is maintained with someone with whom frequent disagreements have occurred or who appears to have a different cultural heritage. Another suggestion is to increase the number of owning statements made and to decrease the number of blaming statements. The interpersonal skills of owning feelings and self-disclosure often facilitate attempts to become more behaviorally flexible in difficult situations.

DESCRIPTIVE LISTENING

Descriptive listening is the ability to provide feedback in a manner that is not evaluative or judgmental. It is particularly useful in interpersonal relationships when individuals are seeking to understand their own feelings about matters of important concern. The descriptive listener serves as a sounding board, in a sense, as the troubled individual seeks a solution. The individual practicing descriptive listening will react to what is heard by paraphrasing the speaker's message (i.e., saying it in a different way).

Since the goal of descriptive listening is to help the speaker make decisions about specific issues of concern, descriptive messages from the listener must focus on behaviors that can be seen directly. Concrete, specific, and descriptive messages from the listener are encouraged. For example, note the following two approaches to the same situation.

Speaker: I've just found the car that I have to buy, but it's about $5000 more than I can afford.

Judgmental feedback approach:

Listener: John, you shouldn't try to buy such an expensive car.
Speaker: Who are you to try to tell me what car I shouldn't buy?

Descriptive feedback approach:

Listener: John, the car you like so much will cost more than you originally budgeted.

Speaker: I can't really spend more unless I give up something else; the cost of the car is almost twice what I wanted to spend.

The descriptive approach does not include a command but allows the receiver of the message to make an independent decision about how to react.

Nondescriptive feedback goes beyond, or adds to, what is directly observable by interpreting, judging, or drawing conclusions. The major drawback in using nondescriptive feedback is the negative effect on the communication process caused by responding in an evaluative or judgmental manner. Gordon (1970) has identified twelve ways that judgmental verbal responses can be classified.

1. **Commanding**—Telling a person to do something, giving an order or a command. For example: Don't buy the expensive car.
2. **Warning**—Telling a person what consequences will occur if something is done. For example: If you buy the expensive car, you'll go broke.
3. **Preaching**—Telling a person what should or ought to be done. For example: You ought to buy a car that you can afford.
4. **Advising**—Telling a person how to solve a problem. For example: It's my opinion that you should buy a cheaper car.
5. **Teaching**—Trying to influence a person with facts, logic, information, or opinions. For example: The insurance and upkeep on the expensive car will cost you much more than it would for a cheaper car.
6. **Criticizing**—Making a negative judgment or evaluation of a person. For example: You must be out of your mind to think you could afford that expensive car.
7. **Praising**—Offering a positive evaluation or judgment. For example: You are smart to realize that the expensive car is too costly for you.
8. **Shaming**—Making a person feel foolish, putting a person into a category. For example: When you cannot afford to pay for your own lunch, how can you think of spending that much for a car?
9. **Analyzing**—Determining the motivation for why a person is doing or saying something.

For example: The only reason you want that expensive car is to show your old college friends that you've really made it big.

10. **Sympathizing**—Trying to make a person feel better. For example: Don't be upset by not being able to buy the car; most people can't afford a car like that.
11. **Questioning**—Searching for more information to help solve the problem. For example: Why can't you be happy with a car that you can afford?
12. **Humoring**—Trying to get a person away from the problem. For example: There's more to life than cars; aren't you planning to go to London this spring?

In helping a person explore feelings and arrive at conclusions, responses based on the above list are in many cases best avoided. Such responses cause the speaker to react to the feedback rather than face the problem.

Descriptive listening is not a technique that fits all situations. In using the technique, the listener must determine whether or not paraphrasing makes sense. Consider the following inappropriate examples.

I wonder where I should park my car when I get to school?
You're concerned about finding a place to park your car.

My biggest problem is knowing how to pronounce these unusual words.
You seem to be very concerned about knowing how to pronounce some unusual words.

Some statements are just not appropriate for a response based on the descriptive listening technique. To be effective, a listener should refrain from overdoing descriptive reactions and avoid making responses that appear trite or thoughtless.

Agatha Christie's sleuth, Miss Marple, was an expert at descriptive listening. She solved many crimes by attentively listening to and drawing information from persons associated with the crimes. Because she did not contribute any information to the conversation, she was able to learn a great deal from those to whom she spoke. Consider the following excerpts from *A Murder Is Announced* (Christie, 1950).

"Yes, indeed." Miss Brunner sighed. "Very few people would be as loyal to their old friends as dear Miss Blacklock is. Oh, dear, those days seem a long time ago. Such a pretty girl and enjoyed life so much. It all seemed so sad."

Miss Marple, though with no idea of what had seemed so sad, sighed and shook her head. "Life is indeed hard," she murmured.

"And sad affliction bravely borne," murmured Miss Brunner, her eyes suffusing with tears. "I always think of that verse. True patience; true resignation. Such courage and patience ought to be rewarded, that is what I say. What I feel is that nothing is too good for dear Miss Blacklock, and whatever good things come to her, she truly deserves them."

"Money," said Miss Marple, "can do a lot to ease one's path in life."

She felt herself safe in this observation since she judged that it must be Miss Blacklock's prospects of future affluence to which her friend referred. (pp. 151–152)

"I'm sorry," she said. "It—it just came over me. What I've lost. She—she was the only link with the past, you see. The only one who—who remembered. Now that she's gone I'm quite alone."

"I know what you mean," said Miss Marple. "One is alone when the last one who remembers is gone. . . ."

"You understand very well," said Letitia Blacklock. (pp. 193–194)

Descriptive listening is a useful skill in helping others arrive at their own solutions to their problems. It allows the individual to search out

a solution while receiving support from a concerned listener. Descriptiveness requires careful listening and rephrasing without being judgmental. It encourages people to open up, it shows that the listener is indeed paying attention, and it forces the person with the problem to take responsibility for any decision made.

EMPATHY

Empathy is the ability to put oneself in the place of others and experience some of their feelings. One can empathize with positive as well as negative feelings. Empathy involves not only the emotional response of sympathy in unfortunate circumstances but also the sharing of joyful experiences. Empathy and sympathy are quite different responses. Sympathy implies feeling sorry for or feeling badly for someone in a state of distress. Empathy implies sharing

---

GOAL
Distinguish between empathy and sympathy.

Who's Wavin'

I ain't wavin babe, I'm drownin'.
Goin' down in a cold lonely sea.
I ain't wavin' babe, I'm drownin'.
So babe quit wavin' at me.

I ain't laughin' babe, I'm cryin'.
I'm cryin', oh why can't you see?
I ain't foolin' babe, I ain't foolin',
So babe quit foolin' with me.

This ain't singin' babe, it's screamin'.
I'm screamin' that I'm gonna drown.
And you're smiling babe, and you're wavin',
Just like you don't hear a sound.

I ain't wavin' babe, I'm drownin'.
Goin' down right here in front of you.
And you're wavin' babe, you keep wavin',
Hey babe, are you drownin' too?

Oh.

—Ric Masten
Stark Naked published by Sunflower Ink, Carmel, CA

sharing common feelings with others. It is easier for individuals to empathize with emotional states that they have experienced than to empathize with unfamiliar emotional states.

Observations of the actual behavior of the other person, what the other person says, and personal experiences with similar situations provide the information required to empathize. It is useful also to listen with eyes as well as ears and to note such nonverbal clues as facial expression, body position, posture, and gestures. An analysis of the match between verbal and nonverbal behavior will be helpful in determining the true meaning of the other's feelings. It is very important, also, in empathizing with another to attempt to remain objective and avoid emotional reactions. Empathic listening, a skill very similar to descriptive listening, is very appropriate for receiving another's self-disclosures in situations where individuals attempt to put themselves in the place of others.

Empathic listening involves making noncommittal responses like the following in an attempt to draw information from another person.

I see.	Really.
Oh.	You don't say.
Mm Hmm.	No fooling.
How about that.	You did?
Interesting.	Is that so.

These are responses that do not communicate ideas, judgment, or feelings that might change the meaning of the message. The responses do, however, invite the other person to share judgments, ideas, and feelings. The responses open the door and invite the person to talk. Other useful, more explicit responses include the following.

"Tell me about it."
"I'd like to hear more about it."
"Tell me more."
"I'd be interested in your point of view."
"Would you like to talk about it?"
"Let's discuss it."
"Let's hear what you have to say."

Often people are more than willing to share their joys and sorrows if only given the chance; and to empathize, the listener needs information. Descriptive listening, where the speaker's

Barbie Doll

A slender little waist.
A pretty little face.
That's Barbie with every hair in place
There's no rebellion in a Barbie Doll
There's just a little empty space.

Barbie Doll, Barbie Doll.
Oh, what a perfect world
This would be
If every little girl were a Barbie!
She loves to look her best
In a new expensive dress.
For Barbie this is happiness.
Invest your money in a Barbie Doll,
She's not the kind to protest.

. . . .

There's not a bit of strife
With a Barbie in your life
With a Barbie for your daughter or a wife.
No, there's not one problem with a Barbie Doll,
And also not a bit of life.

—Ric Masten
They Are All Gone Now published by Sunflower
Ink, Carmel, CA

ideas are restated in other words by the listener, can be useful too in gaining the information needed to empathize.

Listed below are some basic attitudes that must be present when one is attempting to empathize. When these attitudes are present one can more readily experience the feelings of another person.

1. You must want to hear what the person has to say. This means you are willing to take the time to listen. If you do not have time, you need only say so.
2. You must genuinely want to share the other's experiences at a given time. If you do not want to share at that time, wait until you do.
3. You must be genuinely able to react without judgment to feelings, whatever they may be or however different they may be

from your own feelings and from the feelings you think a person "should" have. This attitude takes time to develop.

4. You must have a deep feeling of trust in the person's capacity to handle feelings, to work through them, and to find solutions to problems. You'll acquire this trust by watching the person solve a given problem, not by trying to take responsibility for solving the problem.

5. You must appreciate that feelings are transitory, not permanent. Feelings change—hate can turn into love, discouragement may quickly be replaced by hope. Consequently, you need not be afraid to express feelings, since they will not become forever fixed.

Empathy implies caring, understanding, and valuing differences.

In addition to caring and understanding, empathy is dependent on recognition of others' values. If the empathizer can identify the values of the other person, data are gathered that contribute to other past observations and personal experience. The feelings of the other person can be more readily experienced if it can be assumed that the person's behavior results in part from a specific set of values. Generally individuals can more readily experience the feelings of others when their own experiences and values are similar to those of the other person. The question might arise as to how individuals empathize with others whose values differ significantly from their own. The interpersonal skill of behavioral flexibility can be quite useful in such situations. When two individuals do not share similar values, behavioral flexibility allows the empathizers to leave their own frames of reference and more accurately perceive the feelings experienced by others. It is a nonrigid response to an unusual or different experience.

With empathy, we must put the other person first. In many communication domains, we are trying to achieve our own goals and the other person is secondary. Covey (1989), in his *The Seven Habits of Highly Effective People*, suggests that empathy requires seeking first to understand and then to be understood. The

emotional bank account is an important concept that Covey ties to empathy. The emotional bank account is just like a financial bank account. We make deposits and withdrawals with those with whom we interact. We deposit kindness, courtesy, honestly, dependability. Actions like disrespect, interrupting, ignoring, taking advantage represent withdrawals.

In a relationship which typifies reciprocity there is a mutual trust and understanding along with an equal give and take of rewards. The relationship is based on equality. A relationship of reciprocity is contrasted to one where the give and take is out of balance. Sometimes, in a physician/patient or a teacher/student relationship, reciprocity is not a reasonable expectation. In most lasting friendships, however, reciprocity is evident.

If there is no reciprocity (give and take that is nearly equal) between two people, we tire of the relationship. Most of us will tire of always giving and getting nothing in return. Relationships where you do all the driving, pay for all the meals, do all the clean-up, and your companion does not reciprocate become one-sided, tedious. There is no empathy, no seeking first to understand, no sensitivity to another's needs.

GOAL
Demonstrate styles of conflict management.

Conflict Management

All communicators have experienced conflict, that is, situations where our desires and intentions are in opposition to those of another person and the alternatives seem to force one of the persons into a losing position. The situation should be viewed as a chance for finding new solutions rather than an angry response expressed by avoidance or aggression. Focus on solutions not on blame. Everyone can relate to previous experience with parent/child conflict, public authority conflict, conflict with rules, conflict with traditions of other cultures, supervisor/subordinate conflict, or professional conflict among peers. Conflict is to be expected in all of our relationships in which mutual respect for differences exists. Consider the following examples of conflict situations.

A child wants to stay up and watch TV; the parents want the child to go to bed.

The city bus company will not provide service on Sundays; some residents of the city will not be able to go to church.

Girls cannot wear shorts to school; they want to wear shorts so that they can participate in active sports in physical education.

An employee feels obligated to participate in a religious service on a Friday; Friday is the busiest day of the week at work.

A supervisor wants an employee to take a morning break at 10:15; the employee's friends take their breaks at 10:45.

One teacher believes that students should receive credit for class participation; another believes that grades should be based only on examination scores.

With the exception of hermits who isolate themselves from society, no one has been able to eliminate conflict from life. Most people feel that conflict is a bad and unhealthy state. Children are told to be polite and not to get angry or no one will like them. In some television and literature, the ideal family is portrayed as living happily ever after. In reality, every interpersonal relationship of any depth has conflict at some points in time. No matter how close two people seem to be, there will be times when their ideas will not match.

Conflict is generally viewed as a negative experience. Feelings often associated with conflict are anxiety, stress, tension, resentment, anger, disappointment, depression, and frustration. However, some positive outcomes can result from conflict situations. Conflict can provide a stimulus for the development of new and creative ideas and can, in fact, tend to strengthen interpersonal relationships. Therefore, learning to deal positively with conflict is one of the most important skills a communicator can acquire.

The common approach in conflict situations is for each participant to strive to defeat the other. Competitiveness generally results in the win-lose situation where one individual is pleased with the outcome and the other is displeased. A more appropriate outcome would be a win-win situation where both individuals are pleased with the solution. In fact, one of Covey's (1989) habits in *The Seven Habits of*

Highly Effective People is "think win/win." Although the previous win solutions for which both parties were striving might not be realized as originally conceived, both parties will leave the situation with positive feelings and channels of communication will remain open. Consider the following example.

Ed travels in his job and is home only on weekends. His wife, Susan, stays home all week with their two children. Susan does work part-time while the children are in school, but looks forward to going out or having guests on Friday and Saturday evenings. Ed would like to spend his weekend evenings at home alone with his family. The win-win solution on which they decided was to spend one evening out and one evening at home alone. The evening at home alone, however, would be planned with the same care as evenings with guests and would, therefore deviate from the normal routine that Susan found so boring.

The key to positive outcomes in conflict situations is a form of compromise, more specifically, collaboration. It requires a willingness to consider the values motivating the involved individuals, the ability to empathize with the other person's position, a desire to be behaviorally flexible in reacting to the expectations of the other individual, and accepting a modification of one's own expectations. Successful resolution and management of conflict REQUIRES all parties to be willing to consider a variety of options and solutions. Conflict management strategies WILL NOT WORK when one or more of the persons involved refuses to be flexible, avoids the issues by refusing to confront them, or just assumes a role of accommodation. Dealing with difficult people (see activity 9) requires different, although similar, approaches to reaching acceptable outcomes.

One way to handle conflict situations is to look at the problem objectively, that is, as if it belonged to someone else, and then to list as many solutions as possible. To provide meaningful alternatives the two parties in conflict must be willing to abandon their original objective and to attempt to develop some creative solutions. Once the possibilities have been identified they should be discussed for their possibilities as win-win solutions. That is, can the two parties in conflict be happy with the outcome? If so, then the proposed solution can be tried with both parties maintaining flexibility as the situation is worked out in a positive manner.

Conflict can be constructive or destructive depending on how you manage it. Some communication skills that are particularly useful in managing conflict are listed below. Try some of these as you attempt to achieve win-win solutions in areas of disagreement.

1. Be sure the timing is right and both parties are ready and willing to listen. Then, allow both parties to state the problem as each perceives it. Use "I" statements and avoid name calling or other put-downs. Both parties MUST be willing to consider compromise.
2. Actively listen in your role of receiver and use nonverbal signals to acknowledge the other person.
3. Ask clarifying questions and wait for an answer. "Why?" "Why not?" "Why are you saying this is the only answer?" "Have you considered an alternative?" Avoid accusatory questions like "How can you be so stupid?" Be sure that you have accurate information.
4. Keep the dialogue in the present and future. Avoid bringing up past transgressions.
5. Maintain focus on the topic of conflict. Avoid introducing other problems that will delay resolution of the current problem.
6. Search for areas of intersection—where agreement occurs.
7. End the discussion if it gets out of control but attempt to set a future time to resolve the conflict.
8. Consider asking your partner to use descriptive listening skills until you are comfortable that your position has been understood.
9. Request behavior changes not changes in attitudes or feelings.
10. Rather than suggesting that someone stop a behavior, suggest an appropriate substitute behavior.

11. Avoid conflicting verbal and nonverbal messages. Rely more on words to reflect negative feelings.

Conflict can arise from perceptions of reality emerging from different sets of experiences, from goals which are not complementary, from incompatible likes and dislikes, and from fear of the unknown. Collaboration can be facilitated by following these steps:

1. Eliminate "false" conflicts. Many seemingly important issues, when really considered, are actually not worth pursuing. Other major problems are reduced to insignificance when parties attempt to explain the problem in somewhat objective, less emotional contexts.
2. Analyze the interests of both parties and discover areas where goals coincide. Often the similarities which emerge will make a solution obvious.
3. Create an environment which will facilitate discussion. Sit side-by-side and treat each other as equals. Suggest possible solutions without passing judgment; be flexible and open-minded.
4. If mutually acceptable solutions do not emerge from any of the strategies above, consider making some low-priority concessions. Say, "I'll forego . . . What will you do for me?" Keep negotiating until a solution begins to emerge which has some appeal to both of you. It will not work to say, "I've already made concessions, now you have to give in." Be prepared with information that will help in solving the problem. Do your homework.

Much has been written on conflict as it occurs in a variety of settings. For instance, *Parent Effectiveness Training* (Gordon, 1970) treats parent-child conflict; *The Intimate Enemy* (Bach and Wyden, 1968) introduces the "fair fight" as a technique marriage partners might use to reduce conflict; and *Interpersonal Conflict Resolution* (Filley, 1975) treats conflict as it relates to business relationships. In the book *Men Are from Mars, Women Are from Venus* (Gray, 1992), the author explains gender differences in communication styles, emotional needs, and modes of behavior that often result in conflicts. Some material from Gray's book (pp. 11–13) that might help to resolve conflicts between men and women is listed as follows:

1. Men mistakenly offer solutions and invalidate feelings while women offer unsolicited advice and direction. . . .
2. Men tend to pull away and silently think about what's bothering them; women feel an instinctive need to talk about what is bothering them. . . .
3. Men are motivated when they feel needed whereas women are motivated when they feel cherished. . . . Men need to overcome their resistance to giving love and women must overcome their resistance to receiving love. . . .
4. A Martian/Venusian Phrase Dictionary translates misunderstood expressions. Women will learn what to do when a man becomes silent and men will learn to listen better. . . .
5. Different needs for intimacy exist. Men are like rubberbands—they get close and then pull away. . . . Women are like waves—they have low points and high points which men do not understand. . . .
6. Men and women give the type of love they want not what their partners want. Men primarily need love that is trusting, accepting, and appreciative. Women need love that is caring, understanding, and respectful. . . .
7. Men and women keep score differently in their emotional bank accounts. For women, the score is increased the same amount for any kind of positive gesture, whether big or small. Men feel that big gestures deserve more points. Also, men wait to be asked. Men want to be appreciated; women, to be supported. . . .
8. Men and women hide feelings differently. Rather than a direct confrontation, writing letters may work in expressing feelings. . . .
9. Women have a difficult time asking for support. Men commonly resist requests. . . .

Gray points out that conflict—problems, resentments, communication breakdowns, mistrust, rejection, and repression—can ruin even the most loving relationship. Perhaps he is right to suggest that much of what happens is the result of communicating from your own perspective rather than realizing that men and women are different. The next chapter on cross-cultural communication includes gender as a cultural difference and offers more possibilities for overcoming the gender communication barrier.

As in all communication situations, John Gray and other authors stress the importance of keeping open the channels for exchange of feelings and ideas. We can all change the way we deal with conflict. There can be no management of conflict if communication stops. When people fail to deal with conflict in a positive way a great deal of hurt can result. By using interpersonal skills to keep communication channels open, the possibility of a suitable solution for both parties exists. Remember, it is natural that the other party to the conflict perceives you to be in the wrong. Mark Twain said, "Nothing so needs reforming as other people's habits." Ask yourself the following questions as you contemplate what to do when you feel anger and conflict about to get out of control.

• Is conflict a normal part of human interaction in all types of settings? . . . can something good come out of this?
• Are there specific issues or beliefs that are getting in the way of finding a solution?
• What are some of my behaviors that might exacerbate the potential for negative feelings, mine and others, to continue?
• On what issues do we agree or disagree? Can we agree on a process for collaboration?
• How can we avoid a serious, on-going conflict which damages relationships and/or productivity?
• Have I used logic rather than feelings to find a win-win solution?

You have learned by now that you can only change your behavior, including how you react to others; you cannot change the behavior of others.

Summary

Recognition and awareness of one's own values and those of persons with whom communication takes place are important interpersonal communication skills. Messages sent and received are determined by the values—those things recognized as important—of both parties. Communicators can improve their interpersonal relationships by recognizing their own values and those of others and using this knowledge to interpret messages sent and received. Knowing standards of conduct, ethics, expected in specific situations enables individuals to make appropriate choices, also.

The skills of behavioral flexibility, descriptive listening, and empathy affect interpersonal communication. Behavioral flexibility refers to the skill involved in adapting to unfamiliar and possibly distressing situations rather than allowing habitual behavior to be the guide. Descriptive listening relies on paraphrasing to provide nonjudgmental responses to messages from individuals self-disclosing a problem situation. Empathy refers to the ability to put oneself in the place of another and thereby develop an understanding of the other's feelings. Behavioral flexibility, descriptive listening, and empathy are affected by the values of participants brought together in communication situations.

Values, ethics, behavioral flexibility, descriptive listening, and empathy are all important skills in relating to others. They have special importance in the positive management of conflict situations. By using appropriate interpersonal skills to keep communication channels open and providing accurate information on which to make choices, the win-lose outcome common to most conflict situations can possibly become a win-win outcome.

CHAPTER 9

MULTI-CULTURAL DIVERSITY

The purpose of this text and other texts which cover basic verbal and nonverbal skills is to facilitate personal growth in the ability to communicate with others. Communication competence is the ability to use knowledge of language, including grammar and syntax, along with understanding of perceptual processes to increase the clarity and effectiveness of interactions with others. Communication competence improves as language competence improves. Sharing the sound system, vocabulary, and the rules for combining thoughts with others facilitates the sharing of meaning. Communication competence varies from situation to situation. In some contexts, you will find it much easier to express yourself clearly, to give feedback and to feel confident that understanding occurs. With some new acquaintances, difficulty will arise in assuring that exchanges in messages and feedback are accurate.

Humans tend to feel comfort from sameness and similarity. When travelling to new places, why do many Americans flock to McDonald's and other restaurant chains for meals? For one reason, the travellers know and feel confident about the procedures for ordering food and what the product will be. They might live a few blocks from such establishments and seldom visit them at home, yet when away gravitate to the security of familiarity. Taking some risk and making a new acquaintance in food will many times be very rewarding. Likewise, in meeting new people, we tend to seek

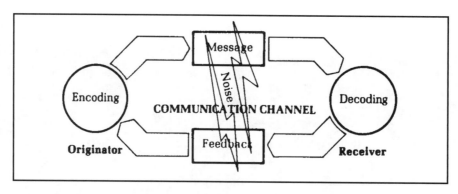

Figure 9.1. "Noise" interferes with understanding and sharing.

out those with whom we can immediately make a connection. Think of the times you have entered a new group, looked around and finally spotted someone with whom you felt you shared a common bond. We seek familiarity in interpersonal encounters because of fear of the unfamiliar and anxiety about accurate interpretations and predictions of others' behaviors.

Culture refers to the values, beliefs, norms, rules, and customs of a group of people that result in a somewhat specialized way of living. Enculturation refers to the passing forward of culture from one generation to the next. Not only parents and family but also peers, schools, religious institutions, and government are teachers of culture. Acculturation refers to acquiring the ways of another culture, usually though direct contact and by modifying native culture. Intercutural or multi-cultural communication refers to communication between persons who have different cultural beliefs, experiences, and backgrounds. To explore the various characteristics of different cultures, the Internet provides innumerable sources. Use your favorite Search Engine such as Google and enter the name of the culture, for example Christian or Muslin or Hindu, and you will find many interesting sites to explore. Investigate values, beliefs, customs, gender roles, family organization, art, food, religions, rituals, artifacts, clothing, and much more.

In establishing interpersonal relationships, common bonds are welcome but a willingness to question and explore will create new opportunities and expand

personal knowledge. Multi-cultural communication requires willingness to take risks and to seek new experiences as relationships with others who seem different are explored. Because the extent of shared values, attitudes, beliefs, and experiences may be diminished, more "noise" interacts with the encoding and decoding processes than would be expected when common bonds are shared. Norms and rules vary across cultures and expectations tend to be violated. To maximize effectiveness in multi-cultural communication domains, both sender and receiver must adopt new strategies and emphasize the skills which contribute to communication competence.

The purpose of this chapter is to show how the communication skills we all possess can be employed outside the context of similarity to increase the ability to communicate with those reflecting obvious differences. Multi-cultural communication is not a smattering of stereotypical elements reflecting identifiable groups. It is not only about global communication. Multi-cultural communication deals with the excitement of exploring differences. Multi-cultural communication deals with relationships within the ever-expanding diversity of communities as technology shrinks the world. Multi-cultural communication relates to a proactive attitude toward exploring differences and toward not automatically discounting those who fall outside our personal comfort zones for interaction. The chapter will include a description of multi-cultural communication, a discussion of communication across cultures, and suggestions for

GOAL

Describe the benefits of embracing a diverse culture.

improving competence in multi-cultural encounters.

Description of Multi-Cultural Communication

The world is populated by approximately six billion individuals who can be described along many dimensions. If we could shrink the earth's population to precisely 100 people, with all the existing human ratios remaining the same, it would look like something like the following (Harter, 2000). There would be:

57 Asians
21 Europeans
14 from the Western Hemisphere, both north and south
8 Africans

52 would be female
48 would be male

70 would be nonwhite
30 would be white

70 would be non-Christian
30 would be Christian

89 would be heterosexual
11 would be homosexual

6 people would possess 59 percent of the entire world's wealth ... and all 6 would be from the United States

80 would live in substandard housing

70 would be unable to read

50 would suffer from malnutrition

1 would be near death; 1 would be near birth

1 would have a college education

As you can see, you are very privileged.

All people share similarities when compared with some groups and reflect differences when contrasted with others. Multi-cultural communication relates to differences along such obvious dimensions as race, nationality, and geographical origins. It relates, also, to such readily discernable factors as gender, age, religion, education, and economic status. Areas such as interests, talents, ideologies, opinions,

---

A Memo from the Past

at 25
you can't imagine how frustrating it is
to be over 50
trying to explain something
to someone 25

to someone—who is twice as far away
from tomorrow
as i am

to someone—on whose person
things have not begun growing
and/or
started dropping off
and falling out of

to someone—who hasn't yet discovered
that being old
feels exactly like being young
with something wrong

and so
for those of you who maintain
chronological age is irrelevant
i have prepared a statement
to be opened and read when
they themselves turn fifty
a memo that goes:

greetings
know-it-all
and don't say i didn't tellya so.

(the anticipation of an event such as this
is incentive enough to keep me alive
for another 25 years)

—Ric Masten
Notice Me! published by Sunflower Ink,
Carmel, CA

and experience can create cultural differences, also. Even family backgrounds, health, sexual orientation, and physical abilities can create the impression of differences among people. In multi-cultural communication, decoding by the receiver is controlled by cultural variables not necessarily present in the encoding of the sender.

Culture is not defined by the differences listed in the paragraph above. Rather, culture evolves through reflections of such differences. Culture is the specialized lifestyle, the dynamic feature of relationships, of a group of people that has evolved from one generation to the next. Culture includes language, art, law, religion, artifacts, and beliefs and values. Culture is transmitted through learning not through inheritance. Culture is continually evolving and changing. The entire history of the world has been characterized by the transfer of advances from one group to another.

Multi-cultural communication refers to the ways that people share verbal and nonverbal symbols as they attempt to share perceptions of the world and achieve goals. By sharing across cultures, we can all gain. We can value the individuality of others without becoming like them or without asking them to change. We can choose to engage in transactions which reflect respect, esteem, and love of life or we can choose to engage in indifference, suspicion, apprehension, and reticence. We can know others without reflecting prejudice or expecting specific behaviors from them. Difficulty in communication arises because no two individuals share the same life experiences; differences are magnified as cultures are more diverse.

For some individuals, there is an ingrained resistance to change, a fear of what cultural diversity will do to the life they know and like now. Four types of anxiety in interactions with strangers have been identified (Gudykunst and Kim, 1992). Negative expectations arise from anticipating loss of self-esteem through feelings of discomfort and inadequacy—a self-fulfilling prophecy. Anxiety arises from the thoughts that strangers may attempt to take advantage of us, exploit or dominate us. Fear arises from anticipation that others may negatively stereotype us or reject and disapprove of us. Further, we may feel that our associates may disapprove of our interactions with strangers. Negative expectations,

anxiety, fear, and threat of disapproval, are generally diminished as multi-cultural experiences increase and confidence in embracing diversity grows. Again, the unknown causes anxiety when viewed negatively and causes excitement if viewed positively.

A useful model for studying multi-cultural communication (Beamer, 1992) includes the following five steps: acknowledging diversity, organizing information according to stereotypes, posing questions to challenge stereotypes, analyzing communication episodes, and generating other culture messages.

1. **Acknowledging diversity**—A most important step in multi-cultural communication is developing an awareness of differences. Often communicators rely on habit to respond or deny interest in order to protect a vulnerable self-image. Allowing natural curiosity and qualities of openness to emerge will enable one to transform culturally conditioned behaviors into the new behaviors of an interculturally competent person.

2. **Stereotyping**—Stereotypes provide limited insights into the characteristics of an individual identified by a label. Some stereotypes are simple and others contain layers of complexity. To communicate interculturally, one must recognize stereotypes and proceed beyond them. Stereotypes usually are based on easily identifiable variables such as gender, race, or signifiers of economic background. The stereotype is usually assigned to all members of the group and we assume all members of a group to be similar. We tend to stereotype our own group with positive descriptors; we tend to stereotype other groups with more negative descriptors. Stereotyping is helpful in that it allows us to categorize and systematize information. It provides a starting place in understanding a new acquaintance.

3. **Questioning stereotypes**—Questions must be asked in order to confirm or invalidate the stereotype. Stereotypes give the communicator a beginning, a way to formulate and test hypotheses. The outcomes of inquiry will create a new, more accurate

image of the other participant in the communication encounter. One must be careful, however, of the tendency to see behavior that conforms to expectations and to ignore behavior that does not fit. It is critical to question unconscious assumptions and to increase the complexity of the identities we assign to strangers. Constantly reevaluating your impressions is essential as familiarity can often disprove initial perception.

4. **Analyzing communication episodes**— After learning about the individual from generalized characteristics, specific communication domains can be analyzed more accurately. This stage goes from the generality of an impression to the distinctiveness of a specific message. In this step, we begin to relate to a new acquaintance as an individual and to interpret messages based on our knowledge of the person and not the group.

5. **Generating other culture messages**—Finally, the communicator acquires the competence to "walk in the other's shoes." In both sending and receiving messages, the communicator is able to initiate and interpret messages from the context of the different culture. We tend to attribute the behavior of others to their association with specific groups. As we learn more about others, we can see that their behavior is a product of the situation as well as their traits. We can shed the image that their behavior occurs due to their group membership.

Understanding that group memberships have affected the behaviors of an individual because of the role models, experiences, and teachings of the group is important. To become interculturally competent as a communicator takes an effort at applying communication skills that at first may not be automatic. To experience cultural diversity as a positive takes caring concern and commitment to personal growth and development. Remember the following communication skills as you meet and interact with people of diverse backgrounds: accept responsibility for your problems and

behaviors, work on productive pursuits rather than culture clash, and enhance relationships through mutual respect. You have the following choices when you observe someone from a different cultural background being mistreated.

1. You can ignore it.
2. You can pretend it did not happen—denial.
3. You can get involved with the other person and do something to help.
4. You can go to a higher authority about it but remain anonymous if you need to.

Communication across Cultures

Communication problems across cultures often occur because of two reasons: variations in norms of behavior judged to be inappropriate and misinterpretations of messages due to differing views and expectations of the world. Communicators who are experiencing difficulty will often try to adapt their behaviors and messages to their perceived expectations of the differing cultures. They will attempt to gain approval by acting less as themselves but more as they anticipate others would expect. They shift their communication style to become more like those with whom they are interacting. It is common to see television segments where an investigator is trying to get information from someone in a subculture. The investigator will often adopt the speech patterns of the person from whom the information is being sought. Some research has shown, however, that too much adaptation will be viewed as presumptuous whereas moderate adaptation is viewed as sensitive and respectful.

Even when the obvious signs point to an individual from one culture adopting some of the symbols of another culture, assuming that cultural differences have been erased is probably an error. In the early 80s, women's business dress mirrored that of men's. Women often wore two-piece gray, tailored suits; crisply starched blouses with silk bows; and dark, low-heeled pumps. That women adapted the style of the stereotypical, successful business man

GOAL
Discuss how cultural differences affect the way we communicate.

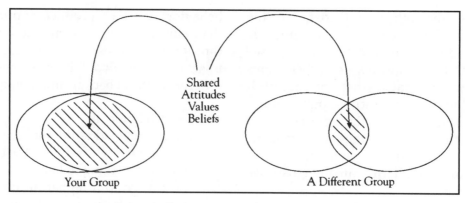

Figure 9.2. Intersection of Value, Attitudes, and Beliefs

did not make women perform in business roles in the same way as men. Women still had a background of very different role-models and experiences which enabled them to achieve success in different ways. Rather than letting appearances dictate perceptions, it is important to increase sensitivity, give more attention to detail, and perhaps even change basic behavioral patterns. Many women, dressed in business suits, did not relate well to the locker room humor that they were sometimes subjected to. We all bring our cultural baggage with us—conjecture, images, biases, and perspectives.

Recognize that new acquaintances are often different than you in attitudes, values, and beliefs. Recognize, understand, and respect the fact that differences in perceptions and motivations exist. Attempt to be neutral as you explore the other individual's characteristics. Be non-judgmental and recognize that different norms are guiding the behavior of others. Attempt to learn about others and savor the excitement of expanding your horizons. This is not to say that you must adopt the values and behaviors of another culture. Your critical listening and thinking skills will enable you to openly view the behaviors of the other culture and determine how you relate to them. Multi-cultural communication skills require that you avoid the mindless assumption that others' ways are categorically wrong. Multi-cultural communication skills do NOT suggest that you mindlessly assume others' behaviors are always right. Once you understand another's culture, you may decide that some mores are senseless or even cruel. That is your right as an independent thinker.

Consider the fact that in some cultures unwanted children are left in the elements to die—this is often a female child born into a family who desires a male heir. In some countries, children are forced to work long hours under conditions that most Americans would perceive to be lacking in adequate nutrition and education. Does multi-cultural communication mean that we must accept infanticide, slavery, or such atrocities as Hitler and his followers committed? Absolutely NOT! It suggests that we might attempt to understand the conditions that lead to behaviors we perceive to be atrocities and, therefore, exercise the critical choices that we all make about what we will value.

Ethnocentrism plays a role in difficulties that arise in multi-cultural communication. Ethnocentrism refers to identification with our own cultural group and our tendency to apply the values and mores of our group to individuals from other groups. We tend to judge the behaviors of our group to be the correct way, the right way, the moral way. We view the ways of our group as superior to the ways of other groups. Establishing group identities is important in forming our self-image and in moving up the scale of Maslow's hierarchy of needs toward self-actualization. We like to feel wanted and a part of society. Ethnocentrism becomes negative when it leads to hostility and conflict between groups or when one group feels that they must change others to their ways of behaving. High levels of ethnocentrism can cause individuals to make inaccurate assumptions about individuals from other groups and can contribute to the misinterpretations that so often occur between people who cannot shed their stereotypes of others.

Multi-cultural communication requires some effort. Passive listening, habitual speech patterns, and perceptual constancy are not the characteristics of one who is delving into the excitement of diversity. Some personal characteristics of importance in multi-cultural communication are flexibility, adaptability, tolerance of ambiguity, empathy, high self-esteem, sensitivity, caring, and willingness to adjust and change. Risk-taking is perhaps paramount since the similarity/acceptance paradigm is abandoned and the chances of rejection are increased. A script is a term that reflects rule-governed, habitual behaviors that we automatically use often without thinking. We adopt such pattern of behavior through our culture, geographical location, ethnicity, religion, gender, age, parents and other role models. A good communicator uses critical analysis to determine which scripts are valid and which need to be discarded.

Suggestions for Multi-Cultural Communication

Cultural similarity is not a prerequisite for establishing effective interpersonal relationships. Multi-cultural communication opportunities can occur in many different circumstances. Often one happens into a situation where habitual communication patterns will not suffice or language barriers exist. Other times, individuals make a concerted effort to broaden their cultural perspectives and seek opportunities for enrichment. Sometimes business and professional responsibilities will require negotiation with someone from another culture. Some suggestions for dealing with these different situations follow.

GENERAL SUGGESTIONS

All of the communication skills in this book and other similar books are even more important as you attempt to improve your ability to send and receive messages within the more complicated arena of cultural diversity. Several of the skills are repeated here for reinforcement.

1. Practice the concept of equality when experiencing differences rather than the more personally safe inclination of superiority.
2. Demonstrate a sincere attempt to empathize and seem caring of the other person.
3. Increase the accuracy of your interpersonal perceptions by formulating hypotheses not conclusions, by analyzing contradictory clues, and being aware of your own biases.
4. Encourage others to self-disclose by demonstrating a sincere interest in what they have to say.
5. Use descriptive listening skills to learn about another as that person self-discloses.
6. Reveal a willingness to be behaviorally flexible even when your initial reaction is to reject the other's position.
7. Adopt a demeanor which expresses a tendency toward being objective as opposed to being valuative—be non-judgmental.
8. Emphasize collaboration, cooperation, and support and a willingness to experiment and be spontaneous.
9. Reject signs of status or supremacy.
10. Phrase your viewpoints with tentativeness rather than certainty.
11. Consider the various angles of perceiving an event—be adaptable.
12. Appear active, energetic, enthusiastic and dynamic.
13. Arrange for opportunities to include the other and to experience enjoyable activities together.
14. Display characteristics of trustworthiness, be someone that can be depended upon.
15. Be aware that others with whom you attempt to communicate may not be open-minded and willing to explore differences.

GENDER DIFFERENCES

We interact with those of the opposite sex so often that we might not think of such relationships as multi-cultural. Men and women do look at the world through different eyes and numerous interpersonal conflicts arise due to different styles of communication. Although scientific evidence is

> **GOAL**
> Employ strategies for overcoming cultural barriers to communication.

not available for confirmation, some writers and comedians like to present gender differences. In early civilization, women were viewed as "gatherers" and men as "hunters." These roles have perpetuated even into the present where a look at the shopping behaviors of men and women confirms the hypothesis. A common stereotype shows women wandering through the shopping mall evaluating the merchandise before making a final selection. Men, on the other hand, zero in on the object of their search, make the kill, and go home. Are we still living the roles of hunter and gatherer?

Some of the commonly cited research findings about gender are the following:

1. Gender differences in communication are not biological. They are learned behaviors resulting from your own and others' reaction to your biological sex.
2. Males tend to be ambitious, deliberate, aggressive, logical, stubborn, outspoken, and dominant whereas females tend to be sophisticated, tactful, gentle, kind, sentimental, lovable, and moody.
3. Males tend to talk to other males about business and sports. Females talk to other females about men, clothing and furnishings, and other women. Males and females

---

GOAL

Discuss the impact of gender differences on communication between males and females.

---

tend to talk about amusing events and themselves. Both males and females tend to self-disclose more to females than to males. Males tend to have difficulty verbalizing emotions and expressing intimacy. Females are better at decoding nonverbal messages than are males.

4. Differences occur in the choice of vocabulary. Men are more direct and more likely to express hostility and use profanity. Women have larger vocabularies, tend to soften messages, use qualifiers like "maybe," and make statements in the form of questions (e.g., "Are we going to be late?" when they know that they will be late).
5. Men are more likely to dominate a conversation and interrupt; women are more sensitive to turn taking.
6. Voice quality, which is biological, affects perception of a message. A deeper, louder, quality is perceived as more assertive than a softer, higher-pitched quality.
7. Differences in same-sex touch are common. For example, women are more likely to hug other women than men are likely to hug other men. Males interact at larger distances than females whereas females are more willing to tolerate violations of personal space.

Gender Differences

Females	Males
Tend to ask questions.	Feel questions are intrusive meddling.
Share secrets.	Conceal personal feelings.
Use words to keep conversation flowing.	Use words to dominate.
Use more nonverbal listening signals.	Use listening signals when in agreement.
Use "silent protest" to counter interruptions.	Comment throughout conversation.
Avoid sounding mean and controlling.	Give orders to show dominance.
Base friendships on equality.	Base friendships on status and power.

8. Females must be aware that their voices may not be heard. Females have softer, quieter voices and tend to be more polite and sensitive to the other side in a dispute. Females who are competing in a male-dominated situation should increase proactivity and be less passive. Males who are competing in a female-dominated situation should appear more understanding and sensitive. This is not to say that either gender should adopt the patterns of the other, but rather to be aware of the expectations that might exist when opposite gender communication has high stakes.

Keep in mind that the research findings just summarized are based on generalities and that many males and females provide examples of exceptions. Also, gender communication is changing. As the traditional roles of women and men have changed in the last half century, the communication between men and women has evolved to the expectation of equality. Women expect to have a voice and to be listened to. Likewise, men have the same expectations. When one gender dominates a group, both men and women are wise to keep in mind that gender can create a bias.

PEOPLE WITH DISABILITIES

The Americans with Disabilities Act of 1990 brought to the attention of mainstream America the importance of inclusion for those with mobility, auditory, and visual disabilities. This landmark civil rights legislation pointed out the importance of providing accommodation to a group that had often been excluded in the past. Many types of buildings and spaces are covered by the legislation such that disabled Americans must be provided access. In the time since the legislation was adopted, evidence of accessibility abounds in our society. Look around you to see ramps (e.g., cut curbs for parking), braille (adjacent to numbers in elevators), and sound cues (ringing in an elevator to indicate floors). As you read the above sentences, you should have noticed that the word handicapped was not used at all to describe inclusion of those with disabilities. No one wants to be handicapped. Handicapped refers to inability to fulfill the normal functions of

daily living—bathing, dressing, using a toilet, preparing food, running errands, enjoying entertainment, and much more. Although you might enjoy occasionally being pampered and waited on, no one wants to be handicapped. Design professionals have made enormous strides in developing products and spaces to allow people of all ages and physical status to be independent. Be sure that you use the proper vocabulary.

1. Handicapped—a negative word that you should remove from your vocabulary, to indicate physical limitations resulting in the inability to fulfill normal, daily activities.
2. Disability—physical condition which needs accommodation to permit independence. Sometimes used interchangeably with the term impairment.
3. Accommodation—the condition of being made suitable in order to reach an objective.
4. Accessibility—through appropriate design considerations, a space is made useable by someone with a disability.

Many of us are visually *impaired*. Through the *accommodation* of glasses or contact lenses, we are able to have *access* to such aspects of daily living as driving a car or viewing a film. Without the *accommodation*, we might very well be *handicapped* and dependent on someone else to transport us or to describe the scenes in a film. Proper use of the terminology requires, therefore, that we refer to an *accessible* parking place or an *accessible* toilet.

LANGUAGE BARRIERS

Language specialists have developed some suggestions for negotiating meaning without knowledge of another's native language. The techniques make it possible for non-English speakers to use knowledge of English that they already have to acquire information from you.

1. Speak at a slow, but natural rate of speech.
2. Use clear, but not exaggerated articulation.
3. Use longer strategic pauses between phrases, but not words, to allow time for decoding.

4. Project slightly louder than usual, but at not an offensively loud volume—no yelling.
5. Incorporate exaggerated, but culturally acceptable, intonation and gestures, for emphasis or clarification.
6. Reduce use of idioms, slang, and regionalism.
7. Use words that are heard most commonly in English. Try synonyms.
8. Use nouns rather than substituting pronouns with implied antecedents.
9. Define terms, by listing examples and drawing analogies and parallels.
10. Use gestures, pictures, and the immediate surroundings, including the persons themselves, to illustrate a point. Be visual.
11. Use simplified syntax, avoiding use of complex sentences requiring transitions.
12. Help the listener complete utterances by providing a possible answer to a question.
13. Use their language even if you know only a few phrases.

CULTURAL PERSPECTIVES

Learning about the customs and rituals, fiestas and folklore of specific groups is useful but not enough to develop a cultural perspective. Rather than accumulating a knowledge of isolated bits of information, it is enlightening to experience cultural diversity and sensitivity in your own life. Several recommendations for accomplishing this follow:

1. Remember that the words you use convey images not only of the referent but of you. The casual use of terms that promote prejudice makes a big impression especially on young children who are developing language skills.
2. Get a globe, a map, or an atlas. When events occur or you meet people from other countries, you can identify the location and better relate to the event or person.
3. Investigate the origins of the food you eat. Many American regionalisms exist— Virginia ham—and many popular foods have very specific foreign origins—tortillas that exist in various forms in Tex-Mex food.
4. Participate in the many festivals and events that celebrate the traditions of other countries. Most areas have some sort of Oktoberfest. Where did this originate?
5. Analyze your friendships. Most of us have cherished relationships with some others who are different. How did these relationships evolve and what do they mean to us?

The Punch and Judy Show

trying hard to understand human nature
i
having pacifist leanings
find my son learning karate
breaking bricks with his bare hands
so that he could kill a man
in two seconds
he says smiling
as i go up the wall
and i
being the son of militant ex-catholic
atheist parents
*   get myself ordained a minister*
much to the disgrace of my old mother
whose reedy voice calls me on the phone

*   ricky!—she squeaks*

as always speaking
like a Punch and Judy show
and i as always looking
for the alligator to jump up
and hit her with a stick

*   ricky!—she squawks*

*   you're not gonna let them*
*   put Reverend in front of your name*
in the phone book are you?

now
i suppose all this explains
why the grandparents and the grandchildren
usually get along so well

they have a common enemy

—Ric Masten
Notice Me! published by Sunflower Ink,
Carmel, CA

6. If your community offers few opportunities for cultural diversity, seek other avenues. Consider getting a penpal or participating in a foreign exchange visit. Buy the Sunday paper from a large city near your home and find out what events are planned that would broaden your perspective on the world.

7. Recognize that the ways that historical facts are presented sometimes portray events self-serving to a dominant group. Liberty and justice have not been readily available to all Americans. Women did not have the opportunity to vote until 1920. Be flexible as you reflect on history.

8. Explore your own cultural history. We all like to focus on ourselves and we often find interesting facts in our ancestral heritage. Very few Americans have all their ancestors from the same nationality. For example, people born in some regions of the country are quite likely to have a Native American ancestor. We can expand our relationships with others by learning more about ourselves.

9. Use media and library resources as an avenue for growing culturally. Reflect on news and literature as they communicate differences among groups.

10. Examine your feelings about cultural differences. Consider descriptors that might set people apart—gender, religion, age—and reflect on your culture and experiences.

BUSINESS AND PROFESSIONAL SUGGESTIONS

Many business and professional dealings in our shrinking global economy include elements of cultural diversity. Often language is a major factor with the need for translation as well as an understanding of the differing systems of conducting business and cementing relationships. Below are a few do's and don'ts for cross cultural negotiations (Herbig and Kramer, 1992).

1. Do know your subject and be well prepared.
2. Do specify clear objectives and know your bottom line.
3. Do develop personal relationships but be careful not to be manipulated.
4. Do seek opportunities for informal get-togethers since that is where initial contacts will be made.

5. Do meticulously follow protocol: foreigners may be more status conscious than Americans.
6. Do understand national sensitivities and do not violate them.
7. Do assess flexibility of your opponent and the obstacles he or she faces.
8. Do understand the decision-making process and build up your position by taking advantage of each step.
9. Do pin down details.
10. Don't look at everything from your own definition of what determines a rational and scientific viewpoint.
11. Don't press a point if others are not prepared to accept it.
12. Don't look at things from your own narrow self-interest.
13. Don't ask for concessions or compromises that are politically or culturally sensitive.
14. Don't stick to your agenda if the other party has a different set of priorities.
15. Don't use jargon that may confuse the other side.
16. Don't skip authority levels since you will need middle management to implement the agreement.
17. Don't ask for a decision that you know the other side can't or isn't ready to make.
18. Don't differ with members of your own team in public.
19. Don't stake out extreme positions; be consistent in your approach.

One might argue that Americans (since the United States is only one nation among many in the Americas, do we have the right to use this name?) have no choice but to learn skills to facilitate multi-cultural communication. Readily available statistics emphasize such realities as the growth in the so-called minority populations, the numbers of non-English speaking groups that have immigrated to the United States, the growing global economy, and the rapid rate at which messages can be carried to all corners of the Earth. No one today can afford to bury themselves in a homogeneous subculture and expect life to continue without change. This necessity of adapting to a changing world is motivation enough to improve multi-cultural communication competence. On the other hand, the excitement of willingly learning about yourself and about others is more exciting! Living the full richness of a diverse world ensures a closeness with others and avoidance of a lonely existence.

Summary

Multi-cultural communication occurs in situations where we attempt to communicate and interact with others whose backgrounds and values are different than our own. Such diversity is not only associated with country of birth or national origin but also emerges with age, gender, religion, socio-economic, and educational variables. Humans tend to find comfort in the familiar and often hesitate to initiate new experiences. Multi-cultural communication occurs when we make a proactive attempt to explore differences and remain open to communicating with others whose values, attitudes, and beliefs may differ from our own. Multi-cultural communication competence builds on the interpersonal communication skills used in familiar encounters. Multi-cultural communication requires greater effort, however, because the greater differences create noise in the communication channel. Being flexible, open, and non-judgmental are very important characteristics in multi-cultural communication.

Loneliness

Standing by a highway
Waiting for a ride
A bitter wind blowing
Keeps you cold inside.
A line of cars is passing
No one seems to care
You look down at your body
To be sure you are there.
Sitting in a hotel
Staring at the walls
With cracks across the ceiling
And silence in the halls,
You open up the window
And turn the TV on
Then you go down to the lobby
But everyone's gone.
    And this is loneliness
    The kind that I have known,
    If you've had times like this
    My friend
    You're not alone.
So you leave the empty city
And go down to the shore
You're aching to discover
What you're looking for.
The beaches are deserted
In the morning time
A solitary figure

You walk the water line.
Come upon a tidepool
And stand there peering in.
And when you touch the water
The circles do begin.
They lead to where a seabird
Lies crumpled on the sand
So you take a single pebble
And hold it in your hand.
    And this is loneliness
    Another kind I've known,
    If you've had times like this
    My friend
    You're not alone.
You come back up the beaches
At the end of day
And see how all your footprints
Have been washed away.
No
Nothing lasts forever
We are born to die,
So may I say I love you
Before I say goodbye.
I must say I love you

And now I'll say goodbye.

—Ric Masten
Notice Me! published by Sunflower Ink, Carmel, CA

Activity 1

Information about
Interpersonal Communication

Preparation: Read Part 3: Interpersonal Communication. Prepare for a test by answering the practice items given below.

Practice Items

PART 3: OVERVIEW

1. Where is the emphasis placed in interpersonal communication?
2. What are several variables that affect the outcomes of interpersonal communication?

CHAPTER 7

1. Where do individuals often place blame for unsatisfactory interpersonal encounters?
2. What does owning feelings and thoughts imply?
3. To what does denial of feelings refer?
4. What is one goal for effective communication?
5. Why is it useful to consider the message, the feelings, and the intent of the sender in interpersonal communication?
6. What is meant by an operational description?
7. How would you define self-disclosure in interpersonal relationships?
8. Why does self-disclosure require courage?
9. What are the five levels of self-disclosure according to Powell?
10. What are eight of the most common suggestions in the list of assertive rights?
11. What is the purpose of assertive behavior?
12. How is assertive behavior different from aggressive behavior?
13. What are four aspects of the assertive personality?
14. What is often a first step in becoming more assertive?
15. What are three areas that are especially important in creating a positive image in a potential employer's eyes?
16. What is the purpose of the letter of application?
17. When the interviewer begins to talk about a position, what should the applicant keep in mind?
18. What differentiates behavioral interviewing from requests for factual information?

CHAPTER 8

1. What are "values"?
2. How can values be faked?
3. What are five ways that people acquire values?
4. What is the purpose of the "values clarification" movement?
5. How are values directly related to self-esteem?
6. Why should a communicator consider others' values?
7. What are two professions that follow a code of ethics?

8. What forms the basis for trust in interpersonal relations?
9. How do people demonstrate they are behaviorally flexible?
10. What is descriptive listening?
11. What is the goal of descriptive listening?
12. What is meant by non-descriptive listening?
13. What is empathy?
14. What are several basic attitudes that must be present when one is attempting to empathize?
15. What are the feelings that often accompany conflict?
16. What is meant by a win-win solution in a conflict situation?

CHAPTER 9

1. What is the definition of communication competence?
2. What are the names of 10 dimensions used to describe differences in cultural identity?
3. What are some characteristics of culture?
4. What are the four types of anxiety which occur in interactions with strangers?
5. Why is stereotyping described as good and why is it described as bad?
6. What are two reasons for explaining why communication problems occur across cultures?
7. Why is it an error to assume that cultural differences have been erased when you observe someone adopting the characteristics of a different culture?
8. Why should you avoid the automatic reaction of assuming that characteristics of other cultures are automatically right or automatically wrong?
9. What is the meaning of ethnocentrism?
10. What are some characteristics of an individual who is multi-culturally competent in communication?
11. What are four general suggestions for improving multi-cultural communication across genders?
12. What are the meanings of the terms handicapped, disabled, accommodation, and accessibility?
13. What are four suggestions for overcoming language barriers in multi-cultural communication?
14. What are four suggestions for developing a broader cultural perspective?
15. What are four suggestions for becoming more competent in business and professional interactions involving varied cultures?

Group Activity: Follow course instructions to complete the test for Part 3.

Individual Activity: Make arrangements with your instructor to complete the test for Part 3.

Activity 2

Critical Communication Skills in the World of Work

Preparation: Important tasks of college students include gaining general knowledge as well as preparing for entering the work force upon graduation. Employers will often look for employees with specific speech communication skills. A Task Force on Competencies for Speaking and Listening was commissioned by the Educational Policies Board of the Speech Communication Association in Arrandale, Virginia. The result of their study was the development of the following survey reporting evidence that people in career areas feel communication activities play an important role in the job success of entry-level workers. It lists essential and necessary skills but does not report what is considered a minimum level of communication competency.

Read the following survey. Respond by placing a plus by those speaking and listening skills in which you feel adequate. Place a zero by those areas in which you feel additional work is needed.

What Are the Critical Communication Skills?

Three groups of oral communication skills were identified by respondents to the survey as Absolutely Essential or Very Necessary to those entering the work force. Over 80 percent listed the first group of eight skills in this category. The second group of 10 skills was identified as Absolutely Essential or Very Necessary by 70 percent to 80 percent of respondents, and the third group of 10 skills was identified as such by 60 percent to 70 percent of respondents. Over 50 percent of respondents felt that the fourth group of 16 skills was Necessary, Very Necessary, or Absolutely Essential.

Over 80 Percent Response

SPEAKING SKILLS
_____ Use words understood by others.
_____ Use words, pronunciation, and grammar which do not alienate others.
_____ Phrase questions in order to obtain information.
_____ Explain specific requirements to others.

LISTENING SKILLS
_____ Understand directions.
_____ Obtain necessary information.
_____ Identify important points when given oral instructions.
_____ Recognize when another does not understand a message.

70–80 Percent Response

SPEAKING SKILLS
_____ Provide thorough responses to others.
_____ Organize messages so that others can understand them.
_____ Use appropriate rate, volume, and clarity in face-to-face situations with others.
_____ Use appropriate rate, volume, and clarity when talking on the telephone.
_____ Use language appropriate to different listeners.

LISTENING SKILLS
_____ Understand suggestions of others.
_____ Understand questions of others.

_____ Understand complaints and needs of others.
_____ Distinguish between facts and opinions.
_____ Understand expectations of others.

60–70 Percent Response

SPEAKING SKILLS

_____ Teach others to perform tasks.
_____ Explain/demonstrate a process or technique.
_____ Use appropriate facial expressions and tone of voice when talking to others.
_____ Use a chronological order to explain a complex procedure.

LISTENING SKILLS

_____ Restate information given by others.
_____ Recognize intent of others, for example: threats, commands, promises.
_____ Make a clear/concise oral report.

INTERACTION SKILLS

_____ Maintain friendly relationships with clients, customers, co-workers.
_____ Be able to resolve conflict.
_____ Work cooperatively in groups.

Over 50 Percent Response

SPEAKING SKILLS

_____ Use questions which aid others in learning to perform a specific task.
_____ Express and defend points of view with evidence.
_____ Use appropriate persuasive strategies.
_____ Use sufficient volume when making a presentation to a large group.

LISTENING SKILLS

_____ Distinguish between informative and persuasive messages.
_____ Recognize specific persuasive techniques.
_____ Express and defend views in meetings.

INTERACTION SKILLS

_____ Ask questions in a manner that results in cooperation.
_____ Recognize feelings of others.
_____ Express reactions to supervisors about changes in job.
_____ Suppress feelings in appropriate situations.
_____ Describe opposing points of view.
_____ Express satisfaction to co-workers about their work.
_____ Express feelings of satisfaction/dissatisfaction to appropriate persons.
_____ "Break the ice" in first encounters with people.
_____ Describe differences in opinion between selves and others.

Group Activity: After completing the Survey, evaluate your responses. In groups of four discuss your responses and a specific plan for improving your communication skills.

Individual Activity: After completing the Survey, evaluate your responses. Write a one page paper listing a specific plan of action for improving specific weaknesses you have noted in the areas of speaking, listening, and interaction.

Activity 3

Interpersonal Video Project

Preparation: Popular movies are a great source of examples for illustrating interpersonal communication techniques and theories including cultural patterns. As you watch popular films, notice the interpersonal interactions and cultural variables that are portrayed and select one that you feel illustrates an interpersonal skill from this section of the book. Limit your selection to a scene that is from two to seven minutes long. To save time in class, cue the video to the exact place that you want to start the illustration. If you think the class will not follow the scene without some background, be sure to fill in VERY BRIEFLY the critical information needed to understand your example. Some examples of film titles follow:

Warning—Be respectful regarding the subject matter and rating of the film.

- When Harry Met Sally—Relationship Stages
- Guess Who's Coming to Dinner—Flexibility
- Shirley Valentine—Owning Feelings
- Remember the Titans—Descriptive Listening
- Twelve Angry Men—Stereotyping
- Million Dollar Baby—Gender Identity
- Hotel Rwanda—Values
- The Breakfast Club—Self-disclosure
- Mambo Kings—Goal Setting
- The Big Chill—Intimacy
- Father of the Bride—Conflict
- Rudy—Confidence

Analyze the following points of the scene you choose to show.

1. Record the name of the film and the year of its release.

2. Briefly state the names of the characters who appear in the scene.

3. Is humor used to make a point?

4. What is the level of intimacy that exists among or between the characters?

5. Which interpersonal skills—empathy, self-disclosure, assertiveness, owning feelings, and so forth—are evident in the scene?

6. What nonverbal behaviors have you noticed that seem essential to the message?

7. What level and type of listening skills are evident?

8. What cultural factors—gender, age, religion, national origin, other—emerge?

Group Activity: Bring your film to class, show your segment, and then lead a discussion to determine if the class drew the same conclusions that you did about the scene. Reveal answers to the above questions as needed. End your discussion by briefly explaining what you have learned about your own interpersonal communication style from analyzing this scene.

Individual Activity: Follow the instructions for the group activity. Convene your own audience of about two to four people to comment on your example. Write a summary of the scene, the answers to the questions, and the reaction of your audience. End with a written paragraph about what you learned about your own communication style.

Activity 4

Empathy

Preparation: Recall an event in your life where you used or SHOULD have used one of the following communication concepts.

1. Assertiveness	6. Credibility	11. Self-disclosure
2. Behavioral Flexibility	7. Empathy	12. Stress Management
3. Body Language	8. Ethics	13. Time Management
4. Communication Style	9. Listening	14. Values Clarification
5. Conflict Management	10. Self-esteem	15. Owning Feelings

Using the first person, write and be able to tell your story. An example of one individual's story is given below.

EXAMPLE: Self-esteem

I asked my husband what he wanted for his birthday and as usual did not get a specific answer. This made me think about sharing some of the knowledge I was acquiring in college. I came to this class thinking that I was fairly together and had been unable to perceive any changes in my communication skills. I decided to ask some family members if they had noticed any changes. I was surprised by their comments because they told me about improvements in areas that I had not realized were problems.

1. I have become more assertive and better able to deal with intimidating people, especially on the phone.

2. I have improved in finishing one thought per sentence.

I laughed with my family about these problems. They said that they had been able to tell to whom I was talking on the phone just by my non-verbal actions and pitch and rhythm of my voice. They also told me that I had spent a lot of time speaking and never getting my point across. I now realize this class is a "starter kit" that helps people get what they want from life. Effective communication tools are a most wonderful gift to acquire.

Group Activity: In front of the entire class, if time permits, or in small groups, tell your story. As you listen to the stories of others, attempt to empathize and experience another's feelings. Totally absorb all of the data, both verbal and nonverbal that are being communicated. Resist the temptation to be judgmental. Strive to listen with empathy to what is being said.

Individual Activity: Locate a friend or relative to serve as your partner. Ask your partner to reveal an experience about one of the topics listed above. Remember to be understanding as you listen. Totally absorb all of the data, both verbal and nonverbal that are being communicated. By "hearing" both content and effect of each statement, you can assist your partner in expressing thoughts and feelings in a clear and complete fashion. Resist the temptation to judge or evaluate the comments. Strive to listen with empathy to what is being said. Then repeat the process as you reveal your responses to the questions above and your partner empathizes. Finally, prepare a written report of both experiences and your experience at self-disclosure and empathizing.

Activity 5

Values Clarification

Preparation: Use the format below to express some of your values.

1. In column 1, list ten areas that you value. Examples might be money, love, sex, marriage, family, freedom, education, religion, leisure time, and health.

2. In column 2, describe what you learned about each value as you were growing up.

3. In column 3, write the name and relationship of the person from whom you learned the information in column 2. If you learned on your own through experience, write "EXP."

4. In column 4, indicate the extent to which you now agree with the statement in column 2 by writing strongly agree (SA), partially agree (PA), neutral or don't know (DK), partially disagree (PD), or strongly disagree (SD).

Value	Statement about Value	Name and Relationship	Agreement
EXAMPLE Education	It's essential to obtain a college degree.	Ms. Rogers, teacher	PA
1.			
2.			
3.			
4.			
5.			
6			
7.			
8.			
9.			
10.			

Group Activity: In groups of four discuss the areas that you value and the reasons you acquired the value.

1. Did someone moralize to you about the issue?

2. Was the belief imposed on you by someone?

3. Did you adopt the belief from someone who serves as a role model for you?

4. Did you acquire the value from your own experience?

5. Did you weigh several alternatives and make your own free choice?

6. Did you acquire many of your values in the same way?

7. Discuss with your group similarities and differences that you identify within your own list and through comparisons with your list and the lists of your group members.

8. How do your values differ from people of other cultures with whom you interact on a regular basis?

Individual Activity: Give your lists of ten areas that you value to someone who knows you well. Ask that person to provide the information about you for columns 2, 3, and 4. Briefly describe in writing the similarities and differences in the two perceptions of the areas you value.

Activity 6

Descriptive Listening

Option 1—Interpersonal Communication Situation

Preparation: What areas in your life are you willing to share with others? Listed below are topics you may or may not feel comfortable discussing. Give thought to several topics so you can express feelings to a listener who will try to be nonjudgmental.

1. Religious doubts	11. Taking drugs
2. A first love	12. Abortion
3. Problems with parents	13. Marriage problems
4. Negatives about friends	14. Financial problems
5. Weight control	15. Cost of your house
6. Innermost desires	16. Racial prejudices
7. Present salary	17. Jealousy
8. A personal problem	18. Birth control
9. Health problems	19. Cheating
10. Thoughts of suicide	20. Child discipline

Group Activity: Choose a class member to whom you feel you can relate well. Ask your partner to listen to your feelings about one of the topics from the above list. Watch your partner for signs of making judgments about your feelings. Encourage your listener to be nonjudgmental. Pause to let your listener paraphrase what you have said. Was your listener able to be descriptive or did opinions and judgments enter the conversation?

Then reverse roles so that your partner can express feelings about a topic and you can serve as listener. Use your descriptive listening skills; paraphrase what the speaker says. Be especially careful not to evaluate or give your opinion about what was said.

If time allows, change partners and topics until you have talked on several topics and to several people. After you have practiced descriptive listening return to the full group and discuss the experience. How do you feel as a speaker? How do you feel as a listener? When would this skill be useful?

Individual Activity: Choose someone in your life with whom you can be honest and who will be sensitive to your feelings. Ask the person you select to listen as you explain your feelings about one of the topics from the above list. Ask the listener to be especially careful not to evaluate what you say but simply to listen and then paraphrase what you say in slightly different words. Watch your listener for signs of having made a judgment. Pause as you speak to allow the listener time to describe what you have said. Was the listener completely accurate in describing, or was judgment passed on your ideas?

Now ask your partner to let you reverse roles and allow you to be the listener. Does your partner feel open enough with you to discuss feelings on a subject from the list? As you listen to the explanation, be especially careful not to give your opinion about what is said. Your task is to paraphrase what you hear. This will allow your partner to hear it in slightly different words.

Write a one-page paper to describe the dialogue and the paraphrasing experience. Include your feelings and thoughts about the success of the activity. You may want to tape the paraphrasing activity so it is recorded accurately. Include your opinion about the advantages and disadvantages of descriptive listening.

Option 2—Group Communication Situation

Preparation: Your instructor will assign a controversial topic that can be debated in class. You may choose to be either for or against the topic. Take about fifteen minutes to think through and jot down your ideas about the topic.

Group Activity: With the entire group, begin debating the topic informally. There will be no specific speaking order except that the affirmatives and negatives will alternate. Everyone should get to speak at least once. Each person who speaks may give ideas and feelings about the issue only after accurately restating what was just said. That is, the speaker must use paraphrasing and descriptive listening skills before giving an opinion.
   After the debate discuss the following questions about the descriptive listening experience.

1. How did you feel when you tried to listen objectively and understand the debaters? Do you usually try this hard to listen accurately?

2. How did the listening you did compare with the kind you do every day? Do you usually try to evaluate the messages you receive?

3. As a listener, were you able to paraphrase accurately the other debater's statements?

4. How did you feel when you were the one speaking and the other debaters were trying to understand you? Were you relieved that they could not make critical judgments of your message?

Individual Activity: Find several people who are willing to debate the controversial issue with you. Allow them time to complete the preparation for the activity. Group members will take opposite sides in debating the issue. Once everyone is prepared, take turns stating opinions. However, before you state your opinions each should rephrase what was just heard. Use your descriptive listening and paraphrasing skills. Do not make judgmental reactions to the other debaters' statements.
   Write a short report of the debate. Include major arguments for and against the issue. Describe roles as speaker and listener. Then write answers to the questions following the group activity.

Activity 7

Caring Behaviors

Preparation: A basic human need is to feel loved. In fact, the third of Maslow's Hierarchy of Needs (see page 11) is the need to belong and to be accepted, appreciated, and loved by others. However, people express and receive love in different ways. Chapman (1995) in his book, *The Five Languages of Love: How to Express Heartfelt Commitment to Your Mate*, identified five ways that we can communicate love: words of affirmation, exchanging gifts, physical touching of one another, providing acts of service, and quality time. If one spouse, for example, needs to hear encouraging words and gets served a nice dinner instead, he or she may not feel cared for at all. John Grey (1992) in his book, *Men are from Mars, Women are from Venus*, argues that men and women speak two different languages. Both authors are saying the same thing: one has to express caring about the other in a language that the other understands.

Group Activity: Separate into groups of four students. Discuss and/or role-play examples of each of Chapman's five ways of communicating love. If class time is short, separate into five groups with each group focusing on only one of the five ways of communicating love and then sharing their findings with the total class. These ways of communicating may or may not seem natural to you. Try the ideas—you might find that you can communicate differently than you thought.

1. **Words of Affirmation**—try using encouraging words instead of critical words.

   "You look beautiful in that new dress."
   "I really appreciate your cleaning the kitchen tonight so that I can study for my test."
   "Justin, you put five toys in the box today—that's great!"
   "Thanks for bringing your special cake to work today. Everyone loved it."

   A. With your group, make a list of compliments, words of encouragement, and requests rather than demands that you like to hear from others. Decide which type of communicator you are—requesting or demanding—and self-disclose this to your group.

   B. With your group, role-play a scene from school, work, or home that shows negative, critical communication. Then role-play the same scene but use positive words of affirmation.

C. Plan some changes in your communication style. Think about your use of harsh words rather than affirming words. Think about making suggestions instead of demands. Think about giving a compliment instead of a criticism. Then think of examples in your life where you might change what you say from something negative to something positive. With your group, describe situations where you will try words of affirmation at least twice in the coming week. Give and receive feedback from those in your group.

2. **Giving and Receiving Gifts**—something that you can hold in your hand and feel that someone is thinking about you. Gifts increase the receiver's self-worth because they are visual symbols of caring. The importance is the thought expressed in securing a gift for someone you want to validate. Without a gift to have as a visible symbol, your love for another might be questioned. Gifts can be given anytime, not just at holidays, and they do not have to be expensive. To be a gift giver, you might have to examine your attitude about spending money. If you enjoy spending money, then gift giving will be easy for you. However, as a saver of money, you resist spending. The saving gives you a sense of satisfaction and security which may not be perceived positively by others. Gift giving might be an investment in your most important interpersonal relationships. Some gifts are free—a flower or a task—and can be just as meaningful as a purchased gift.

   A. With your group, discuss your attitudes about giving and receiving gifts. Determine different types of gifts that are family traditions or are given in different cultures. Describe the value of tradition in gift giving. Make a list of gifts you have given and received in the past. Reflect on the value that you gave those gifts. Consider how you react to receiving gifts that have little value to you. Should you reorient your thinking about giving and receiving gifts?

   B. With your group, discuss the different between material and non-material gifts. Can your presence be considered a gift? Making the effort to be with someone can be a gift that is more meaningful than a tangible gift.

   C. Prepare a list to present to the class which expresses what your group has discovered about both giving and receiving gifts in the context of an interpersonal language of caring. Roleplay nonverbal reactions to gifts that are valued and gifts that are disliked.

3. **Physical Touch**—researchers in the area of child development have concluded that babies who are hugged, held and kissed develop happier, more secure personalities. For some adults, physical touch such as holding hands and embracing makes them feel cared for. Without physical touch, they feel they are not valued. According to Chapman (1995), "Physical touch can make or break a relationship. It can communicate hate or love" (p. 105).

   A. With your group, discuss how you react to and exhibit touching behaviors.

      a. What negative forms of touching are expressed in interpersonal relationships? How can these be discontinued? Can verbal apologies make up for negative forms of touching?

b. What positive forms of touching are expressed in interpersonal relationships? Given different circumstances (e.g., leaving a house, going to a funeral), what types of touch can enhance interpersonal relationships?

c. How do you want a significant person to express caring through touch?

d. How does touching behavior differ in various cultures?

e. How can moods and attitudes affect touch on a given day? Do you have a responsibility to be sensitive to the changes in moods of those you encounter?

B. Using the information from your discussion, use role-playing to express the importance of touch in interpersonal relationships of various intensities.

4. **Acts of Service**—in the execution of routine tasks (e.g., taking out the trash, changing oil in the car, cleaning up dishes, doing laundry), we can make requests but not demands of those we love. Gender stereotypes often provide the rules for who does what in a relationship. Men take care of cars; women do laundry. Changing gender roles in the latter half of the 20th Century, however, have made such stereotypes obsolete. Reciprocity is now more of the rule in "equal relationships." By sharing the burdens of life, both persons in a relationship can pursue activities they enjoy independently and can share quality time together. Neither party in a relationship will feel loved if routine tasks are not shared equally. Equal sharing does not mean that one person has the oil changed in January and the other has the oil changed in July. Rather, it means that responsibility for changing the oil is balanced with the other partner taking on another responsibility. By caring for someone else, you will want to provide acts of service to make daily challenges of living easier and more equitable.

A. Consider your own behaviors. What simple tasks do you especially dislike doing? Do you complete those tasks because you care about someone else? What are your unconscious biases about gender-role stereotypes? Do you believe that both sexes should share the routine burdens of daily life? Are there any exceptions to the sense of sharing you feel? What routine tasks would you like someone to do for you?

B. With your group discuss the topics above. Do males and females look at "acts of service" through different eyes? Should courting behaviors—those behaviors which serve to endear one person to another—continue after marriage?

C. Summarize your group consensus on the items above and report your findings to the entire class.

5. **Quality Time**—giving another person our undivided attention. Quality time cannot be forced; it is not merely being together. Quality time means that you have placed the other person before everything else and the time spent with that person is lost from other pursuits. When you receive quality time, you will know that for this moment in time you are ranked #1 with the other person. Busy lives make such focused time a rare commodity and a treasured gift to give.

A. Consider activities that you shared in relationships that provoked strong memories. These experiences need to be those that brought you closer to a significant person and involved quality time shared by the two of you. Be creative as you think about potential activities which would create strong memories.

B. With your group, list activities that suggest quality time to you. Discuss ways that you can manage time so that you have quality time for the people most important to you. Can quality time occur in small groups (e.g., a family) or does it apply only to one other person? Does quality time have to involve interests that both people enjoy? Does giving into the interests of the other demonstrate caring in a relationship?

C. Summarize your discussion and present ideas to the group about how to increase the amount of quality time in relationships.

Individual Activity: Locate five friends or family members. With each person follow the directions from the group activity to discuss one of the caring behaviors. After discussing the five caring behaviors, write a paragraph to summarize your conclusions for each. Conclude with a paragraph which reflects your critical analysis of Chapman's ideas.

Activity 8

Conflict Management

Preparation: One of the major goals of listening is to establish contact and cooperation with others. However, much of our social, family and business contact is filled with conflict, misunderstanding, and failure to communicate. As we live and work together, we continue to have differences of opinion. When more than one person is involved, there are communication complications that must be worked out. Successful people have the ability to listen to one another and to "fight" fairly as they work out differences effectively.

The general principle of fair fighting is to focus on the current problem and to avoid the "baggage" of the past and to avoid "hitting below the belt." No reviving past disputes and no name-calling are allowed. To "fight" fairly as conflict is managed, agree with your partner to follow these steps.

1. The individual with the problem needs to do a self-assessment to evaluate feelings of anger associated with the situation.

2. The individual with the problem needs to express feelings at the beginning of the discussion. If only anger is present, the other person will likely respond with anger.

3. The two persons must discuss what initiated the difference and determine if expectations for solving the problem are realistic.

4. The two persons must recognize the need to compromise. Often two people enter a disagreement with a Win-Lose attitude. Both must feel that the solution makes them a winner. Work toward Win-Win. If both persons do not make changes, there is not a compromise.

5. The two persons must remember that fair fighting is a skill that takes time. In fair fighting, the conflict may not be solved quickly. Breaks are important when the discussion becomes heated.

Locate someone with whom you have had a recent conflict. Go through the following steps and write down the scenario and the results of your conflict management experience.

1. You must introduce the problem and review the details.

> You cannot expect others to read your mind.
> Have a clear understanding of your feelings.
> Stay focused on one issue at a time.
> Do not allow counter demands to enter the picture until the original issue is clearly understood and acknowledged by the other person.

2. State the problem clearly. Say "I'm feeling _____ because of _____."

> Be factual when you introduce the problem.
> Avoid complaining, whining, or blaming.
> Do not be sarcastic.
> Stay focused on the present.

3. Both parties need to listen and understand the problem. The listener can reflect back by saying

   "I understand that you feel _____ because of _____" or the initiator can make clarifying statements like "Tell me what you heard me say." Clarifying statements and questions will help bring out feelings associated with anger.

   > Do not assume you know what the other party is thinking, how they will act, or what they will or will not accept. Always verify your perceptions.
   > Do not put labels on the other person by saying "You always act this way." Do not express your perceptions with judgmental labels.

4. Both parties must understand what is being said before proceeding. This does not mean that agreement has been established but only that positions have been clarified.

5. The person who introduced the problem now takes responsibility for offering a solution that both parties can adopt to make changes. The initiator identifies changes that he or she will make first.

   > Ask for reasonable changes one at a time.
   > Always consider compromise. Remember that the other person's perception is that person's reality even if it differs from yours.

6. Discuss an initial solution first and then allow a counter solution. Remember there should always be changes on both sides.

7. Discuss several options until both parties agree on one proposal that is the most workable. It is neither right nor wrong.

8. When the proposal is agreed upon, discuss how it will be implemented. Who will do what, when, where, and how? Be specific and use descriptive listening. Audio-taping or writing down the changes or the steps can help further clarify the current discussion and serve as a reference in future discussions when memories are not clear.

9. Discuss how each party could sabotage the agreement.

10. Agree to come back to this problem after a specific period of time to reassess how the solution is working. This allows time for change and fine-tuning specifics.

Group Activity: In small groups of four to six discuss the conflicts you described. Also discuss your evaluation of the conflicts. Determine if the parties used "fair fighting." Did you find a Win-Win solution to the conflict? Did both parties follow through with what each agreed to do? Is it possible that the compromise provided a better outcome than either of the original positions? Or did you fall back on the common roles of defensiveness, blaming, and intimidation?

Choose the most interesting conflict from each group to role play for the class. After each scene discuss the way the conflict was dealt with and how you feel it should or could be handled differently. In dealing with conflict situations, which interpersonal skills could you use to keep open communication channels?

Individual Activity: Ask someone you know well to role-play on a cassette tape the conflict scene you described on paper. At the end of the tape include your answers to the discussion listed with the group activity.

Activity 9

Dealing with Difficult People

Preparation: People typically are given the label "difficult" when a conflict arises. Using conflict management strategies is usually the best approach to dealing with difficult people. The problem that arises is that conflict management requires two or more participants who are willing to negotiate and compromise—look for a Win-Win solution. There are times when one or more of the participants in a conflict are not willing to budge. Then you have a situation where you must deal with a truly difficult person.

> For example, one person in the conflict might be so determined to stay with the original position that communication is halted. Some people feel that pride or power keep them from compromising. They say such things as: "If I give in now, people will never respect my decisions;" "I come from a good family and learned that once you start something, you cannot quit;" or "I don't want to look like a spineless, fence-sitter who can't be counted on to stay the course."

Working with such people is difficult but not impossible. We have all tried to work with difficult people and found it frustrating to say the least. If all people had the same life experiences and thought and acted alike, then there would be no difficulties among people. Thinking alike on all issues, we could operate in perfect harmony. No stress based on dysfunctional interpersonal relationships would emerge. Difficulties arise because people see the world differently and they tackle day-to-day problems with different strategies. It might be easier to surround ourselves with similar, like-minded, agreeable people. However, we lose a lot by refusing to interact with people of different genders, ages, religions, cultures, and personality types. Different people, even difficult people, add spice to life and add challenges to our relationships. Without differences, organizations, schools, and families would consist of "yes people." Thus, differences are valuable in our world and appealing but we must develop good working relationships and learn to work together.

Robert Bramson (1981) identified seven types of difficult people in his book, *Coping with Difficult People.*

1. Hostile-aggressives: bully, overwhelm, bombard, belittle, throw tantrums when situations do not go the way they want.

2. Complainers: continually gripe but never do anything to resolve their complaints.

3. Silent and unresponsives: only answer with a yes, no, or grunt.

4. Super-agreeables: seem reasonable, sincere, and supportive with others but never follow through.

5. Negativists: deflate the optimism of others by always pointing out flaws.

6. Know-it-all experts: try to make others feel like idiots by seeming to know about anything worth knowing.

7. Indecisives: always seeking perfection, they stall major decisions until the decision is made by default.

We all know people who fall into the above categories—even ourselves at times. Rather than attaching labels, stating explicit behaviors in relation to specific incidents is often a more productive approach in getting along with a seemingly difficult person.

Group Activity: Separate into small groups.

Part I. Discuss the following questions. Select one person to be the recorder as you draw conclusions.

1. What is going on in our world today that results in so many people seeming to be difficult?

2. What qualities do you equate with calling someone a difficult person?

3. Do you have any of the following characteristics which might make you more vulnerable to the power of difficult people? If so, what can you do to overcome each?

   a. Not Assertive

   b. Not Organized

   c. Naive or Gullible

   d. Not Attending to Detail

   e. Unclear on What to Do

   f. Lack Goals

g. Lack People and Communication Skills

h. Weaker Position because of Status

i. Facts (Too Many or Not Enough)

4. Study the following list of strengths with their counter-productive synonyms. Do you see how the same behavior can be interpreted in a positive way and a negative way?

    Which of these are your strengths?

    Describe to your group an instance when one of your strengths might have been interpreted in a negative light.

Accepting/Passive
Ambitious/Ruthless
Analytical/Nit-picky
Caring/Smothering
Cautious/Suspicious
Curious/Nosy
Fair/Indecisive
Flexible/Easily Influenced
Forceful/Dictatorial
Frugal/Stingy

Helpful/Self-sacrificing
Idealistic/Impractical
Orderly/Compulsive
Organizer/Controller
Persevering/Stubborn
Persuasive/Pressuring
Realistic/Unimaginative
Influenced Risk-Taking/Gambling
Trusting/Gullible
Self-Confident/Arrogant

Part II.   The following sections list strategies to employ when you must interact with someone you perceive to be a difficult person.

1. We train people how to treat us by our responses. If we do not like how we are treated, we need to change our responses. Following are several assertiveness techniques.

    A. Fogging—agreeing in principle to the critic's positive. For example, "It may be true...."
    B. Broken Record—calm repetition of your position.
    C. Prompt the Critic—asking for more information that may be negative. For example, "Is there anything else?"

2. We have three choices in a difficult encounter—avoid, accept, or confront. It is important to assess the situation and determine if confronting the situation is worth the risk. Often we are bothered by such trivial matters that avoidance and accepting make the most sense. When the stakes are high, consider using good communication strategies to confront.

3. Assertive Sandwich Method—You need to feel good about how you have responded. Use the script below, either verbally or in writing, to form your response. This script can be used to re-open a conversation that has not gone well for you.

I Feel

Description: What Caused the Feeling

Request for Change

4. Often we get caught off guard by a difficult person or circumstance. Always start by assessing, not just responding with a "gut" reaction. Then decide if you should accept or distance yourself. Using "one-liners" often helps, too.

   A. Assess—ask yourself, "What am I dealing with? A person, a situation, a momentary flare-up, or a pattern response?" Consider your safety—is involvement likely to be life threatening?
   B. Accept—people sometimes react without thinking. Difficult people may have had NO intention of upsetting you. Remember that you cannot change the other person; you can only change the way you react.
   C. Distance—emotional or physical.

      a. Collect your thoughts. "I'll get back to you."
      b. Get over your initial feeling of distress and let the situation calm down. "Let's meet tomorrow to discuss this again."
      c. Reduce the complexity of the situation. "I'm juggling too many balls here. Give me a moment to focus."

   D. Use one-liners—gives you a chance to collect your thoughts and puts the burden of response on the other person.

      "If you are looking for an argument, you will have to find someone else."
      "What do you want me to do about this?"
      "I can see that this upsets you. Can I be of help?"
      "What is it that you would like to see happen here?"
      "I want to talk through this but not when we are both so upset."
      "I'd like us to get along better. What do you suggest we do?"

Part III: With your group, role-play several scenarios which demonstrate techniques for diffusing a difficult situation. Time permitting, create an example for each of the techniques in Part II. Otherwise, divide the techniques among the groups.

Individual Activity: Answer the questions in Part I above by writing short responses. Study the techniques in Part II. Find a friend who will role-play an example for each of the four strategies in Part II. Write a paragraph to summarize each of the role-plays.

Activity 10

Cultural Stereotyping

NOTE: This activity can be completed using cultural variables other than gender. Gender, however, is a good choice since males and females generally find their differences to be benign.

Preparation: Looking back at chapter 9, you will find that many of the characteristics of communicating across cultures affect male/female communication. The purpose of this activity is to explore the differences between the sexes by looking at stereotypes. Just remember that stereotyping is positive only as a starting point. It is essential that each stereotypical characteristic be evaluated for each individual. No one fits all the characteristics of a stereotype. For example, not ALL males leave the toilet seat up (well, there may be one stereotype that has no exception).

Group Activity: Divide into two groups based on gender. It is better if the two groups can be in separate spaces so that the verbal and nonverbal interaction of one group cannot be observed by the other. Select a recorder to compile a list which can be reported when the group as a whole reconvenes. Keep your sense of humor as you complete this activity and discuss the findings.

In your gender-defined group, begin listing responses to the following:

What I Dislike about the Opposite Sex.

To get the ideas flowing, try using brainstorming where you begin with one person in the group and go systematically one by one adding to the list.

After a given time or when the lists have grown quite long, both groups should return to the same area. The recorder from each group is then given the opportunity to present the list of grievances to the other group. Discussion should follow. If there is any reticence between the groups, the following questions may help.

1. Do the listed elements reflect stereotypes or are they really representative of most males or females?

2. Does awareness of the listed characteristics provide some insight into your own sex as well as the opposite sex?

3. Do you like the generalizations made about your gender? Can sensitivity to these factors affect your behavior in certain situations?

4. Is our culture becoming more androgenous? How do you feel about this?

5. Can you approach gender differences and stereotypes from a humorous angle? Could you do the same if you were to list stereotypes about race, national origin, or religion?

Individual Activity: You may be limited by the size of your group somewhat in doing this activity alone. However, try to assemble at least four people, two men and two women. Follow the instructions above. Turn in a written report which includes the two lists and answers to the five questions included in the group activity.

Activity 11

Paradigm Shifts

Preparation: Paradigm means a model, pattern, or a set of ideas that describes aspects of the world. We think in paradigms. Our minds construct models or ideas about the world and its people: cultural groups, technology, governments, political parties, and even ourselves. We form paradigms about ourselves based on what we believe others think about us. The comments of others are based on their perceptions, opinions, and paradigms about who we are. We are treated either positively or negatively as a result of their opinions. Judgments by others are formed on the basis of past interactions with us.

For example, imagine a high school senior who is told by an academic counselor that she will not be able to get into college because of low test scores. There may be some truth to the opinion in that the student may not be admitted to a highly-selective college. However, she can be admitted to a less selective college where time can be spent in improving skills. Thus, the information that we receive from others can be wrong or only partially correct and as a result of determination and imagination, recommendations can often change.

We do make decisions, judgments, and predictions based on our paradigms. Paradigms can explain cause and effect relationships. Scientists sometimes use these relationships to make predictions. If what they observe does not match their predictions, then they revise their paradigms and begin again to obtain verification. They are willing to test data and then be flexible enough to shift paradigms when the data do not support the paradigm.

Group Activity: In class, view the film, "The Business of Paradigms" by Joel Barker. Answer the following questions individually, using examples where possible, and then discuss your answers with a small group.

1. Define the term "paradigm."

2. List other words, or synonyms, for paradigm.

3. Define "paradigm shift."

4. List six specific examples of paradigm shifts.

5. Describe a "paradigm shifter."

6. List the paradigm pioneers.

7. List examples of "old paradigms" from history.

8. List paradigm shifts that have occurred in technology during the last quarter century.

9. List technological shifts in communication that are on the precipice for the 21st century.

10. List other paradigm shifts that are possibilities for the 21st century. ...subsequent centuries.

11. Define "paradigm paralysis."

12. List excuses used for not making paradigm shifts.

13. Describe what is meant by Barker's comment that when paradigms shift, everyone goes back to zero.

14. List suggestions for dealing with change.

15. Evaluate your understanding of your own paradigms.

16. Interpret what is meant by the following quotation by Proust that "The real voyage in discovery consists not in searching new lands but in seeing with new eyes."

17. Describe how flexibility in paradigms can help you in communication with yourself and with others.

Individual Activity: View the film, answer the questions above, and write a summary of your impression of the implication of paradigm shifting and communication effectiveness.

Activity 12

Speaking Activity—
Employment Interview

Preparation: Review the material from chapter 7 on the Employment Interview. Consider your life goals in terms of work. Reflect on a position that you would ultimately like to obtain. Choose a company to research that you would actually like to work for, but be realistic in setting this goal. Once you have made this important decision visit your campus placement office, a counselor, the Internet, or the actual employment office to research the details of the position. In learning about the company, you will want to receive information concerning necessary educational background, specific qualifications, past work experience, job expectations, salary, benefits, and so forth.

One major California company (Flanagan, 1975) has drawn up the following guidelines for forming interview questions. Keep these in mind as you formulate your own questions. The college career office has additional material for your use.

Subject	Guideline
Sex	Cannot discuss unless sex is a definite requirement for the position.
Marital Status	Cannot ask if single, married, engaged, divorced or living with someone.
Children	Cannot ask if applicant has children at home, ages, child care provisions, or future plans for having children. After hiring, numbers and ages of children may be requested for insurance purposes.
Physical data	Cannot ask personal questions regarding height or weight. A physical exam can be required. Physical requirements of the position can be described.
Criminal record	Unless security clearance is indicated, cannot ask about arrests, convictions, or time spent in jail.
Military status	Can ask if applicant is a veteran and, if so, what job related experiences resulted; cannot ask about type of discharge or branch of service.
Age	Cannot ask or estimate age. After hiring, can ask if employee is over 18.
Housing	Can ask how to reach; cannot ask about housing.

Questions frequently asked during interviews are listed below. Use the questions as a guideline for role playing an interview situation.

Factual questions you might be asked by employers:

1. What are your long-range goals and objectives in regard to your vocation?
2. When and why did you establish these goals?
3. How do you plan to achieve them?
4. Specifically, what would you like to do five years from now?
5. What salary do you expect to earn five and ten years from now?
6. How much money per year do you feel you need to earn to achieve your personal goals?
7. Which is your first consideration—money you will earn or happiness in the job? Explain.

8. What causes you to be motivated to do your best?
9. What do you consider to be your greatest strength?
10. What do you consider to be your greatest weakness?
11. Why did you choose the career for which you are prepared?
12. Based on what you did in school how do you think a professor would describe you?
13. How has college prepared you for this position?
14. What college subjects did you like best?
15. What college subjects did you like least?
16. What grades did you earn in your major field?
17. Are your grades a good indication of your academic achievement?
18. What were your extracurricular activities in college?
19. What did you learn from participation in these?
20. Do you feel you need additional course work?
21. How much education do you plan to obtain?
22. When would you go for advanced course work if that is your choice?
23. Why do you feel this company should hire you?
24. What qualifications would make you an asset to this company?
25. How would you describe success?
26. How could you be successful in this company?
27. Describe the relationship that should exist between you and a supervisor.
28. What led you to this particular company?
29. What do you know about this company?
30. What geographic area do you prefer?
31. Are you willing to relocate?
32. Are you willing to travel?
33. Would you be willing to spend six months as a trainee?
34. What have you done to show initiative and willingness to work?
35. What accomplishment has given you the most satisfaction? Why?
36. What do you feel has been your most rewarding life experience?

Behavioral questions you might be asked by employers (tailored to the job duties):

1. If bids had been submitted for a number of contracts, expecting a 50% hit, what would you do if all bids were accepted?
2. How would you handle an advertising error which indicated your product would sell significantly below cost?
3. What would you do if one of your staff experienced a life-threatening injury on the job?
4. How do you handle conflict situations in the work place?

Questions you might ask your prospective employer:

1. What is the last person who had this job doing?
2. What are the job responsibilities?
3. What skills are the most important for the job?
4. What kind of training is provided?
5. What is the company's history?
6. What are the company's goals?
7. Where does the job lead?
8. What is the salary range?
9. What benefits are offered?
10. Does the company have a personnel and procedures manual?

11. What are the strengths and weaknesses of the supervisor? (Don't be afraid to ask.)
12. What is the management style of the company?

Questions you might ask yourself:

1. Do I understand the job responsibilities?
2. Is the job location within a comfortable driving radius?
3. Does the personality of the company fit with mine?
4. Does the position fit with my goals?
5. If moving to another location, does change in salary cover the difference in cost of living?

Complete the following tasks for both the *Group Activity* and *Individual Activity*.

1. Prepare a description of the employer with at least the following information—what is the mission of the employer, how large is the organization and how many locations are there, what are the qualifications for the type of position for which you want to be considered? For the Group Activity, this information will form the introduction that you give the class prior to your role playing your interview so that the class has an understanding of the type of job for which you are interviewing. For the Individual Activity, this information will support your choice of employer to interview.
2. Fill out an application for the job. Many employers will have information on websites which include an application. You will probably conclude that applications have considerable overlap in the types of information requested. (If you cannot obtain an official application for the position you want, then find an application that is similar and use it.) Consider taking an application that is filled out with you when you apply so you will have correct dates for education and employment.
3. Prepare a letter of application and a resume that fit the employer information and job of interest which were described in #1 above (see Chapter 7 for examples or use the internet to find templates and examples).

When your preparation is complete, you will have a written description of the employer and the qualifications for the job, a completed application, a letter of application, and a resume.

Group Activity: Role Playing an Interview

Purpose: to give students an opportunity to experience both the role of applicant and employer as they verbally and nonverbally communicate qualifications for a job.

1. Select a classmate as a partner to role play an employment interview. Take turns acting the role of the employer and applicant.
2. Formulate two lists of questions which fit the job for which you are applying. The first list will be questions an employer might ask you, and the second will be questions for you to ask the employer. In the employer's list, include at least two behavioral interviewing questions—practical questions that go with the type of job for which you are applying. In the applicant's list, include a question about salary and benefits. Select questions from the previous pages, use materials from the Career Center, or find internet sites to have at least 10 for the employer to ask and 5 for the applicant to ask.
3. Prepare answers to the questions you expect the employer to ask. Give thorough and thoughtful answers and share information even if a "yes" or "no" would suffice.
4. Give your partner your letter, resume, application, and employer questions.
5. Review the letter, resume, application, and employer questions from your partner.

6. On the assigned day, role play your interviews with your partner. Remember to prepare a short introduction to describe the employment opportunity. DRESS appropriately so that you can receive feedback about the nonverbal effect of your appearance. In the role of interviewer, you are in charge of the exchange. Put the applicant at ease by asking some insignificant questions (the weather is always a winner), attempt to maintain the flow of information and ideas, avoid awkward silences but give the applicant time to reflect, paraphrase to show you understand the answers, and act interested in the applicant.

7. As you observe the interviews, take notes of the positive aspects and the negative aspects of what you see. Record at least two positive and two negative comments for each applicant.

8. When all interviews are complete, share your observations about the following with the class.

    a. Nonverbal Body Movements
    b. Nonverbal Appearance
    c. Nonverbal Paralanguage
    d. Verbal Content of Answers
    e. Professional Appearance of Written Materials

9. As a class, write a follow-up letter that would be appropriate for thanking the employer for the interview.

Individual Activity: Field Interview

Purpose: to seek out and interview an employer in a job that you might want to someday fill so that you can experience an information-gathering interview and visit an employment site.

1. Immediately begin seeking out a potential employer. Find someone who is in a job that you might someday want to fill. The individual cannot be a relative or close friend. If you are courteous, most people will take the time to help a student who is aspiring to enter their field.

2. Make an appointment. Let the employer know about how long you will need to meet (no more than one hour) and what kinds of information you are seeking. Explain that the employer will need to fill-out and return a brief evaluation form to the instructor.

3. In addition to the research on the employer, your application form, your letter of application, and your resume which you completed under the *Preparation* Section of this Activity, compile a list of at least 15 questions to ask the person you have chosen to interview. Use the questions listed in the Activity, use the resources of the Career Center, or check one or more of the many websites available to advise about employment. The following three questions, supported with examples, MUST be included:

    a. What educational and professional experience is needed for the position?
    b. What are the general and daily responsibilities of the position?
    c. How does interpersonal communication facilitate the challenges faced?

4. When you conduct your interview, start out with a firm handshake and introduction of yourself. Bring your prepared questions as a reminder but do not read them verbatim or keep your eyes on them. Make good eye contact with the employer. Ask the employer if you can tape the interview on a small audio recorder. If not, keep good written notes.

5. Before you leave the interview, give the employer the evaluation form which is provided in the Appendix. Point out the deadline for the form. Give the employer a stamped envelope with the following address:

    Instructor Name
    Eastfield College
    3737 Motley Drive
    Mesquite, TX 75150

6. Also, obtain a business card from the employer.
7. Immediately after the interview, send a follow-up letter thanking the individual for taking time to work with you on this important assignment for your career growth. Consider this a networking experience and the establishment of a contact person who will help you obtain employment in the future.
8. Review your notes immediately after the meeting and begin your written report. Check the syllabus for the due date. The written report should include the following:

    a. Title Page listing your name, date and time of the interview, the employer's name, the employer's position, and the company name. Attach the business card.
    b. Introduction explaining why you chose the particular employer you interviewed.
    c. The questions and answers to the minimum 15 questions including the three required questions in #3 above.
    d. Conclusion describing the important lessons you learned from the interview.
    e. Attachments including the application form, letter of application, resume, and follow-up letter.

9. Use the following specifications for the format:

    a. Typed using Times New Roman, 12-point Font
    b. Double-Spaced with 1.5 inch margin at the top and 1 inch margins on sides and bottom. Bottom-centered page numbers are preferred.
    c. Use headings for Sections B, C and D—the questions and conclusions.
    d. Staple the pages—do not use plastic binders.

NOTE: Evaluation criteria for the Speaking Activity are located in the Appendix.

SMALL GROUP COMMUNICATION

Overview

Human beings are very social and require contacts with other human beings to be truly healthy individuals. It is the rare individual who does not seek interactions with others as a course of daily living. Gatherings or groups of people generally elicit favorable associations—parties, planning, achieving, understanding, learning—that reinforce involvements. To demonstrate the value humans place on contact with others, consider the case histories of two men who voluntarily sought adventure and isolation in the wilds.

Ned Roesler (Englebardt, 1978) was a successful executive until age thirty-seven when he chose to become a freelance photographer. At age forty he left friends and family to attempt a 300 mile hike and photographic expedition across the north slopes of Alaska—alone. In his diary on the first night of the trip, knowing that civilization was far away, he wrote, "never felt so lonely in my life." It took him twenty-three days to reach his first stop, a village of about 150 people. He recorded his feeling at spotting the village: "The sun reflecting off the village roofs filled me with joy. Soon I would be able to eat, pick up fresh supplies, receive mail, send off postcards and film. And talk to people." He ended the journey nearly dead from exhausting his food supplies. Approximately two days' walk from his final destination he was picked up by helicopter. When he reached camp, "it was his first human

contact in 39 days, so he momentarily forgot about his unfed stomach until the pilot pointed the way to the camp kitchen."

The subject of the second case study is Naomi Uemura (Uemura, 1978), a Japanese adventurer who became the first person to reach the North Pole alone. His travels lasted eight weeks as he and his dog team traveled 800 kilometers across the icebound Arctic Ocean. Four days into the trip his camp was ravaged by a polar bear. He writes of being hidden and barely breathing in his sleeping bag as the hungry bear ripped open his tent, "Then my mind turns to my beloved wife in Tokyo. Kimi-chan, help me somehow." Uemura did have the advantage of being able to radio base camp daily to "discuss his progress, to talk about ice conditions, and perhaps just to hear somebody else's voice." He wrote at the end of the dangerous trip that his thoughts went to the "countless people who had helped and supported me, and the knowledge that I could never face them if I gave up."

These two stories, although emphasizing the struggle of two men against the elements, include references to other human beings, to communication, and to companionship. They endured isolation and hardship for the beauty and the challenge but never forgot their associations with and need for other people. Human beings are very social and spend much of their time with others.

To maximize your study of group communication, consider the following two suggestions as you use the skills you have practiced from your previous work in communication.

- Evaluate carefully ideas that come from the mindset of "this is the way it has always been done or another group does it this way." Balance the concept of "why reinvent the wheel" with creative thinking strategies. Sometimes, but not always, "thinking outside the box" will result in a better outcome than the obvious "cookie-cutter" solution. This paragraph is based on trite phrases which, after careful consideration, will hopefully result in innovation and forward-thinking solutions. The future oriented mindset of our society, in contrast to the past and present mindsets of some cultures, has resulted in the conceptualization of the many of the products that make our society so technologically advanced.

- Consider building teams of people who have many differences in skills and experiences. A team of mental clones would limit thinking to the same ideas from everyone. Building a team where each member has a unique contribution and the outcome could not occur without the contributions of all will maximize the probability that something unique and better will result. Explore the knowledge and skills of your group members and build on their potentials. Our

multi-cultural society makes finding group members who are diverse relatively easy. Look for people who are different as you build your group.

The study of group relationships is essential in a thorough study of the communication process. A study of small group communication is applicable to family situations, informal social groups, organized groups, and many other instances when several people find themselves together. In order to be effective in a group, individuals must be sensitive to their own behavior and the behavior of others. Skill in small group communication can be learned through study and practice.

Pulling a Tiger's Teeth

whenever you feel
like saying:
what did i do?
try saying:
how can i help?

—*Ric Masten*
They Are All Gone Now published by Sunflower
Ink, Carmel, CA

CHAPTER 10

Goodshoot®

SMALL GROUP COMMUNICATION DEFINED

A small group is defined very generally as a gathering of several people who have some common purpose or who are in some way interrelated. Several examples of small groups would be four couples getting together to play bridge; five people standing on a corner waiting for a bus; seven workers meeting to solve parking problems at their plant; or even ten people, representing various organizations, on a council to plan a large meeting. A more useful definition of small groups will include the concept of communication among those gathered together to seek a common goal. This more restrictive definition would possibly eliminate groups like the one at the bus stop, or people sitting in a physician's waiting room. Thus a small group is better defined as a gathering of several people who, through communication, reach a common goal.

The small group has always been an important means for attainment of human purposes. Probably first in the extended family, then the clan and tribe, the guild, the community, and the state, groups have been formed to conduct government, work, war, religion, recreation, education, and even just to maintain life. Very early in the historical development of the human race it was discovered that groups could perform some tasks more efficiently than individuals, and that certain group procedures worked better than others. This resulted in a body of folk wisdom regarding the selection of leaders, the division of labor and procedures for making decisions. During the last few decades of human history the scientific community has done much to research small group communication and develop a body of literature useful to all who strive to improve their communication skills.

Small Group Characteristics

GROUP SIZE

The minimum group size is defined by some authors as two and by others as three. Because of the emphasis in our society today on interpersonal communication techniques, that is, the interaction of one individual with one other individual, it is probably more useful in studying small groups as a distinct area of communication to say that the minimum size of a small group is three.

The maximum size of a small group varies depending on the characteristics of the members and their purpose in being together. A group ceases to be a small group when individual members are no longer able to communicate with every other member. Two very obvious signs of the loss of small group characteristics are the formation of subgroups or the nonparticipation of some members.

Some small groups will function effectively with as many as fifteen or twenty members, but the optimum size for small groups is probably five, seven, or nine. An odd number of members is more effective in case of a split decision because it eliminates the possibility of a tied vote. A small group of five to nine members allows everyone the opportunity to express opinions, provides sufficient input to create ideas for discussion, and allows each member to establish an interpersonal relationship with every other member. Many of the qualities, like cohesiveness, that create optimum small group participation are more readily developed if group size is within the maximum range of eight to ten participants.

Group size affects group performance as well as the satisfaction that each member feels in being a part of the group. Larger groups, for example, take more time to reach decisions, especially if all members express their viewpoints. Factions of the membership may polarize themselves and thus distract the group from the task. Generally, too, dominant members eventually account for most of the input, and in effect create a small group of active participants and a separate group of observers. Even in very large groups, small groups are created to perform certain tasks. Large groups will often elect representatives to governing boards and have

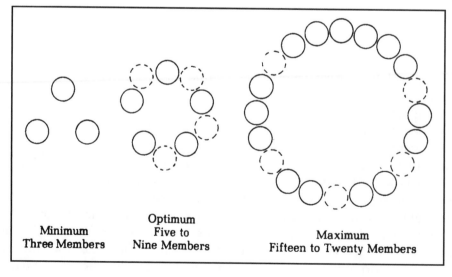

Minimum	Optimum	Maximum
Three Members	Five to Nine Members	Fifteen to Twenty Members

Figure 10.1

```
┌─────────────────────────────────────────┐
│                                           │
│            Functions of Groups            │
│                                           │
│            Problem Solving                │
│            Learning                       │
│            Socialization                  │
│            Therapy                        │
│                                           │
└─────────────────────────────────────────┘
```

many committees to handle specific problems and perform special tasks.

FUNCTIONS OF GROUPS

An effective small group for most situations is composed of five to nine members who communicate with each other in an attempt to achieve a common goal. This definition can be expanded to include the following qualities (Knowles and Knowles, 1959): members are known and can be identified, members think of themselves as a part of the group and identify with each other, members work together to achieve a common goal, members acknowledge that they need each other's help in reaching their common goal, members form interpersonal communication relationships with each other, and members together behave as a single entity. The common goal, or the idea of a common need or objective, has been expressed throughout the narrowing of the definition of a "small group" and "small group communication." What then are some common goals or functions of groups? Although many small groups will have several functions, most will have a primary function that fits in one of the following four categories: problem solving, learning, socialization, or therapy.

Problem Solving

Small groups that have set a task for themselves that will affect their living environment fall into the category of problem solving. Their goal is to carry out the steps it takes to make a change or find the answer to a problem. Examples are numerous. A group of parents who plan and conduct structured after-school activities for their children, a group organized to publish a newsletter for a large corporation, or a group of concerned citizens who organize a clean-up campaign for their neighborhood are

all examples of small groups whose goal includes a problem-solving task.

There are numerous models to help groups in their task of problem solving. The most widely known and, perhaps, used model is one formulated in 1910 by John Dewey. He suggested the following steps as a logical process for solving problems.

1. **Recognizing the problem**—An awareness that something needs to be altered
2. **Defining the problem**—A clear statement of the problem as it is perceived
3. **Analyzing the problem**—Identifying such factors as causes and extent of the problem to gain greater insight into the problem
4. **Establishing criteria for evaluating potential solutions**—Criteria set in advance to help in recognizing the best solutions
5. **Suggesting solutions**—Possibilities for solving the problem
6. **Selecting the solution**—Applying criteria to select the best solution
7. **Testing the solution**—Trying out and evaluating the solution

The problem-solving group may be well advised to consider a model like the one proposed by Dewey and used for nearly a century, or another similar model for attacking a problem situation.

Learning

The task of a small group oriented toward learning is to share or acquire knowledge. Their direct effect on the environment is minimal since they are not seeking to change things or to create an impact. Their goal is to further their knowledge or impart their knowledge to others. Small groups of students who meet informally to discuss their field of interest, groups of collectors who meet to share objects from their collections, and professionals who gather to expand their expertise are examples of small groups who meet for the purpose of learning.

Socialization

Social groups generally form because the participants enjoy being with each other as individuals. Social groups are often more selective than other types of groups in admitting new members. Their goals are related to leisure activities that provide enjoyment and entertainment for the members. A group that has a monthly poker game, several individuals who buy season tickets to the theatre, or a group of neighbors who meet occasionally for coffee are examples of small groups whose functions are primarily social in nature.

Therapy

When several people meet for the purpose of self-disclosure, talking through their problems, or trying to improve some aspect of their personalities, the group serves a therapeutic function. A group of neighborhood women, in some cases, might be more a therapeutic than a social group. If their purpose in getting together is to discuss personal problems rather than to talk about more positive aspects of their lives, then it would be logical to classify them as a therapeutic group. Another example of a therapeutic group is a gathering of individuals who are aided in self-disclosure by a professional counselor or psychologist. Therapeutic groups exist in many situations where the group goal is to solve one member's or the group's personal problems.

Positive Outcomes of Joining Groups

People join groups for many reasons. Often their reasons relate specifically to the group goals. Individuals interested in preserving the environment might join a group merely because of the group's specific purpose. People often join groups because they feel that they cannot achieve their goals as individuals; or groups form because of the common motives of several people who discover their similar

---

The Nouveau Rural

it's why we live here
terry said

this last 4th of july
when we awoke to a water tower
drained dry
useless faucets
and a mile and a half of empty PVC
the mountainside went wild
waving wrenches
running beside the pipe
bumping into each other
Mack Sennett
looking for leaks in the line
and for awhile
till the toilets flushed again
at least
there was meaning
and direction
in the lives
of eight
middle-aged men

—Ric Masten
Voice of the Hive published by Sunflower Ink,
Carmel, CA

---

interests. Individuals will join one group rather than another because they feel that group will be more effective or successful than the other group.

On the other hand, individuals may select groups because of personal values or needs they wish to fulfill. Often the status of a group will be an enticement. If not the group's prestige, it may be the security of belonging to the group or the need to identify oneself with the image that the group creates. Individuals may join groups because they are able to play a role different from other roles they fulfill. A person whose occupation is one of menial labor may be the respected leader of a garden club.

Whatever the motives in acquiring group membership, there is an expected outcome that each individual seeks and that determines satisfaction with the group. A person's self-esteem is affected by groups of significance to the individual—family, church, occupation, service clubs, or social organizations. The positions that individuals hold in each group affect the way others react to them, their levels of aspiration, and how they feel about themselves. Membership in a group is generally perceived in a positive light, but may in fact become a difficult burden. Forced participation in a group or heavy responsibilities may make group memberships more a personal liability than a benefit.

When group membership is a good thing, however, there are several incidental yet positive outcomes that occur (Rosenfeld, 1973). One positive outcome sometimes resulting from group membership is the development of a commitment to achieving the proposed outcome. Generally individuals who have been deeply involved in a group decision feel a sense of loyalty and responsibility to each other. Thus a decision of the group is more likely to be enacted than a decision by an individual. Another positive outcome of group membership is the possibility of learning more about one's impact as a communicator. By carefully noting other members' reactions to one's attempts at communication, impact as a communicator can be studied and improved. A third positive outcome that may result from group membership is the opportunity to develop meaningful relationships. Because of the opportunity within small groups to become personally acquainted with all members, communication can exist on a more meaningful, less superficial plane. Last, problem-solving procedures can be learned through group work. By observing the different approaches to a problem suggested by different members, one can learn to judge ideas critically and to compromise.

Groups are dynamic in that members are continuously changing and adjusting relationships with each other. Because of the potential for developing close interpersonal relationships, there is a continuous restructuring and readjustment to reduce tensions, eliminate conflicts, and reach solutions to problems. In fact, the term "group dynamics" is widely used in reference to the complex interactions that occur in every group throughout its existence, and

which account for the outcomes and decisions agreed upon by the members of the group.

Small Group versus Individual Potential

PROPERTIES OF GROUPS

There are many situations where small groups are more effective than individuals in reaching decisions, but small groups are not always the best means of solving a particular problem. A look at some common properties of groups is useful to develop a framework for differentiating between those situations where the individual can be more effective and efficient than the small group. Consider the following properties of groups (Knowles and Knowles, 1959).

GOAL

Summarize characteristics of a small group.

---

1. **Background**—The history or lack of history of the group influences the way it operates and the confidence placed in it.
2. **Participation Pattern**—Participation among members may vary from none to complete dominance by one member. Generally, groups where all members participate to some extent will exhibit a deeper commitment to the task and outcomes.
3. **Communication**—The clearness with which members express ideas, opinions, and feelings will be directly related to the effectiveness of the group. When members are unable to understand each other, there is little chance of success.
4. **Cohesion**—Cohesion refers to the strength of the commitments that hold the group together. There will be less destructive interaction in cohesive groups.
5. **Atmosphere**—Atmosphere refers to the extent to which group members feel able to be openly and honestly expressive. It will directly affect the ways that members participate.
6. **Standards**—The set of standards determines what is proper and acceptable behavior within the group. They may be openly expressed or be implicit.

7. **Procedures**—The methods that groups use to get things done are procedures. All groups must have some procedures. They affect group cohesiveness, atmosphere, and communication patterns.
8. **Goals**—All groups have goals, their purpose for being. Often goals are vague or merely implicit, sometimes resulting in confusion about what is to be done.
9. **Sociometric Pattern**—Some relationships between and among members of a group are more successful than others. The sociometric pattern refers to the extent of close and not so close relationships that develop. It seems that individuals are more likely to agree with those members they like than those they dislike.
10. **Structure**—Groups have both visible and invisible organizational structures that make it possible to assign tasks and get things done. To further consider the advantages of groups, review Lessons from Geese Box.

These ten characteristics are certainly relevant in differentiating small groups from individuals and make the small group the dynamic force that it can be. They also lead to group ineffectiveness in some situations and the greater effectiveness of the individual.

Deciding between Individual and Group

Group discussion is most appropriate when a goal can be reached more effectively by the interaction of several people than by the thoughts of a single person. Below is a list of questions (Rosenfeld, 1973) that can be used to decide whether a given situation is more appropriate for group or individual consideration. An answer of "yes" indicates group consideration is important; an answer of "no" indicates the appropriateness of individual consideration.

1. Are many steps required to reach the goal?
2. Is achievement of several goals being attempted simultaneously?

3. Will an appropriate procedure for achieving the goal be difficult to establish?
4. Are the group members likely to perceive the goal as impersonal?
5. Would a single individual be unlikely to have the knowledge needed to reach the goal?
6. Does the plan for achieving the goal demand a division of labor?
7. Are many diverse ideas useful to establish a plan?
8. Are many hours of time required to reach the goal?
9. Will there be some risks that are better shared?
10. Is it likely that group members will be motivated to coordinate their efforts in reaching the goal?

These questions as a whole are probably most appropriate for problem-solving groups; some may be inappropriate for learning-oriented, social, and therapeutic groups.

All in all, groups are an essential force in the achievement of the human causes of survival and enrichment of life. Consider some examples of goals that are more appropriate for individuals than small groups, and vice versa. An individual decision is probably appropriate for selecting personal items that reflect an individual personality, fulfilling routine on-the-job responsibilities for which procedures have been developed, and making critical judgments when only one knowledgeable person is available. Group consideration is often useful in solving controversial problems, presenting detailed information about a variety of aspects of a certain topic, and planning a charity ball for 2000 people. The usefulness of groups probably underlies the popularity of the phrase, "two heads are better than one."

There is often strength in numbers. People will perform actions as a member of a group that they would never consider doing alone. Often group strength will be positive. For example, a complaint about destroying wetlands might go unheard if voiced by one person, when a group of 15 will get the attention of

> **GOAL**
> Describe situations in which a group decision is superior to individual decision making.

Lessons from Geese

Facts	Lessons
1. As each goose flaps its wings, it creates an "uplift" for the bird that follows. By flying in a "V" formation, the flock's flying range is 71 percent greater than if each bird flew alone.	1. People who share a common direction and sense of community can get where they are going more quickly and easily because they are traveling on the thrust of one another.
2. Whenever a goose falls out of formation, it suddenly feels the drag and resistance of trying to fly alone and quickly moves back into formation to take advantage of the "lifting power" of the bird immediately in front.	2. If we have as much sense as a goose we stay in formation with those headed where we want to go. We are willing to accept their help and give our help to others.
3. When the lead goose gets tired, it rotates back into the formation and another goose flies to the point position.	3. It pays to take turns doing the hard tasks and sharing leadership. As with geese, people are interdependent on each other's skills, capabilities, and unique arrangements of gifts, talents or resources.
4. The geese in formation honk from behind to encourage those up front to keep up their speed.	4. We need to make sure our honking is encouraging. In groups where there is encouragement, the production is much greater. The power of encouragement (to stand by one's heart or core values and encourage the heart and core of others) is the quality of honking we seek.
5. When a goose gets sick, wounded, or shot down, two geese drop out of formation and follow it down to help and protect it. They stay with it until it dies or is able to fly again. Then, they launch out on their own, joining another formation or catching up with their flock.	5. If we have as much sense as geese, we will stand by each other in difficult times as well as when we are strong.

Taken from a speech given by Angeles Arrien at the 1991 Organizational Development Network and based on the work of Milton Olsen.

officials. Other times group strength leads to negative consequences. Consider looting behavior during a crisis. People who are not prone to criminal activity will break windows or steal property as part of a mob. It is ironic, also, that sometimes a group will take an action that not one of the members really wanted to do. Have you ever joined a group of friends for an evening, gone to dinner or a movie, and later you all admitted that you would rather have stayed home? As you participate in groups, use your critical reasoning skills to be certain that the actions of the group represent actions that you would support as an individual.

Summary

A small group is a gathering of three to fifteen or twenty people who come together and rely upon communication processes as a means of achieving common goals. The optimum group size is probably an odd number no greater than nine. Groups serve a variety of functions, but most groups can be classified by their primary purpose: problem solving, learning, socialization, or therapy. People join groups for a variety of reasons. Several common reasons are the group purpose, status of membership, and opportunity to adopt different roles. Many goals can be more effectively achieved through group participation, yet the potential of the individual should not be overlooked. Groups enable human beings to come together to fulfill a variety of social, psychological, and physical needs.

CHAPTER 11

IMPORTANT FACTORS FOR GROUP PARTICIPATION

During the early stages of forming a small group, it is important to eliminate any barriers to communication. Early gatherings of the group provide an awareness period when members can begin to know each other, set a clear goal, ask questions, discuss possible barriers, define terms, determine research procedures, select a group leader, establish a plan, and set a definite time line for reaching the goal. Each member of the group should be encouraged to make an oral contribution to the group. Members who hesitate to get involved in the early stages are not likely to contribute later. In addition, to be productive and efficient, leadership patterns must be established within the group.

After effective communication channels are established, deeper discussion of ways to achieve group goals can occur. The current situation, time constraints, and appropriate activities to implement a solution become important topics for discussion. There are seldom single causes or solutions to the sometimes complex problems that arise in achieving group goals. Through effective small group communication, groups can reach goals by proceeding from analysis of the problem to determination of a plan, to its implementation, and eventual evaluation. A synergy (Covey, 1989), when the whole is greater than the sum of its parts, will develop as creative cooperation grows among group members. The chapter begins with a conceptual introduction of creativity and then provides some very prescriptive suggestions for how to participate as a group member or group leader.

Creativity

A blank page, a bare canvas, an empty room, nothing for dinner but unrelated ingredients, a speech outline with no content—we have all been there and faced the prospect of failure. However, with a bit of extra effort and with the stress associated with failure as motivation, we usually come through in the end. Creativity is the process of taking the ingredients at hand, sometimes adding to them, and eventually producing a masterpiece. Persistence, the ability to keep going to the point of closure, is a very important component of the creative process. The interaction and synergy of groups makes the creative process easier since the various members can stimulate the ideas of the others.

According to Twyla Tharp (2004) in her book, *The Creative Habit: Learn It and Use It for Life*, creativity starts with small ideas which can be built upon. She suggests some of the following sources as places to find those small ideas.

- Reading—the Internet, of course, can give you numerous ideas to consider.
- Conversation—talk to people, you will be surprised at what they know.
- Observation—look around and notice details which might stimulate ideas.
- Mentors—many successful people are flattered to share their insights.
- Heroes—study those whom you admire, e.g., Frank Lloyd Wright in architecture.
- Nature—be inspired by the beauty around you.
- Variety—use several of the above ideas to get the creative juices flowing.

Do not give up if you get into a rut and seem to be going nowhere. The first thing to do is to admit that you are stuck and try different strategies to get going again.

To be creative in a situation, you have an advantage when you consider some or all of the following character traits.

- Be motivated to keep your body physically fit. You need endurance to go beyond the ordinary to find a creative solution. Being rested and nourished will allow your body to focus resources on your mental activity.
- Compartmentalize any problems or distractions that will destroy your focus. Compartmentalizing, where you mentally refuse to allow yourself to be distracted, is very difficult but tell yourself to focus on the creative process for a short period and then give yourself permission to think again about your distractions. Gradually lengthen the time you focus.
- Evaluate how much risk you can take. Being free to be outrageous in your ideas might be highly creative but might mean you lose a job, alienate an associate, or even earn a low grade on a class project.
- Realize that time is a factor. Few of us have unlimited time to create. We have deadlines that need to be considered in the overall scheme.
- Be open-minded and non-judgmental. Are you one of those people whose first answer to a novel idea is always "No!"? Be willing to change your mind up to the point that a decision must be made.

Most of all, do not give up when faced with the blank, the bare, the empty and be persistent until you find the best solution given the level of risk, the time available, and the resources at hand.

Effective Group Participation

SOME TECHNIQUES

The communication potential of a small group can be enhanced when individuals take some responsibility for interaction among members (Knowles and Knowles, 1959). Group members can encourage each other. This involves being open to what others have to say, praising and indicating agreement when possible, and being responsive to the contributions of all group members. Each member can be a gate keeper and see to it that all members have a chance to make a contribution. This can be achieved by suggesting limits for each speaker or by addressing a member who has not contributed. Group participation is facilitated by paying attention when others express their views. Group procedures bog down when members care to listen only to themselves. Group members can attempt to relieve tension when negative feelings erupt. It is sometimes helpful to ease the situation with humor. It should be obvious by now that communication is the key to effective group participation. Small group work can be accomplished more smoothly when group members use critical and reflective thinking to express their views clearly, listen attentively to others, and strive to seek a solution acceptable to all.

Often rules make events go more smoothly. Defining rules for effective group participation would be somewhat arbitrary. However, the following list includes six statements that could be called rules for effective group participation (Cassels, 1960). Following the statements are questions that group members might ask themselves as they clarify their purpose and seek to achieve their goals.

1. Define clearly the goals of the group. Time is wasted because of ambiguity surrounding what it is the group is attempting to do. What is the specific group goal? What information or research is necessary before a goal can be reached? What questions must be answered to reach the goal? What terms need to be defined so that all members benefit from the discussion?
2. Determine the power the group has in seeking to achieve its goal. This will affect the decisions to be made. Are there any barriers (e.g., time, money, facilities, authority) to overcome in reaching the goal? What specific factors have interfered with reaching this goal in the past?
3. Make it clear that contributions are expected from all group members. The person who simply nods from time to time might be replaced by a more active participant. Who will be involved in the process of achieving the goal?

GOAL
Participate effectively in groups through effective listening and by using critical and reflective thinking.

4. Allow as many potential outcomes to be discussed as possible. Then begin to evaluate the alternatives and make decisions. What are some alternative ways that this goal might be achieved? What are the advantages and disadvantages to each alternative solution? What obstacles may come up to prevent implementing the plan? What can be done to overcome the obstacles?
5. Do not attach ideas to the person who proposed them. Rather than "Ralph's plan," call it "Plan A." Which solution would be best for the group?
6. Allow members to vary roles from time to time by encouraging flexibility. A group leader, for example, might permit other members to conduct parts of the meeting where their expertise is especially relevant. How can the solution be put into operation? Who can facilitate the process of implementing the solution?

The rules and questions listed above are not necessarily applicable to all situations but can be considered in the process of achieving the goals of a small group.

It seems then from this analysis that groups can be more effective when the means for achieving the group goal are given careful consideration. Effective communication patterns and a definite plan for achieving the group goal are probably the two most important factors in achieving a successful outcome for a small group.

ADVERSE GROUP BEHAVIOR

People seem to notice adverse behaviors more readily than effective behaviors. In fact it is all too easy to take effective behavior for granted. Nonverbal cues are especially evident indicators of adverse reactions by members of small groups. Verbal indicators of adverse behaviors are readily definable as well.

Nonverbal Behaviors

Nonverbal cues of dissatisfaction are sometimes sent in obvious ways by those who are not involved with the group and those who disagree with the group. Indicators of noninvolvement include leaning back in the chair, little or no eye contact, fidgeting, and nonexpressive face. This behavior is in contrast to the individual who leans forward, looks at group members, and smiles and nods to reinforce the discussion. Disagreement can be indicated by crossed arms, frowning, and nervous body movements. This is in contrast to nodding the head in agreement and a more relaxed and open body position.

Not listening is certainly an example of adverse group behavior. Before an individual can agree to a solution, it is essential to understand prior messages. The person who constantly asks questions or repeats what has just been said because of failure to listen is certainly a detriment. This is in contrast to the member who seeks to clarify by paraphrasing, or who adds supporting evidence to give credibility to an opinion.

Verbal Behaviors

Verbal tactics aimed at interrupting group progress may be more adverse than the nonverbal tactics. Good examples of this are blocking discussion by bringing in unrelated personal experiences, arguing on a point seemingly resolved, or flat rejection of ideas without a logical reason. Showing hostility or aggression toward specific group members by blaming, criticizing, attacking motives, or deflating egos are other verbal tactics disruptive to group progress. Boasting about personal accomplishments, or calling attention to oneself by excessive talking are other forms of disruptive behavior. Trying to dominate by intimidating other members, withdrawing, whispering to others, and pleading are still other disruptive techniques.

Being an effective group participant is certainly more difficult than being a disruptive one. It takes little practice to acquire the adverse skills listed above. An effective group member may acquire skill in dissipating behaviors that begin to be detrimental to group progress.

RESPONSIBILITIES OF THE GROUP MEMBER

Groups are composed of all types of people, all attempting, it is hoped, to make contributions in their own ways. Many authors have attempted to describe certain types of individuals who seem to surface in numerous small groups. The list can go on and on. A list that seems fairly representative yet not unduly long is given as

---

GOAL

Distinguish between productive and nonproductive behaviors in a small group.

The Teacher Alone

I suppose anyone fat-headed enough
to stand up in front of more
than one person and try to say something
          deserves what he gets
but if you're being rude
because you've spent so much time
with your television set

ignoring walter cronkite
and/or
beating your toy on the floor
in front of captain kangaroo
that you've gone and lost sight
of reality
then i must respond
and call you on it

if i don't
and just let it slide
i might as well be on TV
and this room really is twenty-four inches
wide
and absolutely empty

—Ric Masten
The Voice of the Hive published by Sunflower Ink, Carmel, CA

follows (Arnold and Hirsch, 1977) with brief explanations of the types.

1. **Harmonizer**—This person is responsible for keeping things going smoothly, reducing misunderstandings, and reconciling those who have conflicts. A typical statement: "Wait a minute, we've made some progress, let's not lose it, that argument may clear itself up as we proceed."

2. **Encourager**—The encourager attempts to achieve the full participation of all group members and is generally able to do this by employing outstanding interpersonal communication skills. A typical statement: "Joan, we haven't heard from you yet. What do you think about . . .?"

3. **Clarifier**—The clarifier employs descriptive listening skills to facilitate the group by restating or paraphrasing important points during discussion. A typical statement: "That's a good point, Jim. Let me be certain that I have it right. You said . . ."

4. **Initiator**—This is the person who suggests new ideas when everyone else is exhausted. A typical statement: "Wait until you hear this. How would it be if we . . .?"

5. **Energizer**—This group member is very task-oriented, reminds the group of goals and deadlines, and makes certain that things get done on time. A typical statement: "We've been dwelling on this point for over an hour and I can't see that we're accomplishing anything."

6. **Questioner**—The questioner often brings up issues that the group has overlooked and seeks information that might prove useful in achieving group goals. A typical statement: "Has anyone done any reading on this that might lend support to what we're deciding to do?'

7. **Listener**—The larger the group, the more likely it is that it will contain one or more persons who are truly interested in what the group is doing but who make few verbal contributions. This is generally viewed negatively. However, we've all been in groups where a few listeners would have been appreciated.

GOAL

Identify consequences of roles, skills, and attitudes on group participation.

---

8. **Tension Reducer**—The tension reducer knows the exact place for a joke or a humorous side comment in a small group meeting that is getting tense or dull. A typical statement: "Hey guys, this group reminds me of . . ."

9. **Opinion Giver**—This person is extremely well prepared and adept at making meaningful comments that have a sound basis. A typical statement: "Considering that 95% of . . . we probably ought to . . ."

10. **Dominator**—The dominator uses such tactics as interruptions, long monologues, or long arguments in an attempt to assert authority. A typical statement goes on and on and includes many references to "I."

11. **Negativist**—One who finds fault with everything, refuses to cooperate, and interjects derogatory comments to make a point is a negativist. A typical statement: "That was a dumb idea. Why can't this group ever be creative?"

12. **Deserter**—The deserter is indifferent, aloof, and refuses to become involved with the task of achieving group goals. A typical statement (off the subject in a loud whisper directed to another individual): "Have you seen the movie that just opened at the cinema?"

13. **Aggressor**—This individual's only goal seems to be to achieve personal status within the group. This is often attempted through boasting, criticizing others, deflating egos, and trying to get attention. A typical statement: "Unlike some others in this group, I am able to grasp the subtle implications of such a decision and recommend that we . . ."

Do you recognize any of these typical members in the groups to which you belong?

Most group members will, hopefully, fulfill roles that make positive contributions to the group. In general, however, members of small groups have two main responsibilities. The first of these is to be prepared for meetings. This means completing tasks assigned to the individual or the group as a whole before the meeting. It means completing unassigned tasks if necessary to be adequately prepared. Group members can prepare themselves by reading relevant material, questioning others who might have input, and thinking through relevant issues before meeting with the group. A prepared group member is able to participate. Involvement with and participation in the group is the second general responsibility of group members.

Some more specific responsibilities for effective group memberships are given below.

1. Be on a first name basis with members of the small group and remember the names of all members.
2. Be active, energetic, and dynamic; be a good, serious listener.
3. Be willing to share knowledge and experience.
4. Give active nonverbal responses when someone else has the floor.
5. Speak up when you feel strongly about an issue.
6. Think critically and reflectively; ask questions to clarify points of view that are difficult to understand.
7. Do not only sit and listen but propose new ideas, activities, and procedures.
8. Encourage others to participate and get involved; be careful not to dominate.
9. Show respect for the opinions of others even when you do not agree.
10. Develop relationships among the ideas presented rather than dwell on independent details.
11. Demonstrate the ability to examine your own personal opinions and prejudices as they apply to the issues, and to change if evidence and reasoning prove you wrong.
12. Evaluate the facts and ideas presented by others rather than merely accept them.
13. Encourage members to undertake worthy projects for which they can enthusiastically share responsibility.
14. Do what you can to keep all members active and involved in group activities.

15. Contribute to such meeting preparations as arranging furniture, serving refreshments, and cleaning up.

If, as a group member, you can perform the fifteen tasks above, you will make a contribution to the final achievement of the group goal that far surpasses that of the average member.

Group Leadership

Some groups function quite well without a leader. These are generally very small groups where all members are motivated and interact well on an interpersonal level. Most functioning groups will have a leader who accepts responsibility for keeping the group organized and productive. The leader of a group may be appointed by some higher authority (e.g., the executive that establishes the committee); may be elected by a larger group that it serves in some capacity, or by the small group itself; or may emerge as group members learn to interact with each other. The leader may serve for a specific term, or an unspecified length of time, or even change with each meeting. The permanent leader gives the group a greater continuity from meeting to meeting. Achieving tasks may be easier as each member and the leader learn specific roles. If leaders change frequently, however, group members feel more equality and more self-motivation since there is no

The Top Seeded

he perfected his service
his opening statement
until it could not be returned

he entered many conversations
but he died alone

center court
in his spotless whites

—Ric Masten
The Voice of the Hive published by Sunflower Ink,
Carmel, CA

dependence on a single leader. There are several different leadership styles, a number of responsibilities that the leader will accept, and some behaviors that lead to more effective leadership.

LEADERSHIP STYLES

Authoritarian

The authoritarian leader dominates the group by employing the various instruments of power that are vested with the position. For the extremely authoritarian leader, these powers often include punishment, reward, denial, and intimidation. Group members are viewed by the authoritarian leader as subordinates who are unable to formulate ideas and who are certainly unprepared to make decisions. The authoritarian leader, therefore, dictates all policies. The concepts of persuasion, discussion, and group consensus are unknown to persons who serve such leaders. In fact communication generally takes place only through the leader, with virtually no interaction among members.

Democratic

Although democratic leaders may retain the right to make the final decision, they are interested in working with group members to achieve a collective goal. The democratic leader is not interested in power over others but in bringing out the best that all members have to offer. Responsibilities are distributed to all group members. Decisions are discussed and often made by the group as a whole. The democratic leader is primarily a coordinator or a resource person whose success depends

on facilitating the efforts of the entire group in achieving its goal. The democratic leader is accepting of others and is generally an expert in the art of effective interpersonal relationships.

Laissez-faire

Laissez-faire leadership in-volves a minimum of control or possibly no control at all. The group functions more as a spontaneous group of individuals with a common goal. Laissez-faire leadership generally evolves when the leader is withdrawn, unskilled in the tasks, or believes that direction stifles creativity. It is a rare group that can function effectively in the absence of leadership. Generally, the group will achieve little, or the tasks of leadership will be assumed by one of the more dominant members.

GOAL
Identify application of leadership styles to real-world situations.

Comparison of Styles

From this brief analysis of the three leadership styles, it probably seems that the democratic style is the only one that can be effective. In many situations this is true. However, the authoritarian style has the advantage of efficiency when the time allotted to reach a decision is short. Because the need for discussion under democratic leadership and the possibility of total floundering under laissez-faire leadership, neither is as effective when time is a factor. Consider the coach of a football team determining a crucial play. Which leadership style would you choose? Without a highly respected person in the role of leader, the authoritarian style often leads to poor motivation, discontent, and lack of individuality among group members. It is probably best, when being authoritarian, to be benevolent and consider

Leadership Styles	
Authoritarian	You will write the letters.
Democratic	Who will write the letters?
Laissez-Faire	There are some letters to be written.

group members as human beings with distinct feelings and needs.

Under democratic leadership members are generally more creative and work harder than under the other leadership styles. The group process is more rewarding to members when all feel they have a place. As they learn to know and respect each other, group members under a democratic leader will develop closer, more satisfying relationships with each other. The good feelings of the group may be viewed as more important than achievement of the task. Becoming an effective democratic leader is probably more difficult for most people than becoming an effective authoritarian leader.

Is there no place for the laissez-faire leader? There is in groups that are most likely small and composed of individuals with very similar expectations and working styles. Each member is a leader and each a follower as they work closely together to achieve the group goal. Generally, however, the laissez-faire style leads to the eventual discontent of all members when the group seems to be getting nowhere.

RESPONSIBILITIES OF LEADERS

Leaders may of course delegate responsibilities to other group members. Ultimately, however, the group leader will probably be the one held accountable for certain tasks that must be done to enable the group to proceed. There are two major types of leadership responsibilities: those relating to arrangements and plans for meetings, and those relating to facilitation of group interactions. These will be described in a general context probably more appropriate for the democratic leader than the authoritarian or laissez-faire leader.

Meeting Arrangements

The leader is responsible for locating a place to conduct the meeting and for arranging seating to provide an optimum environment. The facility in which the group assembles can enhance the process and possibly the outcome of the meeting. When it is obvious that the planners have given thought to meeting arrangements, group members often feel a greater responsibility toward achieving the task

of the meeting. Generally, comfortable seating that allows all members to relate interpersonally with all other members will be most suitable. This can be done by arranging chairs in a circle or semicircle, or around a square or round table. Having regular meeting times and places helps members schedule attendance.

Agenda

The leader should plan the discussion and activities of the meeting prior to the meeting time. This necessitates an awareness of the critical topics to be discussed and advance contact with other officers or committee leaders. It is probably wise to prepare an agenda for the meeting. Copies of the agenda can be sent to members in advance or can be distributed at the beginning of the meeting. If agendas are distributed in advance, members are reminded of their responsibilities and are better able to prepare for the meeting. Along with the agenda, the leader should distribute copies of other relevant materials such as minutes and financial reports. If making copies of the agenda and related materials is impossible, it is extremely important that the leader, at least, have knowledge of the meeting plan and have a copy of important materials.

Facilitator

Once the meeting is in progress the leader's role often becomes that of facilitator. The leader should introduce new members to the group, get each member immediately involved, watch the time and indicate progress, restate opinions for clarity, offer fresh ideas when appropriate, summarize the transactions of the meeting, and provide a transition to the next meeting. The leader is especially important when conflicts arise. The leader might try to get at the source of the problem and get members to talk about the conflict, move on to a new topic, call a recess, or perhaps ask an extremely hostile member to leave the meeting. To facilitate participation of all members, the leader might attempt to draw quieter members into the discussion during early meetings (i.e., before the wrong pattern becomes set), be especially attentive when less active members speak, direct questions specifically to less involved members, use eye contact and nonverbal language to get the reluctant member involved, or prevent any one individual from monopolizing the conversation. Leaders must develop individual styles as they fulfill their responsibility for keeping the group moving toward its goal.

EFFECTIVE LEADERS

An effective leader might be defined as one whose group manages to achieve its goals while maintaining good feelings about one another. It is doubtful that significant goals can be reached without all or most group members assuming some responsibility and being accountable for results. Although no recipe for effective leadership has been found, much has been learned and written about leaders. It is probable that a good leader will have abilities in the areas of decision making, communication, and motivation of others. Although many leaders seem to have natural abilities, many effective leaders have studied, learned, and practiced the skills that helped in achieving their success.

Decision Making

In order to be an effective leader it is necessary to be able to make decisions. Too often decisions are made by default. That is, no decision is made but events go on until something that must be lived with occurs. Some helpful hints for making decisions (Engstrom and Mackenzie,

1968) include the following: do not make decisions under stress; base decisions on adequate data; do not put off decisions; consult other people who will be affected by the decision; do not be afraid to make a wrong decision; and do not worry about the decision once it is made. It is important that leaders have confidence in their ability to make decisions. A decision backed by confidence is more likely to succeed than one broached with timidity.

Communication

All groups seem to complain about poor communication. Much has been written about communication and it makes good reading. Many leaders, and others as well, make the mistake of overlooking the essential role of practice. One cannot learn the skill of playing tennis solely from reading; likewise, communication skills must be practiced repeatedly to become a subconscious force in interaction with others.

Human minds often race at two to three times the speed of the spoken word. Thus people continually tune in and out on conversations. Often poor listening habits result in the missing of important details. Some key points for leaders to consider as they listen (Engstrom and Mackenzie, 1968) are the following: evaluate what is being said (i.e., use critical listening skills); consider the credibility of the speaker, and whether statements are supported with evidence; ask questions to confirm the relevance of and to clarify a point; and do not rule

---

Agenda for March 1

1. Call to Order
2. Minutes from February 15
3. Report
   - A. Treasurer
   - B. Committees
4. Old Business
5. New Business
6. Program
7. Announcements
8. Closing

out the relevance of a subject because it appears uninteresting.

Leaders are discussion facilitators as well as listeners. In this role they keep the meeting going or let it bog down and perhaps end in failure. Some hints for improving skill as a discussion leader (Brilhart, 1965) are the following: have a clear understanding of group goals; become skillful in organizing the results of group thinking; remain open minded; be an active group participant; be democratic and consultative; have respect for and sensitivity to others; be self-controlled and show restraint; and share rewards and give credit to the group.

Motivation

The leader's role extends beyond the meeting time and place. The effective leader is able to generate an enthusiasm that carries on after meetings are over to times when members must accomplish tasks on their own. How does a leader get members of a group to do what has to be done? It is, of course, important to be sensitive to and aware of the feelings of others. Some suggestions the effective leader might study in an attempt to eliminate behaviors potentially harmful to the interest and motivation of the group (Feinberg, 1965) are the following: never belittle, as this destroys self-worth and initiative; never criticize a group member in front of others even if tempted under pressure; never fail to give a group member your individual attention; never seem preoccupied with your own interests; never play favorites; never fail to help your members grow; never be insensitive to small things; never embarrass a weak member; and never vacillate in making a decision. To summarize these nine suggestions, the best way for group leaders to motivate group members is to demonstrate a consciousness of individual needs, ambitions, fears, and worth.

The insensitive leader, who is perhaps unintentionally aloof, cold, impersonal, and uninterested in individuals, usually finds it difficult to get group members to exert that extra effort. Some suggestions for what the effective leader might do to enhance motivation among group members (Feinberg, 1965) are the following: let people know where you stand; give praise when it is due; keep members informed of

A Sleeper

to be a poet reading
is chancy work at best
tough enough to face rejection
but worse
far worse this:

you fell asleep
even as i read you closed your eyes
and dropped your head upon your chest
and to this day i marvel
that you kept your seat
           nodding
           east and west

and although i find it sad
i guess it's only human
that looking back upon a sea
of open faces
i can best recall the one that slept
and wonder were you overtired
        or simply bored
           with all that i expressed
only now writing this
years later
have i thought to ask about the dream
you might have had that day
           and all
           i may have missed

—Ric Masten
Dragonflies, Codfish and Frogs published by
Sunflower Ink, Carmel, CA

changes that may affect them; perceive people as ends, not means to an end; confirm the feeling that group goals and members are important; be caring, tactful, considerate, and courteous; be willing to learn from others; show through behavior and speech that the tasks of the group can be accomplished by the group members; allow freedom of expression; delegate responsibility; and allow group members to make as many decisions as possible, learn from mistakes, and be proud of successes. The effective leader, therefore, does not motivate through threats or authority but by building the self-esteems and expectations of the group members. Like the comments dealing with leader responsibility, these on group motivation are most likely appropriate primarily for the democratic leader.

Summary

The effectiveness of small groups often depends on the communication skills and contributions made by members and leaders. Group members have two general responsibilities: to be prepared to participate in group activities and actually to participate in a positive way. All small group members must remain alert to what is said and decided as plans are made to achieve group goals. Leaders, whether authoritarian, democratic, or laissez-faire, are responsible for seeing that meeting arrangements are made, for preparing an agenda for conducting meetings, and for facilitating discussion during meetings. Group leaders must possess skill in decision making, communication, and motivation of others.

CHAPTER 12

SOME APPLICATIONS OF SMALL GROUP COMMUNICATION

Although small group communication occurs spontaneously in a variety of everyday settings, there are special techniques in group communication settings that can be used for specific purposes. One of these is brainstorming, a technique useful in providing creative alternative solutions for problem solving. A second type of small group activity occurs during the meeting of a committee or small organization. Ground rules appropriate for conducting a meeting can contribute to group productivity. Another example is the round-table discussion, where a small group comes together to talk about an issue of interest or importance. A fourth type of activity involves small groups who discuss a topic or make coordinated presentations in front of an audience. Some of the more formal presentations of this type are the panel discussion, forum, symposium, or colloquium. In addition, a small group might form to make a more informal and perhaps creative presentation about some topic of interest to an audience. In this latter case, presentation strategies can be varied to provide greater interest and even audience involvement.

Brainstorming

Brainstorming is a special technique used primarily in problem-solving groups. It is one of the most creative ways to generate ideas in a small group setting. It can be applied to any problem if there is a wide range of possible solutions, not one of which can be said in advance to be right or wrong. The group simply starts with a problem stated in the form of a question. Each member of the small group, preferably limited to three to five persons, answers with the first thought that comes to mind. One group member, serving as recorder, makes notes on each member's ideas. There is no evaluation of the suggestions during the idea-generating phase of the process. Thus, brainstorming is a technique of quickly generating as many possible solutions as the individuals in the group can think of.

Let's look at an example of the brainstorming process. Picture a group of five elementary school teachers seated at a table brainstorming the question, "What types of equipment should we include in the school's proposal for a creative playground?" Remember, one member of the group is the recorder.

Person 1: I'll start. Parallel bars with ladders at each end.

Person 2: A fort with a wall and a small garrison that can be crawled into.

Person 3: A twisted tube that the kids can crawl and slide through.

Person 4: A sandbox made from railroad ties.

Person 5: Rocking horses, but with other animals like fish, chickens, and elephants.

Person 1: Stacks of tires of different heights in a rectangular area.

Person 2: A slide that twists around and around like a spiral.

Person 3: A raised platform with a ladder leading to it through the middle.

Person 4: A rocket ship with ladders and platforms inside and out.

Person 5: A tall rocket ship with ladders and platforms inside and the spiral slide on the outside.

GOAL
Demonstrate use of brainstorming to generate possible solutions to problems.

The process goes on until time or ideas are exhausted. Early in the process, when all members are generating fresh ideas, it is probably better to go around the table person by person. Later, when ideas are harder to generate, people can respond out of turn as ideas come to them. During the brainstorming process, it is essential that there be no criticism, either verbal or nonverbal. The wilder, more free-wheeling the ideas, the better the process is working. Quantity of ideas is the goal—the more suggestions the better. Combinations of ideas and improvement of ideas are encouraged.

When the idea generation process is ended, the group should examine the advantages and disadvantages of each suggestion. The least effective should be discarded immediately, leaving a group of plausible alternatives to be discussed, built upon, and improved until a final decision can be made. It is sometimes better to delay the review process for several days. With fresh minds and a new look at the ideas, it is often easier to make a final decision.

If there is creative interaction and spontaneity during the idea-generating session, the alternative solutions to the problem will provide a unique set of potential outcomes. As long ago as 1926, Walls, in his book *The Art of Thought*, suggested the following five steps to enhance the creative process.

1. **Preparation**—sensing and defining a problem, gathering needed information
2. **Concentration**—focusing attention, excluding other demands—BRAINSTORMING
3. **Incubation**—withdrawing, sorting, reflecting

4. **Illumination**—"Aha" phenomenon where ideas emerge "out of the blue"
5. **Verification**—testing and evaluating, implementing, explaining worth of the idea

With the emphasis in American education today on preparation of students for high stakes testing, often creative classes and activities are excluded. Students are taught to follow protocols for solving problems, a good strategy for passing a test but a strategy that limits consideration of new ways to solve problems. Brainstorming is a great technique for letting the mind run wild. Brainstorming is an effective intrapersonal strategy to use with yourself when you need to find alternatives to a personal problem.

Ground Rules for Meetings

Meetings occur when people assemble for the purpose of working together to make decisions, collect or disseminate information, plan, or problem solve. Many meetings are conducted under circumstances which lead participants to conclude that their time was wasted. The leader of a group has some responsibility for planning and conducting meetings; participants must also share this responsibility by fulfilling their commitments and assigned tasks. Meetings are much more productive when a suitable environment has been arranged, when an agenda is developed and shared, and when participants enter the meeting having completed expected preparations (see chapter 11 on Responsibilities of Leaders).

Numerous suggestions for running meetings are available. It is helpful if a group will discuss rules of communication like those listed as follows and decide on those which are acceptable behavior for fulfilling the mission.

1. Members will perceive the meeting as a safe zone—repercussion will not occur from input by the various participants.
2. Members will not assume superior/inferior roles.
3. Members will all participate and no one will dominate,
4. Members will share responsibility for keeping the group on track.
5. Members will listen as allies, not adversaries.
6. Members will speak one at a time.
7. Members will practice active listening skills.
8. Members will give freely of their experiences.
9. Members will maintain other's self-esteem.
10. Members will agree only when it makes sense to do so.
11. Members will keep an open mind.
12. Members will maintain confidentiality.

Members of groups who wish to have effective, productive meetings will often establish an issues bin. The issues bin, a way of listing suggestions and concerns, provides a way for all members of the group to have input into the topics to be included on meeting agendas. The issues bin allows the group to stay on task while insuring that topics of relevance to the group are not forgotten. Members of the group can submit topics that may or will be addressed at a subsequent meeting, questions that can or should be deferred until the end of the current agenda or to the next meeting's agenda, or that can or should be the subject of future agendas. It is important that anything submitted to the issues bin be associated with a member of the group who will be able to justify inclusion and present factual information associated with the issue.

Most people who participate in group activities, whether at home, work, or in the community, feel that time in meetings is often wasted and that better planning would result in greater satisfaction with time spent. Common problems with meetings (Culpepper and Forrest, 1997; 34) are listed below.

- **Unclear Roles and Responsibilities**—Who is supposed to be doing what?
- **Participation Problems**—Getting some members to be quieter and other members to say more

---

GOAL
Conduct an effective meeting through the use of organized planning skills.

- **Recording Syndrome**—Going over the same old ideas again and again
- **Shotgun Syndrome**—Everyone wants to discuss something different and discussions do not build on each other
- **Problem Avoidance**—Everything is fine; there are no problems to discuss
- **Win/Lose Decision Making**—General negativity about others' ideas and little willingness to compromise
- **Communication Problems**—Not listening or understanding, jumping to conclusions, making faulty assumptions, lack of openness and trust, underlying tensions
- **Poor Meeting Environments**—Cannot see, cannot hear, cannot breathe comfortably
- **Confused Objectives and Expectations**—Why are we here and what are we doing?

Because meetings are so prevalent and consume so many hours of time, consideration should be given to making the best of the opportunity for progressing on an issue. The following list summarizes several of the factors which meeting participants have described as favorable characteristics.

1. Clear role definitions that enable participants to know what each is supposed to do and what the overall goal is
2. Time control, which starts and ends the meeting on time with enough time to get the work done. People today, who effectively budget their time, schedule their entire day; meetings which do not end as announced force busy people either to leave or to be late to a subsequent appointment
3. Participants who are sensitive to others and who listen and respect other's views
4. Informal, relaxed atmosphere instead of formal exchange
5. Good preparation by leadership and participants which provides necessary information and materials
6. Members who are qualified and interested with a definite commitment to the group's mission
7. Interruptions avoided or held to a minimum
8. Good minutes or records so that decisions are not lost

9. Committee work that is accepted, used, and makes a contribution
10. Recognition and appreciation given to reflect the contributions of the members
11. Assessment of the group goals and performance with willingness to change or improve

Problems with meetings usually occur when role expectations are unclear or one or more members dominate or appear reticent. Following is a list of ways to "kill your group" (Culpepper and Forrest, 1997; p. 47)—in other words, do NOT be guilty of the following behaviors:

1. Do not attend every meeting.
2. Arrive late and "forget" your notes.
3. Do not speak during the meeting—wait until you get outside.
4. Vote for everything, then do nothing.
5. Find fault with everyone.
6. If asked to help, say you do not have the time.
7. Take all you can get, but give nothing in return.
8. Never ask anyone to join your group.
9. Do not accept a little until you are satisfied with everything the group is doing.
10. Threaten to resign all the time, or give up your job if it gets too rough.

Meetings can be viewed as productive time periods when the combined minds of interested persons achieve more than any of the individuals could achieve alone.

Round-Table Discussion

The round-table discussion occurs when a small group of individuals come together for a formal conversation. The goal is often to reach a solution to a problem or to come to consensus about an attitude or position on a controversial issue. The round-table discussion differs from discussion in general in that there is one specific issue of importance about which the group expects to reach some agreement.

Since interaction among members is essential for a round-table discussion, individuals in

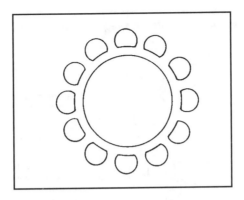

Figure 12.1. Round-Table Discussion

the group must arrange themselves so that eye contact with every other member is possible. Depending on the composition of the group and past experiences together, a leader may or may not be selected. Generally, however, some summary of the outcome will be required. The leader or another designated individual should probably be assigned the responsibility of taking meeting notes and/or summarizing the outcome. And too, a leader or designated individual is sometimes required to keep the group focused on the topic of concern.

The participants in the round-table generally make no formal preparation for the discussion. That is, members do not make formal remarks as a matter of procedure. Members will often prepare, however, by making certain that they are well informed on the topic to be discussed. Most of us will find ourselves involved in round-table discussions at one time or another. A common experience is to attend a lecture and be told to form small groups for more personal involvement with the topic.

There are several techniques that group members can suggest or use to get a more vigorous discussion going in a quiet group. First, a member might suggest that all participants introduce themselves and reveal something about their backgrounds. As people become better acquainted, they are more likely to share ideas. Second, it is sometimes helpful to suggest preparing a list. Often people can think of something to add to a list, and too, a list provides a stimulus for focusing the initial discussion. Another suggestion is to make a provocative or controversial statement. This is a sure

way to generate some response. However, the discussion may turn into a heated argument instead of an orderly discourse. A fourth suggestion is to address someone with a specific question. This can work well if you know that a member of the group has some relevant experience that might provide meaningful input, or at least form a basis for further contributions by others. Round-table discussions often have time limits and silence proves wasteful.

A buzz group is an adaptation of the round-table discussion that allows members to experience the opinions and thoughts of many individuals in the small group setting. Buzz groups consist of four to eight individuals who meet for short periods of time, approximately three to five minutes. At the end of the time limit, several designated individuals leave the group and join a new group. The rotation process is repeated several times as people are exposed to the thoughts of many more individuals than possible in the round-table discussion. When more superficial but varied input is useful, the buzz group can be an interesting approach to group discussion.

Small Group Communication in a Public Setting

Many small groups meet privately, that is, they have no audience or observers. These small groups would include club meetings of many types, meetings of committees, social get-togethers, and brainstorming sessions. Some small groups, however, meet in front of an audience. Their ultimate goal is generally to

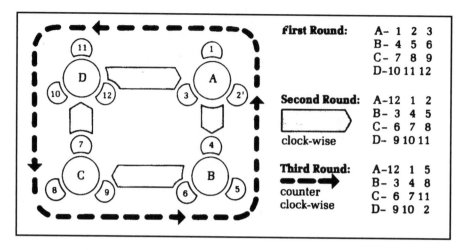

Figure 12.2. Buzz Group

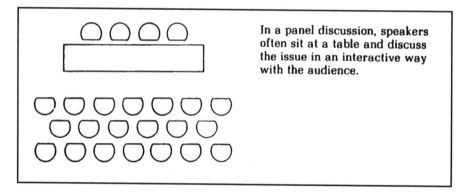

Figure 12.3. Panel Discussion

make a presentation or participate in a discussion for the benefit of another group, possibly quite large, that will assemble for the purpose of listening to the program.

Small group presentations can be described by different titles depending on the exact nature of the program. A few of the formal types of small groups that meet in public for the benefit of other groups are panel discussions, forums, symposia, and colloquia. Often these groups will come together for the first time during the presentation. They will have been selected or organized by a program coordinator.

PANEL DISCUSSION

A panel discussion consists of a group of speakers (usually four to six) who are well informed on an issue. The speakers are generally seated informally at a table. The success of the panel depends on the spontaneity of the speakers as they react to one another and interact with the audience. A panel discussion will usually begin with a short and possibly prepared message by each of the panelists. The audience then begins participating by directing questions to panel members. It is important that the room arrangement be designed to facilitate the speaker-audience interaction. This can be done by placing the panel closer to the audience than in a more formal speaking situation. A moderator is often used to help direct questions and limit the length of questions and answers. The nature of the messages is often informative.

FORUM

Audience participation is not an essential part of a forum. The forum is characterized by a group of experts who present their viewpoints on a topic. The speakers may be organized in a

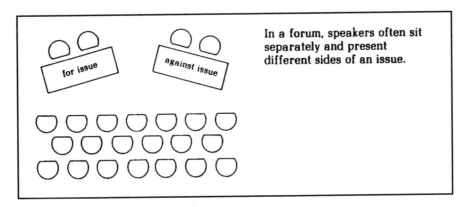

In a forum, speakers often sit separately and present different sides of an issue.

Figure 12.4. Forum

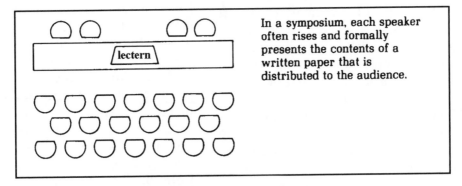

In a symposium, each speaker often rises and formally presents the contents of a written paper that is distributed to the audience.

Figure 12.5. Symposium

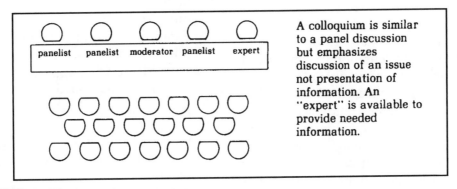

A colloquium is similar to a panel discussion but emphasizes discussion of an issue not presentation of information. An "expert" is available to provide needed information.

Figure 12.6. Colloquium

debating format with speakers designated to present different sides of an issue. The speakers generally give prepared presentations. Interaction with the audience is primarily for clarification of points and not to develop discussion.

SYMPOSIUM

Experts on related topics present prepared papers to an audience during a symposium. Often printed copies or summaries of the presentation are given to the audience. Other times the proceedings of the symposium are posted on the Internet. Audience participation, if allowed, is generally limited to questions to clarify content.

COLLOQUIUM

A group of individuals assembles to discuss an important issue. Experts in the area of discussion are present to provide details that the discussants need to clarify particular points. Generally a moderator is present to call on the experts when appropriate. The topic of discussion is generally a complex or highly specialized topic of interest to the discussants and audience.

Planning and Rehearsing a Small Group Presentation

Small groups may also join forces to present more informal programs for which group members rather than outside coordinators are responsible. In this type of presentation the group members themselves work together in private meetings to establish a plan and to assign and accept responsibilities. These presentations may borrow from the format of the forum, panel discussion, symposium, or colloquium, but are characterized by close planning and rehearsal by the group as a whole.

Many authors of communication texts dismiss the small group presentation as a special case of public speaking. They perceive the several speakers as giving independent presentations which rely on the theory and methods appropriate for public speaking. This is true to some extent, yet the small group working together to make a presentation can provide a program of much more variety than an individual can. The program presented by a small group can move faster and audience interest can be held more easily as the program shifts to different speakers and presentation strategies. Diversity, variety, and faster pace are easier for the small group to achieve than for the individual public speaker. The choice of presentation strategies and systematic process for planning and rehearsing the program are the two keys to a successful presentation. Creativity and enthusiasm should be taken for granted.

PRESENTATION STRATEGIES

Presentation strategies are the ways the speakers use to present information or provide examples. The innovative small group may develop its own strategies of presentation. For the group that needs some ideas, a list of 12 common presentation strategies follows. Keep in mind too that many of these can be useful for individual speakers as well as groups.

1. **Demonstration**—Actual objects, including the human body, are used to show the audience what something is or how something is done. Example: Conflict between verbal and nonverbal messages might be demonstrated by someone saying "I am not angry" through clenched teeth and with a tense posture.

2. **Discussion**—Exchange of viewpoints occurs under the direction of a leader. Example: A member of the presentation team might ask the audience their reaction to something that was just said or open the floor for general questions.

3. **Lecture**—An oral presentation of facts or principles is given to an audience, the members of which will use active listening skills. Example: A member of the team presents concepts associated with assertiveness.

4. **Role-Playing**—Two or more presenters, and/or selected members of the audience, take on the behaviors of others as they act out real or hypothetical situations. Example: A conflict between two people might be shown as it often happens and as it could happen if appropriate communication skills are applied.

5. **Modeling and Imitation**—The audience listens to and watches a demonstration with the intention of copying the demonstrated behaviors thereby improving skill in a task. Example: A technique for participating in a handshake that conveys confidence is demonstrated and the audience attempts to imitate.

6. **Skill Practice Session**—Modeling and imitation is taken a step further as the audience is given the opportunity to practice skills demonstrated by the group and to receive feedback concerning their performance. Example: A technique for initiating an interpersonal encounter might be shown; the audience role plays the skill and is given feedback by the group.

7. **Sensitivity Training**—A group examines feelings about themselves and each other in a straight-forward and honest manner.

Example: A group decides to honestly self-disclose their most frightening fear.

8. **Problem Solving**—A step-by-step procedure is listed which when followed will provide possible solutions to a problem. Example: A process is presented which an individual can use to handle conflict in interpersonal encounters.

9. **Tactile Activity**—Sense of touch is used to present manipulation or perceptual skills as the audience is creatively involved in the content being presented. Example: In describing ways to communicate with children, placing an arm around the shoulder and hugging are demonstrated to show intimacy.

10. **Visual Aids**—Material presented orally is made clearer through the use of posters, charts, chalkboard, felt boards, overhead transparencies, slides, films, or handouts. Example: A chart showing common nonverbal signals using flirtation is distributed to the audience.

11. **Costume and Props**—Artifacts and environment are used to communicate characteristics or reinforce verbal images. Example: In demonstrating effective interview skills, members of the team wear business attire instead of their usually more casual classroom wardrobe.

12. **Staging**—Creativity is used in the movement of the group within the presentation area. Example: Presenters arrange themselves in a panel discussion format and move to the side to role play examples of behavior relevant to their topic.

It is useful for small group members to draw on several of the presentation strategies as they prepare and rehearse their program. Again, groups have the advantage over individuals in that some members can work with equipment and props while others are speaking. A balance in varying strategies and speakers generally results in a program that more easily holds the attention of the audience.

PREPARATION

Once a group is formed to make a group presentation, it is necessary to plan, prepare individual parts, rehearse, revise if necessary, and rehearse again. Group members are responsible not only to themselves but to the group as a whole in working toward a successful program. A list of steps suggested for planning and making a group presentation follows:

1. Become acquainted with all group members.
2. Select a group leader to plan meetings, coordinate activities, and facilitate communication.
3. Define explicitly the goal of the group. What exactly are the instructions, purposes, and expected results of the program?
4. Brainstorm possible ways to achieve the goal. What material should be presented? What presentation strategies can be used effectively? How can interest be created and maintained?
5. Determine a solution from among possible alternatives.
6. Individual assignments are agreed on. All members of the group should agree to do a fair share in pulling the program together and presenting it. Members will have different strengths to contribute and should volunteer information to the group about such strengths.

Hands #2

i have these hands

the right one
swings the hammer
     building

the left
holds the nail
    and dreams

they
work together

—Ric Masten
The Voice of the Hive published by Sunflower Ink,
Carmel, CA

7. Individuals complete responsibilities in preparation for rehearsal. It is useful for individuals to prepare notes for use in rehearsals. Members should be flexible in their preparation and ready to adapt remarks spontaneously in case other members present the same material.

8. A rehearsal is held to time the presentation and to make sure that members are prepared and organized. Complete coverage of all material is not necessary, but a brief summary of what each person will say is needed.

9. Program changes are made if necessary and part or all of the program is rehearsed again.

10. Individuals polish their parts in preparation for the actual performance. The leader should check with and encourage members to do their best.

11. After the presentation, it is useful for the group to evaluate the experience. Was the preparation complete? How did members relate to each other and accept responsibility?

The group presentation takes time. The group process often takes longer to reach a goal than it would take an individual to reach a similar goal, but it is expected that the product resulting from the group interaction will be worth the extra effort.

Summary

Small group communication skills are useful in many formal and informal settings. Some particularly interesting applications of small group communication are brainstorming, conducting productive meetings, group discussion, and group presentations before an audience. Brainstorming is a technique for generating creative ideas for problem-solving situations. The brainstorming technique allows group members to suggest solutions without receiving criticism. Unusual suggestions are encouraged. Evaluation of ideas occurs at a later time. Rules for conducting effective meetings are merely common sense. The small group who meets to achieve a goal must come to a consensus and set ground rules for conducting business. Group discussions are often called round-table discussions. A round-table discussion occurs when a small group meets with the specific purpose of reaching consensus on the solution to a problem or expressing a common attitude about an issue. Group presentations may be unrehearsed or rehearsed. The panel, forum, symposium, and colloquium are examples of group discussion formats where participants often meet for the first time immediately before the presentation. Their roles are often coordinated by a single leader. The rehearsed group presentation is made by individuals who have met to plan and rehearse their roles. The rehearsed group presentation can incorporate presentation strategies and variety that are impossible for an individual presenter.

The Voice of the Hive

when
the shadow of death
fell upon us
the queen mother died
and the swarm
        scattered
        far afield
social insects
self-aware now
        feeling utterly alone

        except
        in our dreams
        songs
        and poetry

there
through it all
the voice of the hive

calling us home

—Ric Masten
The Voice of the Hive published by Sunflower Ink, Carmel, CA

Activity 1

Information about
Small Group Communication

Preparation: Read part 4: Small Group Communication. Prepare for a test by answering the practice items given below.

Practice Items

PART 4: OVERVIEW

1. What are some examples of people needing to be considered part of a group?

CHAPTER 10

1. What are the characteristics of a small group?

2. Why is a group of five to nine members the more "ideal" size for a small group?

3. What are four purposes of small groups?

4. What are specific qualities of groups according to Knowles?

5. What are the seven problem-solving steps used in group communication as defined by Dewey?

6. What are some examples of specific reasons people have for joining groups?

7. What are several positive outcomes that can occur when people join groups?

8. What are common properties of groups as defined by Knowles?

CHAPTER 11

1. What techniques can be used to facilitate interaction among group members?

2. What are six suggestions or rules that group members might use to help them achieve their goals?

3. What are specific nonverbal cues of dissatisfaction often revealed by individual group members?

4. What are specific verbal cues of dissatisfaction often revealed by individual group members?

5. What are some descriptions of specific types of individuals that make up groups?

6. What are specific responsibilities for effective group membership?

7. What are the three major leadership styles and some examples of each?

8. What are specific responsibilities of a group leader?

9. What are three abilities that a good leader should possess?

10. What are specific techniques used by a leader to motivate individuals within a group?

CHAPTER 12

1. What is a definition of the brainstorming process?

2. What specific behaviors are acceptable and unacceptable in the brainstorming process?

3. What are the definitions of the four kinds of discussion groups: forum, panel, symposium, and colloquium?

4. What are the 12 presentational strategies often used in group presentations?

5. What are ten suggestions for planning a group presentation?

Group Activity: Follow course instructions to complete the test for part 4.

Individual Activity: Make arrangements with your instructor to complete the test for part Four.

Activity 2

Learning Small Group Encounter

Preparation: Culture appears to be a glue which cements a group of people together. It is also apparent that culture is transmitted, defined, and enforced through communication.

The concept of subculture is equally as important as the concept of culture. Subcultures are simply smaller groups within a larger society. In America, it is important to note that we are not really a melting pot, but rather a multi-cultural nation in which many different cultures live side by side. There are Irish Americans, Italian Americans, African Americans, Native Americans, Hispanics and many others. In addition to these subcultures, it is important to consider males and females as two separate cultures. The possibility that groups such as hard hats, professors, blue-collar workers, and white-collar workers, may exist as separate subcultures with their own norms and traditions must also be considered.

In communication experiences involving different subcultures, one needs to develop the ability as well as the flexibility to be able to relate to people in new and different ways when necessary. Following is a list of questions. Write answers to the questions and whenever possible, make several responses to each question.

1. Discuss the way in which culture and race relate to each other.

2. Discuss the idea that America is not a melting pot.

3. How can males and females be separate cultures even when they live with each other? How different is the male culture from the female culture? Where do the differences exist?

4. What are the differences between the various subcultures involved in the following three major cultural conflicts: the generation gap, with youth and elderly in conflict; various ethnic groups; and males versus females? What are the differences among these groups which cause conflict, and what role does communication play in these three conflicts? What are the communication differences among these groups?

5. How does the subculture in which we have been reared affect our perception of such things as welfare, poverty, discrimination, the draft, the political process in America, and education opportunities? Do we perceive these things differently according to the culture from which we have come?

6. What words cause severe communication problems among members of various cultural groups in the United States because of the effect of culture on word associations?

7. What nonverbal cues can you think of which are significantly different across different cultures in America? How would these differences adversely affect interpersonal communication between people of different subcultures?

8. What examples can you think of in which stereotypes of prejudices on the part of members of the White, African American, and Hispanic groups lead to the self-fulfilling prophecy in communication between and among the different groups?

Group Activity: In class divide into four small groups. Within each group choose a recorder. Discuss the eight questions and the responses each person made to the questions. The recorder should briefly compile the varied responses as the group attempts to increase knowledge of cultural perceptions held by the participants.

Individual Activity: Gather together a small group of individuals who might discuss with you the eight questions above. Acting as a recorder, follow the group instructions above.

Activity 3

An Experience in Observing Group Consensus

Preparation: In many group situations a leader either emerges as a dominant force or is selected by the group. Leaders of groups generally fall into one of three classifications: authoritarian, democratic, and laissez-faire.

Authoritarian leaders are extroverted, dominating, and aggressive. They stress the values of discipline, deference to authority, and the outward symbols of status and power. Authoritarian leaders have little, if any, confidence in those they lead and rely on instruments of power to effect their will. Communication among followers is discouraged if not restricted; communication is accomplished almost exclusively through the leader.

Democratic leaders are not interested in possessing power but in stimulating members to participate in group activities. They work as one of the group to achieve collective goals, and enact their roles in such a way as to facilitate effective role behavior in others. They distribute responsibilities to all rather than strive for personal power over group members. They lead through ability to facilitate others in the attainment of ends.

While they initiate fewer leadership acts than either the authoritarian or democratic leader, laissez-faire leaders are active listeners who sympathetically and lucidly reflect group members' thoughts. They facilitate communication within the group and help bind the group together to strive for a common goal.

"Survival" is a group activity in which leadership and participant roles can be observed. As you participate in the activity, note the qualities of the leader you have selected for your group. Try to determine which category your group and group leader exemplifies.

To participate in "Survival," your group must assume responsibility for the ten inhabitants of the last outpost of humans in a world destroyed by nuclear explosion. The ten people have just realized that life-saving supplies of water, food, and air are adequate for only six of them to survive the three months they must remain in the shelter. A decision must be made to eliminate four of them from the nuclear shelter or all ten will perish.

The information below is all you know about the ten people.

1. Fifty-year-old scientist—a real ladies' man

2. His twenty-eight-year-old wife—four months pregnant

3. Young physician—has terminal illness; male

4. Twenty-year-old jack-of-all-trades—wino; male

5. Thirty-two-year-old architect—homosexual; male

6. Fifty-year-old nurse—too old to bear children

7. Brilliant female—thirty-eight; professor; never married

8. High-school girl—cheerleader, National Merit Scholar

9. Thirty-year-old nun—studied nutrition

10. Farmer—sixty-five years old; male

Without consulting anyone else, rank the persons in the order that you would have them remain in the shelter. Briefly note the reasons for your selections.

Group Activity: Meet with a group and select one member as leader. Discuss the advantages and disadvantages of each person as one of six survivors on earth. In no more than thirty minutes of discussion, it is the leader's responsibility to see that the group has decided on a list of six survivors. Take five more minutes to discuss and select persons who would compose an ideal group of six survivors. Again, the leader is responsible for seeing that a list is completed.

After completing your list, discuss the following questions, which deal with group interaction and leadership roles.

1. Which of the three styles did your leader display at the beginning of the discussion?

2. Did the leadership style remain the same or change as the discussion progressed?

3. What other leadership styles were displayed?

4. How would you describe the participation of each group member?

5. Which of the membership "titles" from chapter 11 best fits each member?

6. What did your selections of survivors and ideal survivors tell you about your values and those of the other group members?

Individual Activity: Choose a group of people that you know outside the classroom. You may choose a family, church, or party group. Explain that you are doing an assignment and that you would like them to help. Explain the difference in authoritarian, democratic, and laissez-faire leaders. You will take the role of one of these types and you would like the group to tell you which type you display and how effective you are as that type of leader.

Pass out the information available on the ten survivors of the nuclear explosion. Ask each group member to rank the persons in the order that they would have them remain in the shelter, and to briefly note the reasons for selection. As group leader, you should direct a brief discussion of the advantages and disadvantages of each person as one of the six survivors on Earth. At the end of the discussion, it is your responsibility to get the group to select only six to survive in the shelter. After reading the list of survivors, discuss what values are apparent in the group's persons who would compose an ideal group of survivors.

Finally, ask them to discuss the style of leadership you display. Were you an effective leader? If not, how could you improve your leadership role? Prepare a summary of the results of this activity in writing. Be certain to include the list of survivors with the reason for their choice and the results of the discussion of your leadership style.

Activity 4

Therapeutic Small Group Encounter

Preparation: Prepare brief notes of several interpersonal conflict situations that you have experienced. Describe your behavior as well as the behavior of the other participant in the conflict. Describe the situation accurately and analyze it.

The situation might be like one of the following.

1. An incident that left you with the reaction, "Why did I say that?" or "I wish I hadn't said it."

2. An incident in which you or someone else reacted defensively to criticism.

3. A situation where "pure" gossip or rumor continued to spread or was stopped by someone who asked for the facts.

Group Activity: In class form groups of approximately four students to discuss your interpersonal conflicts. From yours and those of the others, select one of the conflict situations to role play for the class. After role playing, talk to the class about the conflict. What attitudes were revealed by the people in the scene? Was there a communication breakdown between the people? What might have been done to avoid the conflict? What is being disclosed about the people involved?

Individual Activity: Write down the dialogue between two people who are experiencing an interpersonal conflict. Then find several friends or family members to discuss the conflict situation. At the end of the discussion, answer the questions posed for the group activity. Include your written answers to the question along with the dialogue.

Activity 5

Socializing

NOTE: Complete BEFORE Activity 6

Preparation: Often group work is facilitated when members of the group can relate on a personal level rather than merely on a professional level. Why do corporate employees and public servants have annual picnics or softball teams or retreats? Why are we so impressed when top management leaves the ivory tower and mingles with the workers? Why have communities developed neighborhood watch groups with periodic meetings for members to meet each other? When people know each other on a personal level, they are more supportive, less competitive within the group, and work more as a team than as individuals.

Find out who you will be joining to complete activity 8 of part 4: Group Presentation. At your first meeting, which you will probably have in class, exchange phone numbers and e-mail addresses and make arrangements for at least one out-of-class meeting to socialize and to begin to organize your project. Even a few refreshments and a little time to chat when you get together will set the tone for socialization.

Group Activity: Take some time to get to know your group members, find out about their families, their jobs, who you know in common (it is a small world), and what they hope to contribute to the group project. Find out about the special talents and strengths of each. Discuss the following:

1. Do you feel better about your group when you know something about each member?

2. Did you enjoy self-disclosing so that your group members would relate to you as a person rather than just as a classmate?

3. Do you think that the personal level of interaction increased the level of participation of all members?

Individual Activity: This activity cannot be completed without interaction with your group members. If you missed the group meeting, try to interact with at least part of the group on an informal basis as you fulfill your responsibilities as a group member. Do you feel better about your group when you know something about each member? Did you enjoy self-disclosing so that your group members would relate to you as a person rather than just as a classmate? Do you think that the personal level of interaction increased the level of participation of all members?

1. NAME _____ TALENTS _____ PHONE _____ e-mail _____

2. NAME _____ TALENTS _____ PHONE _____ e-mail _____

3. NAME _____ TALENTS _____ PHONE _____ e-mail _____

4. NAME _____ TALENTS _____ PHONE _____ e-mail _____

Activity 6

<u>Brainstorming</u>

NOTE: Complete BEFORE Activity 8

Preparation: Brainstorming is the process of quickly thinking of all the ideas possible in regard to a particular problem, object, or idea. Brainstorming sessions work effectively only if as individuals and as a group you can temporarily avoid evaluating what is said. The goal is for you and everyone involved to feel free to create. Criticism will inhibit the creativity. Brainstorming is a useful skill for an individual as well as a group. Have an individual experienced in brainstorming take a pencil and notepad and jot down all the ways you can think of to use a tin can. See how many uses you can come up with in ten minutes of time. Remember to avoid personal evaluation of your own ideas.

Group Activity: In class, join the group to which you have been assigned for activity 8, the Group Presentation. You will need to have selected your topic and to be familiar with the content you want to present to the class.

Review the rules for brainstorming. Ask someone to be the recorder as you and your group generate ideas for specific examples of presentation strategies that will result in audience involvement and variety. Do not just say, "let's use a song from a CD" but rather say, "let's use Mary Chapin Carpenter's 'He Thinks He'll Keep Her.'"

1. Decide on the main purpose of the group presentation:

2. Design your <u>GROUP OUTLINE</u>. Expand or contract the outline to fit the size of group and the number of points you plan to cover. See the example outline included with activity 8. Not all parts of the outline will have a presentation strategy but ALL presentation strategies from the end of chapter 12 MUST be used at least once. As you brainstorm, you will generate many more ideas than you can use and you might use each strategy several times. The value of brainstorming is that there is no judgment as you throw out ideas and that many ideas are generated from which a final plan can be implemented. Feel free to use humor and entertainment to achieve your goal.

Presentation Strategy	**Suggestion**	**Location in Outline**
Example: Discussion	Use hypothetical example of intrapersonal organization and have audience evaluate the example	3rd Speech II A
Example: Costume	Wear business suit	3rd Speech Section I A

1.   Demonstration

2.   Discussion

3.   Lecture

4.   Role-Playing

5.   Modeling and Imitation

6.   Skill Practice Session

7.   Sensitivity Training

8.   Problem Solving

9.   Tactile Activity

10.   Visual Aids

11.   Costume and Props

12.   Staging

Individual Activity: Because of the requirement of group interaction and presentation to an audience, there is no equivalent individual activity suggested.

Activity 7

Evaluating Group Participation

NOTE: Complete DURING and AFTER Activity 8

Preparation: The purpose of this activity is to evaluate the effectiveness of working with a group.

Part I: DURING the Preparation for the Group Presentation

Keep a log of the activities that you contribute in preparing and presenting activity 8: Group Presentation. An example is given.

Ex.	HOURS	DATE	TIME	ACTIVITY
	2.25	APR 5	8:00am–10:15am	Reading My Section of Book

1. _____
2. _____
3. _____
4. _____
5. _____
6. _____
7. _____
8. _____
9. _____
10. _____
11. _____
12. _____
13. _____
14. _____
15. _____
16. _____
17. _____
18. _____
19. _____
20. _____
21. _____
22. _____
23. _____

Part II: AFTER the performance of the Group Presentation

Rate each of your Group Members and yourself on the following scale. Attach additional rating scales if needed.

Circle the number that matches your feelings. 1=Agree   2=No Opinion   3=Disagree

Member 1_____

1 2 3   1. Contributed a fair amount of effort to the choice of the topic.
1 2 3   2. Achieved an acceptable level of knowledge concerning the group goal.
1 2 3   2. Contributed a fair amount of effort to the formation of the Group Outline.
1 2 3   3. Contributed a fair amount of effort to the development of ideas to fulfill the presentation strategies requirement.
1 2 3   5. Fulfilled expectations in completing individual responsibilities.
1 2 3   6. Conducted self in such a way that I would like to share group responsibilities again with this person.

Member 2_____

1 2 3   1. Contributed a fair amount of effort to the choice of the topic.
1 2 3   2. Achieved an acceptable level of knowledge concerning the group goal.
1 2 3   2. Contributed a fair amount of effort to the formation of the Group Outline.
1 2 3   3. Contributed a fair amount of effort to the development of ideas to fulfill the presentation strategies requirement.
1 2 3   5. Fulfilled expectations in completing individual responsibilities.
1 2 3   6. Conducted self in such a way that I would like to share group responsibilities again with this person.

Member 3_____

1 2 3   1. Contributed a fair amount of effort to the choice of the topic.
1 2 3   2. Achieved an acceptable level of knowledge concerning the group goal.
1 2 3   2. Contributed a fair amount of effort to the formation of the Group Outline.
1 2 3   3. Contributed a fair amount of effort to the development of ideas to fulfill the presentation strategies requirement.
1 2 3   5. Fulfilled expectations in completing individual responsibilities.
1 2 3   6. Conducted self in such a way that I would like to share group responsibilities again with this person.

Member 4_____

1 2 3   1. Contributed a fair amount of effort to the choice of the topic.
1 2 3   2. Achieved an acceptable level of knowledge concerning the group goal.
1 2 3   2. Contributed a fair amount of effort to the formation of the Group Outline.
1 2 3   3. Contributed a fair amount of effort to the development of ideas to fulfill the presentation strategies requirement.
1 2 3   5. Fulfilled expectations in completing individual responsibilities.
1 2 3   6. Conducted self in such a way that I would like to share group responsibilities again with this person.

Next, answer the following questions about your group experience.

1. Did your group use a structured plan in reaching its goal? Describe.

2. What type of leadership style emerged in your group? Did this change as the due date got close? Was the leadership style effective?

3. What were your most difficult individual responsibilities?

4. How would you rate your contribution to the group efforts? Explain.

5. How would you rate your fulfillment of individual responsibilities? Explain.

6. How would you rate your group members' enthusiasm for the project? Explain.

7. Overall, would you evaluate your group as excellent, good, or fair? Justify your rating.

8. Would you enjoy working with this group again? Explain.

9. Do you prefer individual or group projects? Justify.

Group Activity: Bring your responses to both parts I and II above to class. With the original group, discuss the effectiveness of the group working together as well as the effectiveness of the group activity.

Individual Activity: Talk with at least two members of your original group. The conversations may be by phone or in person, with each alone or all together. Discuss the effectiveness of the group working together as well as the effectiveness of the group activity. Prepare your individual evaluation and summaries of your two conversations in writing.

Activity 8

Speaking Activity
Group Presentation

Preparation: Become a member of a group and select a group leader (Activity 5—Optional). Follow the instructions given at the end of chapter 12 as you prepare and participate with your group.

Option 1: Human Development
The purpose of the group presentation is to inform the audience of the contents of a human development book. The instructor may suggest a book or your group may choose one from the library or bookstore. Several excellent examples are included below. Inform your instructor of the title and author before proceeding further (Activity 6—Optional). To prepare for this activity obtain and review a copy of the book and consider the part of the book for which you want to take responsibility.

Adams, B.	*The Everything Time Management Book*
Alberti, R. and Emmons, M. L.	*Your Perfect Right*
Aslett, D.	*Have a 48-Hour Day*
Baines, E.	*Survival for Busy Women*
Beattie, M.	*Co-Dependent No More*
Beck, A.	*Love Is Never Enough*
Burns, D.	*Feeling Good: The New Mood Therapy*
Carnegie, D.	*How to Stop Worrying and Start Living*
Covey, S.	*Principles of Leadership*
DeAngelis, B.	*Confidence—Finding It and Living It*
Dobson, J.	*Love Must Be Tough*
Downing-Orr, K.	*Get the Life You Want*
Findley, G.	*The Secret of Letting Go*
Garner, A.	*Conversationally Speaking*
Goleman, D.	*Primal Leadership: Realizing the Power of Emotional Intelligence*
Gray, J.	*Mars and Venus in the Workplace*
Gray, J.	*Men Are from Mars, Women Are from Venus*
Helmstetter, S.	*Choices*
Johnson, S.	*Who Moved My Cheese? An Amazing Way to Deal with Change in Your Life and Your Work*
Kassorla, I.	*Go for It*
Lerner, H.	*The Dance of Anger*
Matthews, A.	*Be Happy*

McGraw, P. C.	*Relationship Rescue*
McFarland, R.	*Coping through Assertiveness*
Meier, M.	*Happiness Is a Choice*
Molley, J. T.	*Live for Success*
Peck, S.	*Road Less Traveled*
Schuller, R.	*Tough Times Never Last but Tough People Do*
Ury, W.	*Getting Past No: Negotiating with Difficult People*
Ziglar, Z.	*Raising Positive Kids in a Negative World*
Zukav, G.	*Heart of the Soul: Emotional Awareness*
Zunin, L.	*Contact: The First Four Minutes*

Option 2—Local, National, or International Problem

The purpose of the group presentation is to select the best possible solution to a local, national, or international problem of interest to the group. This will be accomplished by individual preparation and group interaction. To prepare for this activity read any news magazine, and cut out an article to take to class that you feel would be an interesting topic for a problem-solving discussion.

During the first meeting the group will need to select a discussion problem that the students feel is challenging, interesting, and can be solved. As a group you will need to consider the time that you have to solve the problem, the information available, and the expertise of the individuals involved in the process when a general area has been decided on. You need to phrase a question so that there will be open and productive discussion. Inform your instructor of the topic before proceeding further (Activity 6—Optional).

As an individual and as a group discuss and answer on paper the questions below.

1. What is a concise statement of the discussion problem?

2. What terms within the problem need to be defined?

3. What is unsatisfactory about the present situation?

4. Why did the problem develop?

5. Who is involved in or affected by the situation?

6. What previous action has been taken to solve the problem?

7. What specifically has kept the problem from being solved?

8. What criteria must the solution meet?

9. What are possible solutions to the problem (use brainstorming)?

10. Which solution solves the problem?

11. What plan—personnel, costs, time, energy—can be implemented to put the solution into action?

12. What plan might be used to overcome obstacles?

Preparation Continued:

After the initial research and preparation, individuals, with the help of the group leader, will need to decide on a particular topic for the presentation. Review the presentation strategies in chapter 12 and consider how these could be used to clarify and create interest when presenting your material to an audience. Participate with your group to prepare an overall group outline where each group member has an entire speech over a group point and contributes to a group introduction and a group conclusion. EACH GROUP MEMBER MUST PRESENT A COMPLETE SPEECH OVER A PART OF THE CONTENT. NO ONE CAN MERELY PROVIDE A SUPPORTING ROLE SUCH AS HANDLING PROPS OR GIVING GROUP INTRODUCTION. This outline would specify the order in which each person will speak as well as a topic or heading to be covered. In your outline be sure to include any visual aids and equipment needed as well as presentation strategies to be used. To ensure success for the performance of the whole group, accept responsibility for your individual role. At the end of the class the group leader should prepare a written plan detailing the responsibilities of each member of the group.

After completing the outline and assigning responsibilities, plan to meet with your group a final time to complete preparation for your presentation. Review the evaluation form included for the activity to be certain that you are adequately prepared for the presentation. Note that ALL presentation strategies must be used at least once and be noted on the outlines. Briefly rehearse your part with the group to build confidence, perfect timing, and avoid repetition of key items. After a final group meeting, continue to rehearse your part of the group presentation as you would any speech.

Example of a Group Presentation on a Human Development Topic

An example of a group presentation on a human development topic follows. The example includes the group introduction, one of the four speeches, and the group conclusion. The group was composed of those members referred to as First Speaker, Second Speaker, Third Speaker, and Fourth Speaker. Note the Third Speaker and the Fourth Speaker shared the group introduction. Each speaker presented a full speech, only one of which is reproduced. The First Speaker and Second Speaker provided the group conclusion. Presentation strategies are noted in the outline to provide clarification.

Reference: *Men Are from Mars, Women Are from Venus* by John Gray (New York: HarperCollins Publishers, 1992).

Group Introduction

A. and B. Third Speaker Presents
C. and D. Fourth Speaker Presents

Topic Outline	*Script*
A. Gain attention of audience	"Once upon a time Martians and Venusians met, fell in love and had happy relationships together because they respected and accepted each other. They came to Earth and amnesia set in: they forgot they were from different planets."
B. Relate to audience	Martians and Venusians, according to author John Gray, forgot that they were supposed to be different. They became frustrated

with each other and no longer delighted in being together. Divorce increased. Families suffered. The planet Earth was in trouble because men and women were supposed to be different.

The men in the audience mistakenly expect women to think, react, and communicate the way Martians do; the women expect men to feel the way Venusians feel. We often forget that there are gender differences—that men and women are supposed to be different. Life does not need to be filled with stress or friction or with resent and intolerance.

C. Statement of main purpose

The purpose of our group presentation is to explore how Martians and Venusians are different and to present John Gray's suggestions from the book, *Men Are from Mars, Women Are from Venus,* as we explore gender differences.

D. Preview first speech

Our first speaker, Maria, will explain how men are like rubber bands.

E. Preview second speech

Jeremy, our second speaker, will suggest ways to avoid arguments.

F. Preview third speech

Next, Iza will provide an understanding of how difficult feelings evolve.

G. Preview fourth speech

Finally, Brenna will describe strategies for keeping the magic of love alive.

H. Transition

Let us now begin this exploration of gender differences by discovering how men are like rubber bands.

First Speaker—First Speech
"Men Are Like Rubber Bands"

Second Speaker—Second Speech
"How to Avoid Arguments"

How to Avoid Arguments

Topic Outline
I. Introduction

Script

A. Gain attention of audience (role play) (A male and a female group member act out and argument.) Relate to audience

It is likely that all of you have been in a relationship with a member of the opposite sex so everyone in this room can relate to arguments.

B. Main Purpose

The purpose of my speech is to explain why couples argue and how to avoid arguments.

C. Preview First Main Idea

To begin, I will inform you of why women and men argue.

D. Preview Second Main Idea	Next, I will speak about the four F's of avoiding an argument.
E. Preview Third Main Idea	To finish, I will speak about how to express your differences without arguing.

II. Body

A. First Main Idea	Why do men and women in relationships argue? It seems simple—because they disagree though it does go deeper than that. According to John Gray, "Most couples start out arguing about one thing and, within five minutes, they are arguing about the way they are arguing."
1. Support	Men and women argue about money, sex, decisions, children, chores, values, and the list goes on. If it has to do with life, it can and will be argued about. Both sexes have different ways of arguing resulting in hurt feelings, confusion and no solution.
2. Support	During an argument, if one takes time to listen to his or her partner, a lot can be accomplished and the argument can end with positive results. Usually, however, each side gets upset with the other and causes the argument to switch tracks. The original cause of the argument is forgotten and the argument has evolved into nonsense.
B. Second Main Idea (Visual Aid)	According to John Gray, there are four F's which individuals use to avoid getting hurt in an argument.
1. Support	The first F is for "fight." "The best defense is a strong offense." This means that the best way to defend yourself is to fight back harder than you are being attacked.
2. Support	The second F is "flight." This means refusing to talk so that nothing ever gets resolved. Rather than arguing, couples stop talking to avoid hurting one another.
3. Support	The third F is "fake." This means pretending that nothing is wrong so that an argument does not begin.
4. Support	The fourth F is "fold." This means one person giving in and taking the blame to end the argument.
C. Third Main Idea	My final point is to describe two ways to express your differences without arguing.
1. Support	One way to avoid arguments while still expressing your feelings is to give support at difficult times. If your loved one knows you are there for him or her, you can avoid arguments before they start. This trust can also bring you closer to your partner.

<table>
<tr><td>2. Support</td><td>Loving communication can help to avoid arguments. Knowing how easy it is to talk to your partner in a loving manner makes it easier to express deep feelings without fear of causing an argument.</td></tr>
</table>

III. Conclusion

<table>
<tr><td>A. Summary of Main Ideas</td><td>I have expressed why women and men argue, have told you the four F's of avoiding getting hurt in an argument, and have described two ways to express feelings without fear of starting an argument.</td></tr>
<tr><td>B. Closing Remarks</td><td>Understanding how to avoid arguments is a positive step to take in understanding differences in the ways that men and women build relationships.</td></tr>
<tr><td>C. Transition</td><td>Now Iza will explain how to communicate difficult feelings, which in turn can help to avoid arguments.</td></tr>
</table>

Third Speaker—Third Speech
"Difficult Feelings"

Fourth Speaker—Fourth Speech
"Keeping the Magic of Love Alive"

Group Conclusion

A. First Speaker Presents
B. Second Speaker Presents

<table>
<tr><td>A. Summary</td><td>We have described four of the sections of John Gray's book, *Men Are from Mars, Women Are from Venus*. We have described how men are like rubber bands, how to avoid arguments, how to understand difficult feelings, and how to keep the magic of love alive.</td></tr>
<tr><td>B. Closing</td><td>Next time you are frustrated with the opposite sex, remember men are from Mars and women are from Venus. If you do not remember anything else from this presentation, please remember that men and women are supposed to be different. Then you will eliminate blaming and asking only for what you want and you will begin to create the loving relationship you want, need and deserve</td></tr>
</table>

Group Activity: On the day of presentation be adequately prepared to fulfill your responsibilities as a group member. Take an active and enthusiastic part in the presentation to ensure its success before an audience. At the completion of your presentation, reflect on the value and/or frustration of the group process.

Individual Activity: Because of the requirement of group interaction and presentation to an audience, there is no equivalent individual activity suggested.

NOTE: Evaluation criteria for the Speaking Activity are located in the Appendix.

SPEAKER-AUDIENCE COMMUNICATION

Overview

Opportunities to speak in front of groups are feared and avoided by many people. Often people who have long feared expressing themselves in the speaker-audience situation find after experience that such fears are unfounded. Any experienced speaker will admit to feeling some nervousness in speaker-audience situations, but all have learned to deal effectively with anxiety.

In thinking about speaker-audience experiences and feelings, consider the testimonies of several "successful" students of public speaking.

No matter what profession you plan to go into, you are going to have to communicate. A communication course really helps conquer that sick, tense feeling you get before you make a speech. The world's number one fear is speaking in front of an audience. A communication course helps you make that the number three fear.

I was afraid and nervous the first day I walked into class. After each speech, I became more confident of myself. This course helps very much in becoming relaxed and confident of yourself when making a speech. The best cure for "speechphobia" is a communication course.

Being somewhat reserved, I thought giving a speech would be quite difficult. Yet, after only a period of about four months, I found that a speech can be quite easy as well as fun to give. Taking a communication class turned out to be an enjoyment and a learning experience.

I could always talk in front of a few people, but I froze in front of a crowd. After my experiences in a communications course, I feel fairly confident when I talk in front of a large group.

I think we need to know how to communicate well with people today. The future is full of changes and you never know when you might have to give a speech. It could be in other classes or at a banquet, or you might be top salesperson of the year or the recipient of an award.

In the career I am planning, I have to communicate well with the public. I have to be dominant but also soft spoken at times. I think that everyone should take a communication course.

Of the many students asked how they felt about the speaker-audience situation, none expressed greater anxiety after learning how to prepare and deliver such messages. The speaker-audience situation can be a rewarding one in both the personal and professional areas of living. As one student so wisely commented, the future is unknown. The time to learn is today. Then the challenges of tomorrow can be readily met no matter how unlikely future public speaking prospects may seem.

The "expert testimony" of the students about improving communication skills in general and more specifically improving speaker-audience communication omitted reference to listening to and evaluating the speeches and presentations of others. A very important part of the skills you will learn in studying speaker-audience communication will provide you with the evaluative skills that you can use as you listen. You will find yourself looking for main ideas, main points, supporting information, rational arguments and much more. What you will likely find is that many speakers just ramble. Sometimes speakers will possess a certain charisma which makes listening to nothing seem enjoyable but most often, after learning more about speaker-audience presentations, you will feel like saying—take a communication course. Mentioning no names, recently a student mentioned to one of the authors of this text that a prominent politician really did need to take this course if he is to make his points. Even famous people sometimes need help with public speaking. Studying speaker-audience communication will improve your own presentations as well as enable you to be a more critical listener.

As you take more classes as a college student, you will find many assignments to make presentations either independently or in small groups. The section on speaker-audience communication fits right into this scenario. Actually, when given no specific outline for writing a paper, you might find the general public speaking outline to be very useful as a guide for writing as well. When making a class presentation, you have a captive audience but the audience is one that you know well. Often the entire class has a similar assignment, so your introduction might be less detailed than in situations where you are the only speaker on a topic. Timing is ESSENTIAL since classes are required to end on time and the instructor must give all students their opportunity to present. Instructors really hate to tell a student to stop in the middle of a presentation but have no choice if they want to give equal time to all students in the class.

Perhaps one of the best outcomes of being a listener of formal presentations of others is what you can learn. Listening to a good speaker inform or persuade is an enjoyable experience if the message is tailored to the audience and the occasion. You can learn how to do things, you can evaluate the different rationales on both sides of controversial issues, and you can learn about people and places that are outside your normal routine. In our global economy and our technological world, learning about other cultures can be a valuable asset both in your personal life and your career. More and more our multi-cultural society places us in situations which are unfamiliar. Having taken the effort to learn more and to be prepared for different settings will add to your comfort level in new situations.

The material on speaker-audience communication is intended to build on communication skills already acquired. You will learn how to prepare a message for presentation to a large group, and you will experience the anxiety of anticipating the experience and the positive rewards of successfully making the presentation. Afterward you too will be able to offer testimony about the value of communication.

CHAPTER 13

PLANNING THE SPEAKER-AUDIENCE MESSAGE

D uring a lifetime most individuals are on the receiving end of the speaker-audience message many more times than they are on the sending end of the message. Not only should an effective communicator be prepared to deliver messages to an audience, but the effective communicator must develop skill in receiving such messages. As sender, the communicator has the responsibility to present a thoughtfully prepared message designed specifically for the audience, the occasion, and the setting. As receiver, the communicator must avoid irresponsible messages and evaluate carefully those messages meant to change the listener's values, beliefs, or behaviors. A knowledge of speech preparation and practice in speech delivery can do much to enhance a communicator's skill in sending and receiving speaker-audience messages. To begin, consider several ways that the speaker-audience situation can be differentiated from interpersonal and small group communication: (a) characteristics of the listener, (b) advance preparation of the message, and (c) formality of the delivery.

Those who gather to listen to a speaker-audience message generally perceive their role more as receivers of the message than as participants in an interactive process where they both send and receive messages. Although unusual circumstances might produce an audience composed of a single listener, the audience will generally number above the fifteen that is considered maximum for effective small group interaction. The audience size results in the listeners' expectation that they will be able to say little, if anything, during the speaker's presentation. The lack of opportunity to speak is quite a reversal from the expectation in interpersonal or small group communication.

The messages in many speaker-audience situations are prepared in advance and even rehearsed to produce the best presentation possible. Advance preparation is important because the speaker wishes to make an impact with a specific audience in a given amount of time and set of circumstances. Unprepared speakers will often ramble so much that the audience fails to grasp the intended message. Although speakers will sometimes prepare messages before interpersonal or small group interactions, these situations are generally more spontaneous.

The setting in which a speaker-audience message occurs is generally somewhat formal. In most situations the message is prepared with thought given to grammar and the omission of fillers like "uh," slang, and colloquial words and phrases. The speaker is generally set apart from the audience so that each listener can both see and hear the speaker. Much can be done to make the setting somewhat intimate, but the separation of the speaker and the audience and the prepared message make the situation appear more formal than the usual casual setting associated with interpersonal and small group communication.

In considering speaker-audience communication the key is planning. Planning a message for each specific situation is a must. In developing an effective and appropriate message, it is important to be aware of the special characteristics of the different types of speeches that can be presented and to give consideration to the setting, topic, and the gathering and ordering of material.

Types of Messages

Students of public speaking will hear references to informative, demonstration, ceremonial, entertainment, inspiration, eulogy, motivational, introduction, tribute, presentation, acceptance, and many other types of speeches. In any public speaking situation, however, most messages can be classified according to their intent to inform, persuade, inspire, or entertain. The more specific categories listed above will generally fall within one of the four major categories. And sometimes the same speech will include segments to inform, persuade, inspire, and entertain.

INFORMATIVE

When the purpose of the message is to add to the listener's knowledge it is an informative message. Such messages would include a demonstration of how to operate a new type of machine, an introduction of a visiting dignitary, a lecture on child psychology, a news program on television, or the findings of a committee appointed to investigate fringe benefits for employees of a company. In all these examples

Speaker-Audience Messages

Purpose of Speaker	Response of Listener
To Inform	Acquire Knowledge
To Persuade	Change Behavior
To Inspire	Positive Personal Characteristics
To Entertain	Experience Diversion

the speaker is seeking to provide information that listeners will retain as knowledge.

PERSUASIVE

When the purpose of the message is to bring about some action or change some belief on the part of the listener, it is a persuasive message. Such messages include product advertisements presented on television, political speeches to create support for a given candidate, motivational pitches to exercise for good health, inspirational encouragement to become a better person, appeals to donate time or money to good causes, or reasons for taking a certain stand on an issue. In all these examples the speaker is seeking to convince or motivate the listener, and is hoping the listener will react in ways that support the message objective.

INSPIRATION

An inspirational message is designed to provide the listener with a stimulus to further develop some positive personal characteristics. It is intended to motivate individuals to live lives on higher planes. The message can be based on a person's life, a book, or an idea.

The area of interpersonal communication offers many possibilities for topics for inspirational messages. The concept of winners versus losers, for example, might be an appropriate topic. Books on assertiveness provide many ideas for encouraging listeners to develop more active roles in the directions their lives will take. Actually, all aspects of life provide a basis for inspiring messages. The speaker's aim is to inspire with optimism, hope, and encouragement to reach higher goals.

ENTERTAINMENT

The purpose of a speech to entertain is diversion—it is not to impart knowledge or provide a rationale to acquire certain beliefs or take specific actions. The speech to entertain should not be confused with the stand-up comedian's performance or a humorous monologue. Although it will frequently produce laughter or wild applause, this is not a requirement. The speech to entertain might include a description of a mountain climbing expedition, the perilous adventures experienced as an undercover police detective, and humorous stories about children in a preschool. The speech to entertain will occupy the minds of the listeners but will not obligate them to retain any knowledge or consider beliefs or actions. Facets of the speech to entertain can be very useful in creating interest or attracting attention in informative and persuasive speeches.

OTHERS

Hopefully, the speech types mentioned above and those the public speaker will hear mentioned in the future can be classified as speeches to inform, persuade, inspire, or entertain. The demonstration speech, where a procedure is actually shown, is an informative speech. However, if the ultimate purpose is the sale of the object being demonstrated, the speech would include persuasive elements as well. The eulogy, a formal speech praising someone who has recently died, is most likely informative in nature. Likewise, introductions of or tributes to someone are likely to be informative. Speeches to motivate and inspire will probably contain elements of persuasion to change behavior or perform some action. The ceremonial speech, traditionally made to celebrate some event, will be informative or persuasive if given in a serious vein, or entertaining if given lightly. The speeches accompanying presentation and acceptance of awards can be either informative or entertaining depending on the occasion.

It is difficult to determine the nature of a speech by its title. The important point to consider is the special techniques public speakers can use to enhance the informative and persuasive aspects of their messages. These will be discussed in more detail in the last two chapters. The purpose of this chapter is to inform the reader about general principles of speech planning and preparation, and to persuade the reader that public speaking skill can be enhanced by giving attention to these principles.

Preparing the Material

Adequate preparation for delivery of the message is extremely important. Unprepared speakers may alienate their audiences as well as damage their own self-esteems. It is the exceptional person who can consistently address new audiences without prior preparation. Consideration must be given to the setting, topic, gathering of materials, ordering of materials, and supporting materials.

GOAL
Adapt to the purpose, occasion, and audience of a public speaking situation.

SETTING

Each occasion for public speaking will involve a speaker, an audience, a time, a place, and a purpose. Before beginning work on the organization of the message, a thorough analysis of these factors is important. To be effective the message must be tailored to the setting.

Speakers know themselves well and should consider their own backgrounds, interests, and experiences as they prepare their messages. It is important to ask, "Is this speech suited to me? Do I know enough about the topic? Can I relate to the needs of the audience?" Audiences often appreciate getting to know the speaker as well as learning the message. Ideas discovered through research can be more meaningfully presented when they are related to the experiences of the speaker and the audience. It is important too to display a positive attitude about the speaking experience. Making excuses or mentioning shortcomings has only a negative effect on the message.

Setting = Speaker + Audience + Time +
Place + Purpose

The message must be adapted to the audience. Would you deliver the same message on "home insulation" to a junior high school science class, a neighborhood association of home owners, the local chapter of the home builders' association, and the national society for insulation research? Hopefully, you would tailor your message to suit the background, knowledge, and experience of each group. The good speaker will find out as much as possible about the audience. The presentation must not be so simple as to be boring, or so complex that it cannot be understood. It is a good idea too to have information about the receptiveness of the audience toward the topic. Since speakers will probably receive a more favorable response from audiences whose views are similar to their own, the message can sometimes be developed in ways that will make audience attitudes more favorable. Each audience will be unique and will require special consideration in message planning. Such characteristics as size of the audience, age and sex of the audience members, educational level, cultural backgrounds and socioeconomic factors, memberships and affiliations, experiences with the topic, and values and interests are often relevant to message planning. How do speakers learn audience characteristics? They ask questions and more questions until they learn enough to prepare messages to gain the attention and hold the interest of the audience.

In our multi-cultural society of the 21st century, the speaker must avoid any type of reference which could be offensive. Locker room jokes and undignified references have no place in the social and professional world today. Do not even be tempted to make comments that could be offensive. You never can tell if a member of your audience represents the group you are demeaning, and many others will be offended even if the reference does not directly relate to them. Show respect and you will be respected. Often offended people will be good sports or they will understand the mentality of the speaker, but awkward situations can be easily avoided by showing respect to all people of all backgrounds. Demeaning comments related to gender, race, and religion are particularly hurtful and those who use them to attract attention are generally viewed as ignorant. As you relate to your audience, consider the following:

- Avoid taboos or issues that are forbidden in a given culture.
- Avoid ethnocentrism or making your way seem like the only way or the right way.
- Avoid jokes which make fun of subgroups of the population.
- Avoid sexist language such as placing men in positions of power and women in subordinate roles.

Consider, also, the special needs of the disabled. You might have a person who is deaf, blind, or has mobility impairment in your audience. With awareness, you can sometimes make the message more easily accessed by the person with a disability.

The time and place will affect the preparation and delivery of the message also. The speaker has a responsibility to others sharing the same program to stay within the time limits agreed on in accepting the speaking responsibilities. Lack of attention to time can result in a rushed, possibly flustered, conclusion to the speech. The place in which the speech is delivered has an effect also. Characteristics of the location can affect the use of visual aids, the speaker's attire, the distance between speaker and audience, and physical comfort of the speaker and audience. Often a request by the speaker for changes in the setting can make a possibly unpleasant atmosphere more suitable.

When delivering a speech that you have spent considerable time preparing, you expect your audience to give you attention. The audience will likely be planning to given you attention as well. However, comfort and distractions impact the attention level of the audience. As a speaker, you will be well served by taking the extra effort of examining the area in which you will be speaking. You should ascertain that adequate quantities of seats are available and that they are comfortable enough for sitting through your speech. You should determine if the acoustics of the space and the noise levels of the surrounding areas will be adequate for people to hear your message. Also, consider the air quality including temperature. Determine if your audience will need refreshments especially water and that there will be rest room facilities conveniently available. You will have occasions, also,

to evaluate the lighting especially if you have visual aids that require viewing. Consider the setting in relation to your visual aids and be sure that visual aids will be viewable.

The purpose of the speech will affect the message. It will often determine whether the topic is presented in an informative or persuasive manner. Speeches are a part of many different occasions in our society. As guest speaker at the monthly meeting of an organization, you may decide it will be more appropriate to develop an informative message. On the other hand, you may be selected to deliver a persuasive message to the membership of your own organization on the importance of consistent attendance; or you may be invited to speak as a recognized expert on a subject and discover that a persuasive message would immediately alienate your audience. Purpose, like other considerations discussed above, is important in planning a message that will be worthwhile and interesting for the audience and rewarding for the speaker.

TOPIC

Once an analysis of the setting is complete, the next step in speech preparation is determining the topic. What exactly will be the subject covered by the speech? What is the main purpose of the presentation? The topic statement represents the goal of the speaker. It is essential for guiding the speech development and determining if, in fact, the message fulfills the initial purpose. Once determined, the topic statement or speech objective is not set in cement—it can be modified or discarded. Its importance may be expressed by considering the following question: If you do not know where you are going, how will you know when you have arrived? The topic statement tells you where you want to go, and a comparison of the prepared message with the topic statement tells you if you succeeded in getting there.

Finding a suitable topic for the audience, the occasion, and your personal expertise can be daunting. You can consult numerous library sources as well as the Internet to find possibilities. Use your favorite Search Engine, Goggle perhaps, and search on "speech topics" in quotations marks. Ideas abound. In beginning topic selection it is common to be very general, but

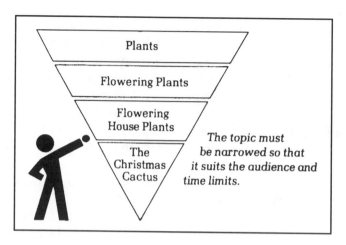

Figure 13.1. Topic

eventually the topic must be narrowed to suit the setting and especially the restraints of time limits. Another important advantage of a narrower topic is that it can reduce time in researching materials and it can help in organizing ideas. The speaker's interests and those of the audience may relate to the great leaders of World War II. Volumes have been written on this topic. To narrow such a general topic, a speaker might consider leaders of a specific nationality, of a specific campaign, or even one leader as he or she functioned in a specific situation. A good topic is like a good photograph—the image must be sharp and clear. Several specifics may be more meaningful to the listener than vague generalities. Some examples of general areas and topic statement are given below.

General: Auto tune-up

Topic statement: The audience will understand the importance of spark plug gap and timing as it relates to fuel economy.

General: Shakespeare

Topic statement: The audience will recognize the relevance of *A Midsummer Night's Dream* to modern society.

General: Photography

> GOAL
> Demonstrate ability to use research and data bases to gather support material for speeches.

Topic statement: The audience will realize the value and simplicity of recording their lives in photographs.

GATHERING MATERIAL

Once a topic that fits the parameters of the setting is selected, gathering materials for preparation of the message is the next task. There are many ways to gather materials and most good speeches will include several of these. In fact, in public speaking and other communication situations, the more knowledge at the speaker's command, the more interesting the message will probably be. Some of the more common sources for gathering information are review of personal experiences; conversations with others; conducting experiments; courses taken; mass media—television, films, magazines, and newspapers; library search; and, with the proliferation of personal computers, Internet search.

Personal Experience

Speakers will often prepare a public message based on experience they have had. In fact, many speaking invitations are made because of the knowledge and experiences for which individuals are known. As a potential source of information on a topic, it is useful for the speaker to review direct personal experiences and perceptions that relate to the topic.

Interviews

Other people are good potential sources of information in preparing a public message. Conversations with acquaintances are a good way to develop ideas and increase knowledge of the topic. Appointments can be made with people in the community to gather information from those who are knowledgeable. It is wise to prepare specific questions in advance of an interview. The initiator of the interview should be prepared to take responsibility for getting the kinds of information needed. (See the section in chapter 7 that relates to the interview process.) Telephoning, writing letters, and sending e-mail messages to request information are three additional means of gathering information from others.

Experiments

Conducting experiments may seem too sophisticated for the public speaker. Experimentation does not always require years of dedicated work or intricate equipment, but can be quickly and easily done for some topics. Consider the topic relating to auto tune-ups given above. As an experiment, the speaker might adjust the spark plugs on several cars in several ways and compare the approximate miles per gallon for each car with the miles per gallon when spark plugs on the cars were set appropriately. Other simple experiments can often be devised to provide useful and interesting information for a public speech.

Course

The public speaker can gain knowledge each day while taking advantage of the many learning experiences available. Information presented by instructors, news media, performers, and writers, encountered as a routine part of life, can be useful in preparing a public message. Attention to available learning opportunities can lead you to a special program on campus or in the community, to a news program or film, or to a recently published article relating

to the topic. This type of information is up to date and gives credibility to the speaker.

Library

Library search probably comes first to the mind of the speaker who is gathering material for a message. It is useful and important to supplement other types of information with support from journal articles, books, and reference materials. Within a very short time, the speaker who is familiar with library use can systematically collect a list of sources relating to the topic. The speaker who does not learn efficient ways to use the library will expend much more time and energy and possibly discover nothing of relevance. And too, the skills learned to find speech materials in the library will be useful in other academic, professional, and personal quests for materials.

Internet

Most colleges are making access to computer networks available to all students. Most college students will be given an e-mail address as a part of their enrollment process. Some colleges or programs within colleges require the purchase of a computer in order to enroll. For students who do not have their own hardware, software, or access capabilities, libraries, dormitories, and computer laboratories will all give access to students who are searching local and world-wide databases for materials to facilitate study and research. Computer literacy is an underlying objective of many classes which are taught outside computer and mathematics departments. If you are not able to access the Internet on your own, visit your college or public library or the computer laboratory associated with your department or college. Trained librarians, media technology specialists, and computer technicians will help you access the Internet. Once signed on to the Internet, it is fairly easy to figure out how to search for information. As with other types of research, use of key words and persistence will be the key to success.

Either through your library networks or the Internet, several of the sources which might be available for you in your searches are listed below:

1. State Gateways to the Information Highway (e.g., TEXSHARE)—periodical abstracts.
2. SIRS—Social Issues Resource Series—includes journal and magazine articles on current topics which would be very useful for undergraduate English, social science, and speech communication classes.
3. Newspapers—local city and state newspapers plus *The New York Times* are generally available in their entirety.
4. Netscape and MSExplorer as well as other similar browsers which access the Internet—these programs are a direct link to the world-wide web (WWW) and are part of the operating systems of many personal computers. Once you are connected, you can choose from various "search engines" like AOLNetFind, Excite, Infoseek, Lycos, Google, and Yahoo. After choosing one of these, you may begin selecting from menus or merely enter a topic name. Consider the menus listed in Figure 13.2 which are navigated in order to find listings of Bed and Breakfast establishments in Valley Forge, Pennsylvania. These entries resulted in listings of B & Bs in the vicinity of Valley Forge. Some listings were directly linked to e-mail and inquiries could be made on-line. Others just gave information for mailing or telephoning. The same or similar information might have been retrieved by entering Valley Forge as a topic and sorting through a dif-

ferent set of choices. The use of web browsing is so prevalent for finding information that "google" has become a frequently used verb. How often do you need resources and say or think, "I'll goggle that"?

If you find a source on the Internet that you plan to use in a presentation or paper, consult your Modern Language Association (MLA) or American Psychological Association (APA) handbooks to determine the proper way to indicate the citation in your reference list. You can easily find links to MLA and APA formats by using a search engine to find sites. Some sites will even take you step-by-step through the documentation process. Use the websites to check for changes in format rules each time you document your literature searches. Just like the reference for a book or magazine, you must give sufficient information to enable someone else to locate your source. When using material verbatim or paraphrased from an Internet source, you must document the original author or source.

Internet material is likely to be copyrighted just as a book or journal. Unlike professional journals, however, the publications on the Internet may NOT have been juried or reviewed by professional peers. It is entirely possible that you will find a term paper written by a fourth grader along with a scholarly article written by a leader in a field. Be certain to use credible sources and to acknowledge others' work when appropriate. The general consensus among scholars in speech communication and composition classes is that .com sources should

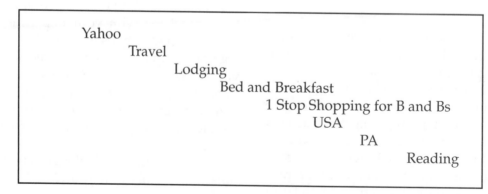

Figure 13.2. Sequence of Steps for InterNet Search

Documentation of Internet Sources

MLA FORMAT:
Krut, Amy. "Skiing vs Snowboarding." *Adventure Time* 1997. 2 Dec. 2001. <http://www.adventuretime.com/featurearticles/skivssnowboard.html>.

APA FORMAT:
Krut, A. (1997). Skiing vs snowboarding. *Adventure Time*. Retrieved December 2, 2001, from http://www.adventuretime.com/featurearticles/skivssnowboard.html

be avoided if possible. The .com sources can certainly be used to get ideas and to gain general background on topics but need to be avoided when establishing credibility. Keep in mind, also, that many books and journals that would be excellent sources for your presentation are not published on the Internet but must be purchased or accessed via a library.

As speakers gather materials, their goal is to become informed about the topic. They must read widely and study carefully so that the presentation reflects thoroughness and credibility as they present information or seek to persuade. In reviewing materials, it is important to be selective and to make notes that will enable recall of important ideas, figures, statements, or examples. It is important to be aware too that all written and spoken words are not necessarily dependable. It is necessary to question each source and consider the qualifications and honesty of the author or speaker, to determine whether similar information is available from other sources, and to decide if conclusions are justified from the rationale presented. It is a good idea too to document notes with the source—author, title, date, page numbers, web address, for example—so that the original material can be easily obtained for future use or checking of details. It can be quite embarrassing to admit in front of an audience that the source of one's information is not available.

ORDER OF MATERIAL

As speakers gather material, they will often begin to see some order to it. Relationships will become apparent among the random bits of information gathered from various sources.

The Poet Addresses the Western United States Regional Conference of Airport Managers and Their Wives

when i arrived the microphone and stool
said: Barry Manilow
when they should have been saying:
Robert Bly

the chairman of the program committee
suggesting
that i would also play guitar during dinner
there'd be an extra fifty in it for me

to which i responded
with a quick thumbnail sketch
of Vachel Lindsay
later
after the welcome
the awards
and the election of new officers
i was tendered to an audience

filled with Tony Bennett expectations

and for thirty intoxicating minutes
i was the only person
on the face of the earth
who knew
what was coming next

—*Ric Masten*
They Are All Gone Now published by Sunflower Ink, Carmel, CA

There are several particularly useful ways to arrange material for speech: topical, chronological, spatial, causal, comparison/contrast, and problem/solution. By using one or a combination of these orders, a speech can be developed logically and will be more understandable when delivered.

- **Topical**—When parts of the message are organized on the basis of similarities and each component is explained before going on to the next, the order is topical. If all topics are equal in weight their order makes little difference. If topics differ in their importance, ordering will be especially critical to the impact of the message on the audience. The topical order might be used in an informative speech on cats by discussing one breed before discussing another.

- **Chronological**—If information is organized from a beginning to an ending point by numerical logic, a chronological order has been used. The ordering may be based on the steps in a process or a sequence of events. A speech to describe major events occurring in a specific period of time could be presented in chronological order from earliest to latest.

- **Spatial**—When the development of a message is organized around a specific point of reference and follows a logical progression, the speaker has used a spatial ordering. Examples of spatial ordering are left-to-right, top-to-bottom, north-to-south, and center-to-outside. The spatial order would be particularly useful to describe a place or an object.

- **Causal**—When relationships of events are shown as cause and effect, a causal ordering has been used. This is particularly useful in persuasive messages when it can be shown that events can be altered by taking action or changing behavior. Causal ordering would be useful to describe events that lead to various types of traffic accidents.

- **Comparison/Contrast**—If a message is presented by describing similarities and differences between several related objects or events, comparison/contrast ordering has been used. Specific examples of how objects or events are alike and unlike should be given. An informative presentation about different brands of a product might be made using comparison and contrast of each brand on several characteristics.

- **Problem/Solution**—When a message presents an unacceptable situation and a way to improve it, the problem/solution format is being used to present the message. It is important that the situation, the problem, possible solutions, and recommended solutions be included. By clearly developing a plan of action, the speaker will enable the audience to understand the reasoning and to accept the recommended solution.

As speakers consider topics and the nature of messages, it is important to keep in mind the ways the materials can be most effectively ordered. As material is gathered, yet another aid will be available for weeding out unnecessary information. And too, as the message is prepared for presentation, the pieces will tend to fall together.

SUPPORTING MATERIALS

As ideas for speech content begin to develop, it is wise to seek support for the message through the use of examples, statistics, and testimony. Support materials represent information from sources other than the speakers themselves. Appropriate use of support will make the message more credible. The ideas expressed will be backed up by sources other than the speakers' opinions or interpretations and will, therefore, become more believable to the audience.

In considering sources to use and in adapting material from sources to create your own message, you must consider the concepts of plagiarism and ethics very seriously. Plagiarism refers to the taking of another person's work and presenting it as your own. Often people do not realize that they have failed to cite sources to give credit where due. With the ease of cutting and pasting of material from the Internet, failure to synthesize and integrate the work of others is very easy. The authors are hearing more and more faculty members complain that speeches and papers often seem to be disjointed passages taken from Internet sources, sequenced, and presented as original work. The student who is tempted to pull together a speech or paper from the work of others should be aware first of all of the "Student Integrity Codes" that most institutions of higher education have. See your College Catalog for this information. Also, sophisticated software is available for comparing student work with what can be found on the Internet.

Ethics, in relation to preparing a speaker-audience message, refers to taking responsibility for your message and being certain that you adhere to the following inventory (O'Hair, Rubenstein, and Stewart, 2004).

1. Do not distort information to make your point.
2. Acknowledge your sources.
3. Focus on issues rather than personalities.
4. Foster a sense of inclusion of all members of the audience.
5. Present socially constructive topics.
6. Determine that your information is accurate.
7. Consider alternate and opposing views.

Unfortunately, many listeners do not use critical thinking skills to evaluate the messages they receive. As a presenter, you must be certain that you are being honest in the way you present your message.

Example

An example supports the message of the speech by providing a specific instance or illustration of the point being made. It adds interest to the message by allowing both the speaker and audience to use their imaginations as they seek to understand an idea. Examples should be used often in most speaking situations to clarify, provide diversity, and gain acceptance. Examples may be given without elaborate detail. The use of a list will often provide a brief example that is concise and to the point.

> Opportunities for higher education abound in our area. There are four state-supported universities within sixty miles, two large community college systems, and at least five well-known private colleges and universities.

More detailed examples are useful when a specific aspect of the message is difficult to understand. Detailed examples provide depth of meaning and are often complete enough to tell a story. The length of the speech has much to do with elaboration of an example, however. The extent of detail of an example must be kept in proportion to the length of the speech. Generally, a speech that introduced one point and concluded with a detailed example would be ineffective in getting the total message to the audience.

Both brief and detailed examples may be either factual or hypothetical. A factual example is one based on an actual occurrence. It need not include every detail of what occurred; it can be edited to fit the message. A hypothetical example originates in the speaker's imagination and is recognized as a fictional example by the audience. It represents something that could exist or could have happened and is designed to help the speaker make a point. Both real and hypothetical examples are useful speaking tools. Since it actually occurred or existed, a factual example, however, is likely to have more relevance for and be more interesting to a particular audience.

Statement: There are many ways to earn college credits without attending traditional classes.

Factual example: R. Jacobs earned thirty hours credit by passing formal examinations on course content.

Hypothetical example: Imagine a student who was able to earn credit by exam, complete independent study courses, take self-paced options of courses, and never enter the classroom.

Statistics

A second type of support material is statistics. Statistics are summaries of numbers of events, objects, or persons that are similar in some way. Speakers will often use statistics to summarize examples too numerous to mention individually. Statistics are useful for clarifying ideas and helping an audience visualize the size or extent of some occurrences. Percentages and whole numbers are probably the most commonly used statistics in general public speaking. It is probably better to round off those numbers the audience is expected to retain after one hearing. The wise speaker will use statistics sparingly, as too many are hard to comprehend and are difficult for the listener to relate to the main ideas of the message. Statistics should not be used to impress the audience. Speakers must be certain that they know the meaning of statistics used in their presentations. Statistics may sound impressive, but to be impressive they must relate to the message.

Testimony

A third type of supporting material is testimony. Testimony refers to information, ideas, or opinions that originate from a source other than the speaker. Few speakers find themselves the sole authority on a topic and most audiences realize that speakers take material from books, periodicals, television, films, and so forth. Such material is either presented exactly as it was originally written or is restated in the speaker's own words. The exact replication is called a quotation; the restatement, paraphrasing. The quotation is appropriate when the original source has stated something in a way that particularly fits the message. When quotations are used, they should be brief (e.g., several sentences) or the listener may be unable to comprehend the meaning intended by the speaker. Longer materials that deserve inclusion should probably be paraphrased. Paraphrasing results in better comprehension. Condensation of material through paraphrasing will permit more than one source to be used. Testimony, whether a quotation or a paraphrase, is especially useful to gain acceptance for a point or to add clarification. Just be certain that credit is given to the originators of unique and specific testimony. A speaker who attempts to take credit for another's ideas will quickly lose credibility with the audience.

In using the three types of supporting materials—example, statistic, and testimony—areas of the speech requiring support must first be determined. Then, as support materials are selected, sufficient sources must be reviewed to allow selection of appropriate and credible materials. Third, support materials must be presented to make ideas clear, interesting, and acceptable to the listeners. And last, the speaker must determine if the message is too heavily dependent on one type of support or one particular source. Consideration of such factors may lead to the discovery of more appropriate examples, statistics, and testimony. Recall too the very important consideration in selecting support materials—they do not necessarily fit the message merely because they sound good.

Once you have located materials and then have read them and judged them appropriate for your presentation, you can ease your burden of content development by writing notecards or using hard copies of relevant segments of the publications. The notecards will take more preparation time but will pay off by enabling you to arrange them in the sequence in which you will present the material. The hard copies, or even computer files containing relevant material, will be quicker to compile but not nearly as efficient for assembling your content. Whichever process you use, be sure to keep all of the information needed to produce the reference list.

Summary

The speaker-audience situation can be differentiated from interpersonal and small group communication by the role of the listener, advance preparation of the message, and formality of the delivery. Generally, public speeches can be classified as informative—the presentation of content, persuasive—an attempt to change opinion or behavior, inspirational—positive personal characteristics, and entertaining—an opportunity to enjoy a message. Some speeches contain elements of all four.

The format for delivery of the speaker-audience message generally permits the originator the opportunity to plan and prepare for optimum presentation. The setting, the topic statement, and the gathering and organizing of material are important considerations in preparing the message. Setting involves the audience, time, place, and purpose for the speech. The topic statement provides the focus of the speech. Gathering materials requires search and selection of materials suitable for developing the topic statement. Organizing the materials involves arranging them in a manner that optimizes audience understanding of the message. Inclusion of supporting materials such as example, statistics, and testimony provides credibility for the message.

Statistics Say

—that each day in America
there is more violent crime perpetrated
than books of poetry purchased

—that in any given period of time
the incidence of child abuse
will exceed the number of poems composed

in this great country of ours
the odds of someone becoming a bard
are a hundred times less
than that
of being blinded by an exploding pop-bottle

and if the figures are correct
i think we can say
without fear of contradiction
that here in the United States
the poetry problem
is clearly under control

—Ric Masten
They Are All Gone Now published by Sunflower
Ink, Carmel, CA

CHAPTER 14

DELIVERING THE SPEAKER-AUDIENCE MESSAGE

Once the topic has been researched, materials have been gathered and ordered, and adequate support has been developed, the speaker's efforts must turn to delivery of the message. It is very useful to prepare a speaking outline that includes all the parts necessary to make an effective presentation. After the material is organized in outline format, the style of delivery must be selected, visual aids prepared if appropriate, and rehearsal must begin. When a well-planned speech is developed around an appropriate outline, and rehearsed until it is adequately learned, a speaker's success is only a matter of having a positive attitude about the experience. Remember, also, to smile. A smile of happiness is one of the few universally understood nonverbal messages. Smiling can help you feel better and can cover up some of the anxious feelings you have in presenting a message to an audience.

Organizing the Message

Most speeches are presented in three parts: the introduction, the body, and the conclusion. In very simple terms, the audience is first told what they will be told, then they are told, and finally they are told again what they were told. To prepare the message, it is suggested that the body be developed before the introduction and the conclusion. The outline presented in the following box is a very general format that could be used in most speaker-audience situations.

GOAL
Draft, organize, revise, edit and present formal public speeches.

Basic Speaking Outline

1. Introduction of the Speech
   a. Gain Attention of Audience
   b. Relate to Audience
   c. Statement of Main Purpose
   d. Preview Main Ideas

2. Body of the Speech
   a. Main Idea
      i. Supporting Material
      ii. Supporting Material
      iii. Etc.
   b. Main Idea
      i. Supporting Material
      ii. Supporting Material
      iii. Etc.
   c. Main Idea (Optional)
      i. Supporting Material
      ii. Supporting Material
      iii. Etc.
   d. Main Idea (Optional)
      i. Supporting Material
      ii. Supporting Material
      iii. Etc.

3. Conclusion
   a. Summary of Main Ideas
   b. Closing Remarks

BODY

The body of the speech is composed of statements of the main ideas and supporting materials. A good speech states a few ideas well. Regardless of the length of the speech, two to four main ideas are usually sufficient. Given more time for presentation, it is better to develop the main ideas in more depth or with more supporting material than to increase the number of ideas to be made. Close attention must be paid to the wording of the main ideas. They must be concise and clear enough for the audience to understand, and they must be vivid enough to make the audience remember them. It is useful to make the listeners feel that each main idea applies to them in some way; that is, to help the listeners identify with the message. If the topic relates to social security, for example, it would be inappropriate to address a group of young adults in the manner a group of retirees would be addressed. Last, as the main ideas are stated, it is often suggested that a similar sentence structure (i.e., similar wording) be used for each so that the listener will readily perceive the progression from main idea to main idea.

Once the main ideas are stated and ordered they must be supported. A message is more likely to be remembered if the important ideas are reinforced by illustrative support materials. When the speech is on a topic the audience finds generally acceptable, examples in the form of illustrations, personal experiences, and comparisons will be most useful for lending support. There will be less need for testimony and statistics. When the audience is totally unfamiliar with, or against the message to be presented, examples, testimony, and statistics will all prove useful. The important point to remember in developing the body of a speech is to limit main ideas to two to four and to provide as much supporting material as time permits.

INTRODUCTION

Once main ideas and support materials are determined, the next step is to develop an introduction to capture the attention of the audience. The introduction is a lead-in to the message. Its purpose is to capture the undivided attention of the audience, to explain exactly what the speech will be about, to point out the value of the message, and to preview the main ideas.

Gaining the attention of the audience is perhaps the most difficult of the four purposes of the introduction to accomplish. Personal experiences are often good for gaining attention. Listeners seem to have an innate curiosity about others' lives. For example, in requesting funds for charity, the speaker might reveal personal help received from that charity. Humorous stories are effective if they fit the audience and the occasion, are relevant to the material, and set the desired tone. Illustrations such as popular songs, stories, pictures, or slides can be used to gain attention if they create an image of the topic presented. A story that begins, "Picture yourself on a dark road on a rainy night with a flat tire . . ." makes the audience want to know what will happen next.

Speakers often use rhetorical questions to gain attention. These are questions that create interest but have no expected response from the speaker or audience. The speaker might begin by asking, "What will you do when our sources of energy are depleted?" The purpose of a rhetorical question is to get the audience thinking, to make the audience curious, to involve the audience, and often to draw the audience closer to the viewpoint held by the speaker. A direct question is one that the audience is expected to answer. A speaker will sometimes gain attention by eliciting brief responses from the audience. This technique can be used to create audience involvement with the message and to gear the message more directly to audience needs and interests. When time is limited, however, the direct question can occupy much more time than the speaker intends.

Unusual or dramatic devices gain attention through the element of shock. The speaker who uses such devices must be careful not to overshadow the intended purpose of the speech.

The objective of the speech will be lost if the audience remembers only the drama and forgets the message. A last suggestion for gaining attention is to use quotations by famous people. It is important that quotations be read slowly, and the important words and ideas be stressed. Whatever the attention-getting device, its selection must be based on the audience, the message, and the setting.

In relating to the audience three factors will make a difference. First, try to find an aspect of your message that will make a difference in the lives of the listeners. Tell people what benefit your message has for them. Second, look the part of a credible speaker. Dress as nicely as you are able. Both men and women should avoid the following: flip-flops, bare midriffs, low-buttoned shirts, caps or any hat that hides the eyes, obvious tattoos or piercings that might distract, and chewing gum or tobacco. Women should avoid wearing skirts that are too short for career wear. Third, recognize any special characteristics of the audience that will make a difference in your message especially persons with physical disabilities and English as their non-native language.

A speech will contain only one main purpose, and it can be derived from the topic objective or statement. The audience should never have to guess the intent of a speech; it should be easily understood and immediately obvious. To point out the value of the message, a statement of the specific relevance of the message to the audience is a very effective device. It is necessary to make the audience feel that the message is important to them in some way. The preview of main ideas can serve to reveal what will be emphasized in the body, and often serves as an effective transition from introduction to body of the speech.

CONCLUSION

The conclusion is as important as the body and introduction. Since the last thing said by the speaker may be remembered the longest, a strong and effective conclusion is needed. The purpose of the conclusion is to provide a brief summary or reminder of the main ideas, to reemphasize the value of the message, and to close the speech with a meaningful sentence that leaves the listener convinced that the message was worth hearing. It is often useful to include parts of the introduction in the conclusion. Many of the introductory techniques, like humorous stories, personal references, examples, and quotations can be used to end the speech. If the conclusion has been effective there will be no need to tell the audience that the speech is over. If the speech has been effective, you will know that the audience was sincerely pleased to have heard your message.

The introduction and conclusion of the speech are essential components of an effective presentation. It is unwise to prepare only the body with the idea that the introduction and conclusion can be developed as you begin and end the actual presentation. The outline presented earlier provides a useful structure to follow in developing speaker-audience presentation skills.

Delivering the Message

All speakers feel some anxiety as the time draws near for the presentation of their messages. The experienced speaker has learned, however, that preparation is the key to minimizing the anxiety felt prior to speaking, to maximizing the enjoyment of making the presentation, and to ensuring a feeling of satisfaction for a job well done. In preparing to present a speech, consideration

of styles of delivery, use of presentation aids, rehearsing the message, and stage fright are important.

STYLES OF DELIVERY

There are four basic styles of delivery available to the speaker in the speaker-audience situation: impromptu, extemporaneous, manuscript, and memorized. They progress from little or no time in preparation to the completely memorized presentation. The situation and skill of the speaker determine the style to be used. A beginner of average skill does well to plan ahead for preparation and rehearsal time.

Impromptu

In the impromptu style, the speaker must rely on knowledge acquired from past study or experience. There is little or no preparation time and ideas are organized as the speaker communicates to the audience. When speakers become adept at impromptu speaking, their skill can be used to advantage in answering questions or volunteering ideas. Impromptu speaking allows spontaneous and natural expression that can effectively reveal sincere feelings. When someone has been called upon to "say a few words," an impromptu speech has been requested.

> **GOAL**
> Demonstrate effective delivery techniques for public speaking.

Styles of Delivery		
Type	**Preparation**	**Verbatim**
Impromptu	No	No
Extemporaneous	Yes	No
Manuscript	Yes	Yes
Memorized	Yes	Yes

Extemporaneous

Extemporaneous speaking is used more often than impromptu speaking because it allows a communicator time to prepare the presentation. The speaker can prepare an outline or notes from research on the topic. Advantages of extemporaneous speaking are the following: (a) brief, topical notes can be used to provide security to the speaker during the presentation; (b) information needed to express the main purpose can be clarified; (c) information to support the main ideas can be documented; and (d) because of practice with the outline or notes, the speaker can communicate more directly and spontaneously than if a script is read or a memorized speech is repeated. Disadvantages of extemporaneous speaking are the following: (a) there is generally no record of what has been said; (b) the speaker can lose track of the flow of thoughts and appear to ramble; and (c) the speaker who has not adequately rehearsed may refer too frequently to notes or even forget what to say.

Manuscript

In the manuscript style of delivery the material is written out. This offers the advantages of providing a complete record of what has been said and of the selection of language to express the message exactly. The disadvantage of the manuscript style is the lack of interaction, through frequent eye contact, of the speaker with the audience. And too, it requires the ability to read effectively from the written page. The speaker must attempt to be spontaneous and energetic while reading. In the manuscript style it is especially important that the speaker employ vocal variety, gestures, and eye contact to communicate with the listeners. The manuscript style is especially appropriate when many exact quotations are to be used. The president of the United States uses this style frequently because his words must of necessity be very carefully chosen.

Memorized

The speaker using the memorization style of delivery completes the research and writing and then memorizes the speech. This is probably the most difficult and least used style because a communicator knows that forgetting any one idea will destroy the entire speech. In the extemporaneous and manuscript styles, the speaker has something to rely on—in the memorized style, only memory. Often speakers are so preoccupied with what will come next that they fail to communicate and totally destroy the objective of the message. An advantage of the memorized style, however, is that the speaker is well rehearsed and can maintain good eye contact with the audience. Other advantages are the use of exact wordings, quotations, and examples, and exact timing of the length of delivery. For effective delivery a memorized speech should appear to be an extemporaneous speech delivered without notes. This results in a more natural speaker who is better able to relate to the audience.

Overall, the best style of speech delivery is the extemporaneous. The speaker has thoroughly researched the topic and prepared the message but is able to be flexible. Good eye contact can be maintained and a conversational manner can be used for delivery. More skilled extemporaneous speakers are able to react to the nonverbal messages of the audience. The extemporaneous message involves memorized ideas, not memorized words. In short extemporaneous speeches, it is best to avoid using any notes at all; in longer speeches, a short outline sequencing the ideas can be used. Eventually, speakers usually gain confidence using this style and feel free to give up lengthy note cards that seem so essential at first.

Whenever you are delivering a speaker-audience message, no matter which of the styles of delivery you are using, consider using a conversational style. Conversational style refers to natural movements and gestures without the barrier created by a podium. The speaker who is adept at conversational speaking style will typically move across the center of the room, stepping closer to the audience to make a point, or stepping out of the way of a projected image. Hands are loosely placed by the side but allow the speaker to use natural gestures, almost as if in an interpersonal conversation. Eye contact, as well, is quite natural since the speaker can move closer and then farther from individual members of the audience. Public speakers were once taught to have feet planted squarely on the floor and to learn gestures to go with each part of the spoken message. This is no longer the case. Although stereotypical, consider the difference in speaking styles associated with the evangelical minister as compared to the traditional, behind the pulpit preacher. At least in the stereotype, there is more audience involvement and excitement by the minister who moves around the stage and reaches out to the audience. Audiences seem to prefer the excitement generated by natural movements and gestures associated with a conversational style of presentation.

PRESENTATION AIDS

The delivery of a speech can often be enhanced by using visual and audio aids. Visual and audio aids add interest, improve clarity, reduce speaker anxiety and reinforce the spoken message. Visual aids are material such as charts, models, films, or even the chalkboard. They permit the listener to see as well as hear and thereby increase understanding of the message. Too often, speakers fail to use a visual aid to clarify points and their impact is lessened. Audio aids help too by providing music and dialog from sources other than the speaker.

Speakers themselves are possible visual aids. They can use movement and dress to help the audience understand the message more clearly. Through gestures and movements the speaker can demonstrate the size and shape of objects, or the correct way to swing a tennis racket. Using dress to enhance the verbal message, a speaker might demonstrate proper attire for disco dancing or skiing in extremely cold weather. Using themselves as visual aids is limited only by the creativity of the speakers.

Posters

Probably the most widely used visual aid for smaller audiences is the chart, graph, sketch, drawing, or picture displayed on a stand or easel. It has the advantage of being easy to prepare and set up. It does require some practice, however. It is quite easy, when several are used, to mix them up and fumble to find the appropriate image. Its major disadvantage can

---

GOAL
Use various types of visual aids in the delivery of public speeches.

---

be the difficulty the audience sometimes has in seeing it. If the image is too small, all the apologies the speaker can render are useless. Also, it is helpful to the audience to print or draw with dark inks on very light backgrounds, and to place the image so that it is completely still during viewing.

Transparencies

For larger audiences the effect of the poster can be achieved by using overhead projectors to show the image on a screen. The overhead projector can be used with charts, graphs, sketches, or drawings placed on a transparent film. Generally the image is created on a sheet of 8 1/2 × 11 inch paper and transferred to the "transparency" by using a special piece of easily operated equipment or a copy machine. For those with access to computer technology, there is software available for personal computers that makes the creation of images for projection a simple and fast process. Similar to the overhead projector is the opaque projector which can be used with pictures or charts without transfer to the special film. Although the overhead requires more preparation than the opaque projector, it is much easier to use during the presentation. Both have the disadvantage of requiring bulky equipment and the possibility of equipment failure. Now with computers and digital projectors, any image can be projected to a screen with the use of a visual presentation device (e.g. Elmo).

Chalkboard

The chalkboard, or marker board, is a medium that is generally available to most speakers. In fact, it may suffer excessive and improper use. Too often speakers will turn their backs to their audiences and spend several minutes writing or drawing on the board. To use the board effectively, the speaker must develop a style of maintaining eye contact and message delivery with the audience while briefly jotting down notes or diagrams. The right-handed speaker should assume a sideways stance to the left of the writing area and maintain eye contact and voice projection by looking over the right shoulder. It may be a better strategy to arrive early, prepare the board, and cover the written message until the appropriate moment in the presentation. Again, audience size will affect the visibility of the message.

Models

Models and objects are sometimes useful visual aids. They are a necessity for many demonstration speeches. If the object itself is too large to be brought before the audience, the use of a model can overcome this difficulty. A model, however, may be difficult and time consuming to create. Smaller audiences can often benefit from close examination of the object. For larger audiences, the speaker again has the difficulty of making certain that the entire group can see the object or model.

Handouts

Handouts, or materials the audience receives and can take with them, are often useful. Handouts can include materials prepared by the speaker or materials the speaker is able to collect from agencies and businesses. Each member of the audience should receive a copy of the materials. To keep the audience from reading handouts while the message is being delivered, they should not be distributed until speech content makes reference to them. If the audience is larger than anticipated, the speaker will often be embarrassed by too few handouts. If the audience is much smaller than anticipated, there may be no use for possibly costly materials. The speaker may wish to have back-up posters or transparencies if the size of the audience is an unknown. Use of handouts can be facilitated by having a colleague or assistant help in their distribution. When quantity of handouts is insufficient, compilation of a mailing list permits the speaker to send handouts to those who did not receive one.

Music

Most people enjoy music and other sound effects that complement a verbal message. Many popular songs have messages associated with them. If the audience listens closely to the words of a song, a part of the speaker's message can be reinforced. Other music has special associations—the Star Spangled Banner, school songs, songs with sports themes, or religious songs like *Amazing Grace* that are popular across denominations. Themes from recent or classic films can also elicit strong emotional feelings. For example, the film *Rocky* is somewhat dated but its theme song still has the connotation that we can win even when the odds are insurmountable. If you choose to use music as an audio aid, it must support your message but be secondary to your message. The sound effects must not distract from your oral presentation or occupy too much of your valuable time. Use of background music throughout a speaker-audience presentation is usually discouraged. The iPod might be a very useful way to bring sound to your presentation but do not let the fun of technology lead you to overemphasize background sound.

Film

Slides, filmstrips, movies, videotapes and DVDs are another category of visual aid that speakers will sometimes use to complement verbal messages. These media have in common the need for projection equipment, a darkened room for viewing, and possible breakdown during use. Most visuals of this type will be accompanied by audio materials. They lend a very professional tone to a presentation but are often quite expensive and lengthy. For the average speaker, slides with personal narration and tapes or DVDs will be the most readily available of the visual aids in this category. Most films used in speaker-audience presentations are available as tapes or DVDs and even slides can be sequenced on videotape for ease of presentation. Today most slides, filmstrips, and videos or DVDs are shown via computer projection.

Technology

Technology, in and of itself, is not a visual aid. However, technology can be used to enhance or provide visual aids that are otherwise impossible. First of all, computer technology can be used to create transparencies, slides, videotapes, DVDs and other visuals. It is possible to sit at a keyboard and type material that is then shown on a screen as it is created and revised. A speaker can be connected to the Internet and project images on a screen as the presentation progresses. Smart Boards permit the speaker to write in front of the group on the Board and save the input in a computer file. Technology makes it possible to link speakers and listeners who are in different locations. Teleconferencing is becoming commonplace. A speaker in one location is projected to several sites where listeners have the ability to interact and question the speaker who can respond just as if the audience were in the same room. Some of the highly technical equipment that requires special studios and processing is not available to everyone. Nearly everyone who reads this text, however, will have access to computer word processors and graphic production programs. You have no excuse for presenting transparencies which have been hand printed at a 15-degree angle or using sloppy posters that won't stay propped up. All of you should begin using computer software to produce transparencies that have a professional appearance. Begin to vary type for emphasis, use color when available, and incorporate drawings and illustrations as you help the listener comprehend your message.

Computerized multi-media presentation strategies are gaining widespread use especially for presentations that will be used with several audiences. According to Parker (2001) Microsoft PowerPoint is found on 250 million computers around the world and is used 30 million times a day. The investment of time in the preparation of a computerized presentation aid will pay off if used a number of times in that it is impressive and professional and, once learned, easier to use. Computerized multi-media presentation strategies are dependent on software like Corel Presentations or PowerPoint (see Inspirational Speech example towards the end of part 5 Activities) to create the visual and possibly audio stimuli but also need specialized projection equipment to present the stimuli to the audience. The visual aids can be charts, graphs, or diagrams like you might have placed on a transparency as well as slides, film clips, drawings, animation, and actual input at the time of presentation. Audio may or may not be present. The use of visual stimuli from CD Rom software can also be coordinated with the computerized presentation or a presenter can teach the use of a variety of software programs by showing step-by-step how the computer commands are entered to obtain the desired output. An example of computerized visual aids that accompanied a speech presentation are shown with the inspirational speech used as an example for one option of the speaking activity for part 5 of this book. The stimuli in the boxes would be projected from the computer to a screen as the speaker progressed from point to point in the presentation. As you begin incorporating computer-based aids in your presentation strategies, you may want to think of the projected images as a sophisticated way to project a poster or transparency image. As you improve skill in developing and coordinating the simple images, you may begin to use pictures or slides that have been scanned into the program. You might even use a digital camera which downloads still images directly from the camera to the computer—no film, developing, and scanning necessary. Eventually, you could be producing animated images with audio dialog to accompany your messages. Smart classrooms are becoming commonplace. These have computer-driven equipment permanently installed so that set-up time is considerable less and is much simpler.

Any point that can be made clearer by the use of a presentation aid should probably not be made without one. The presentation aid, however, should be carefully prepared in advance. There are few things more irritating to an audience than a speaker who does not know how to operate equipment, has to shuffle through a stack of posters, or addresses the chalkboard instead of the audience. The list below outlines some important considerations for using presentation aids in a speaker-audience situation.

1. Keep the aid simple—do not confuse yourself or your audience. Use color to add excitement.
2. For print materials, use easy to read print styles (fonts) and limit print to 6–10 lines. Do not use compact text that you read verbatim to the audience. The use of bullets is a good way to keep text in the right proportion.
3. Use two or more simple aids rather than one complicated aid.

4. Make the visual aids such as posters and models twice as large as seems necessary.

5. If using more than one aid, number them consecutively.

6. Place the viewing point of the visual aid in the center of the audience's viewing area.

7. Keep the aid at the eye level, or slightly higher, of the audience.

8. Do not block the view of the aid by standing between it and the listener. Use a pointer or computer arrow rather than pointing with your hand. When using visual presentation software, such as PowerPoint, attempt to arrange your computer screen so that you can face your audience at all times. Do not turn to check the projection screen. Use the technology properly and trust it.

9. When showing visual aids consecutively, allow time for the audience to view each one completely. Do not rush.

10. Look at the aid only when making specific reference to it. With computer projection, use your computer screen to keep track of what is projected to the audience.

11. Reveal the aid at the specific time when it coincides with the speech content.

12. Consider the capacity of the audience to experience the aid, make sure all can view or hear the aid, and facilitates the access of the aid to those with disabilities.

The audience will benefit from good visual and audio aids. The speaker will benefit too, since they serve as reminders of what should be said and help relieve tension by shifting attention away from the speaker to the presentation aids. Use your visual aids as you rehearse. Always test euipment to be certain your input devices are compatible with the hardware.

REHEARSAL

By now it should be obvious that preparation is the key to a successful speaker-audience presentation. Preparation includes rehearsal or practice in delivering the message. Practice does not mean merely reading your outline several times or memorizing the main ideas. It means standing up and speaking the message and using the gestures and

visual aids just as if there were an audience assembled. A good method for rehearsing the extemporaneous speech is given below:

1. Complete your outline of introduction, main ideas, supporting materials, and conclusion.

2. Study the outline until you have no problem remembering the sequence of ideas.

3. Once the outline is committed to memory, begin presenting the speech to some friendly objects in your surroundings. Use your visual aids. Go over and over those areas that cause you problems.

4. If you have difficulty remembering the sequence, statistics, or quotations, prepare several 3 inch by 5 inch note cards. Place only key phrases, statistics, and quotations on the note cards. If more than one card is needed, number the cards. Use bulleted phrases as reminders of the sequence of your ideas. NEVER use cards as a script!

5. Once the problems are overcome, find some friendly volunteers (e.g., friends, family) to listen to your performance. Use your visual aids. Use audiotape and/or videotape to hear and see your performance.

6. If you have the opportunity, practice your delivery in the room where the actual presentation will be made. Definitely, test any equipment that you intend to use and be thoroughly familiar with the methods of operation.

7. As you become more and more adept at delivering the message, begin concentrating less on the message itself and more on the audience. Be certain that you are meeting the time requirements. As you become more familiar with your material, you will tend to talk faster.

8. Develop a conversational, natural speaking style. Avoid using a podium (unless an integral sound system is needed) since the podium places a barrier between speaker and audience. Use natural movements (not pacing) to emphasize points.

GOAL
Develop strategies for building speech confidence.

As speakers practice their extemporaneous speeches, they should vary the words used to express the message. Any major changes in message should be made early in practice. A speaker who is involved with the message will be more likely to involve the listeners. Practicing vocal variety will aid audience involvement. If an emotional point is being made, the speaker's voice should reflect this. If a point needs to be made emphatically, the speaker's voice should be louder and more abrupt. Above all, practice in changing rate, pitch, and inflection is important to develop a good delivery of the message. A speaker should be sure that words can be distinctly and easily understood without making the presentation appear memorized by speaking in a continuous monotone. A conversational style should be developed; gestures and movements should be natural. Members of the audience must feel that they are being spoken to directly. Dress appropriately for the occasion and use good posture. Never lean on furniture or stand stiffly in one spot. React to the nonverbal message the audience sends to you and adjust your message to fit looks of boredom or confusion. You cannot please everyone but do your best to recognize negative messages from your audience.

STAGE FRIGHT

What about stage fright? Nearly all speakers experience stage fright or communication apprehension to some extent, but find that they can successfully present a speech. In fact, as speaking experiences increase, the ability to handle the anxiety increases until many people find speaking to an audience enjoyable. Early in speaking experiences, however, it is hard to accept the idea that one can do an adequate job of presenting a message to an audience. It is imperative to prepare, to rehearse, and to think about the satisfactions and rewards the experience will bring. In fact, successes are likely to result in the seeking out of speaking opportunities!

The apprehension of giving a public address is similar to apprehension that people feel at music recitals, stage productions, athletic events, and even interpersonal encounters like asking someone out for the first date. The communicator in all these situations is being placed in a position where others will make judgments and fear of failure can be overwhelming. In a

---

To Cough

to cough—according to webster
    is to expel air suddenly and
    noisily from the lungs through
    the narrow opening between the
    vocal cords and the larynx, this
    as a result of an involuntary
    muscular spasm in the throat

it happens most often at poetry readings
music recitals
and/or other dignified public events

there are coughers and coughees

the cougher (usually singular)
is the one who engages in this activity
the one who struggles to keep the mouth
clamped over the sound while desperately
looking around for an easy way
out of the room

the coughees (usually plural)
are the ones who bend forward pretending
that nothing is happening
but whose interest
has left the front of the room and is now

down in a pocket wondering
if that stray lozenge
is still in there somewhere
but even if it is
it will have gathered so much lint
as to be an embarrassment
and like a teenage son with too much hair
go unintroduced
    and all of the above is happening
    while pablo casals gallantly
    tries to play cello in a kennel
    and it is such a truly human moment

it is beautiful

—Ric Masten
The Voice of the Hive published by Sunflower Ink, Carmel, CA

speech communication class, you have an advantage—your audience has empathy for you and is not likely to be judgmental. Your success in the class will carry over into other situations, thus reducing your future anxiety. You are expected to and are allowed to make mistakes in the speech communication class. You will receive feedback from the instructor and the other students which will enable you to grow and be better prepared for future presentations.

What can you do to alleviate anxiety? First, admit that you feel anxious. Covering up the anxiety is sometimes the most difficult part of the presentation. It might be that you need only to admit to yourself that you are apprehensive. Sometimes, in extreme situations, the speaker might open with a statement to the audience that he or she is very nervous in giving speaker-audience presentations. What a relief when the anxiety no longer has to be hidden. Stage fright can be helped by manipulating the setting. Sometimes, the fear is more of standing exposed in front of a group than in actually speaking. Hiding behind a podium is not the answer. However, you might develop very effective visual aids so that the focus of the audience is on your materials and not on you. In fact, Parker (2001) suggests that "PowerPoint can be an impressive antidote to fear—converting public speaking dread into moviemaking pleasure" (78). In delivering a message to a small group or small audience, you might arrange the seating in a circle so that your audience feels more involved and you are not facing rows of lined up eyes. Working on a conversational speaking style where you can move around in front of the audience often helps. You avoid the awkward feeling of staying in one place. Use the audience involvement strategies that you learned in the section on small-group presentations. If the audience is focusing on a handout, is speaking and interacting with you or others, or is formulating answers to rhetorical questions, again the focus is removed from you. Delivering a speaker-audience message does not mean that you must stand in one spot and flawlessly deliver a prepared message with all eyes staring you down. Be creative and think of ways to be yourself and engage the audience in your message. You are in control and only you know what is planned. If you make a mistake,

do not let it cause panic. Most times, your audience will not even realize that your presentation was different than you had planned.

In addition to such psychological preparations as really knowing your topic through adequate research, planning and organizing, and rehearsing, you may want to try several physiological preparation techniques. Often in times of stress you might feel your stomach churning, your mouth might feel dry, you might start coughing or clearing your throat, you might have trouble breathing, you might perspire, you might shake, or you might even feel faint. Deep breathing exercises and relaxation techniques are unobtrusive strategies that can help you gain control over unintended physiological responses to stress. You must practice these strategies before the time of your presentation so they will be second nature as you wait for your turn to present your message. Deep breathing exercises merely require that you learn to fill your lungs with air. Instead of shallow inhaling, take deep breaths and feel the air reach your diaphragm (i.e., the lowest part of your lungs). Relaxation techniques require the tensing and then the loosening of your muscles. One successful strategy is to tense your entire body and then, starting at your head, relax muscles a few at a time until you reach your toes. You can focus on just one area such as your calves; the tightening and loosening of the calves will often cause the rest of your muscles to relax. When outside public view, you might try rotating your head to loosen your neck muscles or yawning to loosen your throat muscles. If these techniques seem to have potential for you, try researching them to find variations and more complete instructions.

If the strategies of the previous paragraphs and the positive experiences you will have in this speech communication class do not reduce your apprehension to an acceptable level, you may want to visit the counseling center of your college. The trained counselors have developed desensitization methods to use with students as well as other group and individual counseling techniques. Counseling is very successful in helping students who have dropped classes, taken zeroes, or even run away in order to avoid speaking assignments. Ask your instructor to tell you about some of his or her success stories in defeating communication apprehension related to speaker-audience presentations. Just remember that everyone experiences some anxiety and that YOU CAN DO IT! Use positive self-talk. Thorough preparation and rehearsal will give you confidence.

Summary

There is more to speaker-audience communication than knowing a subject and/or pulling materials together. The information, thoughts, and ideas must be arranged in an organized manner and then delivered in the most effective way. We have all experienced the discomfort of listening to an "expert" who did not deliver the message in a meaningful way. We might forgive such individuals by saying, "he is a well-known scientist," or "she is a learned scholar." Most of us, however, are not so renowned and simply make a poor impression when we fail to prepare adequately to deliver a speaker-audience message.

Nearly all speaker-audience messages can be effectively organized by using the format of introduction, body, and conclusion. It is best to limit the body of the message to two to four main ideas and expand the message by incorporating varied and appropriate supporting materials. Style of delivery—impromptu, extemporaneous, manuscript, or memorized—must be considered in preparing to present the message. Extemporaneous is generally the best approach since it requires preparation but allows for flexibility. Visual aids like charts, models, and films are helpful in presenting some aspects of the speaker-audience message. They must be selected to complement, not detract from the message. Last, in preparing to deliver a speech, rehearsal is important to help the speaker gain confidence and project a positive self-image. Remember, also, to use words and phrases only on your notecards—no scripts to be read are allowed in extemporaneous speaking.

The Weiner in the Bun

i have just hung up the telephone
but the bad news will have to wait

right now
i must deal with the lump of tension
that has just been thrust into my body
like a frankfurter into a sliced roll

stuffed with stress
my own intestine
swells like a boiled sausage
till it gets all the mustard and relish
leaving the leavened bread
the staff of life
stuck with a red-hot

as a creative person
I try to be thankful
for the sudden presence
of this annoying intruder
knowing that a gut full of anxiety
can be a useful motivator
and knowing also that a bun
all by itself
would never make it at coney island

and certainly
i want to make it
i'd love to be an oscar meyer weiner
singing and dancing
a real hot-dog!

but that doesn't mean
i enjoy being eaten

—Ric Masten
Stark Naked published by Sunflower Ink, Carmel, CA

CHAPTER 15

INFORMATIVE SPEAKING

A n important purpose of communication is to collect and provide information. When the giving of information that will be useful to the listener becomes the primary purpose of a speaker, the resulting speech may be classified as informative. People like to know things and they are curious. It is the fun of telling people something they do not know that makes informative speeches popular.

GOAL
Deliver an effective informative speech.

Part of the task in developing an informative message depends on the ability to avoid vague, ambiguous, misleading, or unproved statements, and to use examples, illustrations, statistics, quotations, and paraphrasing to support what is said. Care must be taken to avoid statements of feelings and opinions. Learning to select and present relevant information is a valuable skill to acquire. The aim of an informative speaker should be to add to the knowledge of the listeners, to give them useful information. The informative speaker must explain and clarify material that is vital to the understanding of the topic. The information must be accurate, objective, and clear. The response from the listeners should be one of understanding and interest in what was said.

Some authors feel that all speeches include some exchange of information, whether they are labeled informative, persuasive, inspirational, or entertaining. The persuasive speech includes information as background to gain listener acceptance; the inspirational speech motivates; the entertaining speech adds information to the pleasant passing of time. The distinction between an informative speech and the transfer of information lies in the purpose of the message. The purpose of an informative speech is to have the listener receive, comprehend, and retain the message. Clarity and the creation of interest while providing useful information should be the goal. There is no question of listener acceptance and no attempt to convince or stimulate the listener. When the listener must be convinced or stimulated to accept the message and act on it, the speech is persuasive in purpose even though it includes information. If the informative message is uplifting and invigorates the positive attitudes of the audience, the message might be better labeled inspirational. If the informative message is not retained but is merely a pleasant means of passing time, the message would more likely be classified as entertaining. An informative speech will have a focus and provide valuable information to be retained and used by the listener.

In developing informative speeches, many skills discussed in the previous chapters will be needed. To expand further the ability to deliver effective informative speeches, it is useful to become familiar with several specific types of informative messages, and some evaluation criteria to apply to informative messages. An example of an informative speech is included in the activities section of this part of the book.

Types of Informative Messages

Although informative messages have been discussed as one of four types of speeches, achieving the goal of an informative speech, that is, increasing useful knowledge, can be fulfilled in several ways. Consideration of ways to inform an audience may give added direction to the preparation of informative messages. There are four common ways to approach an informative speaking situation: (a) description, (b) demonstration, (c) definition, and (d) reporting. As these are discussed, it is obvious that there is much overlap among categories and that a single speech could easily include several categories. Many topics can be located within each category by searching the Internet or by using library computerized indices. Your best choice, however, is chosing a topic to which you really relate.

DESCRIPTION

Description is common in everyday conversation and reading. As listeners learn about a place, an object, an organization, or a process, they seek to recreate it in their imaginations. It is the vividness of details that determines how closely the listener's mental images match the actual place, object, organization, or process. In an informative speech that emphasizes description, it is particularly important to determine the audience's familiarity with the topic. The audience that has greater experience will benefit more from specific details, whereas the audience with less experience requires more general information.

In describing a place, an object, an organization, or a process, the speaker might use personal observations to create the description, or rely on other sources to create an image that is

---

Types of Informative Messages

Description
Demonstration
Definition
Reporting

then recreated for an audience. The National Gallery of Art in Washington, D.C., a famous Van Gogh painting, the Association for Patrons of the Gallery, or the best way to tour a museum might provide informative speaking topics for one who has been to the museum, seen the painting, supported the organization of patrons, and made the tour, as well as one who used library search, interviews, and other sources to create an image. The following is a list of some informative speaking topics that rely on description.

- The varied terrain of the state of Texas
- America's palace—a tour of the Biltmore mansion
- My day at Disney World
- The unique characteristics of the steel-belted tire
- The teeth of the shark
- The sculpture of Henry Moore
- The Society for the Prevention of Cruelty to Animals
- How your heart and lungs work together
- Applying for financial aid in college
- Creating an old-fashioned birthday party

DEMONSTRATION

When the object or process can be shown directly to the audience the need to create verbal images is significantly reduced. A speech that informs by showing or by doing is a demonstration. The purpose of the spoken message is to introduce and clarify the demonstration. Demonstrations are often used in advertisements for products or to teach skills in fields like cooking, athletics, and carpentry. The demonstration may be used in more creative ways as well. For example, it might be used to reveal the absurdity of a process or to prove the correctness of an unlikely idea. The demonstration is especially effective for topics difficult or impossible to describe, for audiences that especially benefit from visual stimuli, or when a special impact is needed. Some examples of demonstration topics follow.

- The New Magic Cook 21-in-1 kitchen gadget
- An inside look at a Swiss watch
- Setting a formal dining table

- How to tune your guitar
- The Heimlich Maneuver—saving lives
- Anyone can pound a nail
- You don't think your pocket could be picked?
- Recognizing a counterfeit twenty
- What is a hot dog really made from?
- How to fix your hair for that special party

DEFINITION

Definition, of course, is explanation of the meaning of a word. Many definitions include descriptions of places, objects, or processes. To distinguish the definition speech from the descriptive speech, it is confined to the definition of ideas—concepts and constructs. Concepts and constructs are intangible and cannot be seen or heard. They are experienced. Examples of such ideas would include love, trust, fear, intelligence, sophistication, and insecurity. There are many observable behaviors associated with such constructs. A hug is a behavior associated with love, but a hug in itself is not love. We use the observable behaviors to help define the concept or construct. There are concepts and constructs associated with specific fields as well as human experiences. Examples would include gravity, refraction, and inertia. Such ideas are generally operationally defined, that is, defined in terms of events or behaviors, so that people who use the words will attach similar meaning to them. Informative speeches will often provide such operational definitions of ideas so that an audience will acquire a better and more useful understanding of a particular concept or construct. Some examples of informative speeches to define are listed below.

- The meaning of self-esteem
- Reality versus fantasy
- Intimacy versus isolation
- Photosynthesis—the key to life
- A better life through complex numbers
- State and trait anxiety
- Sustainable design and development
- Empathy—can you recognize it?
- What is articulation in speaking?
- Implications of cognitive style and learning

REPORTING

The fourth type of informative speech is reporting. Reporting should be viewed as a very objective process. The speaker is, in a way, the intermediary between an event and the telling of an event. A report should be based on the direct relay of an observation from one source to an audience. Judgment and critical analysis, if they occur at all, are left to the listener. The subject might be a personal experience; a problem or critical issue; or a book, movie, or exhibit, as well as specific occurrences.

Many topics appropriate for the informative report could easily become persuasive topics. If the speaker takes a position on one side of an issue rather than giving a balanced treatment of all sides, the speech purpose becomes persuasive. In considering nuclear power plants, for example, an informative speaker would do nothing to convince the audience to favor or disfavor the issue. Some examples of informative speeches to report are given below.

- My day as an elementary school volunteer
- An experience—twenty-four hours of blindness
- Ways to secure your home or apartment
- Apartment dwellers versus absentee landlords
- Eliminating smallpox from the face of the earth
- The films of Sylvester Stallone
- The King Tut exhibit in retrospect
- The future of mass transit in Dallas, Texas
- Tornadoes, hurricanes, and blizzards of 1978
- Progressive country music appeals to all

Informative speaking can be fun and a learning experience for speaker as well as listener. Remember, sharing useful knowledge is the purpose. An informative speech makes no attempt to change the listener's attitudes, values, or behaviors. The message should be so neutral that listener acceptance is of no concern to the speaker.

The Potluck Circuit

a tossed salad
lost in a field of tossed salads
i try to distinguish myself
by describing the flavor of tarragon
with gestures
i long to be experienced

like Langston Hughes
i too have wilted
watching a house erode
between the potluck
and the poetry reading

"we'd love to stay
but we really must go
the ostriches you know . . ."

and it's just as indigestible
at the head table
where the fancy covered dishes
congregate

"look out for this one Sidney
it has liver in it . . ."

everyone sneaking a peek
to see what a poet looks like
eating cole-slaw
marveling
at how smoothly his jaw moves

staring straight ahead
i ask myself why
just being at the table
has never been enough

—Ric Masten
They Are All Gone Now published by Sunflower
Ink, Carmel, CA

Developing the Informative Speech

AUDIENCE NEEDS

In informative speaking, the prior knowledge of the listener is extremely important in formulating the message. The speaker must consider the audience's present knowledge of the topic so that this knowledge can be adequately built on. Knowledge of special audience interests is helpful in selecting supporting materials. Too often the audience fails to understand a message because of inadequate background, or becomes bored with the message because of its simplicity. Audiences may be generally informed on the topic, basically uninformed, or a combination of informed and uninformed. The last, of course, is the most difficult of the three for which to prepare. Because the speaker-audience setting allows little opportunity to determine audience needs at the time of presentation, investigation of audience characteristics must be done prior to preparation of the message.

Spending time on elementary generalities wastes both speaker and listener time if the audience is generally well informed on a topic. To provide adequate and appropriate stimuli for the knowledgeable listener, it is suggested that the speaker present new information, introduce a different facet of the subject, or discuss it in relation to a similar area. The knowledgeable listener will appreciate a presentation that builds on current understanding yet stimulates further thinking.

The uninformed listener should not be classified as stupid. There are many topics of which we all have little knowledge. A good informative speech can be a stimulus in creating new interests. The uninformed listener requires the basics, the fundamentals, the elementary. It is wise to limit coverage of the topic to a narrow aspect and use repetition to reinforce learning. The most important thing for the speaker to avoid is the demonstration of a superior attitude or a tendency to talk down to the audience.

The audience with a mix of informed and uninformed listeners is the most difficult for which to prepare. The message must include the generalities as well as the specifics. The correct balance is challenging and difficult to achieve.

The speaker can subtly introduce the basics in the guise of a review as a means of ensuring that all listeners have common background. The specifics might be introduced as unusual applications or interesting asides. However the goals are accomplished, the message must be prepared in a positive way so that all listeners find satisfaction in receiving the content.

COMMON LEARNING PRINCIPLES

Much has been done in recent years to discover ways to facilitate human learning. An informative speaker is a teacher whose goal is to provide the opportunity for acquisition of information. Some general principles of effective teaching are briefly listed as follows:

1. Make the atmosphere pleasant. If the experience is enjoyable the learner will be more likely to pay attention than to drift away with seemingly more interesting private thoughts.
2. Open the presentation with an attempt to involve the learner. Unless the learner's attention is caught, the message will be lost. Continue relating the message to the learner's needs and interests. Help the message fit into an already established area of the learner's mind.
3. Information can be more readily acquired when it is presented in an organized manner. It has been discovered that learners themselves will attempt to organize material that is presented in an unorganized fashion. The impact of an informative speech will be greater if the organization is provided by the speaker. Review the ways of ordering material (i.e., topical, comparison/contrast) presented in chapter 13.
4. Teach the principles underlying your message. Do not merely cite many specific examples. Each principle may appear as one main idea of the informative speech and some of the specifics as supporting details. The demonstration speech dealing with the twenty-one-function cooking aid might be presented under principles of blending, chopping, grinding, and slicing, with the twenty-one functions as specific examples of each.

5. Introduce information in small amounts. The human mind needs time to deal with facts and figures and cannot assimilate too much at one time.

6. Use repetition to help the learner retain relevant information. The more often a thing is heard, the more likely it is that it will be remembered. In speaker-audience communication, repeat the main purpose at least three times—in the introduction, body, and conclusion.

These six points sound simple but underlie the information-giving aspects of public speaking.

METHODS OF EXPLANATION

Speakers generally develop quite detailed knowledge of their informative speaking topics. Their search for materials is often a learning experience. Because of their familiarity, they sometimes prepare their messages without considering the way explanations familiar to them will sound to the listener. In other words, the speaker will generally have a more sophisticated command of the topic than the audience. To be certain the audience grasps the meaning of the message, the informative speaker must clearly explain words and phrases essential to the message.

Definition is the most common method of explaining words and phrases. The purpose of the definition for clarification is to explain complex words and phrases in terms the audience is more likely to understand. The definition should be brief, probably a single sentence, and should be stated in the speaker's own words (i.e., not the dictionary's words). Listener comprehension will be decreased considerably if the audience misses key points because of unfamiliarity with the terms used. It is particularly important to clarify complex or technical terms and terms that have different meanings depending on usage. An example of a definition to clarify content is given below.

A greenhorn is an inexperienced person who can be easily fooled into believing something that is untrue.

Several other ways to clarify the meaning of speech content are expressed in the following list.

1. **Synonym**—A synonym is a word that has basically the same meaning as another word. Infuriate and enrage are synonyms.

2. **Antonym**—An antonym is a word that has basically the opposite meaning as another word. Infuriate and soothe are antonyms.

3. **Analogy**—Analogy clarifies an unfamiliar word or phrase by comparing it to something that is familiar. Remember the analogy used in an earlier chapter to describe an effective speech? An effective speech is like a clearly focused photograph. Analogies are either literal or figurative. A literal analogy is a comparison of things in the same categories. Polyester carpeting has many of the same qualities long valued in wool carpeting. Figurative analogies compare things in different categories and, therefore, provide some of the more creative visual images. That movie was as exciting as watching two snails run a mile.

4. **Negation**—Negation means explanation by describing what the word or phrase does not mean. Rehearsal of your speech does not mean memorizing the outline. (Remember?)

5. **Classification**—Classification relates the word or phrase to other words or phrases that form a more general set. An informative speech is one kind of speaker-audience message.

6. **Rephrasing**—Rephrasing means stating the same thing in different words. It offers the listener several ways of relating one idea to another idea with which they have had prior experience and it serves as reinforcement just as repetition does. It can be boring, however, if overused. Consider the following two sentences as acceptable examples of rephrasing. Supporting materials add credibility to your message. When you use examples, statistics, and testimony, what you have to say will be more readily accepted by your audience.

During preparation and rehearsal of an informative speech, it is important to pay attention to the words and phrases used. Speakers are wise to ask themselves if they would have understood the words and phrases before they developed the message, and to ask their friendly listeners during rehearsal to point out difficult words and phrases. To confuse in an informative message is certainly not to impress.

Evaluation of Informative Speeches

Many times listeners accept a message and give little, if any, thought to the quality of the message. Some speakers secretly hope that their listeners are among that group of people that fails to consider the worth of the message. Well-educated persons, however, should develop skills that enable them to evaluate activities in which they participate, and they should use credible evaluations received from others as a means of personal improvement. First of all, evaluate the quality of the information itself and second, assess the effectiveness of the speech as a whole.

Consider the sources and types of information that you draw together to formulate your message. The following points are particularly useful in assessing information used in an informative speech or used to provide the basis for a persuasive, inspirational, or entertaining speech.

- Current? Although many facts remain relevant, current literature should be searched to discover new findings.
- Verifiable? Does more than one source provide similar information on a topic?
- Comprehensive? Is enough background given to determine if the findings are accurate?
- Unbiased? Is the information presented without slanting it to make a particular point?
- Credible? Has review been adequate enough to substantiate the findings? Consider the unreliability of much of what is presented in the .com websites on the Internet.

- Factual rather than Opinion? Expert opinion is often given the respect of fact but the reputation of the expert must be established.

A critical thinker will not accept findings based only on anecdotes or testimonials but will require some objective verification of the information which is the basis of an informative speech. Reporters, for example, must verify all findings by securing at least two and sometimes more sources who tell them the same information.

There are a number of criteria to consider in evaluating an informative speech. Many relate to vocal delivery such as volume and physical delivery such as eye contact as well as personal qualities of the speaker. Other criteria relate to the general speaking outline with appropriately prepared introduction, body, and conclusion. Criteria of major importance in considering informative speeches are listed and described as follows:

1. Did the message provide the listener with useful information?
2. Did the message present information in a non-biased way? That is, was the speech informative, not persuasive?
3. Was the supporting material relevant for each main idea?
4. Did the supporting material help to maintain listener interest and attention to the message?
5. Was the supporting material adequate enough to establish listener confidence?
6. Were visual aids used where appropriate?
7. Were visual aids of acceptable quality?
8. Was repetition used sufficiently to reinforce the main ideas?
9. Did the message deal with one main purpose?
10. Did the message include two to four main ideas?

These criteria should be applied to informative messages as final preparation is completed and while listening to others' informative messages. Consider them while reviewing the examples of informative speeches and the evaluation form for an informative speech included with the following activities.

Summary

An informative speech has the specific purpose of providing the listener with information. Because of the enjoyment and excitement associated with sharing knowledge, informative speeches are very popular. To inform requires clear and vivid description as material is explained and clarified. There are several types of informative messages: description, demonstration, definition, and reporting. Audience needs are important considerations in developing informative messages at the appropriate level of difficulty. Listeners must not be bored by a message that they have often heard before, or confused by a message that assumes prior experience with the topic. A speech becomes persuasive when a speaker shares feelings and opinions in an attempt to change the listener's behavior.

CHAPTER 16

PERSUASIVE SPEAKING

The goal of the persuasive speaker is to have the listener take action on an idea or issue, accept or strengthen a belief, or change a point of view. A persuasive message generally includes some information that serves as background for the true purpose of the speech. The remainder of the persuasive message is designed to create a feeling of discomfort in the listener. The dis-

comfort may result from embarrassment over graying laundry, from the desire to possess some very appealing item, from guilt over a belief, or from a realization that something is perceived by an authority figure to be wrong. If the persuasive message is effective, the listener feels compelled to eliminate the discomfort by changing to a different brand of detergent, by buying that appealing item, by changing the belief, or by correcting what was perceived as wrong.

Persuasion is a part of everyone's life at all levels of communication and in many different situations. At an interpersonal level, persuasion is sometimes used in asking permission to do something or in getting someone else to do something. In small group communication, many attempts are made to gain acceptance for recommendations or actions to be carried out by the membership. In the interactive environment of interpersonal and small group communication, the speaker is often placed in a defensive role as others attempt to refute the underlying rationale of the request. In the more formal speaker-audience situation many of the same types of persuasive messages occur, but generally the speaker receives the attention of the audience during the time allotted for delivery of the message. Since most individuals deliver and receive many persuasive messages, it is useful for everyone to know effective ways to classify, prepare, evaluate, and receive them.

Types of Persuasive Messages

Persuasive messages can be classified in three ways: according to the type of behavior expected from the listener, the purpose of the message, or the nature of the topic. Possible behaviors resulting from persuasive messages are adoption, continuance, discontinuance, and deterrence. The purposes of the message are either to stimulate or convince. Two classifications of the nature of topics for persuasive messages are policies or problems, and beliefs or values. The three classifications for persuasive messages will be reviewed with examples of topic statements that reflect each category. Many more topics can be located by using Internet search engines and by using computerized indices available in your library.

Expected Behaviors

Persuasive messages are intended to have some effect on what the listener will do or believe. Some persuasive messages are presented with the purpose that the listener will adopt the belief or action being expressed. The speaker's message is intended to become part of the listener's value system. For example, adoption is intended when the speaker encourages the listener to accept the government's policies to curb inflation. When the message is aimed at maintaining some behavior or attitude, continuance is sought. At a meeting of a weight reduction group, a speaker might urge members to continue working toward their goal of slimness by following their diets. The goal of the message would have been discontinuance had the speaker discussed those habits that lead to overweight.

Persuasive messages of deterrence warn against potentially negative outcomes. The speaker hopes to change behaviors or beliefs before a negative situation occurs. Messages urging smokers to give up their habit before permanent lung damage occurs are examples of messages of deterrence. Some further examples of persuasive topics focusing on the behaviors of adoption, continuance, discontinuance, and deterrence follow.

Adoption

- Individualism—why be afraid to be different?
- Develop your own physical fitness program
- Four ways that you can help decrease the crime rate

Continuance

- Parents keep it up—childhood diseases are nearly gone
- Preservation of our American heritage must not be stopped
- Keep working towards college graduation

Discontinuance

- Give up your biggest contribution to pollution, your car
- The increase in teenage alcoholism must end
- Everyone needs to fight pornography

Deterrence

- Don't lose your family in a home fire
- Recognize these signs of drug abuse before it's too late
- Avoid nuclear contamination—stop those power plants

Purpose of Message

The speaker can consider persuasive messages in relation to their intent. Some persuasive messages are intended to stimulate. These messages have the purpose of motivating listeners to some action that is consistent with their existing beliefs and values. Most successful students, for example, realize that studying is an important part of achieving academic goals. However, some students who would not argue about the value of studying would benefit from stimulation to study. Those students who are unsuccessful might benefit from a persuasive message on the value of studying. They need to be convinced that studying is worthwhile. The persuasive message to stimulate is directed primarily toward specific action or behaviors; that to convince, toward values and beliefs. Several examples of topics are given below:

Stimulate

- Everyone must conserve energy
- Attend your place of worship regularly
- Join the armed forces and see the world

Convince

- Our energy is a valuable resource
- The value of religious affiliation
- The importance of the U.S. armed forces

CLASSIFICATION OF TOPICS

Persuasive topics are sometimes classified as relating to solutions to problems or to values and beliefs. Many situations arise where groups of all sizes come together to agree on a solution to a problem of mutual concern. Small groups may discuss the solutions informally; large groups may recognize speakers who formally present their views to the group. The nature of the solution is such that speakers will employ techniques of persuasion to gain acceptance for their views. The suggested solutions will nearly always relate to some specific action to be performed in the name of the "group," whether it numbers two or 2000. The other category of messages relates to values and beliefs. These messages attempt to bring the listener's values and beliefs in line with those of the speaker. The immediate result may not include an observable action, but a change might occur within the listener. Such changes are generally subtle and will often require continued persuasive messages over an extended period of time. A speaker may argue in favor of the death penalty with the intention that the listener will accept specific arguments and support the same viewpoint. Any change will be unobservable unless the members of the audience take some action like writing to their state's governor. Some examples of policies/problems and beliefs/values topics are given below:

Policies or Problems

- To beat inflation, we must freeze prices and wages
- Call your dentist today and save your teeth
- How you can halt the decline of the inner city

Beliefs or Values

- Synonyms—murder and abortion
- The value of cultural differences among neighbors
- The importance of patience in everyday living

Developing the Persuasive Speech

The persuasive message might be considered an extension of an informative message that seeks to gain listener acceptance. As in developing informative messages, thought must be given to audience characteristics. In addition, it is important to be familiar with ways of gaining listener acceptance and to understand modifications of the general speaking outline when applied to persuasive messages.

Aristotle developed the concepts of ethos, pathos, and logos which are relevant to the development of the persuasive message. These concepts provide three types of proof—personal, emotional, and logical—that can make a persuasive message more effective.

1. *Ethos* refers to personal proof. In terms that we have used throughout this book, ethos is your credibility with your listener. Are you trustworthy and honest? Do you display a high energy level and enthusiasm for your topic? Are you presenting your message as a gesture of goodwill, with the best interests of the audience in mind? Can you demonstrate a personal connection with the topic? Speakers cannot assume

that the audience knows that they are credible. Speakers must take the effort to explain and demonstrate ethos.

2. *Pathos* refers to emotional proof. In terms that we have used before, pathos is the audience involvement with the topic. Can you get your receiver to identify with the message? Can you elicit an emotional response that will engage the audience? Speakers must be careful to adjust the strength of the emotional appeal to the audience background. If an emotional appeal is too graphic or horrendous, the audience might tune out in order to avoid the pain of the appeal. If an emotional appeal is too weak, the audience will not be convinced to take the action you suggest.

3. *Logos* refers to logical proof. In terms that we have used in previous sections, logos refers to your supporting materials. Is your message based on verifiable facts? Is your evidence strong? Is your evidence directly relevant to the topic? Most Americans have been trained to use the scientific method throughout their education. The scientific method uses inductive reasoning which is based on sufficient and representative samples from which conclusions can be drawn. To establish logos use representative examples from which a generalization can be drawn to support the action you wish your audience to take.

Use ethos, pathos, and logos as you develop the various parts of the persuasive speech.

In preparing persuasive messages, it is important to recognize that persuasion is different from coercion. Coercion is different from persuasion in that it leaves no alternatives. It forces the listener to accept the message. Persuasion can be dangerous, too, if listeners are convinced or stimulated to do something that they do not want to do. The best defense against a persuasive communicator is the recognition that persuasive techniques may distort the truth and be unethical, that a choice between alternatives exists, and that you can say no.

Types of Persuasive Messages

1. Expected Behaviors

   A. Adoption

   B. Continuance

   C. Discontinuance

   D. Deterrence

2. Purpose of Message

   A. Stimulate

   B. Convince

3. Types of Topics

   A. Policies or Problems

   B. Values or Beliefs

AUDIENCE CHARACTERISTICS

To be effective, the persuasive speaker must develop a message that allows the listener to be accepting. This requires a careful analysis of the audience background and values. For example, it might be ineffective always to assume that an audience has deep religious beliefs. Religious references as supporting materials would have less impact with some groups than with others. In fact, an audience inclined to accept a persuasive argument might reject the message entirely because of the wrong choice of supporting materials. A group of working mothers, for example, might not hear a message on the benefits of reading to young children if it were introduced with the assertion that working mothers typically fail to read to their children.

Persuasive speakers are sometimes undecided about whether or not to present both sides of an appeal. If time restrictions permit, there are audiences for which hearing both sides will benefit the speaker's purpose. These are listeners who are known to react unfavorably toward a specific viewpoint or who are likely to hear the other side from the other speaker. When the audience strongly favors the other side of the argument, the speaker's credibility will be improved if the audience sees that the speaker has considered the opposite view. If it is known that the audience will be likely to hear the other side, it is useful to present the other side and then immediately show why it should be rejected. When several speakers are scheduled to follow each other, it will generally be advantageous to be the last speaker—that is, to make the last impression.

For some audiences presentation of only one side of an issue is probably better. When the listener is known to favor the message, as in the persuasive situation intended to stimulate, it may be more useful to develop only one side of the issue. When the persuasive speaker is fairly certain that the listener will hear only one side of a controversial issue, it may be advantageous to present only one viewpoint. Care must be taken, however, to remain very objective and ethical in the choice of arguments. Also, if the message intends an immediate action on the part of the audience—for example, a financial contribution—the message will generally be more effective if only the speaker's side is presented.

The point to consider in preparing the persuasive message, as well as any other message, is how it will be perceived by the audience. Many speakers think only of their own reaction and feelings. Speakers are wise to put themselves in the place of the audience and ask themselves what the message is saying to them. Typically, as in the following example, it is advantageous for the speaker to indicate, when stating the main purpose, which side of an issue is being taken.

Review of issues relating to immigration in the United States leads to the conclusion that stricter laws must be passed and enforced to safeguard our national security and standard of living.

OR

Review . . . that more flexible laws must be passed and enforced to provide objective criteria to be used in qualifying immigrants for legal states in our nation.

GAINING LISTENER ACCEPTANCE

Persuasive messages include a recommendation for some change or action. Some goals of persuasive speaking that require major changes or actions will require a series of messages delivered over a long period of time. The anti-smoking campaign of the American Cancer Society is an example of a series of related messages continued over an extended time. Other persuasive messages are intended to have immediate results. The persuasive message, whether alone or in a series, will generally include the following five components: awareness, dissonance, resolution, reinforcement, and action. These five components reflect the motivated sequence of Alan Monroe (1935) who proposed and refined these concepts.

Awareness

The awareness step of the persuasive message is designed to gain the listener's attention. Also, the awareness phase of the persuasive message is necessary to call the listener's attention to a discrepancy between what the speaker favors and what the listener favors. It is the initial attempt of the speaker to cause discomfort in the listener. The more obvious the awareness of the discrepancy, the more the listener will pay attention. Awareness may be developed through a shocking statement or visual aid, a rhetorical question, an example, a literary quote, or any means that attracts the attention of the listener.

Dissonance

Dissonance is a strong feeling within an individual that something is wrong. There is a lack of harmony between two forces that include behaviors and/or attitudes. For example, a health foods advocate can create a great deal of dissonance by implying that people are poisoning themselves through what they eat. When dissonance is created in the listener, the speaker has gone beyond gaining attention and making the listener aware of a situation. The listener feels a great deal of tension or urgent need for action. Nonverbal messages from the audience can be useful indicators that the speaker has created dissonance.

Resolution

The resolution phase of a persuasive message tells how to reduce the tension or discomfort being felt by proposing a solution. The attitude or desire to follow through with the speaker's intention is established. The speaker should inform the audience how to overcome any barriers that stand in the way of relieving the tension or discomfort. It is helpful to present an actual plan that the listener is likely to accept with gratitude.

GOAL

Define the concept of dissonance as it is used in persuasive speaking.

Reinforcement

The reinforcement step in the persuasive message motivates the listener by describing the positive outcomes likely to result from acceptance of the speaker's message. The reinforcement will often refer to the future and the positive rewards the listener is likely to receive. Listeners visualize in their minds the suggested behavior and feel satisfaction. The nonverbal message of the audience after the reinforcement step should be very different from that resulting from the creation of dissonance.

Action

This step is a specific command the speaker can use to end the message. This will generally be brief and suggest an immediate behavior or value change. It gives the listener a specific task to perform. It is more effective if it can be tied to the listener's daily routine. To improve the probability that the action step will be performed, it should not require too much extra effort on the part of the listener.

Consider the following example of the five steps of persuasion:

1. **Awareness:** Police files are full of descriptions of children in our own community who are physically and psychologically harmed by their parents—sometimes to the point of death.
2. **Dissonance:** Consider the worst tortures you can and imagine experiencing such treatment from the persons in your life you trust and depend on.
3. **Resolution:** Observant citizens of the community can significantly reduce child abuse

---

Parts of the Persuasive Message

Awareness or Interest
Dissonance or Need
Resolution or Satisfaction
Reinforcement or Visualization
Action or Challenge

by being responsible enough to report suspected cases to authorities.

4. **Reinforcement**: If you improve the life or even save the life of one abused child, you will have made a significant contribution to your community and to society in general.

5. **Action**: When you suspect child abuse, pick up your phone and call XXX-XXX-XXXX, your child welfare office.

PERSUASIVE SPEAKING OUTLINES

The general public speaking outline presented earlier is not abandoned in persuasive speaking. A persuasive speech, like an informative speech, requires an introduction, body, and conclusion. Within this format, the steps of persuasion—awareness, dissonance, resolution, reinforcement, and action—must be incorporated. Generally the awareness step will be included in the introduction; dissonance, resolution, and reinforcement will be a part of the body; and the action step will be the last statement of the conclusion. These are generalizations, of course, and a creative speaker might very well develop an innovative format that includes the five persuasive steps in other locations within the introduction, body, and conclusion of the speech.

To demonstrate several ways of developing persuasive messages, possible outlines for a problem-solution message and a values message follow:

Problem-Solution Outline

1. Introduction
   a. Gain attention—create *awareness* of problem
   b. Relate problem to audience
   c. State the problem (main purpose)
   d. Preview main ideas

2. Body
   a. Nature of the problem (main idea)—*dissonance*
      i. Causes of the problem (support)
      ii. Effects of the problem (support)
      iii. Extent of the problem (support)
      iv. Personal experience (support)—optional
   b. Solution to the problem (main idea)—*resolution*
      i. Procedure to be followed (support)
      ii. Realistic expectations (support)
      iii. Success in similar situations (support)
      iv. Personal experience (support)—optional
   c. Outcomes to be expected (main idea)—*reinforcement*
      i. Elimination of problem (support)
      ii. Advantages that will result (support)
      iii. Personal experience (support)—optional

3. Conclusion
   a. Problem restated
   b. Summary of main ideas
   c. Closing remarks
      i. Challenge audience
      ii. Ask for *action*

Values—A Beliefs Outline

1. Introduction
   a. Gain attention of audience
   b. Relate problem to audience
   c. Describe the value, the ideal (main purpose)—*awareness*
      i. What it is
      ii. Why it is important
   d. Preview main ideas

2. Body
   a. Absence of value (main idea)—*dissonance*
      i. Familiar example (support)
      ii. Statistics (support)
      iii. Testimony (support)
   b. Benefits of the value (main idea)—*resolution*
      i. Familiar example (support)
      ii. Personal experience (support)
   c. Audience adoption of value (main idea)—*reinforcement*
      i. Procedure to be followed
      ii. Rewards to be realized (support)

3. Conclusion
   a. Description of value restated
   b. Summary of main ideas
   c. Closing remarks
      i. Challenge audience
      ii. Ask for *action*

In using these outlines, remember that they are merely guidelines. Every speech will be unique and require its own adaptation of the general speaking outline.

Evaluation of Persuasive Speeches

The evaluation of a persuasive speech is similar to that of an informative speech. In any speaking situation, the personal qualities of the speaker, eye contact, vocal delivery, and physical delivery are important considerations. Adequate preparation and rehearsal is one way to ensure success on these criteria. The message itself and the appropriate visual aids require consideration also. Some questions of major importance in evaluating persuasive messages are listed as follows:

1. Does the message create discomfort in the listener? That is, was the speech persuasive, not informative?
2. Did the speech create awareness of a discrepancy between listener and speaker?
3. Was dissonance created?
4. Did the speech provide for resolution of dissonance?
5. Did the message demonstrate a positive outcome from accepting the message?
6. Did the message provide the listener with an appropriate action to perform or attitude to adopt?
7. Did supporting materials relate to audience beliefs and values? Was support recent and relevant.
8. Were visual aids used appropriately to support the speaker's goals?
9. Was listener interest maintained throughout the message?

10. Was the speaker ethical and truthful in developing the persuasive message? Did the speaker distort information in order to be convincing? Did the speaker resist personal attacks?

These criteria should be considered in preparing persuasive messages and in listening to those of other speakers. Consider them while reviewing the example of a persuasive speech and the example of an evaluation form for persuasive speeches included in speaking activities in part 5 of the book.

Receiving the Persuasive Message

Because persuasive messages intend to bring about behavioral change, the receiver must develop skills that permit rational choices rather than blind following of suggested actions. One way to resist persuasion is to not listen. This approach, however, eliminates the possibility of receiving beneficial persuasive messages and willingly adopting suggested behaviors. Rather than not listen, it is useful, in receiving persuasive messages, to rely on critical listening skills.

Critical listening skills (see chapter 4) enable the listener to assess the ideas and supporting materials that form the basis of a persuasive message. Critical listening involves more than merely receiving and understanding a message; it means evaluating and judging the message. By critically listening, the receiver of a persuasive message can decide whether or not to be made uncomfortable by the speaker, and whether or not to reject the suggested action. In

---

Veg-O-Matic

your body speaks to my cynic
    skeptic
slouching down there folding the arms
protecting the vitals
from what must be some new kind of

    old shell game
well squint those watchful eyes
lone ranger
and sit there behind your hand
    your mask
and bite your silver bullet and forget
the wisdom of that simple indian
on your color set
for what you see is what you get

as for me it's been nine years in a row
i have gone down front
    and stood slack-jawed
before one of the great men of our time
the guy who demonstrates and sells you
the vegetable slicer
at the county fair

now i know that thing is not gonna cut
a potato for me like it does for him
whomp! ... french fries
with an attachment that carves radishes

into Christmas trees
i know when i get that thing home
it's just gonna take the end of my thumb
off
for me it don't slice tomatoes
it smashes 'em
    but i have bought
    nine of those things
    nine years in a row

so who's buying a vegetable slicer
i can tell a worthless piece of junk
when i see one
i'm simply paying the man a paltry sum
for giving me a few truly golden moments
trying to be like a kid i once knew
who was free
    free to enjoy
almost everything
because you know
he really didn't care
if he was a sucker
    or not

—*Ric Masten*
The Voice of the Hive published by Sunflower Ink,
Carmel, CA

listening critically to a persuasive message, two considerations are relevant: analysis of fact versus opinion and intent of the speaker.

FACT AND OPINION

Fact

Facts are certain. There is evidence available that lends unquestionable proof to the truth of a fact. For example, it is a fact that there are fifty states in the United States, that the earth is round, and that Dallas, Texas, is not a seaport. Something accepted as a fact at one point in time may be shown to be incorrect at a later date. For example, it was once accepted as a fact that the earth was flat. There are several tests that can be applied to help in verifying statements as facts: (a) Is there any evidence against the statement? Or can it be verified as truth? (b) Do other already established facts agree? (c) Do the experts in the area confirm it as fact? Sometimes speakers who are seeking to persuade by whatever means they can make nonfactual information, or opinion, seem factual. The conscientious listener must analyze persuasive messages carefully to determine if statements are supported by evidence sound and sufficient enough to judge them factual.

Opinion

A sound opinion is a judgment based on the best available, although unverifiable, information; the three criteria used to judge whether a fact exists cannot be shown to be true. When evaluating materials, the speaker and listener must be aware that all that is written is not fact. Opinions based on the best information available are useful and acceptable as support for a speech, but should be presented as such. Both the speaker and listener must guard against the use of unverified facts and unsound opinions. The dishonest persuader can be quite effective in making a lie appear to be an informed opinion or even a fact. The speaker or listener must consider the source and the soundness of statements used in preparing or listening to messages intended to persuade. Without sounding disrespectful, listeners who are uncertain about persuasive statements might ask, "how do we know this is true or this will happen."

GOAL
Differentiate fact and opinion.

INFERENCE

Somewhere on the continuum between fact and opinion lies inference. Inference refers to assumptions based on incomplete data. When gathering information to be used in a persuasive argument, speakers must rely at times on their own judgment to synthesize information for efficient delivery. The speaker and listener must be wary in distinguishing among fact, opinion, and inference. "My car broke down and was towed to a garage" can be verified as a fact. "My car will probably break down again soon since I cannot afford the complete repairs" is an inference. "My car is a piece of junk" is an opinion. Be wary, also, of the echo-effect. Just

---

How to Present Ideas in a Way That Gets Attention

P   Polish your presentation—plan, prepare, practice
E   Engage your audience—make the answer to "what's in it for me?" easy.
R   Realize your outcome—ask for a realistic action.
S   Simplify—have a clear introduction, few main ideas, and a dynamic conclusion.
U   Understand the audience feedback—they might say "no."
A   Anticipate possible objections—have some answers ready.
D   Display enthusiasm—believe in what you say.
E   Energize—involve your audience in your message.

because many people repeat an inference or an opinion does not turn it into a fact.

INTENT OF THE SPEAKER

When listening to a persuasive message, it might be wise to ask the following question: What does the speaker have to gain by my performing the suggested action? Many persuasive messages are delivered for the well-being of the listener, but many others are based on a profit motive or to otherwise benefit the speaker. Advertising is a multimillion dollar business with the sole purpose of convincing individuals to purchase one product or service rather than another. Advertising agencies rely on psychological research and the power of suggestion to sell products. They can present their messages via the powerful channels of visual as well as audio media. How often do individuals buy products, visit places, participate in activities, and generally behave in ways that are not in their best interest? Even in interpersonal encounters, persuasion can be used to manipulate to benefit the interests of the speaker. Consider the classic persuasive device of the teenager that "everyone else gets to do something." Parents must suffer the dissonance created when they deprive their child of what is presented as a "right." There is interpersonal persuasion going on constantly. Most of it probably does not amount to much—a few dollars as a donation, an expensive lunch that was not in the budget—but some consequences can be disastrous—unprotected sex, riding with a drunken driver, committing perjury to protect a friend. As a consumer and as a listener, consider the intentions of the speaker before accepting the message. Become sophisticated and remember that many persuasive messages have more than one side to consider before important decisions are made.

Summary

The persuasive speech has the specific purpose of changing the listener's behaviors. Persuasive speeches are designed to convince the listener to adopt a belief, continue a behavior, or avoid a potentially negative outcome. Persuasive speeches attempt to convince individuals to change values or beliefs or stimulate them to some action based on current values and beliefs. Persuasive speeches are often directed toward a specific solution to a problem or toward specific values and beliefs. Effective ways to develop persuasive speeches are: to create an awareness of the purpose; to create dissonance, that is, discomfort; to offer a suggestion for eliminating dissonance; to show the positive outcome resulting from eliminating dissonance; and to indicate a specific action for removing dissonance. In developing effective persuasive speeches, the speaker must include supporting materials that are ethical and honest. The receiver of a persuasive message must develop skills in critical listening.

Activity 1

Information about Speaker-Audience Communication

Preparation: Read part 5: Speaker-Audience Communication. Prepare for a test by answering the practice items given below.

Practice Items

PART 5: OVERVIEW

1. Do people ever overcome fear of making a formal speech?

CHAPTER 13

1. What are four ways that speaker-audience communication can be differentiated from interpersonal and small group communication?
2. What are four major classifications for most public speeches?
3. What does an informative message attempt to do?
4. What does a persuasive message attempt to do?
5. What is the purpose of a speech to inspire?
6. What is the purpose of a speech to entertain?
7. How would you adapt a message to a particular setting?
8. What is the advantage to narrowing a speech topic prior to beginning preparation?
9. What are six common sources for gathering material for a speech?
10. What are six ways used for ordering material for a speech?
11. What are three types of supporting materials?

CHAPTER 14

1. What are the three major parts composing most public messages?
2. Regardless of speech length, how many main ideas are sufficient?
3. What is the purpose of the introduction to a public message?
4. What are specific methods for gaining attention of an audience?
5. How many main purposes should a speech contain?
6. What is the purpose of the conclusion to a public message?
7. How can anxiety be minimized prior to delivering a speech?
8. What are the four basic styles of delivery?
9. Which visual aids are most often used with smaller audiences?
10. When are overhead and opaque projectors more likely to be used?
11. What are important guidelines to follow when using visual aids?

12. How can technology be used to improve a speech?
13. What is a good method for rehearsing the extemporaneous speech?
14. How can a speaker overcome psychological stage fright?
15. How can a speaker overcome physiological stage fright?

CHAPTER 15

1. What are four common approaches to informative speaking?
2. What audience characteristics are important when informing?
3. What are general learning principles to consider when informing?
4. What are some ways to clarify the meaning of speech content?
5. What presentation qualities should be considered when evaluating an informative speech?

CHAPTER 16

1. How is persuasion used at various levels of communication?
2. What are the three ways to classify a persuasive message?
3. What are the behaviors resulting from persuasive messages?
4. What is an example of a persuasive message to stimulate?
5. What is the purpose of a persuasive message that relates to the listener's values and beliefs?
6. How do ethos, pathos, and logos help in creating a persuasive message?
7. How can persuasion be dangerous?
8. What audience characteristics should be considered in planning a persuasive message?
9. When should both sides of a controversial issue be included in a persuasive speech?
10. What are the five components of a persuasive message?
11. What are questions of major importance to consider in evaluating a persuasive message?
12. How are fact and opinion different?
13. What should be considered in accepting a persuasive message?

Group Activity: Follow course instructions to complete the test for part 5.

Individual Activity: Make arrangements with your instructor to complete the test for part 5.

Activity 2

Learning to Use
Library and Computer Resources

Preparation: The following exercises are designed to help you increase familiarity with library and computer resources. Go to the library you plan to use to prepare your speeches and complete the exercises. Ask either the librarian or your instructor for help if needed.

Group and Individual Activity: Use a standard format (i.e., Modern Language Association or American Psychological Association) to provide complete documentation of sources. Review the example which follows and complete the exercises on the topic of your choice.

Example

1. Select a possible topic for your informative or your persuasive speaking assignment.
    The Library has a handout entitled **General Topics** *if you need help determining your topic.*

    <u>Educational Research</u>

2. Narrow that topic, if necessary, to focus on resource materials that will apply to the topic.

    Example: drug abuse   *Example: adoption*

    Narrow: cocaine and addiction   *Narrow: adoption and race*

    <u>Teacher as Researcher</u>

3. Use the computerized library catalog to locate one circulating book with a title relevant for your topic.
    a. *Click on Library Catalog on left side of main screen*
    b. *Click on Keyword*
    c. *Type in your topic with the word "and" connecting multiple terms*
    d. *On Drop down menu choose Eastfield*
    e. *Click Search*
    f. *Locate book in the main collection and pull this book for Question #8*

    CALL NUMBER: <u>LB1028.B75</u>

    DOCUMENTED SOURCE: <u>Brodinsky, B. (1985). improving math and science education. Arlington,</u>
    <u>Virginia: American Association of School Administrators.</u>

4. Use the *Oxford English Dictionary (Ref PE 1625.M7)* to locate the definition of one word that has relevance for your topic. Copy one segment of the definition.
    You may not find your particular topic as a word in the dictionary. You may have to broaden or narrow the term.
    Example: Michelangelo. Use: artist   Example: Feng Shui. Use: design

    WORD: <u>Research</u>   DEFINITION: <u>The act of searching (closely or carefully) for or after a speci-</u>
    <u>fied thing or person.</u>

5. Use a book of famous quotations (e.g., Ref PN 6081) to locate a quotation that has relevance for your topic. COPY THAT QUOTATION: <u>"Seek till you find and you'll not lose your labour."</u>
    You may not find your particular topic as a word in the index. You may have to broaden or narrow the term.

a. Look in the index at the back to locate the term
b. Find the page and line number (or stanza number) for the appropriate quote
DOCUMENTED SOURCE: Ray, J. (1967) In B. Stevenson (Ed.), The home book of quotations. New York: Dodd, Mead and Company.

6. Locate one source of statistical information about your topic (e.g., *Statistical Abstracts of the United States*—Ref HA 202. U5).
   You may have to be creative in choosing a term to use when looking in the index.
   Example: Martin Luther King   Use: civil rights
   a. The source might provide a chart number NOT a page number
   b. Chart numbers are on the left side of each chart
   STATISTIC: Influence of high school on college success was among top 3 issues.
   DOCUMENTED SOURCE: Yager, R. E. (1986). What kind of school science leads to college success? The Science Teacher, 53, 21–24.

7. Locate a book in reference collection (not a dictionary or book of quotations) relating to your topic.
   a. Using guide labels at the end of shelving rows, browse for your topic subject area
   b. You may use an encyclopedia
   CALL NUMBER: REF LB15.543
   DOCUMENTED SOURCE: Shafritz, J. M., Koepper, R. P., and Soper, E. W. (1988). Facts on file dictionary of education. New York: Facts on File.

8. Locate one source which provides expert testimony about your topic and choose a quotation from the source.
   The rule of thumb is that any writer of a book is considered an "expert" for this assignment. *You may use the circulating book from question #3.*
   QUOTATION: "Conspicuous by their absence from the literature of research on teaching are the voices of teachers themselves."
   DOCUMENTED SOURCE: Lytle, S. L. and Cochran-Smith, M. (1990). Learning from teacher research: A working typology. Teacher's College Record, 92, 83–103.

9. **This question has two parts and requires use of the databases on the computer.**
   Part I: Using a Periodical database, print 3 citations about your topic
   a. Click Online Databases on left side of main screen
   *b. Choose **Masterfile Premier** or **Mas Full-text** (both very general)*
   c. Type in your topic and press enter or search
   d. Click "Add to Folder" on right side
   e. Choose Folders at top of screen
   Part II: Using New York Times database, print one entire article about your topic
   a. Click Online Databases on left side of main screen
   *b. Click on "I" in alphabetical list to choose **Infotrac Newspapers***
   c. Type your subject in entry box at top of screen
   d. At center of page, find "Limit to Journal" and type "New York Times"
   e. Click Search at top of screen
   ATTACH THE COMPUTER PRINT-OUT TO THIS ASSIGNMENT.

10. Use the Internet to locate at least one source of information on your topic. Do Not use a .com site. Copy up to one page of the text. Make sure you have the Internet address to use in a reference list if needed.
    You may use any of the search engines available.
    Example: Alltheweb.com   Example: Yahoo.com   Example: Altavista.com
    a. Type in your subject in the search box
    b. Choose one site—Do Not use a .com site for this exercise
    ATTACH THE COMPUTER PRINT-OUT TO THIS ASSIGNMENT.

LIBRARY REFERENCE WORKSHEET

NAME _____

COURSE _____ SECTION _____

1. Select a possible topic for your informative or your persuasive speaking assignment.

   _____

2. Narrow that topic, if necessary, to focus on library resource materials that will apply to the topic.

   _____

3. Using the library catalog, locate one circulating book which has a title with some relevance for your topic.

   CALL NUMBER: _____

   DOCUMENTED SOURCE: _____

   _____

   _____

4. Use the *Oxford English Dictionary* to locate the definition of one word that has relevance for your topic. Copy one segment of the definition.

   WORD: _____ DEFINITION: _____

   _____

   _____

5. Use a book of famous quotations to locate a quotation that has relevance for your topic.

   COPY THAT QUOTATION: _____

   _____

   DOCUMENTED SOURCE: _____

   _____

6. Locate a book in reference collection (not a dictionary or book of quotations) relating to your topic.

   CALL NUMBER: _____

   DOCUMENTED SOURCE: _____

   _____

   _____

7. Locate one source of statistical information about your topic.

   STATISTIC: _____

   DOCUMENTED SOURCE: _____

   _____

8. Locate one source which provides expert testimony about your topic.

   QUOTATION: _____

   DOCUMENTED SOURCE: _____

   _____

   _____

9. Use the computerized search function available in the library to locate at least three sources from periodicals that have relevance for your topic. In addition, locate at least one newspaper article from the *New York Times*. ATTACH THE COMPUTER PRINT-OUT TO THIS ASSIGN-MENT.

10. Use the Internet to locate at least one source of information on your topic. Do not use a .com site. Find a reference with .edu, .org., or .gov. Copy up to one page of the text. Make sure you have the Internet address to use in a reference list if needed. ATTACH THE COMPUTER PRINT-OUT TO THIS ASSIGNMENT.

Activity 3

Speaking Activity—Informative Speech

Preparation: Your instructor will give you instructions about which type of informative speech you may present and an acceptable time limit for presenting your message. Instructions to use for preparing and delivering different types of informative speeches include the following. An example of #1 is provided on pages 306–309 to illustrate informative speaking formats.

1. Description or demonstration
2. Definition
3. Report of personal experience
4. Report on a famous person
5. Report on a book
6. Report on a thought-provoking article
7. Report of a problem situation

As you research a topic, remember to document your sources for further possible reference. After you have selected and researched a topic, use the Basic Speaking Outline presented at the beginning of Chapter 14 to complete an outline of your speech. Transfer the topical outline ONLY to 3-by-5 inch cards and practice your speech until you are prepared to deliver it. As you practice, work toward eliminating the cards or reducing them significantly. DO NOT write a script on the cards—only words or phrases to keep you on track. Be certain to include appropriate visual aids. Practice with your visual aids and keep in mind the following points:

1. Do not hand out visual aids while you are speaking. Ask a colleague to assist you.
2. Do not speak to the aid when using it. Maintain eye contact with the audience.
3. Keep models covered until you are ready to use them. After using them, cover them again.
4. When writing on the blackboard or poster board, use large, clear, simple images. Make sure material can be seen by everyone. DO NOT turn your back completely to the audience.
5. When using visual presentation software, position the computer screen so that you can easily see it. Trust that the image on the computer screen is being projected to the audience. DO NOT turn to check the projected image; maintain eye contact with the audience.

Keep the following guidelines about informative speaking in mind as you prepare and eventually deliver your informative message.

1. The speech is a factual report, not an opinion piece (image—newscaster not analyst).
2. Do not assume that the audience has a great deal of previous knowledge on the subject.
3. Support your message with facts, figures, statistics, and surveys.
4. Use visual aids such as pictures, graphs, evaluations, and surveys to support your message.
5. Quote or paraphrase accurately from sources used, avoid vague generalizations, and mention COMPLETE citations as you quote or paraphrase material.
6. Choose a topic that is timely and of interest to your audience.
7. Concentrate on using correct grammar and pronunciation.
8. Follow the guidelines you have been given especially concerning time limit, format, use of note cards with topical outlines, and development of visual aids.

1. Informative Speech to Describe or Demonstrate

The purpose of this speech is to convey descriptive information to the audience in an interesting way from subject areas like the following:

1. An organization: A labor union, the Federal Reserve System, a beehive, the New York Stock Exchange, the Peace Corps, a scout organization, the National Labor Relations Board.

2. A place: A city such as New York, Berlin, a region such as the Canal Zone or French Riviera, a famous monument, a cathedral, a national park, a beach.

3. An historical event: A famous battle, the rise of Hitlerism, the Arab-Israeli war of 1967, recent stock market trends, a famous trial, the fight for civil rights, a presidential election.

4. A process: Making perfume, raising vegetables, studying, collecting stamps, building a plant terrarium, collecting butterflies, building stage scenery, refinishing furniture.

5. An object or mechanism: A computer, a vacuum cleaner, a human organ (heart, lungs, etc.), a printing press, a watch, a camera, a shotgun, a hi-fi set, a slide rule, or any other invention.

If your speech topic is a description of an organization or place, you may want to use a spatial ordering of material by describing the relationship of various parts to the whole. A comparison/contrast ordering of material would be useful too in telling your listener how the organization or place is like one that might be more familiar or easier to visualize.

If your speech topic describes a historical event or a process, you may want to use a chronological order. You would begin at the beginning of the event or process and follow through the succeeding steps until you reach the end. Because one step logically follows another, you should have no difficulty remembering your material, particularly if you have rehearsed it.

If you choose an object or mechanism, consider a topical ordering of material. Begin by mentioning the origin and common uses of the device and then explain the device by (1) pointing out its theoretical basis, (2) describing its various parts, (3) showing how its parts interact and function as a unit, and (4) demonstrating how the device functions as a whole in a larger system.

2. Informative Speech to Define a Concept

The purpose of this speech is to define an abstract concept. Some suggested topics are: democracy, courage, academic freedom, beauty, existentialism, romanticism, communism, pride, puppy love, humor, common sense, self-reliance, autonomy, liberalism, conservatism, prejudice, anxiety, anti-Semitism, nationalism, idealism, materialism, culture, ethnocentrism, and acculturation.

In writing a speech of definition, consider the following ideas.

1. When possible explain the derivation of a word. The word "democracy" comes from two Greek words, demos, meaning "people," and kratein, meaning "rule." Thus, the two words together mean "rule by the people."

2. Give a brief history of the words. Show how the meaning has changed or how the present meaning relates to the old meaning.

3. Give concrete examples to illustrate the concept.

4. Compare or contrast the concept with other closely related concepts.

5. Cite the views of various writers.

6. Explain common misconceptions about the concept.

7. Explain what the concept does not mean.

8. Be objective in explaining the concept. Do not let personal prejudices distort definitions.

9. Do not be overly technical in explaining the concept.

10. Vary your sources of information. Do not use series of encyclopedias or dictionaries.

11. Research the word. Paraphrase quotations that you found. Remember to mention the source even when paraphrasing.

12. Be as specific as possible.

3. Informative Speech to Report on a Personal Experience

The goal of this speech is to report on a personal experience to an audience. The message should have a specific purpose and should make the audience think as well as feel. The experience could provide insight about people or could suggest a moral. A moral to a story could be that those who lie chronically will not be believed even when they tell the truth. Your story may be a simple experience; it does not need to be dramatic or unusual. The most natural organization for this kind of speech is generally chronological order. Avoid talking about a series of events, such as places visited on a trip. Concentrate on one incident or key event. You may want to choose a frightening experience, an embarrassing incident, an educational experience, or an eye-witness account.

After choosing your subject you will need to outline your experience. The following references to the general public speaking outline might be used to help in organizing your material.

I. Introduction: the setting of the experience.

II. Body: the elements of the experience in chronological order

III. Conclusion: the significance of the experience

By using narrative details, you should bring the audience immediately into the experience. The events should be told in the sequence in which they occurred. Use language that will describe the incident vividly. Make your audience feel as if they had been present. Appeal to their senses of sight and sound. Arouse in them the same feelings that you experienced. Do not be inhibited as you express your feelings and recreate the experience.

4. Informative Speech to Report on a Famous Person

The goal of this speech is to give a brief biographical sketch of a famous person's life. In preparing for the speech you should complete the following tasks.

1. Read a biography of a person, living or dead, who interests you.

2. As you read, list the major forces or interests that seemed to shape the person's life. Be particularly aware of significant factors in the person's life (e.g., a specific belief or attitude, an insecure childhood, a specific talent, or an influential person who helped shape his or her life).

3. Look at each period in the person's life and choose events that support your overall judgment of the person.

4. Since this is a brief biography, insignificant dates and minor events should not be considered. When outlining your speech, use personal sayings, conversations, excerpts from letters, various idiosyncrasies, and quotations by the person.

5. Using the outline, orally rehearse the speech. Be familiar enough with any quoted material so that you can maintain eye contact with your audience.

As you deliver your informative biographical sketch before your audience, remember to include only those materials that illustrate your dominant theme and do not include extraneous materials. Since your time is limited, be careful not to dwell too long on any one story or event. Be enthusiastic about your subject and try to motivate your audience to want to know more.

5. Informative Speech to Report on a Book

The purpose of this speech is to present material from one book and is usually referred to as a book review or lecture-recital. Choose a book that really interests you. Read the book and choose a theme to develop. Phrase the specific purpose or theme carefully and keep this in mind as you search for material. Choose quotations from the book to amplify and clarify your theme. If the meaning of the quotation is not clear, you will need to paraphrase it or explain briefly how it relates to your conclusion. Alternate brief commentaries with brief quotations rather than presenting long quotations. Be careful that the quoted material does not comprise more than 50% of the speech. Type the quotations on note cards or in a manuscript and rehearse with the quotations until you are completely familiar with the author's words.

Possible ideas for speeches are listed below.

1. The Jazz Age as seen in F. Scott Fitzgerald's *Tender Is the Night*.

2. Mark Twain's humor in *Innocents Abroad*.

3. Dostoyevsky's concept of punishment in *Crime and Punishment*.

4. Thomas Wolfe's view of America in *You Can't Go Home Again*.

5. Ernest Hemingway's attitude toward the sea in *The Old Man and the Sea*.

In order to be an effective interpretive reader you must have a complete understanding of your material and reflect this in your voice. Vary your rate, pitch, and volume. Use proper phrasing and meaningful pauses. Use a variety of facial expressions and gestures to help get messages across to the listener. Although you have not memorized the material, you must maintain steady eye contact with the audience as you speak and read.

6. Informative Speech to Report on a Thought-Provoking Article

The purpose of this speech is to inform the audience of a thought-provoking article from a reputable journal like *Saturday Review, Harper's, Atlantic Monthly*, or *New York Times*. Do not choose an article that has already been summarized. Choose a well-researched article in which the author draws responsible conclusions. Do the following to prepare for the speaking assignment.

1. Read the article to get general meaning.
2. Read the article again slowly. Look up difficult words and concentrate on difficult parts.
3. Read the article through a third time and outline the material on note cards. If you plan to use direct quotations, transcribe the quotations to the cards or plan to read from the work itself. In an informative speech of this type, it is a good idea to select key passages from the article that substantiate your main points. However, do not let more than one-third of your speech be material that is directly quoted from the article.
4. Since the content of the speech will be limited by time available, you will not be able to cover all the points of the article. Go over the outline that you have made of the article and decide the most important points. What can be omitted without destroying the author's purpose?
5. Outline the speech again keeping only the necessary material and quotations. Rehearse the speech with notes in hand and put the ideas in your own words. When reading the author's words, maintain audience contact. When reading directly quoted material, hold the cards or magazine up to a level that facilitates reading but does not block you from the audience. Read all quotations with feeling, understanding, proper emphasis, and eye contact. Remind the audience that you are presenting only the views of the author and not your own. Make comments like "As the author concludes . . ."

Some additions to the general speaking outline are suggested below.

I. Introduction

   A. Title of article, source, name of author, date of publication

   B. The significance of the article

II. Body: a summary of article

III. Conclusion

   A. Summary of author's main points

   B. Quotation from article

7. Informative Speech to Report on a Problem Situation

The purpose of this speech is to report on a problem situation or issue. You will be focusing objectively on a problem situation or issue of political, social, or economic significance. The goal is to explore the nature and dimensions of a problem without trying to formulate a workable solution for it. The speaker spells out the problem in some detail without inserting personal judgments.

While noncontroversial subjects tend to lend themselves more readily to informative speech topics, controversial subjects can be persuasive or informative depending on the approach the speaker takes. Informative and persuasive speeches both require careful explanation or background, but persuasive speeches are intent on convincing an audience and not merely on informing them. Many of the techniques used in informative and persuasive speeches are basically the same. Each provides explanations and evidence and draws conclusions from these. In an informative speech, the writer would describe the content of the problem, indicate the growth of the problem, the people who are directly involved, and some of the consequences of the problem. A persuasive speaker goes further and usually advocates a change or the acceptance of a new policy.

In writing your speech, keep the following suggestions in mind.

1. What is the significance of the problem—social, political, economic consequences?

2. What is the extent of the problem? Is the problem getting better or worse?

3. What factors have contributed to the problem?

4. Do you have concrete evidence to support these conclusions?

5. Have you been specific indicating the source of the evidence?

Choose a topic that interests you. Suggested topics might be: unemployment and NAFTA, poverty and welfare reform, high school dropouts, environmental pollution, juvenile curfew, alcoholism, abortion, censorship codes for television, suicide rate, cults, extremist groups, homosexuals in the military, women in combat, legal defense and the justice system, or raising speed limits.

Group Activity: Give a copy of the outline of your speech to your instructor when it is time to speak. Go to the front of the room and begin to inform your audience. Use your visual aids to help you summarize or reinforce facts and information. Deliver your speech with confidence, eye contact, and vocal variety. Your goal must be to transfer your interest in your subject to your audience.

Individual Activity: Make an appointment with your instructor to evaluate your speech. Often your instructor will videotape your presentation so that you can attempt a self-assessment. Report to the video studio at your appointed time. Give your instructor a copy of your outline. At the conclusion of your speech, review strengths and weaknesses by using the "Informative Speaking Self and Peer Evaluation" form in the Appendix. Also, your instructor will often require you to review the informative presentations of one or more of your classmates. Using copies of the same evaluation form, that is, "Informative Speaking Self and Peer Evaluation," obtain videos and complete assessments of the assigned number of class speeches.

NOTE: Evaluation criteria for this speaking activity are located in the Appendix.

Example of an Informative Speech to Describe

Note: Example of an Informative Speech to Demonstrate is included with Part II Activities.

Amish People (or the Plain Folk)

Topic Outline	*Script*
I. Introduction	
A. Gain attention of audience	(Show two scenes from *Witness,* a feature film. First, pleasant scene on farm; second, argument in village.)
B. Relate to audience	Sixteen is the special age for teenagers of this unusual group of people. Unlike the culture to which you are accustomed, when these particular young people reach sixteen they are given a courting buggy and a beautiful spirited horse.

C. Statement of main purpose — The main purpose of my speech is to inform you about a different culture, the Amish people or the Pennsylvania Dutch as they are sometimes called.

D. Preview first main idea — I will begin an explanation of the Amish culture by giving a brief history of the Amish.

E. Preview second main idea — . . . by sharing some of their unique and unusual customs, and

F. Preview third main idea — . . . finally by describing their contributions to this country.

II. Body

A. First main idea — The history of the Amish goes back nearly 400 years.

   1. Support — The Amish were born from the religious turmoil of the Anabaptist movement in the sixteenth century in Switzerland. They did not believe in war or any other violent act. Because of this they were often subjected to a violent death. In one town there were so many Amish caught, who were considered to be heretics, that a huge bonfire was built in the Town Square to accommodate all the offenders. To make things easy, these people were tied to long ladders and dropped one by one into the flames.

   2. Support — Approximately 300 Amish came to America before the Revolutionary War. After the American constitution was ratified, they came in larger numbers.

   3. Support — The Amish people settled not only in Pennsylvania, but in many areas of North America. Wherever they chose to settle, because of their shrewd judgment of land and methods of farming, they were always successful in producing above-average crops.

B. Second main idea — Life for the Amish is very simple.

   1. Support — The home is the pulse of their life. Their house is plain, curtainless, and without pictures on the walls. The kitchen is very large. Simplicity and cleanliness are the order of these homes. Color is captured by the vividly colored rugs, pillows, afghans, quilts, and glassware.

   2. Support — The red, one-room school house is still in use among the Amish where they go through the eighth grade. That is considered enough education for the Amish young people. These schools are usually taught by a young unmarried lady who has an eighth-grade education. Until the first grade children speak German. English is learned in the school and in the fourth grade the students begin to learn high German.

3. Support

An unmarried man is clean-shaven. When he marries he grows a beard. Most weddings are in November after the harvest. The husband and wife do not live together until spring. However, every weekend the young husband collects his bride from her parents' home and visits family members for the weekend. This is a festive time and gifts are given to the young couple. Then on Sunday evening or Monday morning the young man returns his wife to her parents' home. This continues until the spring when the young couple have collected enough gifts, and they are ready to set up housekeeping themselves. The entire first year is spent mainly building a relationship with one another. This custom comes directly from Deuteronomy 24:5, "When a man takes a new wife, he shall not go out with the army, nor be charged with any duty; he shall be free at home one year and shall give happiness to his wife who he has taken."

4. Support

The Amish women and girls wear long dresses of solid colors. Men's hats must be black felt in winter, and straw in the summer. The dimensions of the brim and crown are strictly regulated.

5. Support

None of the things we simply take for granted are used by the Amish. There are no conveniences, automobiles, tractors, electricity, refrigeration, radio, central heating, or hot and cold running water in homes. These plain people worship in private homes, using German as their common language.

C. Third main idea

The Amish are hard workers.

1. Support

Next to the Bible and his religion, the land is the most important thing in an Amish man's life. He knows that this land may one day be in the hands of his great-great-grandsons. They regard themselves not as landowners, but as guardians of the land for future generations. They are careful to give back what they take from the land.

2. Support

The teenage boys are instructed in the essentials of prosperous farming. By the time a young man is seventeen or eighteen he has the basics of animal husbandry, crop rotation and farm finances equivalent to a college agricultural student.

3. Support

The Amish till miles of black earth, which yields one of the lushest agriculture bounties of an unirrigated region in the nation.

4. Support

Their farms are among the most prosperous of any in the nation. Each year extra land is planted and the produce is canned, preserved, and given to charitable organizations. In fact, most of the food used by the Amish is produced on their own farms.

5. Support	There is virtually no divorce among the Amish. They are hard working, thrifty, prosperous, and there is no need for welfare.
6. Support	According to the Religious Movements website, the total Amish population in North America is estimated to be 134,000 with three quarters living in Pennsylvania, Ohio, and Indiana. Because of their unique customs and lifestyle, the Pennsylvania Dutch country of Pennsylvania draws four million visitors annually, creating a large tourist trade for the area.

III. Conclusion

A. Summary of main ideas	You have heard about the Amish, their history, their culture, and their contributions to this country. These are people of the earth, who regard themselves as guardians of the land for future generations.
B. Transition	I would like to leave you with the following thought.
C. Closing remarks	The Amish, within their communities, exemplify love, nonviolence, goodness, and simplicity. Their unity comes from within the community.

References:
Bender, S. (1990, September–October). Everyday scared: a journey to the Amish. *UTNE Reader*, pp. 91–99.
Coleman, B. and Walter, R. (1989, July). Amish odyssey. *Reader's Digest*, pp. 88–94.
Cowan, D. E. (2005, May 22). The Amish. *The Religious Movements Homepage Project.* Retrieved August 31, 2005, from http://religiousmovements.lib.virginia.edu/
Ganett, R. I. (2003). *My Amish heritage.* Paducah, Kentucky: Turner Publishing Company.
Lange, G. (1989, September). In country: imagine a world without MTV . . . where teens dress alike, don't talk back, and actually like to work . . . welcome to Amish country. *Seventeen*, pp. 182–187.
Ruth, J. L., Miller, I., and Good, M. (1990, October 25). America's Anabaptists: who they are. *Christianity Today*, pp. 25–29.
Whalen, W. J. (1988, May). Why some faiths want the world to go away. *U.S. Catholic*, pp. 32–38.

Activity 4

Analysis of a Persuasive Situation

Preparation: Select a persuasive situation such as a film, television documentary, newscast, advertising campaign, political campaign, or commercial. Consider the creators as persuaders who are selecting and emphasizing details in ways designed to sway your opinion. A good persuader will contrive situations and events that seem harmless and require little effort or concentration on the part of the viewer. Be objective as you survey the situation; analyze the motives of the creators and the devices set up to convince the viewer of a point of view. After you choose a persuasive situation to analyze, write a summary or description of the situation. Answer at least eight of the following questions as fully as you can using specific examples whenever possible.

1. What was the purpose or message of the persuasive situation?

2. What common premises were apparent (values we seemed to share, basic beliefs, things we believed in before or things that the persuader thought we believed).

3. Was dissonance produced by a violation of basic beliefs or shared values? How was this done?

4. Did acceptance of the message alleviate the dissonance? Did you feel differently about anything afterward?

5. What attention devices were used to focus your attention, voluntarily, involuntarily, or in anticipation, on what the persuader wanted to emphasize?

6. What basic needs were appealed to?

7. How did the situation produce an emotional response in you? Were you motivated to accept the message because of your emotional response? When you experienced a feeling-response, did you participate vicariously in the situation?

8. What attempts were made to gain viewer involvement? Did you remain aloof from the action? Were your own traits recognizable? How did you feel if you recognized yourself?

9. Were any group appeals made? Did you identify with any of the groups? If so, did you feel pressured to accept the message because of the group identity? Analyze your feelings about negative reference groups if they were used.

10. What did the persuaders use as symbols of their message? Look for objects, scenery, climate, color, analogies, ways of speaking. Identify what the symbols represented.

11. Did the situation provide you with an awareness that you did not have before viewing it? Did it make you want to say, I never thought of it that way before?

12. Did the situation motivate you toward any action, or did it only suggest a change in belief?

13. If you already believed in the central message, consider the ways in which your belief was reinforced.

The preceding questions are answered in relation to the Avis car rental commercial.

Example of Persuasive Activity

1. The persuasive purpose is to get you to rent from Avis.

2. Common premise is that travellers want to rent cars quickly.

3. Dissonance is produced from observing people running through the airport. Avis shows this by making fun of Hertz.

4. The message implied that travellers who use Avis can walk.

5. Attention device is the man sprawled on the floor with papers scattered saying he was running to rent a car.

6. Basic need appealed to is enjoyment and ease of travel.

7. Motivation occurs by saving time and energy in car rental.

8. Involvement occurs in helping the viewer prefer Avis.

9. The message appeals to travellers who want to avoid rushing.

10. Symbols used are glamour, frustration of travel, and crowds.

11. The situation indicates that Avis might be better than Hertz.

12. The message provides motivation to rent from Avis.

13. It reinforces belief by making an obvious choice more apparent.

Group Activity: In class orally summarize the persuasive situation that you have analyzed. Using information and specific examples in the questions as guidelines, discuss the motives of the persuaders. Have they been successful in convincing the viewer of their views? Were you swayed to their opinion? Why? Why not?

Individual Activity: Find at least one person with whom to discuss the persuasive situation that you have summarized. Write a one-paragraph summary of that person's impression of the situation.

Activity 5

Establishing a Common Premise

Preparation: Make a list of all the areas that you value. For example, you might include love, freedom, security, family, and money. Make your list complete and be prepared to share it.

Group Activity: A volunteer should begin writing values on the board. Class members are to volunteer their values until a list is composed of all the values included on the individual lists. Then the volunteer should cross off values that are not common to all members of the class. Even disagreement by one person will eliminate a value. The result will be a list of common values.

Each common value can be used as the premise for a persuasive speech. The premise is the basic assumption on which the speaker's argument is built. Note the example below.

VALUE:	Good Health
PREMISE:	Good health is something to strive toward.
ARGUMENT:	Smoking has been shown to damage health.
ACTION STEP:	Stop Smoking!

Determining common values of your audience may improve your effectiveness as a persuasive speaker. For each of the common values, suggest a premise, argument, and action step that might form the basis of a persuasive speech.

Individual Activity: Select five friends or relatives to help you compile a list of common values. Use the process suggested in the group activity. Write down the common values; discarded values; and the premise, arguments, and action steps for persuasive speeches.

Activity 6

A Mini-Persuasive Speech

Preparation: An outline for a mini-persuasive speech is included in the left column of the example below. Refer to the outline as you formulate ideas on a subject of your choice. Write a statement beside each heading as you attempt to persuade the listener. The idea may be researched in more depth and used for a longer persuasive speech.

Driving under the Influence

Outline	Statement
I. Gain Attention:	Do you know when to say when?
II. Establish Credibility:	The National Highway Traffic Safety Administration has released the statistics for 1999. Total traffic fatalities: 41,611. Total alcohol-related traffic fatalities: 15,786. Percentage of total traffic crashes that are alcohol-related: 38%.
III. Establish Common Premise:	Can you be 100% sure that the next time a drunk driver has an accident that it will not involve someone you love?
IV. Produce Dissonance:	Would you let a friend get behind the wheel after having too much to drink, or better yet, would you get behind the wheel after having too much to drink?
V. Reduce Dissonance:	So, the next time, think of the consequences before you let a friend or loved one get behind the wheel after having too much to drink.
VI. Personal Experience:	I've seen the twisted metal and mangled bodies of accident victims. I've also seen the look on a driver's face after he has been responsible for ending someone else's life.
VII. Action:	The next time a friend or loved one has too much to drink and wants to drive, assert yourself and offer to drive for them, take their keys, or call a cab for them.

References

National Highway Traffic Safety Administration. Retrieved March 1, 2002 from National Highway Traffic Safety Administration on the World Wide Web: http://www.nhtsa.dot.gov.
Mothers Against Drunk Drivers. http://madd.org.

Group and Individual Activities: Present your mini-persuasive speech in class or to a friend. Ask for ideas for making your statements more persuasive. Turn in a copy of your mini-persuasive speech with notes about changes. Consider further developing this idea for your Persuasive Speaking Activity.

Activity 7

Analysis of a Famous Persuasive Speech

Preparation: Your instructor will provide you with the background information about an issue or event and will provide you with a film or textual copy of a famous speech. You are to label the sections of the speech which you interpret as examples of Aristotle's ethos, pathos, and logos—personal, emotional, and logical proofs which form the basis of the persuasive premise of the speech.

For example, a film of Martin Luther King delivering his famous "I Have a Dream" speech might be shown. The film might include the history of the Civil Rights Movement in the 1950s and 1960s which led to the historic speech. As you listen to King's message, you would use the historical background, his nonverbal message, and his verbal message to identify ethos, pathos, and logos.

Group Activity: With your class, discuss examples for each of ethos, pathos, and logos.

1. Which example best exemplifies the concept of ethos? Is there uniform agreement about this or do opinions differ?

2. Which example best exemplifies the concept of pathos? Is there uniform agreement about this or do opinions differ?

3. Which example best exemplifies the concept of logos? Is there uniform agreement about this or do opinions differ?

4. Which type of proof—personal, emotional, or logical—was strongest in the speech?

5. Has the speech stood the test of time? That is, do the arguments have validity in the new century or are the arguments obsolete?

6. If you had been the speaker's editor, what would you have changed in the speech to make it more relevant for its time and what would you change to make it more relevant for today? Which type of proof are you adjusting?

7. Continue your discussion with issues that have particular relevance for your class.

Individual Activity: Join with at least one other person to study the history and text associated with a famous persuasive speech. After identifying the ethos, logos, and pathos of the speech, discuss the questions from the group activity with your partner or small group. Write out your answers to items #1–6. Write at least two more questions and answers to fulfill item #7 above.

Activity 8

Speaking Activity—Persuasive Speech

Preparation: Your instructor will give you special instructions about the type of persuasive speech you are to prepare and an acceptable time limit for presenting your message. See topic ideas listed below.

After you have selected and researched a topic, complete an outline of your speech. Be sure to include quotations, personal experience, examples, and statistics as support. Use the format presented with the persuasive speech outlines in the text and the persuasive speech examples included with this activity. Transfer the key words to 3-by-5 inch cards and practice your speech until you are prepared to deliver it. As you practice work toward eliminating the cards or reducing them significantly. Be certain to include appropriate visual aids.

Suggestion for Persuasive Topics

The Environment

Acid Rain
Litter
Greenhouse Effect
The Ozone Layer

Animals

Pet Altering
Abuse in Animals
Euthanasia
Hunting

Life Maintenance

Time Management
Volunteering
Etiquette for Dating
Being Happy
Procrastination
Buckle-Up

Nutrition

Eating Disorders
Fat in Diet
Obesity
Diet

Addictions

Smoking
Alcoholism in Teens
Drug prevention
Drug Testing

Children and Teens

Day-Care Centers
Sexual Child Abuse
Foster Parenting
Teen Pregnancy

Sports

Athletic Scandals
Baseball
Basketball
Weight Lifting
Fitness

Women

Women's Need for Education
Rights of Women

Education

Defensive Driving
Sex Education
Computer Literacy
Education
Support Teachers
Scholastic Aptitude Test

Social Issues

Pro-Choice
Labor Unions
Retirement Age Laws
Credibility of the Media
Welfare Reform
Aid the Homeless

Cultural Diversity
Discrimination
Social Security

Crime

Death Penalty
Gun Control
Terrorism
Drinking and Driving
Rape

Health Issues

Suicide
Co-dependency
Organ Transplants
Donating Blood
Preventing Cancer
AIDS
Aided Suicide
PMS
Safe Sex
Medicare
Stress
Schizophrenia
Health Insurance

Miscellaneous

Genealogy
Space Program
Heavy Metal Rock
Talk Shows

Examples of Persuasive Speeches—For and Against a Topic

To show the examples of persuasive speeches, both sides of a controversial issue are presented. Some topics, such as cloning, do have valid arguments for and against. Other issues, such as driving and drinking only have one side—nobody is going to give a speech to support driving while drinking.

Support Cloning Research

Topic Outline   *Script*

I. Introduction

   A. Gain attention of audience—AWARENESS

Imagine a world free of disease. Imagine being able to bring a loved one into a hospital and that person being able to leave with a new heart or kidney.

   B. Relate to audience

We all want to cure those who are sick. We want to wipe out disease. No, we demand it! Most of us in this audience have either lost loved ones or have seen loved ones suffer debilitating disease. We are waiting for the time when we no longer have to suffer such things.

   C. Main purpose— Statement of problem

Could cloning be the answer to incurable disease? My purpose is to persuade you to support cloning research.

   D. Preview of first main idea

First, I will briefly explain the process of cloning and describe the significance of the first successful animal clone.

   E. Preview of second main idea

Second, I will explain how this breakthrough could potentially change how we practice medicine.

II. Body

   A. First main idea

A clone is like an identical twin; an identical twin occurs when a single fertilized egg splits in two, creating an exact genetic duplicate of the first. Whether it is creating a duplicate cell or duplicate animal, cloning is the same concept. Scientists have been successfully cloning frogs since the 1970s.

     1. Support

The basic cloning process is very easy. In a lab setting, a viable cell, such as a skin cell or hair follicle, is taken from a donor. The DNA from the viable cell is removed and transferred to an egg, taken from a second donor. The egg is then implanted into a surrogate. The result is a clone of the original donor.

     2. Support

On July 5, 1996, the most famous lamb in history entered the world. It took 277 tries to create Dolly, who was the result of a decade-long research project lead by Ian Wilmut, of the Roslin Institute in Scotland. His goal was to "develop animals that could produce drugs for human use."

3. Support—
DISSONANCE

Cloning is not a perfect science, but successful cloning of a lamb marked a significant change in attitude among the scientific community. This marked the beginning of a new era in science, a step towards creating new medicine and new cures. The problem is that some politicians and scientists want to put a stop to this research that could make the quality of life so much better for those who need cures that medical science currently cannot produce.

B. Second main idea—
RESOLUTION

How does the scientific breakthrough of cloning a lamb affect our society? Funding for and support of research on cloning could solve our organ replacement shortage. With this new research scientists may develop a way to create new drugs, to grow healthy cells of specific DNA, such as new skin for burn victims and new organs for transplants.

1. Support—
REINFORCEMENT

Latest research is yielding findings that result in genetically matched replacement cells for patients without creating a viable embryo. Cells are tricked into dividing without being fertilized to produce such specialized tissues as heart, muscle, and brain cells that are a perfect match to the donor.

2. Support—
MORE DISSONANCE

Do tissue and cells have rights? If science is permitted to advance in finding cures for debilitating diseases, it is likely that processes will be found that void the arguments about the rights of embryos. Put the shoe on your foot. What will you do if you need to replace a kidney? Suffer the agony of frequent and painful dialysis while your body slowly wastes away? Pray for the death by accident of an innocent person whose tissues provide a match to yours? Snatch a kidney from your parent, sibling, or child to keep yourself alive? Wouldn't you rather use your own DNA to produce a perfectly matched kidney in a laboratory?

III. Conclusion

A. Problem restated
(reinforcement)

In summary, I have reflected on how the science of cloning co could improve our world through medical breakthroughs to enhance the quality of life.

B. Summary of main ideas

I have explained how the concept of cloning came to be and the basics of the cloning process. I have explained the potential impact of this science on the medical world of the future.

C. Closing remarks

1. Challenge audience

Our society may not be ready for the reality of cloning. In fact, some people in our society will fight hard to oppose it. Many are ready, however, to cure cancer, AIDS, and all the other deadly diseases.

2. ASK FOR ACTION
(Hand out addresses)

Write your representatives in the U.S. Congress today and ask them to support this innovative medical research that could provide the cure you or one of your loved ones needs to fight deadly disease.

Stop Cloning Research Now

Topic Outline

Script

I. Introduction

A. Gain attention of audience—AWARENESS

Cloning is being touted as the medical wave of the future—the answer for wiping out disease and suffering in the 21st century. Of course, we want to save endangered species, solve the organ transplant shortage, and cure disease—but at what cost to humanity?

B. Relate to audience

We all cling to the hope that science will come up with a way to cure Alzheimer's disease and diabetes, especially when those we love are suffering. That cloning will solve these terrible problems has given us hope, but we must wonder if we are being seduced by this new technology.

C. Main purpose—Statement of problem

What does cloning involve? Cloning is not only a scientific issue, but it is also a moral issue.

D. Preview of main ideas

I will first present the scientific research about cloning and then I will describe the ethics involved in this issue.

E. Transition

You must decide for yourself whether the end justifies the means.

II. Body

A. First main idea

Scientists have been successfully cloning animals since a lamb known as "Dolly" was engineered. This success did not come easily. It took 277 tries that resulted in many deformed lambs.

1. Support

How many tries will it take to create a human clone? Are we willing to let deformed human clones be developed in the name of science? To the scientific community the potential to cure disease is reason enough to continue cloning research.

2. Support

On November 25, 2001, Advanced Cell Technology, Inc. of Worcester, Massachusetts, created human embryos through cloning. Dr. Michael West said, "I'm just trying to help people who are sick." This is very admirable but what about the embryo? Is this not a life that was created only to be destroyed for research purposes? According to President Bush, "We should not as a society grow life to destroy it and that's exactly what is taking place."

B. Second main idea— DISSONANCE	There are many risks involved with cloning research. Scientists will not stop with embryos when the potential for human cloning is possible. Extremists will take this technology and use it for their own benefit.
1. Support	For example, could Hitler or the Incan ice mummy be brought back to life? Could terrorists create clones on a large scale to be used for military purposes? These ideas are far-fetched and have been the stuff of science fiction movies but the technology is there. I have seen web sites that support the idea of cloning Jesus, Hitler, and even Elvis.
2. Support— RESOLUTION	These are the crazy people who make this technology so controversial. That our government would use taxpayer dollars to fund such nonsense is beyond belief.
3. Support— REINFORCEMENT	An ethical look at cloning research results in a clear answer that it must be stopped. Cloning, to many people, is like playing God. For scientists to create a being is unnatural. People question where we will draw the line in getting involved in natural events. If cloning is successful, how will this development impact society? What rights would a human clone have? Some say that the rights of clones will be dismissed because clones are manufactured, not naturally born. What will become of physically deformed clones who develop mental cognizance? Or vice versa, what will become of mentally deformed clones who are physically normal?

III. Conclusion

A. Problem restated	Fertility clinics will offer cloning as a solution to infertile couples and to grieving parents who hope to recreate the same child. These future babies will be our future freak show. The psychological impact would be an enormous burden on cloned children who would be expected to live up to the idea that they were created to be someone else. How many deformed babies will it take to be successful? We cannot afford to find the answer to this question. We must put a stop to this nonsense now!
B. Summary of main ideas	Technology labs are painting a pretty picture of the future of cloning but they are ignoring the great risks involved. There is a potential of good coming out of this research; but with the good, inevitable bad outcomes will occur.
C. Closing remarks	It is important that we remember that cloning has the potential to damage our society as we know it by taking nature into our own hands and playing God. Be sure that you can live with your decision to accept what is "morally wrong" if you do embrace this technology.

1. Challenge audience	When you hear of breakthroughs in cloning technology, remember that life was used and then discarded in the name of science. When you are presented with the hope of a cure for your loved one, remember it comes with a price, the life of another. I urge you to follow your basic beliefs that life is precious and that God is the only one who can take and give life.
2. ASK FOR ACTION (Hand out addresses)	Write to our representatives in the US Congress today and ask them to STOP the research that will result in deformed human embryos and manufactured humans with no rights.

References (for both for and against sides of the cloning issue)

Couric, K. (2001, November 26). Cloning: Research company claims first successful test. *MSNBC*. Retrieved December 1, 2001, from MSNBC on the World Wide Web: http://www.msnbc.com

Fischer, J. (2002, February 11). Science trumps politics. *US News & World Report,* 132(4), 60.

Human embryo created through cloning. (2001, November 26). *CNN*. Retrieved December 1, 2001, from CNN on the World Wide Web: http://www.cnn.technology.com

Kolata, G. (1998). A clone is born. *Breaking the News,* 1–22.

Group Activity: During class, deliver your persuasive message to your classmates.

Individual Activity: Make an appointment with your instructor to plan a specific time to deliver your persuasive message.

NOTE: Evaluation criteria for the Speaking Activity are located in the Appendix.

Activity 9

Speaking Activity—Inspirational Speech

Preparation: The purpose of the inspirational speech is to cause the audience to feel excited, motivated, encouraged, or uplifted. Speakers must use such nonverbal characteristics as tone of voice, posture and facial expressions along with well chosen words to inspire the audience to adopt a "winning" attitude. After selecting an inspirational topic, use the Basic Speaking Outline presented at the beginning section of Chapter 14 as a guide for preparing your message. Use definition, examples, and quotations to support your main points. Use visual aids to create and hold audience interest. Rehearse your message so that you can deliver it with confidence. Remember that the image of the speaker is critical in convincing a group of listeners to change their life styles.

To help in your preparation, an example follows. The example includes slides that could be used with a computerized graphics program like PowerPoint or Corel Presentations. The slide would be shown simultaneously while the text which immediately follows it would be spoken. Some explanation of text appearing on the slides would be spoken, also. The example summarizes a number of points presented as Habit Four in Stephen Covey's (1989) *The Seven Habits of Highly Effective People.*

Principles of Interpersonal Leadership
Think Win/Win

Topic Outline   *Script*

I. Introduction

   A. Gain attention of audience

   B. Relate to audience

All of you have encountered many different types of bosses, teachers, and others who seem to give you a hard time—who want to make you lose.

C. Statement of main purpose

The purpose of my presentation is to describe six different paradigms, with real life examples, that you could face as you interact with others to solve problems.

D. Preview first main idea

First, I will describe paradigms where one or both parties end up as losers. These are:

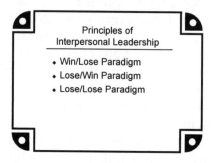

E. Preview second main idea

Next, I will describe paradigms where winning is the goal. These are:

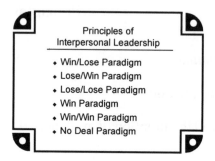

II. Body

A. First main idea

Many people face situations where one or even both parties think that someone has to win and someone has to lose.

1. Support

Consider a sales manager who is trying to motivate a staff to increase sales.

The manager shows a chart with the sales record of each staff member. The highest achiever will win a trip to a tropical paradise.

Which paradigm fits this example? It fits the Win/Lose paradigm since one employee wins and others lose. This will result in less cooperation and eventually less sales. Win/Lose is typified by people who want to control and to compete.

2. Support

Consider a work situation where an employee has filled in every weekend for several months and is looking forward to some free time.

The boss asks the employee to fill in for several more weekends. The employee protests, but the boss prevails. The employee gives in.

The scenario fits the Lose/Win paradigm. Lose/Win is typified by people who want to please, to be accepted.

3. Support

Next, consider two determined and stubborn individuals who must interact to get through a divorce.

The husband must sell his assets and give half to his wife. He sold his $10,000 car for $50 and gave $25 to his wife.

This fits the Lose/Lose paradigm since both lost several thousand dollars. People like this are so obsessed with making the other person lose, that they are willing to lose also.

B. Second main idea

In other situations there is an emphasis on the position—what solution will be the best for everyone involved?

1. Support

Consider a situation now where the individuals involved are thinking only about themselves. There is no goal to have a loser, but there is no focus and interdependence of working together.

These are persons who focus on themselves and leave others to do the same.

This is the Win Paradigm where people avoid involvement with others.

2. Support

Consider a situation where a husband and wife decide where to go on their vacation.

They discuss options—Disney World, Puerto Rico, Lake Tahoe, San Francisco—and finally decide that both would like Lake Tahoe, with a side trip to San Francisco.

The mutual choice fits the Win/Win paradigm. One person's success is not achieved at the expense of another. Sometimes a totally new solution evolves.

3. Support

Last of all, the objective might be deciding between the lesser of two evils. A solution to benefit both parties just does not emerge.

Two partners in a company are trying to decide whether or not to accept a contract. All solutions seem to lead to overwork for one partner and a small profit for both. The partners decide the job is not worth the effort and turn it down.

The partners wanted each to win—a Win/Win situation. They could find no way to do this, the result is No Deal. If both parties do not profit from the solution, it is often best not to do anything.

III. Conclusion

A. Summary of main ideas

I have described to you six scenarios that can occur as we attempt to find solutions that are mutually agreeable. The first three represented solutions where one or both parties were losers. The last three presented the more positive approach of winning. Ideally, you will use your interpersonal communication skills to find a Win/Win solution.

B. Closing remarks

As you grow from a perspective of independence to one of interdependence, it takes courage and commitment to seek Win/Win solutions in a competitive world where Win/Lose often dominates.

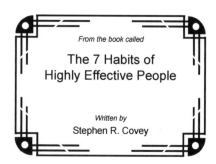

Stephen Covey (1989; p. 216) has said that "effective interpersonal leadership requires the vision, the proactive initiative and the security, guidance, wisdom, and power that come from principle-centered personal leadership."

Reference

Covey, S. (1989). *The Seven Habits of Highly Effective People*. New York: Simon & Schuster.

Group Activity: During class, deliver your inspirational message to your classmates.

Individual Activity: Make an appointment with your instructor to plan a specific time to deliver your inspirational message.

NOTE: Evaluation criteria for the Speaking Activity are loacted in the Appendix.

Activity 10

Speaking Activity—Entertaining Speech

Preparation: Using a subject of your choice prepare a speech to entertain. Use the Basic Speaking Outline presented at the beginning of Chapter 14. Topic suggestions are listed below.

Women	Getting married
Dating	Hippies
Television commercials	Being youngest in family
Liars I have known	Sex education in schools
How not to study	Being myself

Many subjects can be approached in an entertaining way. The speech to entertain can be informative, stimulating, even convincing as long as these goals are not the chief aim of the speaker. The example included is an informative speech on Burma-Shave signs. This speech catches attention and interest of an audience by developing a trend of thought about a chosen topic. The subject will not necessarily make listeners laugh out loud. It may bring only smiles of amusement and still be entertaining.

When organizing your thoughts you will want to put ideas together in an entertaining way. The audience should see that a definite trend of thought has been developed yet should not feel that they must recall facts or consider changes in behavior. Techniques that you may want to use are exaggeration, juxtaposing incongruous statements (e.g., appending a frivolous afterthought to a serious statement), using humorous or unusual figures of speech, making a play on words by using clever phrasing and puns, telling humorous anecdotes, and using humorous examples.

In delivering a speech to entertain, you must approach your subject with more objectivity and less emotional involvement than you do in a serious speech. When you speak to entertain there is a feeling of thoughtful fun that you must catch and transfer to the listener. In creating humor, you must strive to achieve a comic sense or spirit of fun and realize what might be laughed at. Humor can come as a result of an intellectual turn of a phrase. The line must then be projected in a witty way that communicates its humor. Audiences often laugh at incongruities. These are extremes that exist and you as a speaker will need to emphasize the difference between the expected and the actual.

Laughter can also be provoked when the audience has experienced the situations presented. As a speaker, you would try to get the audience to visualize the happening and think that "something like this has happened to me." Through wise selection and emphasis, your voice and gestures should communicate the comic. You will need to learn the technique of exaggerating without being too obvious. Humor should seem easy and spontaneous. You should vary your line of delivery as well as your gestures and movements.

Finally, an entertaining speaker must possess a good sense of timing. Allow the audience to savor the thought. Point out a humorous line by pausing before the line. Less humorous lines can have a faster pace. Never obviously wait for laughs. When the audience does laugh, wait for laughter to die down. If you do not wait, the audience will be afraid to laugh for fear of missing something. Remember too not to break character and laugh yourself.

Until you actually deliver the speech and see the audience reaction you will not know whether or not your speech is entertaining. Much depends on how your speech is delivered. The only assurance of success you will have is in your preparation. Your effort and ability to select a topic, organize, and rehearse the speech to entertain will be rewarded with warm reception by your listeners.

Example of a Speech to Entertain

Burma-Shave Signs

Topic Outline	*Script*
I. Introduction	
A. Gain attention of audience	"Henry the Eighth/Prince of Friskers/Lost Five Wives/But Kept/His Whiskers."
B. Relate to audience	This little jingle and numerous others have been seen beside our highways by many people. They are what are known as Burma-Shave signs. Signs like these have advertised Burma Shave and have added enjoyment to the trips of many motorists.
C. Statement of main purpose	The background of the signs is an interesting anecdote in American merchandising.
D. Preview first main idea	I will begin by describing the Burma-Shave Company and how it was started.
E. Preview second main idea	I will then tell you how the Burma-Shave signs came into being.
F. Preview third main idea	Finally, I will give you a few examples of some of the jingles.
II. Body	
A. First main idea	The Burma-Shave Company was founded by Clinton Odell, a retired owner of an insurance organization. The company originally manufactured a liniment, the essential oils of which came from Burma.
1. Support	Clint combined the word "Burma" with the Latin word "vita," meaning life or vigor, to name his new company. The liniment, however, was very odorous and did not sell well enough to keep the business going.
2. Support	Meanwhile, one of Clint's sons, Allan, was traveling in England and discovered that many men there were using brushless shaving cream. Allan felt that this would be a good product for them to manufacture, thus, giving birth to Burma-Shave.
B. Second main idea	Burma-Shave was such a new idea that it did not sell well in America. One day while driving along a highway, Allan was trying to think of new ways to advertise.

1. Support	While driving he saw a series of signs about a filling station down the road. Allan believed that the Burma-Shave Company could use the same kind of advertising. The advertising experts said it would not work. You had to sell shaving cream with statistics, testimonials, and smiling, well-shaven faces.
2. Support	Clint, however, decided that anything was worth a try and agreed to spend $200 for the first set of road signs. They appeared in September 1926, near Lakeville, Minnesota. Allan wrote the first jingle which read, "Cheer Up/ Face/The War/Is/Over."
3. Support	Allan and his younger brother, Leonard, took the job of installing the signs. Leonard drove a truck loaded with freshly painted signs and tools for setting them up while Allan raced ahead in a car to find a likely spot and an amiable farmer to rent space. By the time Leonard arrived, Allan had talked the farmer into the deal, and the brothers went to work. The $200 gamble paid off. Sales jumped from almost zero to $68,000 in one year.
4. Support	By 1965 there were over 7000 sets of signs dotting highways all over the country. Souvenir hunters used to carry off entire sets of jingles so they were bolted to fence-high iron or wooden posts. Sites for all Burma-Shave signs were leased from farmers who showed a genuine loyalty toward the signs. They protected them from farm animals, guarded against souvenir hunters, and repaired the broken ones.
C. Third main idea	Burma-Shave jingles are very catchy.
1. Support	Examples of a few of them are: "Are Your Whiskers/When You Wake/Tougher than/A Two-Bit Steak?" "A Peach/Looks Good/With Lots of Fuzz/But Man's No Peach/And Never Was."
2. Support	Wives called their husbands' attention to signs such as "He Played/A Sax/Had No B.O./But His Whiskers Scratched/So She Let Him Go." Farther down the road the husband had his turn: "Soon Shaving Brushes/Will Be Trimmin/Those Screwy Hats/We See on Women."
3. Support	Safety experts soon pointed out that the signs helped slow down drivers. Burma-Shave took the hint, and wrote such jingles as "Don't Take A Curve/At 60 Per/We Hate to Lose/A Customer" and "Past Schoolhouses/Take It Slow/Let the Little/Shavers/Grow."
4. Support	The Odells didn't realize how seriously some people took their jingles until one series of signs suggested: "Rip a Fender/Off Your Car/Send It In/For a Half-Pound jar."

Dozens of toy fenders poured into the Minneapolis office, and jars of Burma-Shave were sent out. But the big surprise came when they began to receive crates with real fenders! Of course they sent the half-pound jars to those people, also.

5. Support

Another motorist responded to the sign which read: "Free, Free/A Trip/To Mars/For 900 Empty Jars." He sent a letter to the Odells saying that he had 898 jars saved up and would report any day now for his free trip. The Odells hastily replaced the signs with: "If a Trip/to Mars/You'd Earn/Remember Friend/There's No Return."

6. Support

Jingles were selected annually from contests open to both professionals and amateurs. Jingles in poor taste were never accepted. Though many of those submitted would amuse many motorists, others might be offended. A few examples of the jingles that were censored are "If Wife Shuns/Your Fond Embrace/Don't Shoot the Iceman/Feel Your Face." "Listen, Birds/Those Signs Cost/Money/So Roost Awhile but/Don't Get Funny." "My Man/Won't Shave/Sez Hazel Hus/But I Should Worry/Dora's Does."

III. Conclusion

A. Summary of main ideas

In summary, I have told you how the Burma-Shave Company was formed. I have also told you how the Burma-Shave signs originated. Finally, I have given you a few examples of Burma-Shave jingles.

B. Closing remarks

In closing, I would like to say that Burma-Shave signs have become a national institution. They have been seen by millions of motorists across the country. These signs have well served their purpose, not only to advertise Burma-Shave, but to make traveling more enjoyable to many.

References:
Bedard, P. (1981, March). Why the government can only get verse. *Car and Driver,* p. 20.
Changing Times. (1965, February). Unsung bards of Burma Shave: sign in the Smithsonian Institution. p. 47.
Rowsome, F. (1965, December). Verse by the side of the road: excerpts. *American Heritage,* pp. 102–105.
Senior Scholastic. (1972, February 7). Texts don't say what you want to know about your Coke or Burma Shave. pp. 11–12.
Zinsser, W. K. (1964, September 5). Good-by Burma Shave. *Saturday Evening Post,* pp. 65–66.

Group Activity: Give a copy of the outline of your speech to your instructor when it is your time to speak. Attempt to capture the attention of your audience. Remember your goal is to provide an enjoyable experience, not to encourage the retention of information or to bring about behavioral change.

Individual Activity: Make an appointment with your instructor to evaluate your speech. Turn in a copy of your outline. At the conclusion of the speech, review your strengths and weaknesses.

NOTE: Evaluation criteria for the Speaking Activity are loacted in the Appendix.

Activity 11

Speaking Activity—Impromptu Speech

Preparation: An impromptu speech is given with little, if any, preparation. The speaker is called upon to inform, persuade, inspire, or entertain, and is given no time for the usual outlining, let alone search for supporting materials. The topic, of course, must be one upon which the speaker has adequate background to present a credible message. The speaker should follow the general speaking format of introduction, body, and conclusion with two to four main ideas and supporting statements. Impromptu speaking can be fun. Experience with impromptu speaking can make that statement, "we'd like to hear a few words from you about . . ." much less threatening.

When your time to speak comes, you should not even think about making a speech. You should simply chat with the audience for two minutes in a spontaneous, natural, relaxed way as you would relate a story to someone over a Coke. To develop the ability to speak effectively, you will conquer your fear and develop courage sooner if you will choose a subject with which you are very familiar. Remember to be yourself as you relate this incident. Do not try to be anything other than what you are. Be as energetic and enthusiastic as you possibly can be. In order to make a successful speech of any kind you must be enthusiastic. Enthusiasm does not mean that you are loud or shout at the audience. You speak with intensity and animation. You have the life and energy that result in a more attractive personality. Genuine enthusiasm is one secret of success in any project, but it is certainly necessary in successful speaker-audience communication.

As you gather your thoughts for an impromptu message, keep the following brief outline in mind. The outline will help you appear more organized and will give some structure, rather than mere rambling, to your message.

I. Introduction—short and simple opening statement to relate to audience and preview message.

II. Body—two to four main ideas, think about key words or concepts to communicate and fill in with supporting material.

III. Conclusion—make a memorable closing statement.

Helpful hints to keep in mind as you deliver an impromptu message are listed below.

1. Do not panic, remain calm.
2. Think in chronological, or some logical, order.
3. Try to be specific and give examples.
4. Think about chatting with the audience in a spontaneous, natural, relaxed way.
5. Do not try to be anything other than what you are.
6. Be as energetic and enthusiastic as possible.
7. Speak with intensity and animation.
8. Try to have the audience relive the experience with you.
9. Use humor if it seems natural.

Select one of the following options for an impromptu speech. Be certain that it has sufficient material to last two minutes. Do not write out what you are going to say. Above all do not attempt to memorize it. When speaking, you need to use facts and actions that produce images in the minds of the audience. Good speakers make their listeners see what they are saying. They do not talk in colorless generalities and without enthusiasm.

Option 1—Childhood Event

To choose a subject, look back over your childhood and select an event that made a special impression on you. What is it? Do you remember a special birthday? A memorable holiday? A childhood sweetheart? A day in school? An incident with a special friend? Think briefly about the incident that you selected to talk about. You must not attempt to cover too much. In preparing your impromptu message, think through the incident in chronological order.

Option 2—Learning a Lesson

Choose a subject based on an incident in your life that taught you a lesson. The speech might be about a lie you told, the day you skipped school, an encounter with the law, an embarrassing experience, or something you wish you've never said. When it is time for you to present your speech, you will need to answer the following questions in some detail.

1. The circumstances—who was involved, when did it occur, where did it happen, what happened, and how did it happen?
2. What effects did the incident have on you?
3. What did you learn from the incident?

Option 3—Frustrating Incident

Choose a subject based on an incident that made you angry. You will need to relive that experience before the audience with all the fervor you felt when it happened. A specific topic might be one of the following: I was cheated, I was jilted, I was criticized, or I made a mistake. The story may be an incident about business, school, community, family, or friends that irritate you. Begin your speech with a specific example. Start by telling what, when, where and how you became angry or excited. What did you do and how did you do it?

A framework for giving an impromptu speech is expressed by the following template. Try using this on your own as you practice thinking on your feet.

My *childhood event, lesson learned, frustrating incident* _____

resulted in the following outcomes:

First, _____

Second, _____

Third, _____

Such outcomes have taught me a lesson and from this, I have drawn the following conclusions:

First, _____

Second, _____

Third, _____

In summary, _____

To close, _____

Group Activity: Present your impromptu message to your audience. To make it an effective experience, do not "cheat" and memorize your speech. If you do, in all likelihood, your audience will know that the message was prepared in advance. It is generally more difficult to make a memorized message appear impromptu than to muster the courage to make an impromptu speech.

Individual Activity: Make arrangements with your instructor to present your impromptu speech. Do not "cheat" and memorize it.

NOTE: Evaluation criteria for the Speaking Activity are loacted in the Appendix.

Final Activity

Speech Communication Skills Inventory

Preparation: Use the following comparisons of intrapersonal, interpersonal, and speaker-audience communication as you summarize your personal growth and achievement. Note that general communication concepts, while taught in relation to a particular area, transcend the three areas (e.g., self-esteem was taught in part I as Intrapersonal Communication but relates to interpersonal and speaker-audience, also).

Intrapersonal, Interpersonal and Speaker-Audience Skills

	Intrapersonal	Interpersonal	Speaker-Audience
1.	Recognize *perception* as it influences communication	Accommodate *perceptional* differences with others	Recognize impact of *perception* in public communication
2.	Identify components of *self-esteem*	Describe components of *self-esteem* to others	*Build self-esteem* to make formal presentations
3.	Use realistic *self-talk* in making decisions	Use realistic *self-talk* in establishing relationships	Use realistic *self-talk* to plan and rehearse formal presentations
4.	Understand the need to establish *credibility*	Select appropriate verbal and non-verbals to establish *credibility*	Reveal personal background variables to establish *credibility* with audience
5.	Recognize the universality of *communication apprehension*	Channel energy produced by *communication apprehension* into productive communication	Channel energy produced by *communication apprehension* into strategies for adequate preparation and rehearsal
6.	Recognize importance of *rapport* with self	Recognize importance of establishing *rapport* in interpersonal relationships	Recognize importance of establishing *rapport* with audiences
7.	Understand and appreciate the dynamics of the communicative act—*active listening* and reading of *non-verbal clues*	Use *active listening*, responding, and reading of *non-verbal clues* in interpersonal relationships	*Display sensitivity* to audience reactions
8.	Understand the source of and the mechanisms of *non-verbal* behavior	Recognize impact of *non-verbal* behavior on another person	Select appropriate *non-verbal* behavior when giving speeches

	Intrapersonal	Interpersonal	Speaker-Audience
9.	*Manage time* based on awareness of priorities	*Manage time* as it reflects priorities to others	*Honor time* commitments based on audience expectations
10.	Aware of *self-motives*	Aware of *other's motives*	Aware of *audience expectations*
11.	Recognize responsible *assertive* communication	Recognize and use responsible *assertive* communication interpersonally	Recognize and use responsible *assertive* communication in formal setting
12.	Identify personal *value* structure	Recognize effect of personal *values* in communication with others	Integrate *value* structure in public presentations
13.	Analyze self as an *ethical* communicator	Communicate *honestly* to one other person	Communicate *honestly* with an audience
14.	Develop *flexible behavior*	*Change behavior* or select appropriate behavior in communication with one other person	*Adjust messages* to fit characteristics of an audience
15.	Identify *conflict*	Select productive responses to *conflict*	Prepare messages to obtain *audience acceptance*
16.	Understand role in a *group*	Apply understanding of *role in group*	Apply dynamics of *group process* when appropriate
17.	Understand the importance of developing positions supported by *rationale and evidence*	Further refine positions supported by *rationale and evidence* in communication with one other person	Provide formal communication of positions supported by *rationale and evidence*

As you complete this course in speech communication, you have a set of feelings about your present skill in various speaking situations. As stated in activity 2, part 1, it is an interesting exercise to record these feelings and to compare them with the feelings about your speech communication skills expressed as you began the course. Without looking at your original responses, retake the survey which is reproduced on the following two pages.

Group and Individual Activities: Go back to activity 2, part 1, and compare the two sets of ratings you gave yourself on each item. Hopefully, you will have gained confidence in many of the skills on the rating form.

To gain an overall impression of your improvement, total all the points you gave yourself on the first rating and total all the points you gave yourself on the second rating. Amount of improvement will be indicated by the difference in the two scores. (Since strong skill is given a rating of "5," remember that the higher score will be the better score.)

Finally, discuss those areas where you gained the most self-confidence and those areas where you still need to improve your self-image.

For each statement below, rate yourself as you feel at this moment. Indicate your feelings by circling the appropriate number to the left of the statement. Think carefully and be honest with yourself. These results are for you alone.

5=Strongly Disagree   4=Disagree   3=Don't Know   2=Agree   1=Strongly Agree

1. 1 2 3 4 5 I am able to define communication.
2. 1 2 3 4 5 I am able to identify elements (communication model) involved in any communication process.
3. 1 2 3 4 5 I am able to recognize how written and spoken communication styles differ.
4. 1 2 3 4 5 I am able to differentiate areas of communication: intrapersonal, interpersonal, small group, and public speaking.
5. 1 2 3 4 5 I am able to describe how perception affects communication.
6. 1 2 3 4 5 I am able to illustrate how the use of language affects communication.
7. 1 2 3 4 5 I am able to identify ways to eliminate barriers to communication.
8. 1 2 3 4 5 I am able to explain how self-concept, self-esteem, and self-image affect communication.
9. 1 2 3 4 5 *I am able to recognize the debilitating effects of stress in communication.*
10. 1 2 3 4 5 I am able to describe ways to improve self-esteem.
11. 1 2 3 4 5 *I am able to recognize the effect on credibility of the different roles that each of us plays.*
12. 1 2 3 4 5 I am able to define and distinguish between hearing and listening.
13. 1 2 3 4 5 I am able to demonstrate and employ appropriate listening skills (passive, active, social, critical, discriminative, empathic) in the family, community, workplace.
14. 1 2 3 4 5 I am able to apply principles associated with various types of nonverbal communication.
15. 1 2 3 4 5 I am able to develop effective nonverbal skills for various speaking situations.
16. 1 2 3 4 5 *I am able to illustrate effective ways to handle time management.*
17. 1 2 3 4 5 I am able to demonstrate ability in the use of appropriate feedback (body motion, vocal expression) to help the listener.
18. 1 2 3 4 5 I am able to recognize the importance of vocal quality when talking on the telephone.
19. 1 2 3 4 5 I am able to develop strategies for improving interpersonal relationships.
20. 1 2 3 4 5 I am able to distinguish between feeling and thinking.
21. 1 2 3 4 5 I am able to explain how self-disclosure enhances relationships.
22. 1 2 3 4 5 *I am able to differentiate among passive, aggressive, and assertive communication strategies.*
23. 1 2 3 4 5 I am able to demonstrate effective interviewing skills.
24. 1 2 3 4 5 *I am able to recognize the impact of values on communication.*
25. 1 2 3 4 5 *I am able to explain the importance of ethics (honesty) on communication exchanges.*

26.   1 2 3 4 5   I am able to describe how interpersonal relationships develop and disintegrate.
27.   1 2 3 4 5   I am able to distinguish between empathy and sympathy.
28.   1 2 3 4 5   I am able to demonstrate styles of conflict management.
29.   1 2 3 4 5   *I am able to describe the benefits of embracing a diverse culture.*
30.   1 2 3 4 5   I am able to discuss how cultural differences affect the way we communicate.
31.   1 2 3 4 5   I am able to employ strategies for overcoming cultural barriers to communication.
32.   1 2 3 4 5   I am able to discuss the impact of gender differences on communication between males and females.
33.   1 2 3 4 5   I am able to summarize characteristics of a small group.
34.   1 2 3 4 5   I am able to describe situations in which a group decision is superior to individual decision making.
35.   1 2 3 4 5   I am able to participate effectively in groups through effective listening and by using critical and reflective thinking.
36.   1 2 3 4 5   *I am able to distinguish between productive and non-productive behaviors in a small group.*
37.   1 2 3 4 5   *I am able to identify consequences of roles, skills, and attitudes on group participation.*
38.   1 2 3 4 5   I am able to identify application of leadership styles to real-world situations.
39.   1 2 3 4 5   *I am able to demonstrate use of brainstorming to generate possible solutions to problems.*
40.   1 2 3 4 5   *I am able to conduct an effective meeting through the use of organized planning skills.*
41.   1 2 3 4 5   I am able to adapt to the purpose, occasion, and audience of a public speaking situation.
42.   1 2 3 4 5   I am able to demonstrate ability to use research and data bases to gather support material for speeches.
43.   1 2 3 4 5   I am able to draft, organize, revise, edit, and present formal public speeches.
44.   1 2 3 4 5   I am able to demonstrate effective delivery techniques for public speaking.
45.   1 2 3 4 5   I am able to use various types of visual aids in the delivery of public speeches.
46.   1 2 3 4 5   I am able to develop strategies for building speech confidence.
47.   1 2 3 4 5   I am able to deliver an effective informative speech.
48.   1 2 3 4 5   I am able to deliver an effective persuasive speech.
49.   1 2 3 4 5   *I am able to define the concept of dissonance as it is used in persuasive speaking.*
50.   1 2 3 4 5   *I am able to differentiate fact and opinion.*

REFERENCES

Adell, A. W. (1976). Values clarification revised. *The Christian Century, 93,* 687–688.

Adler, R. and Towne, N. (1978). *Looking Out/Looking In.* New York: Holt, Rinehart and Winston.

Anderson, W. (1998). *The Confidence Cause.* New York: HarperCollins.

Arnold, W. E. and Hirsch, R. O. (1977). Small group communication. In Arnold and Hirsch, eds., *Communicating Through Behavior.* St. Paul: West Publishing Company.

Bach, G. R. and Wyden, P. (1968). *The Intimate Enemy.* New York: Avon.

Barnlund, D. C. (1962). Toward a meaning centered philosophy of communication. *Journal of Communication, 12,* 197–211.

Beamer, L. (1992). Learning intercultural communication competence. *The Journal of Business Communication, 29,* 285–303.

Bloom, L. Z., Coburn, K., and Pearlman, J. (1975). *The New Assertive Woman.* New York: Delacorte Press.

Bond, L. (1995, Winter). Unintended consequences of performance assessment: Issues of bias and fairness. *Educational Measurement: Issues and Practices,* pp. 21–24.

Bower, S. A. and Bower, G. H. (1991). *Asserting Your-Self.* Reading, MA: Perseres Books.

Bramson, R. (1981). *Coping with difficult people.* New York: Ballentine Books.

Brilhart, J. K. (1974). *Effective Group Discussion.* Dubuque, Iowa: Wm. C. Brown.

Brown, S. M., and Walberg, H. J. (1993). Motivational effects on test scores of elementary students. *Journal of Educational Research, 86,* 133–136.

Burgoon, J. K., Buller, O. B., and Woodall, W. G. (1989). *Nonverbal communication: The unspoken dialogue.* New York: Harper and Row, Publishers.

Cassels, L. (1960, June). You can be a better leader. *Nation's Business.*

Chapman, G. (1992). *Five languages of love: How to express heartfelt commitment to your mate.* Chicago: Northfield Publishers.

Christie, A. (1950). *A Murder Is Announced.* New York: Dodd, Mead and Company.

Covey, S. (1989). *The Seven Habits of Highly Effective People.* New York: Simon & Schuster.

Culpepper, G. and Forrest, M. (1997). *Communication: The key to understanding.* Mesquite, Texas: Unpublished manual of the Eastfield College Speech Communication Club.

Dewey, J. (1910). *How We Think.* Boston: D.C. Heath and Company.

Dimitries, J. and Mazzarella, M. (1998). *Reading People.* New York: Random House.

Eisenberg, A. M. and Smith, R. R., Jr. (1971). *Nonverbal Communication.* Indianapolis: The Bobbs-Merrill Company, Inc.

Englebardt, S. L. (1978, July). Alone across Alaska. *Reader's Digest,* 70–75.

Engstrom, T. W. and MacKenzie, A. (1968). *Managing Your Time.* Grand Rapids, Michigan: Zondervan Publishing House.

Fast, J. (1970). *Body Language.* New York: Pocket Books.

Feinberg, M. M. (1975). *Effective Psychology for Managers.* Englewood Cliffs, New Jersey: Prentice-Hall, Inc.

Fensterheim, H. and Baer, J. (1975). *Don't Say Yes When You Want to Say No.* New York: Dell Publishing Co., Inc.

Filley, A. C. (1975). *Interpersonal Conflict Resolution.* Glenview, Illinois: Scott Foresman.

Flanagan, W. (1975, May 26). How to keep bias out of job interviews. *Business Week,* 77.

Gordon, T. (1970). *Parent Effectiveness Training.* New York: Peter H. Wyden, Inc.

Gray, J. (1992). *Men are from Mars, Women are from Venus*. New York: Harper Collins Publishers.

Gudykunst, W. B. and Kim, Y. Y. (1992). *Communicating with strangers*. New York: McGraw-Hill, Inc.

Hall, E. T. (1966). *The Hidden Dimension*. Garden City, N.Y.: Doubleday, Inc.

Hall, E. T. (1959). *The Silent Language*. Greenwich, Conn.: Fawcett Publications.

Harter, P. M. (2000, April–May). In Bieler, R. B. Inclusion and universal cooperation. *Disability World*. Retrieved March 1, 2002, from International Disability News and Views on the World Wide Web: http://www.disabilityworld.org/April-May2000/IntntalNews/Inclusion.htm

Helmstetter, S. (1986). *What to Say When You Talk to Yourself*. Scottsdale, Arizona: Grindle Publishers.

Herbig, P. A. and Kramer, A. E. (1992). Do's and don'ts of cross-cultural negotiations. *Industrial Marketing Management, 21,* 287–298.

Howe, L. W. and Howe, M. M. (1975). *Personalizing Education: Values Clarification and Beyond*. New York: Hart Publishing Company, Inc.

Jourard, S. M. (1971). *The Transparent Self*. New York: Van Nostrand Reinhold.

Kenyon, S. J. and Knott, A. T. (1953). *A Pronouncing Dictionary of American English*. Springfield, Mass.: G and C Merriman Company.

Knapp, M. L. (1978). *Nonverbal Communication in Human Interaction*. New York: Holt, Rinehart and Winston, Inc.

Knowles, M. and Knowles, H. (1959). *Introduction to Group Dynamics*. New York: Association Press.

Lakein, A. (1973). *How to Get Control of Your Time and Your Life*. New York: New American Library.

Lazarus, A. (1971). *Behavior Therapy and Beyond*. New York: McGraw-Hill Book Co.

Luft, J. (1969). *Of Human Interaction*. Palo Alto, Cal.: National Press Books.

Maslow, A. H. (1954). *Motivation and Personality*. New York: Harper and Row.

Molloy, J. T. (1975). *Dress for Success*. New York: Warner Books, Inc.

Molloy, J. T. (1977). *The Woman's Dress for Success Book*. Chicago: Follett.

Monroe, A. (1935). *Principles and types of speech*. New York: Scott, Foresman.

Narciso, J. and Burkett, D. (1975). *Declare Yourself—Discovering the ME in Relationships*. Englewood Cliffs, New Jersey: Prentice-Hall, Inc.

National Institute for Literacy. (n.d.). National literacy statistics. Retrieved August 31, 2004, from www.nifi.gov/reders/intro.htm.

Nelson, W. (1988). *Willie: An Autobiography*. New York: Simon and Schuster.

Nierenberg, G. I. and Calero, H. H. (1971). *How to Read a Person Like a Book*. New York: Cornerstone Library.

O' Hain, D., Rubenstein, H., and Stewart, R. (2004). *A pocket guide to public speaking*. Boston: Bedford/St. Martin.

Parker, I. (2001, May 28). Absolute PowerPoint. *The New Yorker*: 76–87.

Patton, B. R. and Giffin, K. (1974). *Interpersonal Communication: Basic Text and Readings*. New York: Harper and Row, Publishers.

Powell, J. (1969). *Why Am I Afraid to Tell You Who I Am?* Niles, Illinois: Argus Communications.

Reilly, S. and Ahrens, R. W. (2005, April 22). Paychecks increase with education. *USA Today*: IA.

Rosenfeld, L. B. (1973). *Human Interaction in the Small Group Setting*. Columbus, Ohio: Charles E. Merrill Publishing Company.

Simon, S. B., Howe, L. W., and Kirschenbaum, H. (1972). *Values Clarification: A Handbook of Practical Strategies for Teachers and Students*. New York: Hart Publishing.

Smith, M. J. (1975). *When I Say No I Feel Guilty*. New York: Bantam Books.

Sommer, R. (1969). *Personal Space: The Behavioral Basis of Design*. Englewood Cliffs, N.J.: Prentice-Hall, Inc.

Swift, J. (1949). *Gulliver's Travels*. New York: Grosset & Dunlap Publishers.

Tharp, T. (2004). *The creative habit: Learn it and use it for life*. New York: Simon and Schuster.

Uemura, N. (1978, September). Solo to the North Pole. *National Geographic*, 298–325.

Wallas, G. (1926). *The art of thought*. New York: Harcourt, Brace, and Company.

Whorf, B. L. (1956). Science and linguistics. In J. B. Carroll, ed., *Language, Thought, and Reality*. Cambridge, Mass.: MIT Press.

Zelinski, E. J. (1997). *The joy of not working*. Berkeley, CA: Ten Speed Press.

APPENDIX

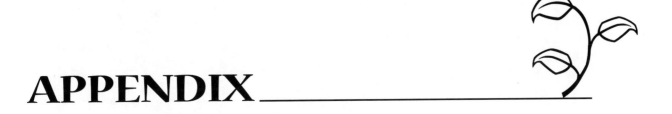

SPEAKING ACTIVITIES EVALUATION FORMS

Evaluation Form

Name _____

Making an Introduction

(Points are given to the right of each criterion.)

I. Attention device

_____ Captures attention (4)

_____ States purpose of presentation (4)

II. Factual details

_____ Statement of factual details (4)

_____ Effectiveness of factual details (4)

III. Summary

_____ Review of relevant details (4)

_____ Conclusion (4)

IV. Personal qualities

_____ Can be heard (1)

_____ Conversational style (1)

_____ Control of fillers—ah's, you know's (1)

_____ Speaker enthusiasm (1)

_____ Looks at listeners (1)

_____ Speaker confidence (1)

_____ Correct posture (1)

_____ Speaker credibility (1)

V. Presentation

_____ Completed introduction of a person (10)

_____ Within two-to-three minute time limit (8)

_____ TOTAL POINTS (50)

Evaluation Form

Name _____

Demonstration Speech

(Points are given to the right of each criterion.)

I. Introduction

_____ Gain attention of audience (2)

_____ Relate to audience (2)

_____ Statement of main purpose (2)

_____ Preview of main ideas (2)

II. Body

_____ Clearly stated main ideas (5)

_____ Shows process (5)

_____ Describes process (5)

_____ Visual aids (5)

III. Conclusion

_____ Summary of main ideas (3)

_____ Closing remarks (3)

IV. Nonverbal speaker characteristics (to facilitate listening)

_____ Appropriate dress (1)

_____ Correct posture (1)

_____ Spontaneous gestures (1)

_____ Eye contact (1)

_____ Facial expression (1)

V. Verbal speaker characteristics (to facilitate listening)

_____ Volume (1)

_____ Vocal energy (1)

_____ Rate (1)

_____ Control of fillers, ah's, you knows (1)

_____ Correct pronunciation (1)

_____ Vocal quality (1)

VI. Presentation

_____ Within four-to-five minute time limit (5)

_____ TOTAL POINTS (50)

Evaluation Form

Name _____

Employment Interview

(Points are given to the right of each criterion.)

Required for Role Playing and Field Interview

_____ Relevant Application Form (5)

_____ Relevant Application Letter (10)

_____ Relevant Resume (10)

_____ TOTAL POINTS (25)

Required for Field Interview Option

_____ Evaluation Form from Employer (printed on the next page) (must be received in order to receive credit for this assignment)

_____ Follow-up Letter to Employer (5)

_____ Paper—Title Page and Card (6)

_____ Paper—Introduction (5)

_____ Paper—Questions and Answers (15 at 2 points each = 30)

_____ Paper—Relevance of Questions (2)

_____ Paper—Breadth of Questions (2)

_____ Paper—Conclusion (5)

_____ Paper—Format and Editing (10)

_____ On-Time (10)

_____ TOTAL POINTS (75)

Required for Role Playing Option

Introduction

_____ Gain Attention (2)

_____ Relate to Audience (2)

_____ Statement of Purpose (2)

_____ Company Background (2)

_____ Preview of Parts (2)

Interviewer

_____ Puts Candidate at Ease (3)

_____ Uses Paraphrasing (3)

_____ Keeps Momentum Going (3)

_____ Salary Question (3)

_____ Smooth Ending (3)

Interviewee

_____ Good First Impression (3)

_____ Well-Prepared Answers (3)

_____ Adds Free Information (3)

_____ Specific Answers (3)

_____ Stresses Qualifications (3)

_____ Expresses Interest (3)

_____ Salary Question (3)

_____ Smooth Ending (3)

Personal Qualities of Interviewee

_____ Poise and Confidence (2)

_____ Enthusiasm (2)

_____ Avoids Slang (2)

_____ Controls Fillers (2)

_____ Articulates Well (2)

_____ Eye Contact (2)

_____ Conversational Style (2)

_____ Credibility (2)

_____ Appropriate Dress (5)

_____ Well Groomed (5)

TOTAL POINTS (75)

_____ TOTAL ASSIGNMENT POINTS (100)

Evaluation Form

Name _____

Professional Interview

Thank you for taking the time to help this student with the Professional Interview Assignment. The classroom environment exposes the student to a limited view of the business and professional world. Through people like you, educators are able to give students real-world interviewing experience. Please take a few moments to complete this evaluation of the interview. Your responses will provide the student with valuable feedback. Use additional sheets if needed.

Please return this evaluation by _____

Student Name _____

1. Comment on the student's professionalism when setting up the interview.

2. Comment on the student's professionalism during the interview.

3. Describe at least one strength of the student's communication style.

4. Describe at least one weakness of the student's communication style.

5. List any suggestions that would help the student in future employment interviews.

Signature _____ Title_____

Again, thank you for your cooperation. Any questions about this form or the interviewing assignment should be directed to Instructor_____ at Eastfield College (214-860-7132, 3737 Motley Drive, Mesquite, TX 75150). Please return in the addressed and stamped envelope.

Evaluation Form

Name _____

Group Presentation

GROUP EVALUATION

I. Presentation strategies (2 points each; 24 points total)—make notation on outline to show where used

_____ Demonstration

_____ Discussion

_____ Lecture

_____ Modeling and imitation

_____ Problem solving

_____ Role playing

_____ Sensitivity training

_____ Skill practice session

_____ Tactile activity

_____ Visual aids

_____ Costume and props

_____ Staging

II. General comments (2 points each; 16 points total)

_____ Was a group goal evident from the presentation?

_____ Was there a meaningful message communicated?

_____ Did each individual accept group responsibilities?

_____ Did the group succeed in getting the audience actively involved?

_____ Did the group seem enthusiastic over the project?

_____ Were the presentation modes well coordinated?

_____ Did the group introduction prepare the audience to receive the message?

_____ Did the group conclusion provide adequate closure?

INDIVIDUAL EVALUATION

III. Message (3 points each; 30 points total)

_____ Gained attention

_____ Related to audience

_____ Stated main purpose

_____ Previewed main ideas

_____ Relevant support

_____ Interesting support

_____ Adequate support

_____ Summarized main ideas

_____ Closing remarks

_____ Transition to next speaker

IV. Presentation (3 points each; 30 points total)

_____ Poised and confident

_____ Use of gestures

_____ Eye contact with audience

_____ Correct posture

_____ Conversational style

_____ Speaking rate

_____ Volume of speech

_____ Vocal variety

_____ Control of fillers

_____ Pronunciation and articulation

_____ TOTAL POINTS (100)

Evaluation Form

Name _____

Informative Speech

(Points are given to the right of each criterion.)

I.   Introduction

_____ Gain attention of audience (2)

_____ Relate to audience (2)

_____ Statement of main purpose (2)

_____ Preview of main ideas (2)

II. Body

_____ Statements of two to four main ideas (2)

_____ Relevant supporting materials (2)

_____ Interesting supporting materials (2)

_____ Adequate supporting materials (2)

III. Conclusion

_____ Summary of main ideas (3)

_____ Closing remarks (3)

IV. Visual Aids

_____ Appropriateness of aids (2)

_____ Ability to use aids (2)

_____ Quality of aids (2)

V.   Presentation

_____ Useful information (10)

_____ Informative not persuasive (10)

_____ Sufficient repetition (2)

_____ Adequate transition between parts (2)

_____ Within time limit (4)

_____ Adquate documentation included (2)

VI. Personal Qualities

_____ General poise and speaker confidence (4)

_____ Expression of warmth and friendliness (4)

_____ Rapport with audience (4)

_____ Speaker credibility (4)

_____ Appropriate dress and appearance (2)

VII. Vocal Delivery

_____ Rate of speech (2)

_____ Volume of speech (2)

_____ Vocal variety (2)

_____ Control of fillers (ah's, you know's, etc.) (2)

_____ Tonal qualities (enthusiasm, sincerity) (2)

_____ Pronunciation and articulation (2)

_____ Conversational style (4)

VIII. Physical Delivery

_____ Use of gestures (2)

_____ Eye contact (4)

_____ Correct Posture (2)

_____ TOTAL POINTS (100)

Evaluation Form

Name _____

Informative Speech
Self and Peer Assessment

SPEAKER'S NAME: ASSIGNMENT:

EVALUATOR'S NAME: DATE: ____/____/____

INSTRUCTIONS: AS YOU VIEW THE VIDEOTAPE, PLACE A CHECK IN THE BOX CORRE-SPONDING TO YOUR RATING. TO OBTAIN THE SUMMATIVE SCORE, GIVE ONE POINT FOR "SATISFACTORY," AND TWO POINTS FOR "EXCELLENT." ADD THE RATINGS TO GET A TOTAL SCORE.

EIGHT PUBLIC SPEAKING COMPETENCIES	SPEAKING PERFORMANCE RATINGS		
	Unsatisfactory(0)	Satisfactory(1)	Excellent(2)
Competency One: CHOOSES AND NARROWS A TOPIC APPROPRIATELY FOR THE AUDIENCE AND OCCASION Comments:			
Competency Two: COMMUNICATES THE THESIS/SPECIFIC PURPOSE IN A MANNER APPROPRIATE FOR THE AUDIENCE AND OCCASION Comments:			
Competency Three: PROVIDES APPROPRIATE SUPPORTING MATERIAL BASED ON THE AUDIENCE AND OCCASION Comments:			
Competency Four: USES AN ORGANIZATIONAL PATTERN APPROPRIATE TO TOPIC, AUDIENCE, OCCASION, & PURPOSE Comments:			
Competency Five: USES LANGUAGE THAT IS APPROPRIATE TO THE AUDIENCE, OCCASION, & PURPOSE Comments:			

Competency Six: USES VOCAL VARIETY IN RATE, PITCH & INTENSITY, TO HEIGHTEN AND MAINTAIN INTEREST Comments:			
Competency Seven: USES PRONUNCIATION, GRAMMAR & ARTICULATION APPROPRIATE TO THE DESIGNATED AUDIENCE Comments:			
Competency Eight: USES PHYSICAL BEHAVIORS THAT SUPPORT THE VERBAL MESSAGE Comments:			

General Comments:

Summative Scores
Of Competencies:

Evaluation Form

Name _____

Persuasive Speech

(Points are given to the right of each criterion.)

I. Introduction

_____ Gain attention of audience (2)

_____ Relate to audience (2)

_____ Statement of the problem (4)

_____ Preview of main ideas (2)

II. Body

_____ Dissonance created (4)

_____ Resolution of dissonance (2)

_____ Support relates to audience values (2)

_____ Support relates to personal experiences (2)

_____ Appeal to common values (2)

III. Conclusion

_____ Problem restated (2)

_____ Summary of main ideas (2)

_____ Challenge to audience (4)

_____ Action step (6)

IV. Visual Aids

_____ Appropriateness of aids (2)

_____ Ability to use aids (2)

_____ Quality of aids (2)

V. Presentation

_____ Persuasive message (10)

_____ Adequate transition between parts (2)

_____ Within time limit (8)

_____ Adequate documentation included (4)

VI. Personal Qualities

_____ General poise and speaker confidence (4)

_____ Rapport with audience (4)

_____ Speaker credibility (2)

_____ Appropriate dress and appearance (2)

VII. Vocal Delivery

_____ Rate of speech (2)

_____ Volume of speech (2)

_____ Vocal Variety (2)

_____ Control of fillers (ah's, you know's, etc.) (2)

_____ Tonal qualities (2)

_____ Pronunciation and articulation (2)

_____ Conversational style (2)

VIII. Physical Delivery

_____ Use of gestures (2)

_____ Eye contact (4)

_____ Correct Posture (2)

_____ TOTAL POINTS (100)

Evaluation Form

Name _____

Inspirational Message

(Points are given to the right of each criterion.)

I. Introduction

_____ Gain attention of audience (2)

_____ Relate to audience (2)

_____ Statement of main purpose (2)

_____ Preview of main ideas (2)

II. Body

_____ Statements of main ideas (10)

_____ Effectiveness of support (10)

_____ Use of transitions between major points (10)

III. Conclusion

_____ Summary of main ideas (2)

_____ Closing remarks (2)

_____ Ends presentation with novel conclusion (2)

IV. Presentation

_____ Provided uplifting message (25)

_____ Appropriate visual aids and/or references (5)

V. Personal Qualities

_____ General poise and speaker confidence (2)

_____ Warmth and friendliness (2)

_____ Speaker credibility (2)

_____ Conviction to subject (2)

VI. Vocal Delivery

_____ Rate of speech (2)

_____ Volume of speech (2)

_____ Vocal variety (2)

_____ Control of fillers (2)

_____ Pronunciation and articulation (2)

_____ Conversational style (2)

VII. Physical Delivery

_____ Use of gestures (2)

_____ Eye contact (2)

_____ Correct posture (2)

_____ TOTAL POINTS (100)

Evaluation Form

Name _____

Entertaining Speech

(Points are given to the right of each criterion.)

I. Introduction

_____ Gain attention of audience (2)

_____ Relate to audience (2)

_____ Statement of main purpose (2)

_____ Preview of main ideas (2)

II. Body

_____ Two to four main ideas (2)

_____ Relevant supporting materials (2)

_____ Interesting supporting materials (2)

_____ Adequate supporting materials (2)

III. Conclusion

_____ Summary of main ideas (2)

_____ Strong and/or novel ending (4)

IV. Visual Aids/references (if appropriate)

_____ Appropriateness of aids/ references (2)

_____ Ability to use aids (2)

_____ Quality of aids (2)

V. Presentation

_____ Entertaining message (20)

_____ Not informative or persuasive (20)

_____ Adequate transition between parts (4)

VI. Personal Qualities

_____ General poise and speaker confidence (2)

_____ Expression of warmth and friendliness (2)

_____ Rapport with audience (2)

_____ Speaker credibility (2)

VII. Vocal Delivery

_____ Rate of speech (2)

_____ Volume of speech (2)

_____ Vocal variety (2)

_____ Control of fillers (ah's, you know's, etc.) (2)

_____ Tonal qualities (enthusiasm, sincerity (2)

_____ Pronunciation and articulation (2)

_____ Conversational style (2)

VIII. Physical Delivery

_____ Use of gestures (2)

_____ Eye contact (2)

_____ Correct Posture (2)

_____ TOTAL POINTS (100)

INDEX